THE ARTLESS JEW

THE ARTLESS JEW

MEDIEVAL AND MODERN AFFIRMATIONS AND DENIALS OF THE VISUAL

Kalman P. Bland

PRINCETON UNIVERSITY PRESS PRINCETON AND OXFORD

Copyright © 2000 by Princeton University Press
Published by Princeton University Press, 41 William Street,
Princeton, New Jersey 08540
In the United Kingdom: Princeton University Press,
3 Market Place, Woodstock, Oxfordshire OX20 1SY
All Rights Reserved

Second printing, and first paperback printing, 2001
Paperback ISBN 0-691-08985-X

*The Library of Congress has cataloged the cloth edition of this
book as follows*

Bland, Kalman P., 1942–
The artless Jew : medieval and modern affirmations
and denials of the visual / by Kalman P. Bland.
    p. cm.
Includes bibliographical references and index.
ISBN 0-691-01043-9 (cl. : alk. paper)
1. Judaism and art—History of doctrines. 2. Ten commandments—
Images. 3. Art, Jewish. 4. Jewish aesthetics. 5. Jews—Intellectual life.
I. Title.

BM538.A7 B55 2000
296.4'6'09—dc21   99-044922

British Library Cataloging-in-Publication Data is available

This book has been composed in Galliard

Printed on acid-free paper. ∞

www.pup.princeton.edu

Printed in the United States of America

10 9 8 7 6 5 4 3 2

To Annabel J. Wharton

Contents

Acknowledgments

PORTIONS OF chapter 1 appeared in *Jewish Identity in Modern Art History*, edited by Catherine Soussloff. A different version of chapter 4 appeared in the *Journal of the History of Ideas*. Chapter 5 appeared in the *Journal of Medieval and Early Modern Studies*. I am grateful to the editors of those publications for their permission to reproduce my work.

Deborah Malmud and her staff at Princeton University Press are unmatched in efficiency, professionalism, and humane support. Collaborating with them in the making of this book was an author's privilege and pleasure.

To the many people who read portions of the manuscript and shared their wisdom with me, I am profoundly grateful. Chief among them is Annabel J. Wharton, to whom this book is dedicated. Sidra DeKoven Ezrahi has a keen eye and a heart for encouragement. Rifaʿat ʿAli Abou El-Haj and Richard I. Cohen know what needs saying. Erich Gruen, Bluma Goldstein, Catherine Soussloff, and Peter Selz were there when I needed them. Robert Alter and Barry S. Kogan gave sage counsel. Daniel Boyarin offered early and constant encouragement. Readers for Princeton University Press made invaluable suggestions. Had I followed more of their advice, I would have repaired all of the remaining fault lines in *The Artless Jew*.

Kalman P. Bland
March 1999

THE ARTLESS JEW

Introduction ⸻

> There is no test that so surely reveals the one-
> sidedness of a philosophy as its treatment of art and
> aesthetic experience.
>
> (John Dewey, *Art as Experience*)

THE ARTLESS JEW studies an idea. It investigates the social origins, intellectual moorings, and cultural implications of Jewish aniconism. Aniconism refers to the ambiguous "historiographic myth that certain cultures, usually monotheistic or primitively pure cultures, have no images at all, or no figurative imagery, or no images of the deity."[1] Jewish aniconism implies that Jews are a People of the Book rather than a People of the Image. Proponents of Jewish aniconism deny the existence of authentic Jewish traditions in painting, sculpture, and architecture. They concede that Jews imitate, in production and reception, the foreign art of their host or neighboring cultures. They claim that Jewish attitudes toward visuality and the visual arts range from indifference to suspicion and hostility.

The grand themes of Jewish aniconism are sounded by innumerable cultural historians who insist that "the Second Commandment and many other restrictions in the Bible undoubtedly had a negative impact on the artistic development of the Jewish people, and subsequently of Christianity and Islam."[2] Similar strains reverberate whenever Jewish artists complain that "monotheism was dearly bought—and because of that Judaism had to give up observation of nature with our *eyes*, and not just with our soul. On religious grounds, Judaism struggled with ancient idolatry, whose remnants are displayed today in all museums of the world, so that [Judaism] remained with no share in the treasures of graphic art."[3] Jewish aniconism echoes whenever scholars declare that "the visual arts never played a central role in the religiously dominated premodern Jewish culture."[4] Almost ubiquitous, the denial is at work when biographers assume that Eastern European Jews seeking to become artists were compelled to "defy the traditional taboo against iconic images."[5] The themes of Jewish aniconism are embellished whenever philosophers and critics propose that "cultures vary greatly in their exploitation of the various senses and in the way in which they relate their conceptual apparatus to the various senses. . . . The Hebrews tended to think of understanding as a kind of hearing, whereas the Greeks thought of it more as a kind of seeing."[6]

Belonging to conventional wisdom, the credibility of Jewish aniconism is reinforced whenever experts in diverse fields declare that "there is an inherent lack of visual talent amongst Jews."[7]

To ascertain the scientific validity of these assertions, to prove Jewish aniconism factually true or false, one would have to consult a battery of empirically minded specialists: cognitive psychologists working in laboratories equipped to measure visual acuity; clinical psychologists and cultural anthropologists willing to tackle the mysteries of artistic creation; historians of philosophy; and historians of art probing the network of symbiotic relationships that link artists, patrons, and collectors with theories of art and artifacts.

Regardless of the empirical findings, several intriguing questions would remain unanswered. Ideas and theories, like all human artifacts, connote their makers. Because human activity is overdetermined, ideas and theories are overdetermined. They "have more reasons for existing than they need."[8] Regarding the denial of Jewish art, what might some of those reasons be? Political campaigns, wishful thinking, and controversies in the history of science warn us of immense gaps between the validity of a proposition and its public acceptance. Is the gap between truth and popularity a clue to understanding the attractions of Jewish aniconism?

What was the environment that allowed Jewish aniconism to germinate, reproduce, edge out its competitors, and become conventional wisdom? What groups of people found it compelling or incredible? What were their educational backgrounds, political loyalties, national identities, and religious affiliations? Denying or affirming Jewish art, did they mean to praise or condemn Judaism? What motivates contemporary discussions of Jewish aesthetics? What motivated premodern discussions? How do the premodern and modern discussions compare? Have Jewish and Gentile perceptions of Jewish visuality and Jewish art been immune to historical change? Have they missed their appointment with the opticians of culture? Have they escaped refraction by the iconoclastic Protestant Reformation of the sixteenth century; the scientific revolutions of the seventeenth century; the American, French, and Russian Revolutions of 1776, 1789, and 1917; the recent emancipation and westernization of the Jews; the rise of political and racial anti-Semitism; the birth of Jewish nationalism; and the bewildering array of modernist, avant-garde, and postmodern developments in all the arts and aesthetic theory? These are the questions to which *The Artless Jew* provides partial answers.

The Artless Jew is chronologically partial. It focuses on medieval and modern developments. Reference is made to the earlier traditions of Israelite culture and Late Antique rabbinic Judaism only insofar as they were received and interpreted by later authorities. *The Artless Jew* is also partial in combining my professional training and love for medieval Jewish thought with my amateur's delight in the musical and visual arts. Writing it broke the senseless and stultified habit criticized by Richard I. Cohen of overlooking "the visual dimension of Jewish life . . . in the study of the Jewish past."[9] *The Artless Jew* satisfied my desire for the pleasures of "critical theory" and confirmed my faith in the advantages of taking a social approach to the history of ideas.[10] It heightened my respect for synchronic and diachronic differences in "ways of seeing."[11] It put and kept me in collegial conversation with new friends and creative scholars from outside my field. It taught me, once again, the humane and liberating lesson that "all ideas have more reasons for existing than they need."

I undertook this project when my initial confidence in the truth of Jewish aniconism was shaken by unfulfilled expectations. I knew that "the Jewish people did not begin to philosophize because of an irresistible urge to do so. They received philosophy from outside sources, and the history of Jewish philosophy is the history of the successive absorptions of foreign ideas which were then transformed and adopted to specific Jewish points of view."[12] I also knew that "there has not been a major philosophical thinker from Plato and Aristotle, to Heidegger and Wittgenstein, who has not had something to say about [the] subject" of art.[13] I therefore assumed that medieval and modern Jewish philosphers were compelled to discuss art. I expected their discussions to be uniformly dismissive, critically negative, derogatory. They would all insist that the "scopic regime" of Jewish culture has always been aniconic.[14] They would unanimously ratify Judaism's preference for the literary and musical arts. They would imply or declare that the trajectory of Jewish thought zigs toward the auditory, the verbal, and the temporal because it zags away from the visual, the pictorial, and the spatial.[15] After all, the Book of which the Jews are the People is a book without pictures.

I maintained these expectations even though I had discarded one of the major premises of Jewish aniconism in the preliminary stage of my research for *The Artless Jew*. I had come to reject the dyadic antithesis between "mentalities," between Hebrew "understanding as a kind of hearing" and Greek "understanding as a kind of seeing."[16] These distinctions are the pernicious product of an outmoded ethnocentric worldview whose political and religious loyalties simplify and absolutize, aggrandize or denigrate, cultural peculiarities.[17] I was certain that hearing and vision are evenly distributed, mutually intertwined, and equally valued in all societies.[18] I therefore concluded that under the playful shade of aristophanic clouds, the owls of ancient Greek philosophy and the eagles of Israelite prophecy might be made to flock together. Greek philosophers and Israelite prophets preferred to speak or write their minds rather than paint or sculpt their ideas. They nevertheless found visual images irresistible and visual metaphors indispensable. According to Plato's *Republic*, Socrates allowed himself to be enticed into a marathon conversation by the exciting prospect of watching an unusual relay race in which horse riders would pass lighted torches to another.[19] Socrates subsequently argued that painters, like poets, misrepresent the truth and therefore are either stringently regulated or altogether banned from society lest they arouse the wrong parts of the human soul and weaken its best part, intellect.[20] The same was true for Moses. According to Exodus, he too was enticed into a marathon conversation by a visual spectacle: He saw a burning but unconsumed bush. He too concluded that society needed to regulate the artists. He subsequently forbade graven images of God for use in worship.

Inheriting the overlapping visual and regulatory traditions of Socrates and Moses, medieval Jewish mystics named their classic texts *Bahir* (*Book of Dazzlement*) and *Zohar* (*Book of Splendor*). Hasdai Crescas, a late medieval philosophizing theologian, named his text *'Or 'Adonai (The Light of the Lord)*. Moses Maimonides (1138–1204) spoke for them all when he couched religious experience in terms of enlightenment: "Sometimes truth flashes out to us so that we think it is day. . . . We are like someone in a very dark night over whom lightning flashes time and time again. . . . There are others [whose] darkness is illumined . . . by a polished body or something of that kind, stones or something else that give light in the darkness of the night."[21] Maimonides also spoke for them all when he likened prophecy to dream images generated by imagination and seen by the mind's metaphorical eye. Not everyone agreed with the Maimonidean equation of ancient prophecy and mere psychological insight.[22] But medieval Jewish mystics and philosophers all cultivated the theatrical powers of their inner "eye." Because they were so engrossed in charting the psychosomatic effects of scenery flashing vividly on the interior screens of their mind, I surmised that they might have been similarly attentive to pictures painted on manuscript pages, figures engraved on coins, images woven into tapestries, and shapes emerging from geometrically patterned walls, even if it turned out that they had nothing favorable to say about them.

I quickly stumbled into a Procrustean bed. My initial expectations were misguided. The evidence told a different story, one that did not conform to the master plot of Jewish aniconism. Nineteenth- and twentieth-century literature was indeed replete with fully elaborated denials of Jewish art. I was startled, however, by a dissonant choir of minority voices. These nineteenth- and twentieth-century minority voices echoed the archaeologists and art historians who were affirming Jewish art. They all defied the conventional wisdom. They declared that the national or religious spirit of Judaism shows deep, native affinities with the visual arts. Several of these voices spoke with Eastern European Jewish accents. Even among the proponents of Jewish aniconism in the West, many were eager to find exceptions proving the rule. People who admired synagogues argued that Judaism has always sponsored religious architecture and favored the decoration of ceremonial objects. People with a taste for secular abstract expressionism or surrealism argued that Judaism has always encouraged nonrepresentational, cerebral paintings and sculptures.

The medieval evidence was even more confounding. My expectations were generally correct about trivial matters and altogether wrong about everything else. Medieval Jews indeed placed the visual arts on their compulsory philosophic agenda; they indeed railed against idolatry. But their travel itineraries, polemical literature, biblical commentaries, and law codes proved that they did not construe the Second Commandment to mean that all visual images were forbidden. Sharing the same culture with medieval Jewish artisans who were commissioned to engrave burial markers, illuminate Hebrew manuscripts, and fashion ceremonial objects, medieval Jewish intellectuals did not act as if Judaism were aniconic.[23] They did not assert that Jewish theology orbits around the auditory and the verbal, avoiding the visual, the temporal, and the spatial. They did not reduce the sensations of sight to mere metaphorical status, since it was apparent that they appreciated physical beauty and cultivated both inner and outer eyes. They propounded and challenged theories claiming that art imitates reality. Some of them realized that beauty subjectively resides in the eyes of the beholder. Often they worked as if their discipline were art history: Their tastes were catholic. They were awed by Christian, Islamic, and Jewish sites. They identified artists and patrons. They described the physical construction of Jewish and Gentile monuments and artifacts, interpreting their symbolic meanings, analyzing their aesthetic properties, speculating on the source of their power, arguing over the regulation of their use.

Alerted by the medieval evidence to the strong possibility that Jewish aniconism was stamped with a strictly modern provenance, I formed a new working hypothesis: If Judaism were in fact aniconic, the oddity of a culture without royal, religious, or secular art would certainly have attracted the notice of interested observers. Gathering evidence to test this tentative assumption, I caught sight of a premodern consensus that included everyone from the ancient Greco-Roman historians and rabbinic sages to the sixteenth-century Protestant reformers and the founders of modern art history, Giorgio Vasari and Johann Joachim Winckelmann. The consensus affirmed that Jews do not fashion artifactual representations of their God. The consensus also affirmed that Jewish culture officially sanctions and adorns itself with all sorts of visual art. Some observers, like the medieval St. Bernard of Clairvaux, complained that Judaism was synonymous with too much opulent visuality.

Chronologically framed by the premodern consensus, Jewish aniconism finally emerged as an unmistakably modern idea. Its modernity suggested more than adventitious temporal coincidence. Its historical origins implied that Jewish aniconism is a barometer indicating the pressure of modern culture and politics on Jewish life. It appeared that Jewish aniconism crystallized simultaneously with the construction of modern Jewish identities.

This historical conclusion reduces the field of "overdetermined" reasons for the genesis and popularity of Jewish aniconism. Without denying other possible factors, chapters 1 and 2 narrow the field even more. These chapters correlate affirmations and denials of Jewish art with specific features of the modern historical context. I argue that were it not for Kant and Hegel, the denial of Jewish art would not have been invented. And were it not for nineteenth-century emancipation and anti-Semitism, the affirmative premodern consensus described in chapter 3 would not have been overturned. Nor would Jewish aniconism have persisted so tenaciously throughout the twentieth century, defying the empirical evidence that indicates the existence of authentic Jewish art. Ironically, Jewish aniconism turns out to have been the partisan opinion of anti-Semites who disparaged Jewish culture and diasporan Jews in Western Europe and America who refused Zionist options. Aniconism eventually became the conventional wisdom for general scholars, art critics, and historians who were unable to overcome the dogmatic lessons of their education. Chapter 2 ends with a coda: It plays a dirge for ahistorical essentialism and postivism, a scherzo to the utter ambiguity of artifactual evidence, and a fanfare to the vagaries of contingency and ideology. I argue that the question of Jewish art is unanswerable apart from the multiple ideological frameworks that construct and stabilize our protean notions of "Judaism" and "art."

Assigning a strictly modern provenance to Jewish aniconism bestows other historiographic benefits, as well. It suggests a fresh understanding of medieval Jewish philosophy. It makes obvious what has been obscured for too long. First, modern textbooks and learned journals in medieval cultural history either ignore or say little about Jewish aesthetics because the mainstream of modern scholarship remains committed to the orthodoxy of Jewish aniconism. The time has come to change all that. Second, medieval conceptions of Jewish art and visuality unfolded without the help of Kant, Hegel, Freud, and Marx. Instead, the medieval conceptions adhered to the precedents of rabbinic tradition and followed the contours of the fully embodied, visually infatuated aesthetics of the Middle Ages. Medieval painting, sculpture, and architecture were crafts. They had not yet been secularized and transformed into the so-called fine arts by the eighteenth-century Romantic mystique of the creative genius. They had not yet been commodified by public museums and commercial galleries.

They had not yet been denatured by ages of mechanical or digital reproduction.[24] Medieval images were not "art" in the modern sense of the
word.[25] Medieval images were appreciated for their beauty, but they were
expected to earn their keep, like medicines, tools, and amulets, by performing specific functions.

Chapters 4 through 7 explicate these medieval topics. Chapters 4 and 5
are devoted to philosophic aesthetics. Chapter 4 redescribes the sensory
underpinnings of Jewish epistemology. Chapter 5 rethinks the concept of
beauty by comparing Maimonides and David Hume. Chapter 6 surveys
twelfth-century trends in the iconographic interpretation and functional
analysis of images. It features a thought experiment involving the notorious golden calf. Were the conventional wisdom correct, the golden calf
incident described in Exodus 32 ought to have elicited stark expressions
of Jewish iconoclasm. Instead, the biblical narrative evoked an unexpected
array of fascinating interpretations that attacked Christian images, rationalized Jewish images, embedded art in politics, and legitimated the
golden calf. Chapter 7 completes the story of the calf, probing multifaceted late medieval perceptions of the power and social control of images.
Chapter 7 allows rabbinic law to have the last, perhaps decisive, word.
Rabbinic law is the Scylla and Charybdis of writing Jewish intellectual
history. To overemphasize the law is to distort Judaism by reducing it
to a legalistic essentialism. To ignore the law is to misrepresent Jewish
intellectuals who cultivated it. To neglect the law is to distort Judaism by
erasing one of its axiological foundations. Topics dealing with the law
therefore permeate the book. No chapter of *The Artless Jew* is devoted
exclusively to the law, and no chapter unfolds without substantial references to the halakhah.

In addition to integrating the law, all the chapters situate concepts of
the visual in their immediate, historical context. Each of the chapters ex-
plores the implications of geographic, chronological, and ideological diversity. I argue that medieval Jewish thinkers were neither prophets who
knew the modern principles of Jewish aniconism nor precursors who recognized an eternal existence of art in the modern sense of the word.

Reversing the conventional sequence in history writing, I have placed
the medieval chapters last and the modern chapters first. I decided upon
this slightly eccentric arrangement for several reasons: I am convinced that
premodern and modern views of Jewish art and visuality differ radically. It
is therefore possible to understand the modern views well enough without
owning a stitch of medieval lore. Conversely, it is impossible even to begin
the study of medieval Jewish culture without knowing what the moderns
have taught. Without being informed by modernity, historical scholarship
would be aimless. One would not know what claims to corroborate, refine,
or reject.

While writing *The Artless Jew*, I was frequently scolded by my academic superego for not being an altogether "innocent eye":[26] Thou art obliged to interpret medieval texts dispassionately, "from their own point of view," merely letting them speak in their "own terms." Silencing that unreasonable wretch of a superego, I reminded it that times have changed. In an earlier and perhaps more innocent era, in 1916, it was still possible for Isaac Husik, a distinguished historian of medieval Jewish philosophy, modestly to declare that "there is not much room for originality in a historical and expository work of this kind, particularly as I believe in writing history objectively. I have not attempted to read into the medieval thinkers modern ideas that were foreign to them. I endeavored to interpret their ideas from their own point of view as determined by their history and environment and the literary sources, religious and philosophical, under the influence of which they came."[27] By now the "noble dream" of neutral, disinterested "objectivity" in history writing has vanished.[28] Whether conservative or radical, modernist or postmodernist, academic historians subscribe to various forms of cognitive relativism. Gertrude Himmelfarb, a conservative modernist, wrote the brief: All academic historians now agree that "ideas and events [are] so firmly rooted in their historical context that history, rather than philosophy and nature, becomes the arbiter of truth." Historians, she declared, now realize that "they themselves live and act and think in their own present, that some of the assumptions they bring to history derive from, and are peculiar to, their own culture, that others may reflect the particular race, gender, and class to which they belong, and that still others emanate from ideas and beliefs that are unique to themselves as individuals."[29]

Husik was therefore well intentioned but naive to deny his originality. Being alive in Philadelphia in 1916, attuned to the conflict between science and religion, he was uniquely positioned to discover "that the philosophical movement in mediaeval Jewry was the result of the desire and the necessity . . . of reconciling two apparently independent sources of truth. . . . religious opinions as embodied in revealed documents on the one hand, and philosophical and scientific judgements and arguments, the results of independent rational reflection on the other." Husik's time, place, and training allowed him to fix his attention on something really "there" in the ancient texts: the medieval struggle between "revelation and reason, religion and philosophy, faith and knowledge, authority and independent reflection."[30] His time, place, training, and predispositions also obscured his view. They did not allow him to notice that medieval philosophers also sought to understand the visual arts.

Being alive in late twentieth-century America, inhabiting a social and academic space in which the topics of multiculturalism, "body studies," and "visual regimes" are preeminent, in which world travel to museums and monuments is easy, in which cameras, televisions, and computer screens await the slightest flick of a switch, I was enabled to imagine *The Artless Jew.* Were it not for the accumulating archival and archaeological evidence of Jewish artifacts ignored by or unknown to Husik's generation, I would not have been aware of what to look for in the medieval texts. Without the modern art historians who disabused me of my mistaken beliefs and taught me that the Byzantine iconoclasts cultivated a visual art of their own, that Islam is not averse to representational art and architecture, that visual art flourished within the Protestant Reformation, I might not have discovered that the Second Commandment theoretically licenses all visual images except one.

Husik lived too early to be shaken out of a dogmatic slumber (as I was) by Linda Nochlin's sociological answers to the question, Why have there been no great women artists? and by Michele Wallace's parallel discussion of African-American art and artists.[31] These controversial essays prompted me to reconsider the conventional wisdom presupposing that Jewish culture produced no visual artists. Their essays also reassured me that I was on the right track in specifically correlating modern perceptions of Jewish art with anti-semitism and the struggle for Jewish identity rather than with vague appeals to an eternally fixed "Hebraic spirit" or ancient biblical prohibitions against fashioning images of God. Their essays finally made me understand that when the ambiguous term "art" is qualified by Greek, Dutch, Italian, or French, it tends to trigger one set of high-minded, canonical associations; but when coupled with Jewish or primitive or feminist or African-American, the terms "art" and "artist" trigger an altogether different stream of conscious stereotypes and unconscious associations. The range and vocabulary of these associations have less to do with timeless (Eurocentric and hegemonic) notions of beauty and more to do with the experience of diasporan minorities and subordinated peoples. Subordinated minorities tend to be excluded from or derogated by the art establishment. They seek cultural effacement ("no such thing as Jewish art") or self-affirmation ("some sort of Jewish art") while engaged in revolutionary struggles against colonialism, sexism, and racism.

Were I not living in late twentieth-century America, I would not have been able to read Nochlin and Wallace. And had I not been taught by Husik's generation that Judaism is aniconic, that Jewish thought favors the verbal over the visual, that premodern Jewish philosophy lacked a full-scale aesthetics, I would not have been astonished to discover that the texts and artifacts of medieval Jewish culture told a different story. In all likelihood, I would not have noticed the medieval story at all.

Were I an art historian, I would have written a different book. It would have contained photographic reproductions of specific images and monuments. The text would have offered critical discussion of those images and monuments, exploring their formal characteristics, provenance, patrons, creators, markets, and iconographic implications. Instead, I am an intellectual historian and this book intentionally lacks plates and illustrations. *The Artless Jew* does not refer to specific images and monuments. It investigates ideas about art, artisans, artifacts, and visuality that are embedded in literary traditions.

Finally, were it not for the contingencies of my personal life, I would not have been visiting Padua in 1993, standing awestruck in Giotto's Arena Chapel, with my partner and significant other. Annabel guessed my envious thoughts and offered a loving, footnoted word of comfort. Ending my ignorance, she mused: "Why so sad? You have your frescoes of Dura-Europos."[32] Nor would I have been in graduate school, long ago, when a mentor informed me that the first principle of historical scholarship requires that "we not smudge our fingerprints all over other people's ideas." Fortunately, there was another mentor, more closely related and far more collegial. Several years ago, in New York, he listened to my paralyzing doubts and said: "Our job is not to write the complete and final word. We just put things on the agenda. We bring things to people's attention, and hope that our work is superseded." *The Artless Jew* is meant to reinvigorate the field of medieval Jewish philosophy. It is designed to show that Jewish bodies no longer "lack eyes."[33] I hope to see my work and intentions superseded.

One

Modern Denials and Affirmations of Jewish Art: Germanophone Origins and Themes

I

In 1922, Marc Chagall was in Moscow and Erwin R. Goodenough was at Oxford University. Chagall, the famous Jewish artist, was preparing to leave for the West; Goodenough, the aspiring scholar, was contemplating the Greco-Roman provenance of Jewish artifacts and symbols. Chagall was musing in Yiddish. Goodenough was conversing with his mentors in English. Chagall remarked that "were I not a Jew (with the content that I put in the word), I would not be an artist at all, or I would be someone else altogether. . . . I know quite well what this small people can accomplish. . . . When it wished, it brought forth Christ and Christianity. When it wanted, it produced Marx and socialism. Can it be then that it would not show the world some sort of art? Kill me, if not."[1] Goodenough was "gently told" by "all" of his dons that "Jewish Scripture and tradition alike forbade the making of images, and so long as a group was loyal to Judaism at all it would have nothing to do with art." Six years later, Goodenough was a junior faculty member at Yale University. His senior colleague, Professor Paul Baur, reassured him "that there was no such thing as Jewish art."[2]

It is customary to resolve the dispute between "some sort of art" and "no such thing as Jewish art" by referring to ancient Israelite laws.[3] This appeal to biblical authority is inadequate. Rather than clarify historical and historiographical complexities, the theological explanation mystifies them. It overlooks the hermeneutical dexterity with which commentators forge anachronisms and graft alien ideas on ancient texts. By themselves, biblical verses cannot explain why Jewish aniconism, the denial of Jewish art, became the conventional wisdom in modern secular scholarship. Biblical verses cannot explain why the idea of Jewish aniconism has persisted throughout the twentieth century despite the apparent evidence to the contrary amassed by a host of archaeologists, ethnographers, archivists, and art historians. Ignoring cultural politics, the theological explanation also fails to explain why so many critics and museum curators deny aesthetic status to Jewish ceremonial or folk art.[4] To fathom the modern denials and affirmations of Jewish art, factors less theological and more recent than ancient biblical laws must be identified.

Consider the authoritative *Jewish Encyclopedia* published in 1902 and the equally authoritative *Catholic Encyclopedia* published in 1910. The *Jewish Encyclopedia* includes an entry "Art, Attitude of Judaism Toward." It was written by Kaufmann Kohler, a prominent scholar, a leading Reform rabbi, and one of the *Jewish Encyclopedia*'s chief editors. Consulting Kohler, we learn that "it is . . . somewhat incorrect to speak of Jewish art. Whether in Biblical or in post-Biblical times, Jewish workmanship was influenced, if not altogether guided by non-Jewish art." As if anticipating Goodenough's mentors at Oxford and Yale, Kohler explained the absence of an indigenous Jewish art by referring to the prohibition contained in Exodus 20:4, declaring that "plastic art in general was discouraged by the Law; the prohibition of idols in the Decalogue being in olden times applied to all images, whether they were made objects of worship or not."[5]

The *Catholic Encyclopedia* was convinced otherwise. Staunchly defending its traditional ritual practice against Protestant iconoclasm, the *Catholic Encyclopedia* argued that the biblical prohibition against idolatry "was never understood as an absolute and universal prohibition of any kind of image. Throughout the Old Testament there are instances of representations of living things, not in any way worshipped, but used lawfully." As if correcting Kohler and Goodenough's mentors, it concluded its richly detailed survey of the copious archaeological evidence by announcing that "when Christians began to decorate their catacombs with holy pictures, they did not thereby sever themselves from the custom of their Jewish forefathers."[6]

The inference is inescapable: When inflected by early twentieth-century Roman Catholic accents, the history of Jewish art was construed positively; when inflected by the contemporary accents of Reform Judaism or Protestant Christianity at Yale and Oxford, it was construed negatively. Kaufmann Kohler was also the leading spirit at the rabbinical convention in 1885 that declared Judaism "no longer a nation, but a religious community."[7] In a historical moment when art was understood to be the expression of national identity, it was reasonable to conclude that nonnational Judaism produced no visual art.[8] A more general inference is also inescapable: Along with everything else in modernity relating to religion, aesthetics, race, and nationalism, the very idea of Jewish art is factious. It is steeped in cultural politics and partisan debate.

In the sections to follow, I argue that anti-Semitism and Jewish assimilation profoundly shaped modern discourse on Jewish art.[9] The argument entails an investigation of nineteenth- and early twentieth-century Germanophone intellectuals who articulated the doctrine of Jewish aniconism and the disciples who inherited and modified it.[10] Coping with Jewish emancipation and anti-Semitism, these intellectuals were intent on dissociating Judaism from the visual arts. Their motives were mixed: Aniconism was both a vice to be condemned and a virtue to be praised. Condemnation mainly served Gentiles who hoped to rid Europe of Judaism. Praise served Jews and Gentiles who struggled to perpetuate assimilated Jewish life in the Diaspora. Regardless of motive, they agreed that Judaism was fundamentally aniconic. Partisans of "some sort of art" were the minority. Struggling in their own way with emancipation and anti-Semitism, they were intent on affiliating Judaism closely with the visual arts. Their motives too were mixed. Some, like Marc Chagall, took secular pride in Jewish national creativity. Most were dismayed or disappointed with assimilated life in Europe. They were inspired by a diverse array of Zionist ideas.[11] Some were merely nostalgic for a lost past.

II

In 1790, not long after the American and French Revolutions, Immanuel Kant, preferring the abstract and the disembodied over the sensate and the sensible, pietistically conceded that "perhaps the most sublime passage in the Jewish Law is the commandment: Thou shalt not make unto thee any graven image, or any likeness of any thing that is in heaven or on earth, or under the earth, etc. This commandment alone can explain the enthusiasm that the Jewish people in its civilized era felt for its religion when it compared itself with other peoples, or can explain the pride that Islam inspires. The same holds also for our presentation of the moral law, and for the predisposition within us for morality."[12]

Hegel closed the pincers of a double bind. Rather than praise Judaism and Islam for their imageless God, as did Kant, Hegel berated them for failing to represent their God visually. In the introduction to the published version of the lectures on fine art he had delivered in Berlin during the 1820s, Hegel spoke for Christian practice. He argued that "everything genuine in spirit and nature alike is inherently concrete and, despite its universality, has nevertheless subjectivity and particularity in itself. Therefore the Jews and the Turks have not been able by art to represent their God, who does not even amount to such an abstraction of the Understanding, in the positive way that the Christians have. For in Christianity God is set forth in his truth, and therefore as thoroughly concrete in himself, as person, as subject, and, more closely defined as spirit."[13]

Acculturated German Jews who remained Jews would seek to escape the double bind by agreeing with Kant and Hegel where it was possible and correcting them where it was necessary. Kant approved of aniconic Mosaic law; Hegel disapproved. Unable to dispute Hegel's empirical observations, German Jewish intellectuals eagerly adopted Kant's awe of aniconism. Finding Hegel's admiration for progressive "spirit" congenial to their own temperament and reformist cause, they used Hegelian categories and principles to prove Kant wrong when he declared Judaism lacking in true religion, ethical significance, and universal concern.[14] When they finished their work, Judaism became fundamentally aniconic, preeminently spiritual, coterminous with ethics, and quintessentially universal.[15]

These major motifs in German Jewry's complex antiphonal response to Kant and Hegel were sounded by Dr. Solomon Formstecher (1808–1889), a liberal rabbi serving in Offenbach. In 1841, Formstecher published *Die Religion des Geistes, eine wissenschaftliche Darstellung des Judenthums nach seinem Charakter, Entwicklungsgange und Berufe in der Menscheit* (The religion of the spirit, a scientific exposition of Judaism according to its character, historical development, and vocation to humanity). He proposed that as long as Judaism "battled" the paganism surrounding it, Judaism would have to consider the plastic arts [*Plastik*] its "severe foe" and "to find its own symbols only in the sphere of the spiritual." Judaism could permit itself the "charms [*Zauber*] of poetry, accompanied by melody and rhythm" that lead people to religious ecstasy, "but no plastic art-form should awaken thoughts of God, no sculptured statues represent Him."[16] Formstecher bluntly asserted that "Judaism is hostile [*feind*] to the plastic arts";[17] he firmly believed that there can be only "ethical, but not aesthetic manifestations of the absolute."[18] The "mysterious [*räthselhafte*] cherubs," the "only plastic art-forms" allowed to stand in the Temple, were no exception to this rule. Formstecher explained that the cherubs were permitted only because they symbolized God's angelic servants but not God Himself.[19]

Ten years later, the same interrelated motifs of Jewish aniconism and Jewish ethical spirituality were orchestrated poignantly by Heinrich Heine (1796–1856), the renowned poet and cultural critic who was born a Jew but underwent a lukewarm conversion to Lutheranism in 1824. In 1854, two years before his agonizing death, Heine recollected his life. Contemplating his rediscovery of Judaism, he acknowledged that Judaism was aniconic, but not without a compensatory art of its own. Heine wrote that formerly he

> could not forgive the law-giver of the Jews for his hatred of all visual imagery [*Bildlichkeit*] and the plastic arts [*Plastik*]. I failed to see that Moses, despite all of his hostility to art [*Befeindung der Kunst*], was himself a great artist [*Künstler*] and possessed the true artistic spirit. In his case, as in that of his Egyptian countrymen, this artistic spirit was directed solely towards the colossal and the indestructible. But unlike the Egyptians he did not fashion his works from baked bricks and granite. He built human pyramids [*Menschenpyramiden*]; he carved human obelisks; he took a poor shepherd tribe and from it he created a people that was also to defy the centuries—a great, immortal, holy people, a people of

God, which could serve as a prototype of humanity. . . . I have learned to appreciate the [Jews] better; and if pride of birth were not a ridiculous contradiction in a champion of the Revolution and its democratic principles, the writer of these pages would take pride in the knowledge that his ancestors belonged to the noble house of Israel; that he is descended from martyrs who have given the world a God and a morality and who have fought and suffered on all the battlefields of thought.[20]

Heine's requiem for Jewish visual art remained popular with German Jewish intellectuals. Sixty years after he composed it, the requiem was transcribed and fine-tuned by Hermann Cohen (1842–1918) in his monumental synthesis of neo-Kantian and existentialist religious thought, the posthumously published *Religion der Vernunft aus den Quellen des Judentums* (Religion of reason out of the sources of Judaism).[21] In the chapter devoted to Law (*Das Gesetz*), Cohen advanced the argument that Jewish observances are not restricted to worship. They pervade the entirety of life, constituting a "yoke of the Kingdom of God that at the same time serves as a "ladder to heaven (*Himmelsleiter*)." The Law is therefore not dispensable; it should not be abrogated, at least not in its entirety. Cohen raised the "great question" then being debated between the reformers and the traditionalists regarding the extent to which the burden of the Law can be "reduced" without destroying its "effectiveness."[22] Searching for guidelines on what can be eliminated safely from Jewish observance, he invoked the precedent of Judaism's traditional abandonment of the visual arts: "The plastic arts [*Plastik*] and painting [*Malerei*] were kept at a safe distance from the pure worship of God."

Formstecher's cherubs had disappeared, but like Formstecher, Cohen did not conclude that Judaism is bereft of all arts. Citing Heine by name, Cohen invoked the "poetically articulated" notion that Moses "carved human pyramids." Cohen explained that this implicitly superior and compensatory "art work of people" (*Kunstwerk der Menschen*) was achieved "by means of the laws." He concluded that "the laws themselves can therefore not be without all artistic value," especially not without the artistic value associated with the verbal art of "poetry." "As poetry," Cohen continues, "the artistic value of the laws permeates all forms, the tragic and the idyllic." Cohen then replayed the complex polyphony of anti-Kantian and neo-Kantian strains in Heine's requiem: "Out of the bounds of the laws, at all times, came forth those Israelites who achieved great things for culture in all of its branches . . . uppermost of all the great moral impulses. The intrinsic connection between the laws and public morality could never be misunderstood."[23]

Cohen repeated these arguments in a later chapter, "The Virtues." Claiming to shed new light on the biblical prohibition against the worship of images, Cohen drew a distinction between the Jewish and Christian use of symbols. The aniconism that Hegel had found to be a deficiency, Cohen pronounced a virtue. He declared that "the veracity of the Jewish consciousness of God is precisely the reason for the aversion to the plastic arts [*Abwehr der Plastik*]." As if echoing Formstecher, Cohen explained that the prophets and psalmists scorned the paganistic visual images of God, but they found their natural ally in the verbal arts of poetry. Cohen assured his readers that "what the religious consciousness loses in the visual arts [*bildenden Kunst*], it makes up for amply through lyrical poetry. . . . Monotheism makes no concessions to the visual arts, for thereby the unique God would come to danger."[24]

Cohen had laid the foundation for these points in the beginning of the book. In chapter 1, Cohen noted the striking fact that "Judaism presents its chief sources in literary documents." In contrast, "polytheism . . . possesses its monuments primarily in the form of plastic arts. Plastic art makes of itself an analogy to nature. Poetry, on the other hand, the original language of literature, is able to make spiritual thoughts more inward than can the visual arts."[25] And again in chapter 2, "Image-Worship (*Der Bilderdienst*), which interprets the Second Commandment, the visual arts are excluded from representing the unique God, for God is "absolutely the archetype for the mind [*Urbild für den Geist*], for the love of reason, but not an object for mimetic reproduction [*Nachbildung*]."[26] Cohen then asserted "there necessarily arises in prophetic monotheism the opposition to, the contradiction of, [visual] art which is the original mode of operation of the human spirit."[27] Judaism was therefore an "anomaly" in the history of culture, and Cohen considered himself obliged to explain why the Jews alone were able to dispense with the visual arts. Not altogether confident in his solution, he surmised that it was the victory of the more powerful art of verbal poetry over the less potent visual art of images. Striking a variation on the theme sounded by Heine, Cohen concluded that "the prophets would not have been able to carry on the fight against art in the visual images of God if they themselves had not been able to lead it as artists [*Künstler*], as poet-thinkers [*Dichterdenker*] in the full power of a poetic imagination."[28]

Perhaps expressing his approval of the efflorescence of synagogue construction in nineteenth-century Germany,[29] Cohen conceded that religious architecture was a noteworthy exception to the rule of a systematic aversion to the visual arts, "for architecture did not fall into the worship of visual images. Rather it can create works for men who serve the unique God, but not for God who might dwell in such a house."[30] Cohen returned to this topic in a later chapter, "Prayer" (*Das Gebet*), which puzzles over the apparent contradiction between prophetic monotheism's aversion to visual images of God and its endorsement of housing this imageless God in an actual building. After all, Cohen argued, "the dwelling of the unique God is a mystery [*Geheimnis*], and building a house for Him seems a violation [*Verletzung*]." He resolved the problem by insisting that the house was built not for God, "not even for His image which does not exist, but only for men who want to pray, not to offer sacrifices."[31]

Unable, then, to improve on the beauty of Heine's formula, Hermann Cohen cited it literally, modulating its poetic excesses. The Mosaic aversion to visual art translates into a repudiation of the polytheistic practice of representing spiritual entities in visual form, regardless of whether those entities are human or divine.[32] Cohen, however, considered Heine imprecise for ignoring Judaism's sponsorship of religious architecture. According to Cohen, religious architecture was compatible with Judaism because it facilitated strictly spiritual acts of verbal and conceptual worship. Heine was right, however, in stressing the idea that Moses was an artist of another kind: Moses shaped a moral society informed by the supreme principles of ethical monotheism.

Moses also left room for a second type of art: poetry. Formstecher agreed. So did Heine, for Heine also boasted that Judaism's literature, especially its Bible, a "portable homeland," was Judaism's supreme contribution to general culture.[33] Franz Rosenzweig (1886–1929), Hermann Cohen's innovative and admiring disciple, also assigned to poetry a preeminent place in religious existence. In *Star of Redemption* (*Stern der Erlöserung*), Rosenzweig declared that

> Poetry . . . comes to be the truly vital art, and a certain human maturity is even more indispensable for the great poet than for the painter or musician. . . . Art and music are still somewhat abstract; the former appears to some extent mute, the latter blind. As a result, oral revelation, beginning with Moses, has never confronted visual art . . . without some misgivings. No such misgivings apply to poetry . . . for poetry supplies structure as well as discourse. . . . Therefore poetry is, because most alive, the most vital art. It is not necessary for every person to have a taste for music or painting, to be an amateur producer or reproducer in the one or the other. But every complete human being must have a taste for poetry; indeed he must be an amateur poet himself. At the very least he must have once written poetry. Even if, at a pinch, one can be human without composing poetry, one cannot become human without having done so for a time.[34]

Formstecher, Heine, Cohen, and Rosenzweig insisted that the spirit of Jewish ethical monontheism was inimical to the visual arts but altogether compatible with the verbal arts of poetry, especially the religious poetry of the Bible. In Cohen's hypothetical formulation, biblical poetry might never have been created "if a stop had not been put to the plastic arts. This characteristic consists in the lyric poetry of the Psalms, which praises neither God alone nor man alone. Plastic art, by contrast, can only depict those two forms in isolation, thus hampering lyric poetry."[35]

Such assumptions and conclusions are not self-evident. It is not obvious that ethical monotheism necessarily excludes the visual arts, that poetry is the supreme art form, that visual art is more sensually provocative than verbal art, that visual art is incapable of depicting God and man together, or that the verbal and visual arts cannot thrive in the same society. It is therefore apparent that these German Jewish intellectuals were convinced by something powerful and authorizing in their culture. When they advanced the cause of Jewish aniconism, they rebuffed Hegel by following the respected lead of Kant who had extolled the biblical prohibition against visual images. When they crowned poetry the supreme art, they were building on foundations laid by Herder in the *Spirit of Hebrew Poetry* (1782). They were also following the prestigious lead of both Kant and Hegel. In *The Critique of Judgment*, Kant had declared that "among all the arts poetry holds the highest rank. . . . It expands the mind. . . . Poetry fortifies the mind: for it lets the mind feel its ability . . . it does not sneak up on the understanding and ensnare it by a sensible exhibition."[36] Hegel had asserted that poetry is the "most spiritual presentation of romantic art . . . Poetry is the universal art of the spirit which has become free in itself and which is not tied down for its realization to external sensuous material; instead, it launches out exclusively in the inner space and the inner time of ideas and feelings. . . . Poetry [unlike the other arts] is adequate to all forms of the beautiful, and extends over all of them."[37] For intellectuals steeped in the German Romantic tradition, then, poetry, philosophy, and religion, in their highest forms, were almost synonymous. As Friedrich Schlegel (1772–1829) put it, "He who has religion will speak poetry."[38]

III

Salomon Ludwig Steinheim (1789–1866), a physician by profession and a Jewish theologian by vocation, also appreciated poetry, but he preferred "hymns and melody." Steinheim was impressed by Aristotle's discussion of the role of music in educating youth, citing at length the discussion in *Politics* 8:5.[39] Steinheim also considered it a scientifically valid fact that hearing was the highest of the the five senses, for hearing does not relate to "spatial entities [*Räumliches*]." It is attuned to "temporality [*Zeitliche*], motion, activity, [and] the work of various powers in the visible world."[40] Steinheim considered hearing the last of the senses to emerge in nature and therefore anatomically the least widely distributed in organic nature.[41] He deduced that hearing has an affinity with "spatial-becoming [*Räumlich-Geschehendes*]" but not with "spatial-being [*Räumlich-Seiendes*]" and that "through hearing, by means of sound, spirit [Geist] recognizes spirit."[42] Praising Kant for being among the very few who "ponder carefully what they assert," Steinheim concurred with Kant's dictum that the ban against visual images of God was the "supreme prohibition in the Old Testament." For Steinheim, as for Formstecher, Heine, and Cohen, "visual and corporeal manifestations belittle and corrupt the notion of God." Unlike them, however, Steinheim affirmed that the "highest and most pure thought regarding God can and should only" take the form of "word and musical note" (Ton).[43]

Comparing himself to Plato, who banned poetry, Steinheim declared that he would not be misunderstood if people thought he was advocating the total elimination of visual art from all worship within the confines of a religious building.[44] Steinheim did not, however, favor the elimination of visual art from all corners of Jewish life. He was not a philistine and did not want to be identified with "rigid Quakerism" (Stockquäkerthum). He appreciated the visual arts for their service to beauty, for their decorative and didactic powers, and especially for their ability to depict historical narratives. He invoked the precedent of the most "devout pietists" (Frommen), holding the most "uncompromising beliefs" (unbeugsamen Glaubens), who allowed art its rightful place in Jewish life. For proof, he mentioned having seen illuminated texts and prayerbooks originating in the fifteenth or sixteenth century adorned with "painted initials" and "decorated representations." Such paintings, Steinheim assured his readers, were used only as an aid to "devotion" (Andacht); they excluded any "sacrilegious depictions of God." For actual worship, however, sculpture and painting lack music's ability to transcend materiality and lead the soul to the spiritual domain of "holiness and everlasting bliss" (Seligkeit).[45]

IV

Heinrich Graetz (1817–1891) admired Steinheim. They both associated Judaism intimately with the verbal and the musical. Destined for fame as the author of the multivolume Geschichte der Juden, Graetz published a programmatic essay in 1846 outlining his thoughts on "the structure of Jewish history." Against the backdrop of a radical distinction correlating paganism with "nature" and Judaism with "spirit," he drew a sharp contrast between pagans who experience the divine as something visible and Jews who experience God "through a demonstration of His will, through the medium of the ear." Carrying this theological distinction into the realms of aesthetics and morality, Graetz absorbed and revised Hegel:

> Paganism sees its god, Judaism hears Him; that is, it hears the commandments of His Will. . . . Furthermore, artistic expression also develops differently ac-

cording to the different concepts of God. The artistic act created in Greek paganism, in accord with its sensuous God-concept, is the art of sculpture, that
lovely fragrant blossom of the pagan form of perception. In Judaism, on the
other hand, which perceives its God in the alternatingly loud and soft sounds of
the movement of the waves, in the rhythm of word sounds, the artistic drive, in
harmony with this particular view of God, gave birth to music combined with
religious poetry. . . . It is unnecessary to dwell on this viewpoint any longer, for
the entire structure of Judaism attests to it. The sharp opposition of Judaism to
a paganism sunk in idolatry and immorality, traits which are conspicuously evident at a single glance, is nothing but the broad antithesis between the religion
of the spirit and the religion of nature, divine transcendence and immanence.[46]

In 1874, writing the introduction to the first volume of his *History*,
Graetz elaborated upon the distinction between licentious Greek visuality
and chaste Hebraic aniconism. "Hellenism," he wrote, "dispersed the
flowers of art and the fruits of knowledge. It unveiled the realm of beauty
and illuminated it with an Olympian clarity of thought." By contrast, Hebraism showed "a certain deficiency in failing to leave behind any gigantic
structures of architectural wonders" because it "probably lacked any architectural skill. . . . Likewise, it did not build temples for its God—the Solo-
monic Temple was built by Phoenicians—because the goal was to trans-
form the heart of man into God's temple. Israel neither sculpted nor
painted gods, for it considered the deity as an object of solemn and devout
reverence and not as a subject of frivolous play." In the realm of literature,
Hebraism did not "excel in artistic epics and still less in tragedy and comedy" because of its "aversion against mythologies . . . as well as against the
levity and theatrics of the stage." But Hebraism did produce "two other
genres which reflected the full richness of its idealistic life: the psalms and
the poetically wrought eloquence of the prophets." According to the
world historical division of artistic labor imagined by Graetz, "Greek literature illuminated the realm of art and knowledge, Hebraic literature idealized the realm of the sacred and the moral." Devoted to holiness and
sexual restraint, the Jews survived history. Devoted to art, philosophy,
and debauchery, "sunk in lewdness and sexual aberrations," the ancient
Greeks, along with all the other nations of antiquity, disappeared. Hebraism entailed the "overcoming and controlling [of] . . . selfishness and animal desires;" it disallowed "animal-like behavior and sexual perversion."
"History provided the test. Nations which defiled themselves through
immorality, growing callous through the use of force, succumbed to
death."[47]

In 1889, chafing under the ever escalating friction of political and racial
anti-Semitism, Graetz polemically applied his stereotypes of ancient civilizations to modern Europe. He fought back in English, writing for an
audience already familiar with the typological distinction between "He-

braism and Hellenism" made famous by Matthew Arnold and inspired by
Heinrich Heine.[48] Writing for the London-based *Jewish Quarterly Review*,
Graetz argued that "whereas the Latin race is more permeated with the
spirit of Hellenism, the Anglo-Saxon race is penetrated with the Biblico-
Judaic spirit because its mind is more directed to truth than to beauty."[49]
Six years earlier, Graetz had been less generous with the Anglo-Saxons and
far less cautious in spelling out the differences between Hellenic "beauty"
and Hebraic "truth." Thinking of widespread prostitution, the number
of illegitimate births, and the ravages of syphillis in nineteenth-century
Europe, Graetz waxed eloquent on the horrid implications of the preference for beauty over truth and virtue. The ancient pagan goddesses of
love, Aphrodite and Venus, according to Graetz, transformed themselves
in modern European culture into the twin ideals of "love" and "beauty."
He remarked that

> the goddess of infamy still continues to ravage the spinal cord of the civilized
> world. Antiquity was little more than a public house of infamy, and modern
> civilization has merely transformed it into private houses. The showing of nudes
> in all art exhibitions whether in the form of Venus or that of the repentant
> Magdalena, the rush to Makart's sensual colors of flesh, and the intense interest
> in so-called academies that destroy any sense of shame and against which the
> police have moved in vain, prove sufficiently that the cult of Aphrodite still has
> enthusiastic adherents in our civilized world. And now, in addition, the filthy
> novels à la Zola.[50]

Convinced that "the survival or demise of nations is determined by
the observance or violation of the laws of sexual morality" and eager to
pronounce that "the palm branch for sexual restraint belongs from antiquity to the present solely to the people of Israel,"[51] Graetz asserted the
moral superiority of Judaism over European culture. Moral superiority
articulated his answer to the urgent questions of his day: How did Judaism
manage to survive endless persecution? How might Judaism guarantee
survival despite racial and political anti-Semitism? To both questions,
Graetz framed one and the same answer: Judaism survives because it es-
pouses the rational sobriety of ethical monotheism. Repudiating paganism, Judaism defies the natural and cultivates the spiritual. It therefore
refuses to indulge in the visual arts.

V

In 1854, Heine anticipated Graetz's austerity. Confessing his former dis-
appointment with Moses for having spurned the visual arts, Heine admitted that his enthusiasm for Greek culture was mistaken. Just as he had

come to realize that Moses was a greater "artist" than any mere sculptor or painter, so too had he come to understand that the "Greeks were only beautiful youths, while the Jews were always men, powerful, unyielding men. This applies, not only to ancient times, but also to the present day, despite eighteen centuries of persecution and misery."[52]

Heine and Graetz developed the interlocking themes of Jewish anti-Hellenism, aniconism, manly restraint, austere spirituality, and survival despite adversity. In *Moses and Monotheism*, so did Freud.[53] Because Freud so neatly encapsulated the nineteenth-century Jewish funicular arguments that elevated Jewish ethical culture while dropping the visual arts, it is worth citing him at length:

> Among the precepts of Mosaic religion is one that has more significance than is at first obvious. It is the prohibition against making an image of God, which means the compulsion to worship an invisible God. . . . The prohibition . . . was bound to exercise a profound influence, for it signified subordinating sense perception to an abstract idea; it was a triumph of spirituality [*Geistigkeit*] over the senses [*Sinnlichkeit*]; more precisely, an instinctual renunciation accompanied by its psychologically necessary consequences. . . . Through the Mosaic prohibition, God was raised to a higher level of spirituality. . . . All such progress in spirituality results in increasing self-confidence, in making people proud so that they feel superior to those who have remained in the bondage of the senses. . . .
>
> The preference which through two thousand years the Jews have given to spiritual endeavor has, of course, had its effect; it has helped to build a dike against brutality [*Roheit*] and the inclination to violence [*Gewalttat*] which are usually found where athletic development [*Muskelkraft*] becomes the ideal of the people. The harmonious development of spiritual and bodily activity, as achieved by the Greeks, was denied to the Jews. In this conflict their decision was at least made in favor of what is culturally the more important. . . . Progress in spirituality consists in deciding against the direct sense perception in favor of the so-called higher intellectual processes—that is to say, in favor of memories, recollection, and logical deduction.
>
> The religion that began with the prohibition against making an image of God has developed in the course of the centuries more and more into a religion of instinctual renunciation. Not that it demands sexual renunciation; it is content with a considerable restriction of sexual freedom. God, however, becomes completely withdrawn from sexuality and raised to an ideal of ethical perfection. Ethics, however, means restriction of instinctual gratification. The Prophets did not tire of maintaining that God demands nothing else from His people but a just and virtuous life.[54]

Heine, Graetz, and Freud combined admiration for Jewish aniconism and ethical restraint with an equally powerful disdain for Hellenic aesthetics and athleticism. In doing so, they were turning the tables on German intellectuals who idealized the Greeks and held the Jews, ancient and modern, in utter contempt. In 1841—the same year that Formstecher announced Judaism's hostility to the plastic arts; eleven years before Heine declared that he had renounced Hellenism in favor of Hebraism; forty years before Graetz claimed truth, music, and morality for Judaism, leaving beauty, visual arts, and sexual perversity to the now deceased Greeks; and ninety-six years before Freud credited Jewish aniconism with initiating the intellectualism and sensual renunciation that eventually gave rise to science—in 1841, Ludwig Feuerbach had declared that

> using the theoretical senses, the Greeks observed nature. They heard heavenly music in the harmonious course of the stars; they saw nature arise from the foam of the all-producing ocean as Venus Anadyomene. The Israelites, on the contrary, opened to nature only the gastric sense; their taste for nature lay only in the palate; their consciousness of God in eating manna. The Greek pursued humanistic studies (Humaniora, the liberal arts, philosophy); the Israelite did not rise above the alimentary view of theology. . . . When Moses and the seventy elders ascended the mountain where "they saw God . . . they ate and drank." Seeing the Supreme Being therefore only stimulated in them their appetite for food. The Jews have maintained their peculiarity to this day. Their principle, their God . . . [is] egoism. . . . Hence, science arises, like art, only from polytheism, for polytheism is the open, ungrudging sensibility for all that is beautiful and good. . . . The Greeks looked into the wide world that they might extend their sphere of vision; the Jews to this day pray with their faces turned towards Jerusalem. . . . Polytheistic sensibility, I repeat, is the groundwork for science and art.[55]

Three years later, in 1844, Karl Marx published an essay, "On the Jewish Problem" (*Zur Judenfrage*). Marx transposed Feuerbach's list of Jewish vices—egoism, carnality, and parochialism—into Jewish selfishness (*Eigennutz*), petty commercialism (*Schacher*), and capitalistic moneygrubbing. Kant had already associated Judaism with the shady practices of commercialism, offering a strictly geographical and historical explanation.[56] Marx went beyond Kant, contending that "money is the jealous God of Israel before whom no other God may endure." He therefore predicted that "as soon as society will succeed in abolishing the empirical nature of Judaism, commerce and its presuppositions, the existence of the Jew will be impossible, because his consciousness will have lost its object. . . . The social emancipation of the Jew is the emancipation of society from Judaism."[57]

In Freud's terms, Marx and Feuerbach had mistakenly defined the Jews as people "who have remained in the bondage of the senses"; Jews were therefore incapable of matching "Greek" achievements in art, science, and philosophy. Heine, Graetz, and Freud disagreed, just as they opposed Marx's call for "abolishing the empirical nature of Judaism," since for

them the empirical nature of Judaism was neither materialistic nor commercial but thoroughly spiritual and chastely aniconic. Defending themselves against the potentially lethal premises of nineteenth-century cultural and political anti-Semitism, Heine, Graetz, and Freud counterattacked aggressively: It is not the monotheistic and aniconic Jews, but
the Greeks and their contemporary admirers who cultivate the merely
physical. It is not the Jews, but the ancient and polytheistic Egyptians,
Phoenicians, and Greeks, together with their contemporary enthusiasts,
who busy themselves with fashioning commodifiable objets d'art. The
counterattack was funicular. It conceded that the spirit of Judaism was
not conducive to creativity in the materialistic visual arts; it stressed that,
in compensation for this deficiency, the Jews have always excelled in the
verbal arts—witness the biblical psalmists and prophets. The Jews also
excelled in music, sexual chastity, manly restraint, and the national capacity
to survive. For Heine, Graetz, and Freud—to which list must now be
added the names of Formstecher, Steinheim, and Cohen—Europe could
ill afford to abolish Judaism, since the elimination of Judaic spirituality
would annihilate the very source of high culture, abstract reasoning, natural science, and morality. Far from being a sign of deficiency, Jewish aniconism was a sign and cause of Judaic virtue.

VI

Speaking for the anti-Semites, Richard Wagner disagreed.[58] In 1849, having absorbed the socioeconomic critique of Judaism and Feuerbach's deri-
sive contrast between Hellenic visual culture and selfish Hebraic taste
buds, Wagner published *Das Kunstwerk der Zukunft* (*The Artwork of the
Future*). This revolutionary manifesto drew a sharp contrast between the
ancient Greeks and the Jews of Wagner's own day. Wagner celebrated the
Greeks who were able to create visual beauty and enjoy sculpture for its
humanistic significance; he bemoaned the nineteenth-century Jews who
produced and appreciated art only for its commercial, pragmatic value
(*Utilismus*). In Wagner's opinion, Jewish aesthetics amounted to nothing
more than the historic "Byzantine . . . Judaic-Oriental notion of profit-
ability" (*jüdisch-orientalische Nützlichkeitsvorstellung*), which had ruined
the free-spirited art of ancient Greece.[59]
    In 1850, Wagner substituted modern German culture for the victim-
ized ancient Greek, added biological inferiority to the list of Jewish socioeconomic defects, and issued a racist's scathing attack against "Judaism in
Music" (*Das Judenthum in der Musik*). Objecting to the "jewification of
modern art" (*Verjüdung der modernen Kunst*), Wagner named Felix Bar-
tholdy-Mendelssohn and Heinrich Heine as proof that composers and

poets of Jewish origin are physiologically and constitutionally unable to contribute anything truly valuable to genuine Germanic culture. Regarding visuality and the visual arts, Wagner complained that

> the sensory capacity for sight [*die sinnliche Anschauungsgabe*] belonging to the Jews was never such as to allow them to produce visual artists; their eyes are preoccupied with matters much more practical than beauty and the spiritual content of things in the phenomenal world. To the best of my knowledge, we know nothing of a single Jewish architect or sculptor [*Bildbauer*] in our own times; as for painters of Jewish origin, I must leave it to experts in the field to judge whether they have created anything real in their art. It is most probable, however, that these artists are no different in attitude toward their visual art than modern Jewish composers are to music.[60]

VII

In 1869, Wagner republished the essay, helping to stoke the deadly flames of racial anti-Semitism that were beginning to engulf fin de siècle Europe. Two of the defensive responses to these flames were a heightened Jewish self-consciousness and Zionism, both of which in turn stimulated the avid production, collection, and public display of Jewish art.[61] Racial anti-Semitism and growing interest in Jewish art compelled Jewish intellectuals and artists to modify their views. Earlier, against Hegel's philosophic objections to Judaism's refusal to depict God visually, German Jewish intellectuals were able to side with Kant, who found Judaism's aniconism sublime. They were also able to point to Judaism's compensatory genius for poetry, music, and universalist ethical monotheism. Against the Feuerbachian-Wagnerian enthusiasm for Greek visuality, German Jewish intellectuals were able to use the same arguments developed for rebutting Hegel. Others, like Graetz, who discredited the visual arts by stressing their carnal, paganistic moral depravity, thereby transformed an apparent ethnic deficiency into an actual aesthetic virtue. Against the Feuerbachian-Marxian-Wagnerian charge that Jewish selfishness and moneygrubbing threatened Europe, German Jewish intellectuals from Heine to Freud were able to stress Judaism's affinity for the temporal rather than the spatial, celebrate its moral self-restraint in renouncing libidinal instinct, and applaud its cultivation of abstract intellectualism. Against Wagnerian-like claims that Jews were unable to produce anything worthwhile in the visual arts, Steinheim acknowledged the didactic and devotional functions of illuminated Hebrew manuscripts and Herman Cohen underscored the spiritual legitimacy of Jewish religious architecture. New arguments were needed, however, against fin de siècle racism and the accumulating

evidence of Jewish visual art. The new arguments would have to neutralize charges of Jewish racial inferiority as well as account for Jewish art
without sacrificing altogether the cherished principle of spiritually driven
aniconism.

One version of these new arguments, clustered with the old, was formulated by Martin Buber.[62] In 1903, Buber edited *Juedischer Kuenstler*, an
illustrated volume of essays featuring six modern Jewish artists: Josef Isra-
els, Lesser Ury, E. M. Lillien, Max Liebermann, Solomon J. Solomon, and
Jehudo Epstein.[63] Buber wrote both a brief introduction for the volume
and the essay devoted to Lesser Ury. He began the introduction by admit-
ting that the sorry state of Jewish visual art justified Wagner when he
"denied to the Jewish sensory capacity for sight [*sinnliche Anschauungs-
gabe der Juden*] the power to produce visual artists." Buber also conceded
that Wagner was not wrong in explaining this deficiency in terms of "racial
characteristics" (*Rasseneigenschaften*).

These concessions "obliged" Buber to defend the publication of the
book and to explore the "causes" for Judaism's "lack of creativity" (*Un-
fruchtbarkeit*) in the visual arts. Buber invoked history. He declared that,
because of racial characteristics, "the ancient Jew had no visual art."[64] He
explained that racial characteristics are not "final and irreversible, but
rather the product of soil and its climatic conditions, the economic and
social structure of the community, the form of life and historical fate." He
then rehearsed the typological distinction between Hebraism and Hellenism made familiar by Heine, Formstecher, Steinheim, and Graetz: "The
ancient Jew was more a person-of-the-ears [*Ohrenmensch*] than a person-
of-the-eyes [*Augenmensch*] and more a person-of-time [*Zeitmensch*] than a
person-of-space [*Raummensch*]. Of all his senses, it was mostly his hearing
which inspired him to form his image of the world."[65] The quintessential
art form of the ancient Jew was therefore "acoustic, music being a barely
adequate means of expression." The impassioned, "lyrical poetry of the
prophets" was its capstone: "The brilliantly gifted Jew of antiquity had to
become a prophet; otherwise he would perish [*untergehen*] in the fullness
of his passion. To visual art, he could not come; his emotion was too fierce
[*wild*] and the way too vast [*weit*]."

From antiquity, Buber passed to a consideration of Jewish culture in the
Diaspora, especially to the "form of life" in the ghetto. He argued that
medieval Judaism was unable to produce art because Jews were buffeted
by life's circumstances, dragged under by the corrupting and exclusive
involvement with moneylending, and hemmed in by the all-powerful regimen of oppressive religious law (*Religionsgesetz*). The law "stifled" creative
impulses at their first appearance. The law made the "human body contemptible. Beauty was an unknown value. To behold [*schauen*] was sinful.
Art was sinful." Buber believed, however, that subterranean "mystical"

forces, percolating beneath the surface of medieval Judaism, made their breakthrough in Hasidism.[66] For Buber, Hasidism "was the birth of the new Judaism" in which "human body was 'marvelous' rather than contemptible;" "beauty an emanation from God, beholding a unification with God;" [and] "love" rather than "law, the goal of life."

Having deflected Wagner's racism by introducing the novel consideration of mythic forces within Judaism that surfaced in Hasidism and by reducing racial characteristics to the "evolutionary" effects of variable historical circumstances, Buber ended the introduction with a brief discussion of the post-Emancipation period, in which the "door to art stood open." In modernity, Buber argued, "the essence of the Jewish race was merely entering a new phase, not undergoing a dialectical nullification [Aufhebung]." First in music, fed by the dominant aurality of the synagogue liturgy and folk art, and then in lyric poetry, in which "subjectivity" blossomed forth, modern Jews gave "new form" to old impulses. Finally in the visual arts, Jews began to experiment with giving unprecedented visual form to the "characteristics of their folk." "They are merely a beginning," Buber concluded, and it is better to observe them than to "theorize" about their work. They will show what contemporary Jewry is capable of producing in the visual arts.

VIII

Wagner and the anti-Semites had claimed that Jews were unable to produce genuine art steeped in communal awareness of divine, mythic beauty because Jews were forever yoked to insidious commercialism. Buber used evolutionary considerations, historical arguments, biblical poetry, and Hasidism to prove otherwise. He granted that Jews produced no visual art until the nineteenth century, but he also insisted that Jewish culture possessed authentically folkish, indigenous aesthetic impulses. Other German Jewish intellectuals were less interested than Buber in the invigoration of Jewish national creativity, but they were equally eager to prove that Jews were no threat to European society. Accordingly, they adopted a different strategy in combating racial anti-Semitism. They too leaned heavily on historical arguments. Unlike Buber, however, they accommodated themselves to the growing body of archaeological evidence. They used the archaeological evidence to prove that Jews have always produced visual art, though they carefully noted that there was no Jewish "look," nothing distinctively Jewish, about it.[67] As formulated by Graetz and the German-educated Kaufman Kohler in the English language *Jewish Encyclopedia* (1902), this historical argument presupposed "that it is . . . somewhat incorrect to speak of Jewish art. Whether in Biblical or in post-Biblical times, Jewish workmanship was influenced, if not altogether guided by non-Jewish art. Roman architecture was invoked in the building of Herod's Temple just as Phoenician architecture was in the construction of those of Solomon and of Zerubbabel." As for the modern Jewish art in which Buber hopefully saw the "characteristics of the folk" in new forms, Kohler emphatically proclaimed that it "no longer bears the specific character of the Jewish genius, but must be classified among the various nations to which the Jewish artists belong."

The *Jüdisches Lexicon*, published in Berlin in 1929, sponsored a similar argument. Written in the light of accumulating archaeological and artifactual evidence, its entry "Jewish Art" claimed that Jews have always produced visual art but also denied that the art is particularly Jewish.[68] Written by Kurt Freyer, a specialist on Spinoza, the entry begins with a Kohler-like proviso: "To speak of Jewish art in the same sense as any other kind of art is not possible without further qualifying details [*weiteres*]." Freyer concludes that one can properly speak of "art by Jews" and "art for Jews" but not of "Jewish art" for a threefold reason: Art by and for Jews lacks a well-defined, "specifically Jewish characteristic, since [it] always employs the forms and motifs of the contemporary host-societies [*Wirtsvölker*]" in whose midst the Jews have lived; it lacks continuity or "internal coherence" because of vast differences in the temporal circumstances of its production; and, finally, it lacks a canon of "extraordinary, brilliant achievements, either by individual artists or an entire epoch." As for the modern Jewish art over which Buber was reluctant to pass qualitative judgments, Freyer concedes that "important things have been achieved." Nevertheless, he is quick to add, these "creations belong more to the art-history of the peoples in whose midst [the artists] live than to the Jewish people."

Regarding the abundance and inferiority of premodern art, Freyer is equally apologetic. He offers two reasons why "Jews have not produced important art of their own." The first reason harks back to the nineteenth-century philosophic and theological arguments polished by Hermann Cohen; it invokes the "special spiritual disposition of the Jewish people," its "anti-Hellenism," which ignored the surrounding world and dedicated itself to the "knowledge of God and the normativity [*Gesetzlichkeit*] of ethical behavior." Were it not for this spiritual disposition, the *Jüdisches Lexicon* argues, the aniconic Second Commandment would never have been able to exert so powerful an influence in Jewish culture. Kohler was saying much the same thing in 1902 when his contribution to the *Jewish Encyclopedia* stressed that "far more potent than the Law was the spirit of the Jewish faith in putting a check on plastic art. In the same measure as polytheism, whether Semitic or Aryan, greatly aided in developing art as it endeavored to bring the deity in ever more beautiful form . . . Judaism was determined to lift God above the realm of the sensual and corporeal and to represent Him as Spirit only." Echoing Graetz's denunciations of lascivious European visuality, Freyer's notion of Jewish art reverberates with assurances that Judaism is neither sexually perverse nor carnally materialistic. Freyer was insistent that Judaism's spiritual essence neither poses a moral threat to its host cultures nor evinces hostility to the fine arts and the universal sciences. This was precisely the argument developed by Freud in *Moses and Monotheism*, and it is interesting to note that Freud's private library in Vienna contained the four volumes of the *Jüdisches Lexicon*.[69]

The second argument advanced by the *Jüdisches Lexicon* folds historical anthropology into the batter of philosophic idealism. Echoing Buber, Freyer maintains that the "political-social" circumstances of the Diaspora were not conducive to the creation of truly important art. Having made all these "qualifications" explicit, Kurt Freyer nonetheless disagrees with Buber and asserts that premodern Jewish visual art did indeed exist. He then outlines its premodern achievements, especially in ceremonial art, synagogue architecture, and medieval illuminated manuscripts.

It would be difficult to understand Freyer's deprecation of premodern Jewish art and his insistence on the lack of national character and stylistic definition in all of Jewish art were it not for the racism against which the German Jews were contending and the Zionist options which the vast majority was refusing. Writing in 1929, Freyer was speaking on behalf of an assimilating, acculturated, besieged community still convinced that the way to defuse racism was to outsmart it with scholarly arguments and that the best way to flatter a host culture was to imitate it.[70] Freyer's affirmation of an assimilative, physically nondistinct, derivative Jewish visual art mirrors European Jewry's desperate and ultimately futile denial of the racist proposition that Jewish bodies differ physically from the bodies of the people in whose midst they live.[71]

Their racist enemies were no figment of the imagination. A "professor of racial hygiene" at the University of Munich typically asked his German readers in 1923 and his English readers in 1931 to "think of the faces of the more refined Jews of southern Europe" in order "to picture . . . the Oriental race [which] is distinguished by its small stature, by a long and narrow cranium, a narrow face with thick and fleshy lips, and a narrow, prominent, equably curved, and not excessively large nose." He asked them to consider the statistically significant, genetically transmitted propensity of the Jews to suffer from blindness, deafness, skin disease, flatfeet, arteriosclerosis, diabetes, obesity, sterility, myomata, Parkinson's disease, lumbago, feeblemindedness, melancholia, schizophrenia, and—like women—all forms of hysteria, especially hypochondria and nosophobia. He informed his readers that "it would certainly seem to be a fact that where the male sex is concerned hysteria manifests itself more often in Jews than it does in the Teutonic races, the explanation being that Jews on the average have in respect to both body and mind a less markedly developed masculine character."[72]

In the *Lexicon* entry, Freyer summarized nineteenth- and twentieth-century German Jewish arguments regarding Jewish visual art. Kohler and Freud fed these arguments into the mainstream of twentieth-century Anglo-American opinion. A review of these Germanophone arguments makes it apparent that the idea of Jewish aniconism was made possible by a combination of Kantian ethics, Hegelian spirituality, Romanticism's enthusiasm for poetry or music, Judaism's traditional veneration of book learning, and the nineteenth-century's nationalistically tinged version of cultural anthropology.[73] What made the idea of Jewish aniconism necessary and persistent was ongoing anti-Semitism in all of its escalating variety, from Kantian and Hegelian philosophic disparagement through Feuerbachian-Marxist socioeconomic vilification, to Wagnerian racism and on to the horrific state-sponsored, genocidal, mass psychosis of Nazi Judeophobia. What complicated the idea of Jewish aniconism were late nineteenth-century cultural Zionism and the collection of Jewish artifacts that were accumulating in ever increasing abundance.

What continues to make the modern idea of Jewish aniconism hopelessly overdetermined and ambiguous is its sponsorship by friend and foe alike.[74] German Jewish intellectuals stressed Judaism's gifts for spirituality and abstract thought. They accounted for these cultural traits by proudly linking them causally to Judaism's renunciation of the instinctual and the physical. They rested their case on Judaism's ban against the sensuality of visual art. Werner Sombart (1863–1941), historian of economics, despised Judaism. Malicious avatar of Feuerbach and Marx, he blamed Judaism's rationality, Talmudic casuistry, and intellectualism for producing the evils of capitalism. He also agreed with German Jewish intellectuals that the Jewish aptitude for abstract thinking is purchased at the expense of visual art. In 1911, describing the "fundamental ideas of the Jewish religion," Sombart proclaimed that Judaism was vastly inferior to Islam and Christianity precisely because they encourage "mysticism" and "emotional feeling" (*irrationale Gefühle und Empfindungen*). Judaism, by contrast, "disdains these fantastic, mystical elements [*schwärmerisch-mystischen Züge*], condemning them all." Sombart rested his case precisely where the German Jewish intellectuals had rested theirs: Judaism's ban against the sensuality of visual art. Alienated from emotion and mystery, Judaism "banished all pictorial art [*alles Bildlich-Sinnliche*] from its cult." Unsympathetic to Judaism and no expert in Jewish law, Sombart concluded that pious Jews in his day perpetuated the ban: "They have no statues made, nor do they set them up in their houses."[75] To Sombart, the ban signaled Judaism's disgrace. To German Jewish intellectuals, the very same ban signaled its pride.

When the future Professor Goodenough was assured by mentors at Oxford and Yale, two bastions of Protestant ethos, that, strictly speaking, there "was no such thing as Jewish art," he was simultaneously hearing the praise of Judaism and its condemnation.[76] Once in place, the double bind invented by Kant and Hegel never relaxed its grip.

IX

The modern idea of Jewish art unfolded differently in Eastern Europe.[77] Chagall's claim for "some sort of art" originated in the non-Zionist, ethnically inspired, secular Jewish nationalist movement that the Russian authorities had encouraged in the early phase of the Bolshevik Revolution. Following Chagall's lead, artists and playwrights sought inspiration in the heritage of Jewish folk art, including medieval calligraphy, illuminated manuscripts, and early modern painted wooden synagogues in Poland. Their multifaceted cultural activities came to an abrupt end in 1922, when Russian policies governing ethnic minorities shifted from support to suppression.[78]

A rival Eastern European notion of Jewish art surfaced in Palestine. Its author was Rabbi Abraham Isaac Kook (1865–1935). Trained in the Talmudic academies of Lithuania and steeped in Jewish mysticism, Rabbi Kook became a "prophet of religious Zionism."[79] In 1907, during his rabbinic tenure in Jaffa and fourteen years before he was appointed the first chief Ashkenazi rabbi of British mandate Palestine, Rabbi Kook sent a message dedicating the Bezalel Academy of Arts and Design in Jerusalem.[80] He began with a lament over the suffering of Jews scattered in exile, particularly in "blood-drenched Russia." Seeking hope of redemption, he remarked that "one of the clear signs of revival is the honorable pursuit that is to emerge from your honored association, 'The Revival of Art and Hebraic Beauty in the Land of Israel.' "

Rabbi Kook had composed a parable for the artists and artisans streaming to Jerusalem. The parable tells the tale of a "delightful daughter" who was seriously ill, burning with fever and close to death. But the child gathers her strength. As if through a medium, she speaks: "Mommy, mommy, the doll, give me the doll, the beloved doll that I have not seen for so long a time." At this sign of life, her family and attendants burst into joy, exclaiming, "Little Shoshanah is asking for the doll." The doctor is called, and he too is reassured of Shoshanah's recovery: "She will grow and become beautiful, and she will be a woman among women. Indeed, the doll is the first request, but she will continue to ask for more . . . for medicine, soup, bread and meat, a dress, necklaces and pins, and then for teachers, pens, books, work and much more." Seeing all this, everyone will "clap hands and dance in delight and say, 'Hurray, beautiful, pleasant little Shoshanah is asking for her doll.' " So ended the parable.

Rabbi Kook then unraveled its meaning: "Shoshanah" portrays Jerusalem. Her near fatal illness resonates with destruction and exile. Her request for the doll represents a "life giving stream . . . which gently shakes the bones" of sickly Jerusalem, whose hopes are raised by the clamoring for beauty and works of art. Rabbi Kook agreed with those who complained that there were perhaps "other priorities and more essential needs," but he refused to see anything but a "sign of hope for salvation and comfort" in Jerusalem's childlike demand for her long hidden "doll." He recognized two immediate benefits attached to the visual arts. Thinking pragmatically, he noted that they "can open the doors to livelihoods and provisions for many" families living in the "Holy Land." Contemplating religious aesthetics, he observed that the visual arts "nurture the sensitivity for beauty and purity" that is innate within the people. He promised that the visual arts "will uplift many depressed souls" and provide them with an "illuminating view of the beauty of life."

Securing these economic and aesthetic benefits in the bedrock of traditional law, Rabbi Kook turned to the strictly "rabbinic point of view." In his expert opinion, the Jewish people have "always related in a positive and pleasant way to artistic beauty made manifest in creations produced by human hands, but within well-defined limits." Jewish art must not imitate "pagan" art, which historically "lacked purity and tenderness." Pagan art puts "blood soaked hands on the delicate flower of beauty and fine art" because it detaches art from the restraints of ethics and morality. Rabbi Kook argued that, in antiquity, Jews were divinely commanded to create visual art so that the "beautiful rose" and the "refinement of beauty" might be safeguarded. The commandment is unchanging, he declared, and creativity must be strictly regulated. He concluded that "the entire realm of adornment, ornamentation, beautification and painting is permitted to Jews." The permission extends to portraits of the human face and even to complete sculptures of the human figure, as long as certain minimal precautions are observed involving the cooperation of non-Jewish helpers. The category of proscribed art, offensive to Jewish sensibilities, which may not be produced or displayed in schools or museums is wide-ranging and significant: "The nation of Israel abhors and will not tolerate pictures specifically characteristic of idolatry, whether from the ancient and present pagan world or from the Christian world." Such images will not be tolerated.[81]

Rabbi Kook's antagonism to the entirety of Christian ritual art and his wide-ranging approval of Jewish creativity are as different from Chagall's folkloristic secularism as they are from German Jewish aniconism. They differed for philosophic reasons. Unlike the acculturating German Jewish intellectuals, Rabbi Kook neither took aesthetic cues from Kant nor gerrymandered principles from Hegel to invent a poetically inspired, ethically motivated, thoroughly spiritual, aniconic Judaism. Instead, Rabbi Kook's thinking was governed by talmudic precedent, kabbalistic speculation, and religious Zionism. Aspects of Rabbi Kook's aesthetics nevertheless resemble aspects of doctrines endorsed by the German Jewish intellectuals. They coincide in rigorously subordinating art to morality, and they find depictions of violence or sexual license repugnant. Being a nationalist, Rabbi Kook also agreed with Marc Chagall in affirming "some sort of art." Rabbi Kook and Chagall were equally persuaded that painting and sculpture spring from the very depths of the Jewish soul. An identical Eastern European affirmation was articulated several decades earlier in a series of Hebrew essays composed by Mordecai Zvi Manne (1859–1886). Manne was a Talmudically trained, religiously observant Hebrew scribe, poet, painter, and "student at the prestigious art academy in St. Petersburg."[82] In Manne's opinion, the artistic achievements and international success of Moritz Oppenheim (1799–1882) proved that traditional Judaism celebrates beauty and historically produces talented painters, sculptors, and architects.[83] Unlike these representative Eastern European Jews who typically anchored visual talent in the Jewish soul, the mainstream of German Jewish intellectuals restricted visual talent to the Gentiles, negating or minimizing Judaism's national genius for producing visual art or artists.

Rabbi Kook differed from German Jewish intellectuals in other respects, as well. He did not claim that talmudic law suppressed painting and sculpture throughout Jewish history. Unlike Hermann Cohen, Rabbi Kook did not assert that the biblical prohibition against images constitutes a normative precedent for abrogating outmoded facets of the law. Instead, Rabbi Kook credited the law for legitimizing visual art and compelling Jews to produce it. He enthusiastically acknowledged the salutary powers of the visual arts. The German Jewish intellectuals tended to suspect that visual art contributes little to the moral enhancement of life. Rabbi Kook also differed from Chagall and the German Jewish intellectuals by strictly forbidding the display or enjoyment of all pagan and Christian art, regardless of setting, whether in situ or within the walls of a museum. Rabbi Kook proudly remarked the artistic prowess of Bezalel, both the biblical artisan and the modern school in Jerusalem. German Jewish intellectuals tended to overlook Bezalel and, with Heine, apologetically explained that Moses was truly a poet and an inspired lawgiver but not a manually skilled craftsman who knew how to chisel an obelisk or build a pyramid with stones.

The philosophically motivated divergence between Rabbi Kook and German Jewish intellectuals also stemmed from economic considerations. Rabbi Kook was preoccupied with the practical question of justifying a form of manual labor: Are Jews religiously permitted to engage in the commercial production of visual art not intended for ritual use or synagogue decoration? He was quick to seize upon the legitimate financial rewards to be gained from encouraging artists and craftsmen to do their secular work. Addressing a different class of constituents, German Jewish intellectuals were apparently unbothered by the challenge of vindicating the crafts as trade.

Politics, however, were the decisive factor. Unlike the mainstream of integrationist German Jewish intellectuals, Rabbi Kook did not refuse Zionist options. Being a religious Zionist, he responded to the threat of anti-Semitism by withdrawing from Europe, energetically and courageously participating in the utopian dream of creating an independent Jewish society governed by the dictates of rabbinic law that embraced the full range of human activities, including the national capacity for a chaste and divinely sanctioned visual art.[84] Dreaming a different utopia, one that promised universal liberation, but contending with the same hellish nightmare—the threat of radical extinction—the mainstream of nineteeth- and early twentieth-century German Jewish intellectuals decided otherwise. Where they were hoping to go, the denial of Jewish art followed.

Two ⎯⎯⎯⎯⎯⎯⎯⎯⎯⎯⎯⎯⎯⎯⎯

Anglo-American Variations

I

In 1897, the London-based *Jewish Quarterly Review* published an art historical study of the paintings and sculpture that adorned early modern Italian synagogues. The study was written by David Kaufmann (1852–1899), a professor at the rabbinical seminary in Budapest, a specialist in medieval Jewish philosophy, and a pioneer in the scientific study of Jewish ceremonial art.[1] Kaufmann's opening lines pulsed with revisionist optimism: "The fable of the hatred entertained by the Synagogue against all manner of art and the new time should at last succumb to the evidence of facts, and literary documents." Fable or not, the ideologically overdetermined notion of Jewish iconophobia withstood Kaufmann's critique. Jewish iconophobia became conventional wisdom and prevailed throughout the twentieth century. The denial of Jewish art was modified, but it never disappeared. Kaufmann himself partially subscribed to it. He conceded that prerabbinic, biblical Judaism lived with the "horror of plastic art" because of the "Lawgiver's" opposition to idolatry. Thinking historically, he argued that as idolatry "gradually disappeared" in Late Antiquity, so did Jewish iconophobia.

Four years later, in 1901, the *Jewish Quarterly Review* returned to the controversial topic of Jewish art, printing an essay by Solomon J. Solomon (1860–1927). Solomon was an English Jew, a future wartime expert in camouflage, the eventual president of the Royal Society of British Artists, and an artist whose portraits included Queen Victoria and Heinrich Graetz, the German Jewish historian who prudishly advocated Jewish aniconism while denouncing the depraved hedonism of European culture. Solomon began confessionally: "Some years ago the Editor of an Art Journal requested me to write for him an article on Jewish Art. I replied that I could more easily write an apology for its non-existence. I shall endeavor to show why Israel has no art."[2]

Solomon displayed no awareness of David Kaufmann's arguments. He also dodged the evidence of synagogal art. Solomon insisted that "the great leaders of the Jewish race have ever been opposed to the artistic reproduction of natural forms, more particularly the human form" and that "none, or practically none of the ancient Hebrews cultivated the plastic arts." Like Goodenough's mentors at Oxford and Yale, Solomon affirmed that "the reproduction of natural forms, more particularly the human form, was forbidden to the Jews." He applauded the antimaterialist spirit of the Protestant Reformation, and he praised the historically affiliated cognates of "Hebrew" and "Puritan" aniconism. Pledging allegiance to the creed of Jewish integration, he observed that "a great part of Israel's mission is fulfilled in the teaching of the Protestant Church." Solomon echoed Graetz in denouncing both ancient Greek "Pagan sensuality" and contemporary "Hellenic Southerners who above most things have pandered to their love of luxury and enjoyment."

Solomon did not risk being misunderstood by England's citizens. He chided the Anglican Church for "stand[ing] midway between the Puritan and Rome." He reprimanded Roman Catholicism for the "Pagan element in its constitution," claiming that "the God at its base is almost obscured by the Madonna, the symbol of the crucifixion, and the saints." Introjecting England's mainstream values, Solomon conformed. He praised what he thought best in his host society.[3] His denial of Jewish art prevailed among the majority of integrationist Jews in Western Europe and America who adjusted their lives to Protestant cadences.

In 1910, the *Jewish Quarterly Review* migrated from private ownership in London to the institutional sponsorship of Dropsie College in Philadelphia, Pennsylvania. With David Kaufmann's essay in one issue and Solomon J. Solomon's in another, the *Jewish Quarterly Review* conveyed contradictory notions of Jewish art to American readers who were sociologically inclined toward aniconism by hegemonic Protestant culture. Later, in the 1920s, Erwin J. Goodenough delivered another shipment of English aniconism to Yale University where the scholarly audience already knew that "there was no such thing as Jewish art."

England continued to export the idea to a receptive America. In 1950, *Commentary* published an article, "Jewish Art and the Fear of the Image," written by Herbert Howarth.[4] *Commentary* was launched in 1945 by the venerable American Jewish Committee, whose ties to Reform Judaism and Jews of German descent were intimate. *Commentary* was "quickly established as one of America's foremost intellectual magazines and a leading voice of liberal American opinion."[5] Howarth was a poet, a translator of Arabic verse, and a British diplomat stationed in Palestine during the mandate. Like Erwin J. Goodenough, Howarth was trained at Oxford University. Like Solomon J. Solomon, Howarth ignored David Kaufmann's attempts to overturn the "fable" of premodern rabbinic iconophobia. A bona fide Orientalist, Howarth maintained that Judaism and Islam impose "a veto on the image." He explained that the biblical prohibition against making "graven images . . . has been understood by the Jewish people themselves as a prohibition against representation irrespective of its purpose—a kind of general exclusion of delight in art." Acknowledging exceptions to this rule, Howarth proclaimed that the "essence of the prohibition was observed in most Jewish communities at most times; and where and when individuals freed themselves of it, they lost touch with their people, worked for aliens, and were left with a rootless art of no real importance."

Sixteen years later, *Commentary* revisited Jewish art. This time, however, the accents were neither Germanic nor British. They were native American, belonging to Harold Rosenberg (1906–1978). Born in New York City, Rosenberg was destined to become a distinguished critic and champion of America's artistic avant-garde. In 1966, the University of Chicago appointed him to its Department of Art and Committee on Social Thought. In 1967, *The New Yorker* selected him its art critic. In the late spring of 1966, Rosenberg lectured at the Jewish Museum in New York City. Several months later, *Commentary* published the lecture.[6] Rosenberg began caustically, with self-mocking wit: "First, they build a Jewish Museum, then they ask, Is there a Jewish art? Jews! As to the question itself, there is a Gentile answer and a Jewish answer. The Gentile answer is: Yes, there is a Jewish art, and No, there is no Jewish art. The Jewish answer is: What do you mean by Jewish art?"

Rosenberg introduced the Jewish answer by repudiating Gentile affirmations and denials. As liberal in his politics as *Commentary* itself, Rosenberg defensively explained that the categorical affirmations and denials were misguided "anti-Semitic" stereotypes that idealized or vilified all Jews. He then unpacked the inquisitive "Jewish answer." Being thorough, he proposed and emphatically discarded five "possible meanings" for the term Jewish art: "[1] art produced by Jews . . . [2] art depicting or containing Jewish subject matter . . . [3] Jewish ceremonial objects: silver menorahs and drinking goblets, embroidered Torah coverings, wood carvings . . . [4] a kind of ceremonial and semi-ceremonial folk art of an ephemeral nature . . . Chanukah *dreidlach* [spinning tops] made out of lead . . . *chaleh* [bread] in the shape of birds with folded tails and whole peppers for eyes . . . [and 5] metaphysical Judaica." Rejecting these five categories, Rosenberg declared that "while Jews produce art, they don't produce Jewish art." He speculated that "metaphysical Judaica" might perhaps be "the Jewish art of the future. Perhaps a genuine Jewish style will come out of Jewish philosophy." He also conceded that Jewish handicrafts and ceremonial objects constitute "what scholars usually accept as Jewish art." He "doubt[ed], however, that this priestly work is art in the sense in which the word is used in the 20th century."

Not to be confused with his anti-Semites or Gentiles, Rosenberg playfully suggested a sixth, "fanciful" possibility: "Jewish art . . . in the negative sense of creating objects in the mind and banning physical works of art. In this sense, the Second Commandment was the manifesto of Jewish art. In our day, an anti-art tradition has been developing, within which it could be asserted that Jewish art has always existed in not existing." Unlike Howarth, Rosenberg recoiled from slandering and dehumanizing the Jews. Howarth ascribed to Jews a "a kind of general exclusion of delight in art." Rosenberg did not. Neither did Rosenberg berate visual creations made by Jews for being an alienated and "rootless art of no real importance." Rosenberg nevertheless agreed with Howarth's fundamental principle. They both affirmed "that there is no Jewish art in the sense of a Jewish style in painting and sculpture." As if aligning himself with Goodenough's instructors at Oxford and Yale, Rosenberg proclaimed that there was "no such thing as Jewish art." Kaufmann Kohler had said much the same thing in 1902, as did Kurt Freyer in 1929 and Sigmund Freud in 1939.

II

Harold Rosenberg was not the first Jewish intellectual educated in America to negate a distinctively Jewish visual art. Bernard Berenson (1865–1959) was born in eastern Europe, but he was raised and schooled in Boston, graduating from Harvard University. Decades before Harold Rosenberg's lecture, the market-making voice of Berenson, a true connoisseur, let it known that neither the ancient "Judeans nor their forebears possessed any kind of plastic or even mechanical ability. . . . As a matter of fact Israel through the ages has manifested nothing essentially national in the plastic arts, neither in antiquity, nor through the Middle Ages, nor to-day."[7] Accounting for the empirical evidence of Late Antique Jewish frescoes and medieval illuminated manuscripts, Berenson reasoned like an assimilationist. He explained that throughout their history "Jews imitated the art of the peoples among whom they were scattered, to the pitiful extent that they made use of art at all." He also declared that "the Jews like their Ishmaelite cousins the Arabs, and indeed perhaps like all pure Semites (if such there be), have displayed little talent for the visual, and almost none for the figure arts." Berenson did not believe, however, that Jews, perhaps himself included, lacked a national compensatory art of their own. Without specifying his authorities, he reinvented or recapitulated the Germanophone arguments fashioned by Heinrich Heine and Hermann Cohen: Berenson proudly acknowledged that "to the Jews belonged the splendours and raptures of the word. Hebrew literature . . . has afforded inspiration and comfort to Christian and Mohammedan [and] has fashioned or reshaped their instruments of expression."

Berenson's pride in sacred Jewish literature and denial of Jewish visual art typified the mainstream of American Jewish intellectuals whose cultural sensibilities conformed to Protestant models. The Jewish literacy of these intellectuals was mainly confined to the Hebrew Bible in English translation. Scholars with advanced learning shared this reverence for biblical literature. They surpassed this reverence, however, by glorying in the luxuriant complexities of rabbinic legend and hermeneutics. In 1989, Geoffrey H. Hartman spoke on their sophisticated and versatile behalf. A literary critic and professor of English and comparative literature at Yale University, Hartman observed that "art, both visual and verbal, has transmitted Catholic tradition with an extraordinary power of illustration. There is, however, no Jewish Dante or Tintoretto. Even in the modern period, when there is a liberation of Jewish thought into forms of art, two matters impede full development. One is a lingering distrust of visual culture, an iconoclastic streak that always—when it comes down to the wire—sides with Abraham. The other is simply the continuing power of a tradition which nourishes that streak. Is not the art of Judaism an anti-art, comprised in what Zunz called 'rabbinic literature,' the great line of Biblical commentary through which the tradition flows?"[8]

Hartman was not alone in asserting that Judaism had no counterparts to Tintoretto. In 1971, Cynthia Ozick, author of fiction and essays, published a feminist critique of misogyny. She found a "curious analogy" between the evidence of "no great female architects, painters, playwrights, sailors, bridge-builders, jurists, captains, composers, etc., etc." and the evidence of no great Jewish artists. "Say what you will about the gifted Jews," she wrote,

> they have never, up until times so recent that they scarcely begin to count, been plastic artists. Where is the Jewish Michelangelo, the Jewish Rembrandt, the Jewish Rodin? He has never come into being. Why? . . . Is it possible that a whole people cannot produce a single painter? And not merely a single painter of note, but a single painter at all? Well, there have been artists among the Jews—artisans, we should more likely call them, decorators of trivial ceremonial objects, a wine cup here, a scroll cover there. Talented a bit, but nothing great. They never tried their hand at wood or stone or paint. "Thou shalt have no graven images"—the Second Commandment—prevented them.[9]

Cynthia Ozick's historical comments anticipated and exceeded Geoffrey Hartman's rhetorical appeal to the singular absence of a Jewish Tintoretto. Her evaluations reiterated Herbert Howarth's dismissive assessment of Jewish ceremonial objects. Like Howarth, she acerbically trivialized the objects and deprecated their makers. Harold Rosenberg was more moderate; he merely denied high aesthetic status to ritual and folk art.

These disqualifications of Jewish ceremonial artifacts reverberated among professionals in the art world. The curator of painting and sculpture at the National Museum of American Art of the Smithsonian Institution typically refused to consider "ritual objects" in reconstructing "a Jewish aesthetic since, even in ancient times, style . . . reacted with the greater world of non-Jewish culture."[10] Given their choice between David Kaufmann's esteem for Jewish ceremonial art and Harold Rosenberg's "sense in which the word [art] is used in the 20th century," art professionals tended to side with Rosenberg, Howarth, and Ozick.[11] The Metropolitan Museum of Art in New York City organizes the display of its collections by historical epoch and national origin.[12] Perhaps because it exclusively ascribes the origin of art to nationalities and considers Judaism a religion rather than a national identity, it has no permanent collection of Jewish artifacts. As late as the summer of 1996, neither did the Museo Arqueológico Nacional in Madrid.[13]

Museums institutionalized the prevailing denial of Jewish art. Bernard Berenson, Herbert Howarth, Harold Rosenberg, Geoffrey Hartman, and Cynthia Ozick articulated the fundamentals of Jewish aniconism. Among others, Max Dimont popularized the denial of Jewish art. In *God, Jews and History*, published in 1962, Dimont assured countless readers that "the Second Commandment . . . had an adverse effect. Because the Jews were prohibited from making images of God, they turned away from painting, sculpture, and architecture. . . . Not until the nineteenth century A.D., when Jews began disregarding the Second Commandment the way the Christians had been doing for two thousand years, did they, too, begin to develop painters, sculptors and architects."[14] Ten years later, in another book, Dimont was hawking the same antireligious and antirabbinic wares.[15] He never tired of proclaiming that Jewish artifacts were heterodox anomalies.

Max Dimont popularized the institutional and scholarly notion of Jewish aniconism. College textbooks in art history enshrined it. Janson's *History of Art* is the best selling. The current edition contains thirteen hundred pages. The five paragraphs devoted to Jewish art teach that the third-century "Graeco-Oriental" frescoes in the synagogue of Dura-Europos are a notable exception to the rule of Jewish aniconism: "Momentarily, at least, the age-old injunction was relaxed so that the walls of the assembly hall could be covered with a richly detailed visual account of the history of the Chosen People and their Covenant with the Lord."[16] *Gardner's Art through the Ages* is Janson's closest competitor. Eleven hundred pages long, the current edition of *Gardner* allocates several sentences to Jewish art in the section devoted to early Christian art. Referring to the synagogue murals in Dura-Europos, *Gardner* blankly assures its readers that "although both Jews and Christians were bound by the Second Commandment against images, the ban was somehow evaded and both sects made use of them."[17] Because they were summarizing conventional wisdom, Janson and *Gardner* did not consider the possibility that neither the Jews nor the early Christians ever construed the scriptural prohibition as a ban against *all* forms of sacred, royal, and domestic art. The *Catholic Encyclope-*

dia of 1910 had sponsored an alternate history of Jewish sacred art, but the authors of America's textbooks were not consulting it. Neither were they aware of David Kaufmann's century-old attacks against the "fable" of Jewish aniconism. Neither did Janson and *Gardner* test their conclusions against Carl H. Kraeling's 1956 monograph devoted to the synagogue in Dura-Europos that might have shaken their dogmatic perceptions of Late Antique Jewish policy regarding the visual arts.[18]

College textbooks perpetuate the notion of Jewish aniconism. A powerful array of philosophers, theologians, and cultural critics refurbish it. Walter J. Ong, S.J., represents the host of twentieth-century intellectuals who merely reiterate nineteenth-century categorical distinctions between Hellenic and Hebraic mentalities. In 1964, Ong delivered the renowned Terry Lectures at Yale University. As if it were Heinrich Graetz or Martin Buber speaking, Ong taught that "cultures vary greatly in their exploitation of the various senses and in the way in which they relate their conceptual apparatus to the various senses. It has been a commonplace that the ancient Hebrews and the ancient Greeks differed in the value they set on the auditory. The Hebrews tended to think of understanding as a kind of hearing, whereas the Greeks thought of it more as a kind of seeing."[19]

José Faur, a rabbinic scholar, was also indebted to nineteenth-century Germanophone cultural anthropology. Claiming that "the Hebrew and Greek types of truth correspond to two different levels of reality," Faur named Greek truth "visual" and Hebrew truth "auditory." Explicitly citing Heinrich Graetz's authority, Faur concluded that the "Hebrew aversion to iconic representation reflects concern with the visual level of expression rather than mere opposition to to representational art."[20] Faur's experiments with semiotics illustrate how the nineteenth-century idea of Judaism's antagonism for the visual arts was reinvigorated by alliances with innovative theoretical systems. The nineteenth-century Germanophone principle of Jewish aniconism remained unchanged throughout the twentieth century, but its rationales varied according to fashion and taste.

Partially to heal the wounds inflicted on the Jews by German culture and genocidal politics, Jürgen Habermas published an essay in 1961 that explored German idealism's philosophic debts to the Kabbalah, the esoteric traditions of Jewish mysticism. He juxtaposed Jewish mysticism's cosmic understanding of the power of language with idealism's "condemnation of language as the instrument of knowledge" and its preference for a "divinized art [*vergötterte Kunst*]." Privileging language over visuality, Habermas expressed his admiration for Judaism's mystically inspired, proto-Heideggerian awareness.[21]

Hannah Arendt (1906–1975) represents the Jewish intellectuals who, like the Gentile Habermas, forged alliances between the original idea of Jewish aniconism and post-Kantian, post-Hegelian developments in Western philosophy. The alliances extended aniconism's life and enhanced its cultural potency. Arendt's "Thinking" was first delivered in 1971 as the Gifford Lectures at the University of Aberdeen. It was published in book form in 1978. In 1977, the *New Yorker* lent its cultivated prestige to the already orthodox denial of Jewish art and visuality by serializing Arendt's lectures. Ever since Kant, philosophers who embrace Jewish aniconism have invoked the Second Commandment. Arendt was no exception. She invoked it in order to draw a familiar distinction. In Western philosophy, she argued, vision is the dominant metaphor for "truth." In the "Hebrew tradition," she asserted, the dominant metaphor is "audition." According to Arendt, "the Hebrew God can be heard but not seen, and truth there-fore becomes invisible." Tipping her hat to Philo, Heidegger, Witt-genstein, and Hans Jonas, Arendt identified the biblical God with absolute truth. The equation between God and absolute truth allowed her to con-clude that *"the invisibility of truth in the Hebrew tradition is as axiomatic as its ineffability in Greek philosophy,* from which all later philosophy de-rived its axiomatic assumptions."[22]

Assuming that José Faur and Hannah Arendt were correct, it would ineluctably follow that Judaism not only forbids visual representations of God but disdains all painting, sculpture, and architecture. Neither Salo-mon Ludwig Steinheim nor Hermann Cohen reached such extreme con-clusions. Steinheim acknowledged illuminated manuscripts and Cohen celebrated synagogal architecture. José Faur and Hannah Arendt outdid their predecessors in denying Jewish art.

Circling conceptual orbit with Hannah Arendt and José Faur, Susan Handelman, a literary critic teaching at the University of Maryland, ad-vanced the cause of Jewish aniconism by enriching it with links to Franco-phone postmodernism. In 1982, Handelman cited Jean-François Lyo-tard's notion that "in Hebrew ethics, representation is forbidden, the eye closes, [and] the ear opens in order to hear the father's spoken word." Apparently in agreement with Lyotard, Handelman incorporated his ste-reotypical distinction between Greek and Hebrew thinking into her own explanation of the "Biblical ban on images."[23] Mining the same philo-sophic vein in 1993, Martin Jay published a study of Emmanuel Levinas that discovered "unexpected links between the traditional iconoclastic Jewish attitude toward visual representation and a powerfully antiocular impulse in postmodernism." Jay, a professor of modern European intel-lectual history at the University of California–Berkeley, cited Levinas's (Kantian) remark insisting that "the proscription of images is truly the supreme command of monotheism."[24]

Associated with the highly respected figure of Levinas, the idea of Jew-ish aniconism preserved its appeal and won new adherents. Jean Baudril-lard, the widely read French theorist of images, also helped propagate new shoots of postmodern aniconism. In his classic essay of 1981, "The Precession of Simulacra," Baudrillard credited religious "iconoclasts" for understanding the paramount importance of forbidding images of the divine "because the divinty which animates nature can never be represented." Knowing that simulacra have the power of "effacing God from the conscience of man," of revealing "that deep down God never existed, even that God himself was never anything but his own simulacrum," the iconoclasts were compelled "to destroy the images." Baudrillard concluded paradoxically that "the iconoclasts, whom one accuses of disdaining and negating images, were those who accorded them their true value."[25]

Underwritten by modern and postmodern philosophy, the denial of Jewish art achieved near unimpeachable status in twentieth-century American thought. Even without philosophy's help, the notion was enshrined in textbooks and museums. Almost ineradicable, the denial of Jewish art was certifed by countless international authorities from across the disciplines, including Freud. The two-hundred-year-old denial conformed to prevailing Protestant discomfort with Roman Catholic visuality. It was bonded to anti-Semitic propaganda. It crystallized the social ideals of Jewish integration. Jewish aniconism therefore became a self-evident certainty. The most scrupulous writers and conscientious editors at the most demanding university presses took it for granted. Let one example testify for them all: In a remarkably thorough biography published in 1993, assurances were made that Mark Rothko's decision to become a painter "defied the traditional taboo against iconic images" but that "such religious prohibitions were less strong for Rothko . . . than they were, say for Marc Chagall or Chaim Soutine, both of whom, born about ten years before Rothko, had grown up in the Settlement of Pale [sic], where their interest in art confronted severe political harassment and religious taboos."[26] Together with Solomon J. Solomon, almost everyone was endeavoring "to show why there is no Jewish art."

III

Intellectuals who denied Jewish art were supposed to have known better. As early as 1897, David Kaufmann had urged the scientific world to renounce the "fable" of aniconism and "at last succumb to the evidence of facts, and literary documents." That many succumbed is obvious. A bibliography published in 1967 registered almost three thousand scholarly articles and monographs devoted to Jewish art.[27] Item 214 refers to passages in the second edition of Salo W. Baron's monumental work, *A Social and Religious History of the Jewish People.* Reiterating the first edition of 1937, Baron noted the recent excavations of Jewish synagogues and cemeteries that have "revolutionized . . . our knowledge of ancient Jewish art."[28] He reported that these empirical data have "greatly qualified the prevalent assumption that the biblical prohibition of imagery had effectively checked all artistic creation."

In his 1942 study, *The Jewish Community*, Baron acknowledged that "it would be pointless to raise . . . the oft debated issue of the capacity of Jews in the graphic arts. This question, which seemed significant in the nineteenth century, lost much of its meaning in the face of the empirical evidence of the recently unearthed ancient synagogues, the plethora of contemporary Jewish artists, and the growing general conviction that a people's artistic achievement is conditioned by social and psychological rather than racial factors." Baron challenged the conventional wisdom by itemizing the " 'genuinely Jewish style' " of richly decorated, wooden synagogues of Poland–Lithuania, the gorgeously illuminated medieval Hebrew manuscripts, and the stained glass windows adorning the twelfth-century synagogue in Cologne."[29]

As for Herbert Howarth, the Oxford Orientalist who had declared authentic Jews incapable of finding pleasure in the visual arts, he was publicly called to task in 1953 by Stephen Kayser, the director of the Jewish Museum in New York City, for confusing "Jewish art and Jewish artists." Kayser complained that critics like Howarth underestimate or "ignore the existence of Jewish ritualistic art."[30] Later, in 1961, objecting explicitly to Howarth's arguments, eminent historian of Jewish art, Joseph Gutmann lamented that "the term 'art'—pictorial or visual—when applied to Judaism, tends to evoke an array of negations. Some critics, claiming that a literal interpretation of the Second Commandment was always the rule in Jewish life, have virtually discounted the possibility of visual art among the Jews." Like Baron, Gutmann surveyed the abundance of literary and archaeological evidence originating in the ancient Near Eastern and Greco-Roman phases of Jewish history. He concluded that a "rigidly and uniformly anti-iconic attitude on the part of the Jews remains as much a myth as the Procrustean bed on which Jewish art history has so often been made to lie."[31]

Another publication issued in 1961 also summarized the empirically based argument against Jewish aniconism. It was titled *Jewish Art*, and appropriately subtitled *An Illustrated History*. It was a collection of essays written by specialists from across the fields and edited by Cecil Roth, the polymathic historian and notable exception to the rule of Anglo-Jewish denials of Jewish art. Toward the end of his introduction, Roth observed that "the data assembled above have made it abundantly clear that the conception of representational art for both domestic and synagogal purposes had become fully familiar in Jewish circles long before the age of Emancipation."[32] Roth also noted that the abundance of Late Antique artifacts had led some scholars to reverse the conventional wisdom regarding influence. It had been commonplace to assume that Jews were absolutely dependent on foreigners and host cultures for their artwork. It was now possible, Roth explained, to "suggest that Christian ecclesiastical art—on which medieval and eventually modern European art ultimately depend—may have developed out of an anterior synagogal art, in much the same way as church music is believed to have developed out of that of the Temple and the Jewish liturgical chant."[33]

IV

Despite the ever growing mass of artifactual evidence and scholarly revision, the denial of Jewish art prevailed and became dogma. Despite three thousand items in a bibliography of studies devoted to Jewish art, despite Marc Chagall's autobiographical remarks and Rabbi Kook's letter, despite Baron and Gutmann, and despite Cecil Roth's illustrated *Jewish Art*, Harold Rosenberg was still adamant in negating Jewish art, Cynthia Ozick was still persuaded that the Second Commandment forever stifled true artistic creativity, and Geoffrey Hartman was still certain that Judaism is partially defined by "a lingering distrust of visual culture, an iconoclastic streak that always—when it comes down to the wire—sides with Abraham." Despite the late twentieth-century scholarship summarized by Bezalel Narkiss and Gabrielle Sed-Rajna in their antianiconic and handsomely illustrated *Ancient Jewish Art* published in 1975 and again 1985, Mark Rothko's biographer was still able to assert in 1993 that Eastern European Jews were compelled to "defy the traditional taboo against iconic images" if they sought to become artists. Fable or not, Jewish aniconism was robust. It was ubiquitous and resistant to attack. It is not easily dislodged.

As the example of David Kaufmann suggests, even scholars who surrendered belief in aniconism were unable to forsake it altogether. Kaufmann was convinced that biblical Judaism was aniconic. Cecil Roth argued that First Temple biblical Judaism was "passionate[ly] iconoclastic" and that the "iconoclastic tendency triumphed in the Orient, the south of Europe, and the Mediterranean area generally," continuing for "as long as Moslem domination and influence lasted."[34] In 1963, Michael Avi-Yonah judiciously explained that Judaism oscillated between periodic episodes of restrictive iconoclasm and lenient creativity. Describing conditions in Late Antiquity, he reasoned that "violence [against visual art] often increased in proportion to the political and social dangers threatening the moral or economic existence of the Jewish nation. Whenever there was a lessening of the external danger, the popular attitude changed and great latitude was allowed in practice."[35]

The durability of confidence in Jewish aniconism despite all the apparent evidence to the contrary also showed itself in peculiar ways. Mordecai Kaplan, founder of Reconstructionist Judaism in America, was a remarkably clearheaded, astute, and learned Jewish intellectual. He knew better than to adopt aniconism. He was nevertheless unable to rid himself of its vestigial attractions. In Kaplan's influential *Judaism as a Civilization*, published in 1934, the denial and affirmation of Jewish art were allowed to stand cheek by jowl. Discussing Jewish folklore, Kaplan added dancing to the funicular refrain cherished by modern German Jewish intellectuals. He proclaimed that "it is true that Judaism did not develop the plastic arts, but it compensated for this lack by the development of music, literature and dance to a remarkably high degree." A mere two paragraphs later, Kaplan's ambivalence surfaced. Contradicting himself, he wrote that "it is not to be supposed that Jewish art was without its plastic expression. With religion as the chief interest in Jewish life, it became the occasion for a rich tradition of plastic adornment, at first in the Temple and later in the Synagogue. . . . In short, the notion that Judaism had not and need not have significant and characteristic art, is an illusion."[36]

A more elaborate form of Kaplan's confused ambivalence surfaced in Raphael Patai's wide-ranging monograph published in 1977, *The Jewish Mind*. On page 55, Patai claimed that the "Cherubim serve as the best refutation of the view that Biblical Yahwism was totally aniconic. . . . [Their] presence in the Holy of Holies habituated the Jews to the idea that their religion, although strictly aniconic where God Himself was concerned, countenanced the visual, two- or three-dimensional representations of lesser superhuman beings, such as angels." On pages 69 and 74, Patai consistently admonished his readers to remember that "the ubiquitous Cherubim figures in both the First and the Second Temples of Jerusalem . . . had long habituated the Jews to the idea and practice of including in their places of worship visual representations of superhuman beings lesser than God and subordinated to Him." Patai therefore differed from the majority of scholars who recognized postbiblical Jewish art but nevertheless continued to assert that Judaism was iconophobic in its foundational ancient Near Eastern phase.

On page 356, however, Patai contradicted himself. He reverted to "no such thing as Jewish art." Referring to the Second Commandment, Patai announced that it "effectively prevented Jews, again in most places and most times, from engaging in sculpture and painting. Moreover, according to the historians of Jewish culture and art, as a consequence of this blanket prohibition, whatever talent Jews may have had for sculpture and painting became stifled, or at least diverted into related but not prohibited fields. . . . The major arts practiced by the Christian artists and developed by them to great heights had no counterpart among the Jews, and for this unquestionably the Biblical prohibition is responsible."[37] Cynthia Ozick had voiced the same opinions six years earlier, as did Martin Buber in 1903 and Marc Chagall in 1936.[38]

The contradictions in Raphael Patai and Mordecai Kaplan are amusing curiosities in the modern history of the idea of Jewish art. Together with dogmatic assertions made in Max Dimont's best-sellers, the curious contradictions define the hardy strain of aniconism in Jewish theology and popular scholarship throughout the twentieth century. A more compelling and profound example of aniconism's resilience is the work of Salo W. Baron. It is apparent from the passages already cited that Baron knew better than to espouse what he knew to be an outmoded nineteenth-century dogma. He acknowledged that Jewish aniconism was anchored in discredited "racial" assumptions. It was unsupported by the artifactual evidence. Baron too was nevertheless unable to resist aniconism's allure. In 1942, he underscored the " 'genuinely Jewish style' of richly decorated wooden synagogues of Poland–Lithuania, the gorgeously illuminated medieval Hebrew manuscripts, and the stained glass windows adorning the twelfth-century synagogue in Cologne. Baron's deduction is startling. Instead of using the evidence to maximize premodern Judaism's affinity for the visual arts, he stressed Judaism's nonchalant disinterest. He reached the incongruous conclusion that "the attitude of the medieval Jew to artistic problems was one of indifference rather than hostility."[39]

By "indifference," Baron specifically meant the German term *gleichgültig* as it was used by Richard Krautheimer in his 1927 study of medieval synagogues.[40] Krautheimer had argued that aesthetic judgments belong to the realm of culture-bound norms. He presupposed that religiosity, as opposed to formalized religion, is preoccupied with individual souls and purely spiritual values. He concluded that medieval Jews "resembled the mendicant friars [*Bettelmönche*] or the early Protestant reformers." He explained that medieval Jews, monks, and Protestants pursued the spiritual and ignored the physical without becoming as ascetic as the early Christians. All three groups, according to Krautheimer, were "indifferent but not hostile to the visual arts."

Krautheimer also perpetuated the argument invented by Heinrich Heine and Hermann Cohen on behalf of Judaism's gift for literature, just as he replayed the theme composed by Ludwig Steinheim and Heinrich Graetz exalting Judaism's gift for music. Perhaps because he was dealing in the conventional wisdom, Krautheimer did not acknowledge his authorities when he sharply differentiated medieval Judaism's indifference to the visual arts from its extraordinary achievements in poetry (*Dichtkunst*) and music.

Given his understanding of religious symbolism and his intimate knowledge of medieval Jewish architecture, it was impossible for Krautheimer to endorse the unqualified denial of Jewish visual art. Because he was a highly assimilated German Jew from a well-to-do bourgeois family, it was equally uncomfortable for him unequivocally to affiliate Judaism too closely with painting, sculpture, and architecture. "Indifference rather than hostility" was therefore an elegant solution to his conceptual dilemmas. "Indifference" simultaneously explained the absence of a distinctive style of Jewish architecture and accounted for the readiness with which Jews casually adapted, or assimilated, the diverse art of the peoples in whose midst they lived. "Indifference" also undercut the arguments developed by the likes of Werner Sombart, who rested his hostile case against Jewish culture on the premise that Judaism was fundamentally "estranged" (*fremd*) from the visual arts. Relying on Krautheimer, Baron had chosen his modern authorities well and followed them faithfully.

Uncharacteristically, Baron was less faithful to the medieval documents from which he extrapolated and tendentiously constructed medieval Judaism's attitudes toward the visual arts. In that same 1942 publication, he referred to "certain rabbis, such as Rabbi Meir of Rothenburg, [who] prohibited illuminated prayer-books lest figures of animals and birds divert attention [during worship]."[41] Had Baron not been misled by his lingering loyalties to aniconism, he might have noticed that Rabbi Meir Rothenburg did not prohibit the practice because it smacked of idolatry. Rabbi Meir merely discouraged it. The opening lines of Rabbi Meir's lengthy and detailed responsum read as follows:

> I was asked concerning those who illuminate their prayerbooks with drawings of birds and animals whether they are behaving properly or not. I replied: It appears to me that they are certainly not behaving properly since when they gaze upon those drawings they are not directing their hearts to their Father in heaven. Nevertheless, there is no trespass here against the biblical prohibition. . . . There are no grounds to suspect [idolatry] with regard to those drawings since they are merely flat patches of color lacking sufficient materiality [*ma-mashut*].[42]

Modern scholars who were less infatuated with Jewish aniconism avoided Baron's misreading of Rabbi Meir's lenient opinion.[43]

V

Baron and Krautheimer were moderates who merely attenuated the relationship between Judaism and the visual arts. They claimed that Judaism was indifferent to painting, sculpture, and architecture. Radical aniconists minimized or sundered that relationship altogether. They claimed that Judaism was officially hostile to the visual arts. Not everyone was satisfied with either indifference or hostility. Believing in Judaism's positive affinity for the visual arts, one group of twentieth-century Americans followed David Kaufmann's precedent. They were attracted to ceremonial objects. Other Americans deprecated the aesthetic status of ceremonial objects. They insisted that sculpture and painting be art "in the European sense" of the term. Or, as Rosenberg formulated it at the Jewish Museum in 1966, they demanded "art in the sense in which the word is used in the 20th century."[44] Seeking a distinctive Jewish art, this group was attracted to avant-garde abstraction and minimalism.

Both of the American groups, the ritualists and the modernists, differed from the Zionists. Cultural Zionists, like Martin Buber, articulated definitions and expectations of Jewish art that were open-ended, experimental, eclectic, and all-inclusive. Without being a Zionist, so did Marc Chagall. Religious Zionists, like Rabbi Kook, sheltered secular handicrafts and folk art under the umbrella of divinely sanctioned creativity. Refusing the Zionist option and affirming Jewish life in the Diaspora, American Jewish intellectuals were less generous than Buber and more restrictive than Rabbi Kook. American options for a distinctive Jewish art were mutually exclusively: either ceremonial objects or nonrepresentational abstractions.

The ritualists tended to be religious practitioners with strong institutional affiliation.[45] Contemplating ceremonial artifacts, Rabbi Mordecai Kaplan, founder of Reconstructionist Judaism, saw proof for the "rich tradition of . . . significant and characteristic art." Meditating on the significance of similar artifacts, Rabbi Louis Finkelstein discerned "tangible witnesses to the love for God and his Torah."[46] Rabbi Finkelstein was chancellor of Conservative Judaism's Jewish Theological Seminary in New York. Rabbi Shubert Spero, a spokesman for American Orthodoxy, examined the artifacts and found proof for the proposition "that the concept of the beautiful does possess the status of a metaphysical category in biblical and rabbinic thought." Like Chancellor Finkelstein, Rabbi Spero quoted the often repeated Talmudic dictum requiring that Jews "make beautiful objects in the performance of [God's] commandments."[47] By 1937, Reform Judaism in America also agreed that ritual art can be distinctively Jewish, proclaiming that "Judaism as a way of life requires . . . the cultivation of distinctive forms of religious art and music . . . in our worship and instruction."[48] The permanent collection of Judaica featured by the Jewish Museum in New York City embodies the ritualists' understanding of Jewish art.[49]

The modernists included an assortment of religious and secular intellectuals. In his 1966 lecture at the Jewish Museum, Harold Rosenberg sympathetically named their project "metaphysical Judaica." Speaking for the

religious metaphysicians, Steven Schwarzschild (1924–1989) articulated
an ethically tinged version of their aesthetics. Schwarzschild was a professor of philosophy and Judaic studies at Washington University in St. Louis.
He was "born in Frankfurt on Main . . . but grew up in Berlin, emigrating
to New York . . . in January 1939."[50] An ardent disciple of Hermann
Cohen, Schwarzschild's philosophy was decidedly Germanic.

In 1987, he published a neo-Kantian essay advocating Judaism's theological "divorce from naturalism." The essay began on the familiar terrain
of Jewish aniconism: "Until recent times . . . no Jewish art was produced,
nor were there Jewish artists of any great significance. There can thus be
no surprise that there never has been a body of Jewish literature on art or
aesthetics. How then Jewish aesthetics—that is, a Jewish theory of art?"[51]
He answered his rhetorical question by stressing Judaism's affinity with
nonrepresentational art. According to Schwarzschild, the biblical ban
against all images, especially representations of God, explains "the striking
poverty of plastic and graphic arts in Jewish history." But this "aboriginal
Jewish aesthetic (for Jews and Gentiles alike)" also explains why nonrepresentational painters like Mark Rothko prove that "in modernism, art is
assimilating Judaism." In Schwarzschild's judgment, modernism eschews
the idolatrous imitation of reality because nonrepresentational art distorts
and disfigures ordinary visual appearance.[52] Modernism thus depicts the
world as it ought to be, not as it is. Idealistic modernism therefore embodies a messianic and utopian morality that refuses to sanctify "physical
nature." According to Schwarzschild, modernism coincides with Judaism's fundamental opposition to pagan idolatry.[53] "In short," Schwarzschild concluded, "true aesthetics, Kantian and Jewish, subsumes art indirectly but decisively to ethics." Calling attention to Hermann Cohen's
approval of French impressionism, Schwarzschild endorsed "Adorno's
writings on music" and championed an "imageless" sort of distinctively
Jewish and "universal" Jewish art. In Schwarzschild's subtle opinion,
there was no Jewish art until Kant made it retroactively possible in theory.
Avant-garde painters, regardless of religious affiliation, made it actually
real in contemporary practice.

Avram Kampf, a more art historically minded exponent of "metaphysical Judaica," explained that artworks like those of Barnett Newman,
Adolph Gottlieb, and Mark Rothko are distinctively Jewish. "Their stern
quality, their lack of atmosphere or tactile details . . . their strict intellectual approach, [and] . . . their quest for the absolute with its inherent
antagonism to the image" make them admirable. According to Kampf,
their "paintings attack the sensuous nature of Western art at its very roots,
and seek to divorce the act of painting from its European tradition."[54]
Ad Reinhardt, an American painter, playfully formulated the universalist,
nonsectarian manifesto of the metaphysicians. He wrote, "Motherwell

said someone said, 'Rothko is the best Jewish artist in the world.' Motherwell and I are Protestant Christians. You don't have to be Jewish to show at the Jewish Museum. . . . How about a Lutheran adopting the Hebraic-Islamic disdain for images?"[55]

In his own reflections on the cultural significance of "metaphysical Judaica," Harold Rosenberg saw things differently.[56] Closing his 1966 lecture at the Jewish Museum, he invoked the problem of the "20th century, a century of displaced persons, of people moving from one class into another, from one national context into another."[57] Perhaps seeking to clarify the immediate unintelligibilty of modern art experienced by viewers expecting to recognize the objects depicted in painting and sculpture, Rosenberg explained that

> in the chaos of the 20th century, the metaphysical theme of identity has entered into art, and most strongly since the war. It is from this point that the activity of Jewish artists has risen to a new level. Instead of continuing in the masquerade of conforming to the model of the American painter by acquiring the mannerisms of European art, American Jewish artists, together with artists of other immigrant backgrounds—Dutchmen, Armenians, Italians, Greeks—began to assert their individual relation to art in an independent and personal way. Artists like Rothko, Newman, Gottlieb, Nevelson, Guston, Lassaw, Rivers, Steinberg, and many others helped to inaugurate a genuine American art by creating as individuals. This work inspired by the will to identity has constituted a new art by Jews which, though not a Jewish art, is a profound Jewish expression, at the same time that it is loaded with meaning for all people of this era.[58]

For integrationist American Jewish intellectuals who were neither Zionists stressing collective identity nor religiously observant people enchanted by ceremonial objects, Rosenberg's combination of deracinated individualism and secular existential universalism spoke eloquently. It simultaneously embraced "no such thing as Jewish art" and "some sort of art." It replaced ceremonial objects with avant-garde modernism, honored the contemporary sense of the term "art," and used nonrepresentational modernism as the raw material for constructing both a "genuine American art" and a "profound Jewish expression."[59]

Not everyone agreed. Speaking for Nazi propaganda in 1930, Alfred Rosenberg deemed modernism a "mongrel" with "bastardized progeny, nurtured by spiritual syphillis and artistic infantilism." Unlike Avram Kampf, who admired modernism and eagerly affiliated it with Judaism partially because of modernism's "strict intellectual approach," the Nazi propagandist reviled modernism. He eagerly affiliated it with the Jews precisely because of its "theoretical bastardized dialectics" and "cerebralism." Alfred Rosenberg looked at the "Chagalls" and recognized "the features of degeneration." He accounted for "this completely chaotic development" by blaming the "democratic, race-corrupting precepts and the *Volk*-annihilating metropolis [which] combined with the carefully planned decomposing activities of the Jews."[60]

Clement Greenberg (1909–1994), the distinguished American Jewish critic, also considered modernist art. His conclusions differed. Unlike the Nazis, Greenberg did not reckon modernism to be "degenerate." Like Steven Schwarzschild, Greenberg admired and championed modernism. Unlike Schwarzschild, however, Greenberg did not discover in visual abstraction the quintessential embodiment of Jewish ethical monotheism and utopian messianism. Neither did Greenberg agree with Harold Rosenberg. Greenberg did not understand abstract visual art to be "a profound Jewish expression." When Greenberg viewed modern art, he discovered that it was precisely that, only modern art.[61] For artists (and perhaps intellectuals) with Jewish origins, modern art therefore transcended parochial Jewish identity. Imagining Chagall in France, Greenberg saw only an "East European in Paris," not an Eastern European *Jew* in Paris. Evaluating Chagall's achievement, Greenberg reiterated the assimilationist's dream: mastery of the host culture without total abandonment of one's traditional heritage, however attenuated. Greenberg wrote that "Chagall's art remains a feat, in oil as well as in black and white. That a man from the Jewish enclave in the provinces of Eastern Europe should have so quickly and so genuinely absorbed and transformed Parisian painting into an art all his own—and one that retains the mark of the historically remote culture from which he stems—that is an heroic feat which belongs to the heroic age of modern art."[62]

VI

The disparities among Clement Greenberg, Harold Rosenberg, Avram Kampf, Steven Schwarschild, and the Nazi propagandists are instructive. Viewing the same painting or sculpture, different critics discovered or invented different entities. The physical properties of the artifact remained constant; its cultural significance did not. Playing grisly ventriloquist to Richard Wagner's hideous dummy, Alfred Rosenberg stared at Chagall's canvases and saw Jewish "degeneracy" and "the shattering of the art of the Nordic West." Contemplating the same Chagalls, Clement Greenberg discerned a "heroic work which belongs to the heroic age of modern art."

Harold Rosenberg studied Mark Rothko's paintings and felt the aura of a "profound Jewish expression." Investigating the same paintings, Steven Schwarzschild recognized a full-blooded Jewish art, the transcendent fusion of Kantian and truly Jewish ideals.

Avram Kampf argued that Barnett Newman's paintings embody "a purely abstract conception, imageless, like the Jewish God. If there were a Jewish style Newman's work would be regarded as it most authentic and classic expression."[63] Attending the same paintings, Clement Greenberg observed that "they constitute . . . the first kind of painting . . . that accommodates itself stylistically to the demand of modern interior architecture for flat, clear surfaces and strictly parallel divisions."[64] Neither a formalist nor a metaphysician, Newman himself declared that his "paintings are not 'abstractions,' nor do they depict some 'pure' idea. They are specific and separate embodiments of feeling. . . . Full of restrained passion, their poignancy is revealed in each concentrated image."[65]

Similar disparities abound in modern discussions of Jewish art. Analyzing medieval Hebrew illuminated manuscripts in the conceptual framework of Jewish aniconism, most scholars have decided that the artifacts "are to be accounted for not by the supposed existence of a specifically Jewish art of illumination, but by the[ir] oriental or semi-oriental provenance."[66] Or, as Bernard Berenson claimed, the illuminations prove that "Jews imitated the art of the peoples among whom they were scattered, to the pitiful extent that they made use of art at all." Or, as Herbert Howarth announced, the manuscripts demonstrate that when the Jews did art "they lost touch with their people, worked for aliens, and were left with a rootless art of no real importance." Other scholars, working with different presuppositions and viewing the same manuscripts, saw indisputable proof for an authentic "artistic tradition among the Jews."[67]

Similarly, when Cynthia Ozick and Rabbi Louis Finkelstein reflected upon ritual art, she perceived "trivial ceremonial objects" and he detected "tangible witnesses to the love for God and his Torah." Similarly, Kant and Hegel agreed that Jewish tradition prohibits the visual depiction of God. Kant praised Judaism for its aniconism. Hegel criticized Judaism for its aniconism. Similarly, Erwin J. Goodenough's mentors at Oxford and Yale pondered Jewish culture. They were persuaded that there was "no such thing as Jewish art." Meditating upon the same culture, Marc Chagall boasted that the Jewish people were fully capable of showing the world "some sort of art."

These disagreements find their parallel in the history of science and their explanation in the sociology and psychology of perception. Faced with identical data, observers with differing points of view reach diverse conclusions, often contradictory ones.[68] Faced with identical data, even the same observer might see one thing now and and a different thing immediately thereafter.[69] Wondering why this should be so, thoughtful persons have concluded "that there is no perception without conception," that nothing in the realm of knowledge is self-evident, that there is no "innocent eye."[70] Regarding the question of when we know we are seeing art at all rather than a mere object, analytic philosophers have discovered that "the eye is of no value whatever in distinguishing art from non-art. . . . One needed, at the very least, some sort of theory to do that; and that in fact the art world must be an atmosphere saturated in theory."[71] Sociologists and historians trace the origin of these art-making theories to diachronic networks.[72] They stress "that our ideas of what vision is, what is worth looking at, and why, are all deeply embedded in social and cultural history."[73] Following the lead of these philosophers and histori-ans, I have been arguing that the factious idea of Jewish art is embedded in the social and cultural history of the factious nineteenth and twentieth centuries.

Breathing an atmosphere saturated in Nazi propaganda, Alfred Rosen-berg affirmed the existence of a Jewish art whose style was abstract and whose features were "degenerate." In atmospheres saturated with Kantian philosophy, premodern Jewish art did not exist. Its nonexistence was a virtue. In atmospheres saturated with Francophone postmodernism, as well, Jewish art does not exist. Its nonexistence is praiseworthy and vital to the "denigration of vision" that accompanies a profound loss of faith in rationalism, positivism, scientism, technology, and capitalism.[74] In at-mospheres saturated with Roman Catholic theology or Rabbi Kook's mys-tically inspired religious Zionism, Jewish art does exist. Its character is sacred and its sanction divine.

In atmospheres saturated with Protestant theology and the poetics of Romanticism, Jewish visual art barely survives. In this prevailing atmo-sphere, Judaism is said to divert the bulk of its creative energies away from visual images in order to specialize and excel in composing music or literature. In atmospheres saturated with the dreams of integration and terrified by the horrors of racial anti-Semitism, Jewish art exists, but it is physically nondistinct. Judaism is said to flatter its hosts by imitating their various styles. In American atmospheres saturated with the apologetics of Reconstructionist, Reform, Orthodox, and Conservative Judaisms, Jewish art exists as ritual object and synagogal decoration. In atmospheres satu-rated with Zionism or ethnic pride, Jewish art also exists, but its expres-sions are eclectic. In atmospheres saturated with the ideas that only nation-alities produce "great" art and that Judaism is a religion rather than a nationality, Jewish art does not exist. Should it nevertheless manage to exist, it is not "great" art worthy of display in important museums.

In social landscapes dominated by the idea of art in the traditional "Eu-ropean sense" of the term, Jewish art does not exist because premodern Jewish artisans were not commissioned to adorn churches, build cloisters, or decorate royal palaces and country retreats. Neither were preemancipa-tion Jews admitted to art academies or apprenticed to Gentile masters who transmitted their craft.[75] In intellectual circles devoted to art in its modern sense, Jewish art simultaneously exists and ceases to be. Living in his "art world," Clement Greenberg viewed Barnett Newman's work formalistically. He saw only a stylistic accommodation to the demands of modern architecture for "flat, clear surfaces and strictly parallel divisions." He did not detect the presence of a Jewish art. Living in an "art world" dominated by metaphysical hunger for the absolute, Avram Kampf viewed Newman's work and discovered the "most authentic and classic expression of a Jewish style," if such a style truly exists. Living in the individualistic artist's "art world," Barnett Newman viewed his work and saw "the embodiment of feeling . . . full of restrained passion" rather than the embodiment of *Jewish* feeling and passion.

These are the sort of socially constructed disagreements that have led politically minded critics to conclude that there is no knowledge without "ideology." The critics mean that partisan thinkers like Clement Greenberg, Barnett Newman, Cynthia Ozick, Rabbi Kook, David Kaufmann, Solomon J. Solomon, Hermann Cohen, Hannah Arendt, Salo Baron, Richard Krautheimer, Richard Wagner, Jean Baudrillard, Immanuel Kant and all the others who participated in the modern debate over Jewish art spoke "forms of thought motivated by social interest," that they are "conscious social actors mak[ing] sense of their world . . . liv[ing] out their relations to a social structure."[76] It is therefore no coincidence that intellectuals living in predominantly Protestant societies persist in denying or minimizing Judaism's sponsorship of the visual arts. Confronted by the archaeological and art historical evidence of Jewish creativity, intellectuals tend to explain it away. Jewish intellectuals tend to emphasize its physical resemblance to the art of the various cultures in whose midst they live. Consciously or not, they make cultural imitation the mirror image of social integration. Consciously or not, they welcome whatever philosophic system offers the most compelling case for aniconism. Neither is it a coincidence that Nazi propagandists despised Jewish art with a vehemence matched by their hatred for Jewish bodies. Neither is it a coincidence that in "making sense of their world and living out their relations to a social structure," Zionists unequivocally affirmed the promise of an all-inclusive national expression of Jewish art.

In 1931, John Dewey lamented "the compartmental conception of fine art . . . [that] sets it upon a far off pedestal." To recapture the "happiness . . . of esthetic perceptions," Dewey followed a "detour" into cultural politics. He argued that the "*theories* which isolate art . . . are not inherent" in the artifacts themselves. The theories arise because they are "embedded . . . in institutions and in habits of life . . . [that] operate effectively because they work so unconsciously. Then the theorist assumes they are embedded in the nature of things."[77] These sociological considerations partially explain David Kaufmann's naiveté when he hoped that a mere consideration of the empirical evidence would dissolve the "fable" of aniconism. By themselves, the empirical data were no match for the dynamics of assimilation and anti-Semitism in West Europe and America. Being neutral, the empirical data were unable to dislodge the prestigious and ubiquitous denial of Jewish art. The affirmation of Jewish art was contingent on the archaeological and art historical evidence. It was equally contingent, however, on theories, ideas, and institutions.

Dewey claimed that "nationalism . . . imperialism . . . capitalism . . . [and] economic cosmopolitanism" determined the contemporary understanding of art in general and the unsatisfying notion of "art of art's sake" in particular.[78] The historical record shows that the modern affirmations and denials of Jewish art were determined by those factors, and by others, as well.

Being a historian of thought, I cannot resolve the partisan disagreement over Jewish art any more than a geometer can square the circle.[79] I cannot affirm or deny the existence of Jewish art. Historians of thought merely account for ideas, plotting them against grids with horizontal and vertical coordinates. The horizontal coordinate situates ideas within their immediate social context. The vertical coordinate compares ideas to "previous expressions in the same branch of cultural activity."[80] The historical record shows that "no such thing as Jewish art" and "some sort of art" are horizontally synchronic with modernity. "No such thing as Jewish art" and "some sort of art" are steeped in nineteenth- and twentieth-century debates over the meaning of visual art and Jewish identity. The vertical or diachronic coordinate remains to be fixed. Do the modern denials and affirmations of Jewish art and visuality perpetuate, modify, or overturn the premodern conceptions of Jewish art and visuality? They overturn it, as I demonstrate in the following chapters.

Three _____

The Premodern Consensus

MOSHE BARASCH, interpreting the controversy between Byzantine iconoclasts and iconophiles, observed that "in the Middle Ages or during the
Reformation . . . whoever dealt with images had to come to terms with
the Second Commandment, to interpret it, and to assess its place in a
comprehensive system of beliefs." Barasch astutely distinguished two interpretations of the biblical law: "comprehensive" and "restrictive." The
comprehensive interpretation "rejects every mimetic image, whatever the
figure or object it represents." The restrictive interpretation "prohibits
the depiction of only one subject—the representation of God." Although
Barasch remarked that the "historical impact" of the comprehensive ban
against *all* images was "broader and more decisive than that of the" restrictive ban, he nevertheless acknowledged that "Christianity was concerned [principally] with the 'restrictive' attitude; it only marginally
touched on the question of whether images as such, regardless of what
they represent, are justified, but it devoted a great deal of intellectual and
emotional energy to discussing the justification or rejection of the image
of God." Barasch therefore informed his readers that the restrictive attitude "will . . . play a more central role in the chapters of [his] book."[1]

In fact, Barasch's chapters are monopolized by the restrictive attitude.
They nowhere adduce a single example of a medieval or Reformation
Christian advocating the comprehensive ban against images. The absence
of such examples in Barasch's monograph might be explained by a parallel
absence in the historical record. The record might show that the comprehensive interpretation was not "possible" in premodern thought in the
way it was "possible," if not ideologically necessary, in nineteenth- and
twentieth-century thought.[2] The record might then suggest that the comprehensive denial of Jewish art be assigned a strictly modern provenance.

What follows is a thumbnail sketch of the historical record. The sketch
traces premodern perceptions of the status of visual art in Jewish culture.
By itself, the sketch does not empirically verify or disprove the actual practice of Jewish art. Only artifacts selected and framed by an interpretive
scheme can verify or disprove that practice, as exemplified by Richard I.
Cohen's studies of the early modern period.[3] The sketch nevertheless supports several historiographic claims, first, as late as the sixteenth century,
neither Jew nor Gentile ever noticed that Judaism was comprehensively

aniconic. Second, as late as the sixteenth century, neither Jew nor Gentile ever understood the biblical law to be a prohibition against the production, use, or enjoyment of *all* visual images. Third, as late as the sixteenth century, neither Jew nor Gentile ever remarked that Jews were constitutionally deficient in visual talent and therefore totally reliant on foreign influence for the production and reception of visual art. Fourth, by the middle of the eighteenth century, minor cracks in the premodern consensus began to appear. By the middle of the nineteenth century, under mounting pressure, the cracks burst apart. By the early twentieth century, the premodern consensus was undone. It had been shattered by revolutions and seismic upheavals in every stratum of Western politics, society, and culture.

The sketch begins with Greek and Latin authors. They confirm that Judaism was not reputed to be comprehensively aniconic in antiquity. Hecateus of Abdera (fourth century B.C.E.) noted that Moses regulated the life of the ancient Israelites "but he had no images whatsover of the gods made for them, being of the opinion that God is not in human form."[4] Hecateus did not observe, however, that the Mosaic prohibition against cultic images of God extended to all forms of cultic, royal, funereal, and secular art.[5] It is also reported that Varro (second century B.C.E.) envied the Jews for their imageless worship of God. Varro wished that the Romans of his day would revert to their former practice of a similar imageless cult: "for more than one hundred and seventy years the ancient Romans worshipped the gods without an image. 'If this usage had continued to our own day . . . our worship of the gods would be more devout.' In support of his opinion [Varro] adduces, among other things, the testimony of the Jewish race."[6] Like Hecateus before him, Varro did not describe Jews as antagonistic to all forms of religious and secular art. Strabo of Amaseia (late first century B.C.E. to early first century C.E.), the widely traveled historian and geographer, observed that

> Moses . . . one of the Egyptian priests . . . went away from there to Judaea, since he was displeased with the state of affairs there. . . . He said, and taught, that the Egyptians were mistaken in representing the Divine Being by the images of beasts and cattle . . . for, according to him, God is the one thing alone that encompasses us all and encompasses land and sea. . . . What man, then, if he has sense, could be bold enough to fabricate an image of God resembling any creature amongst us? Nay, people should leave off all image carving, and setting apart a sacred precinct and a worthy sanctuary, should worship God without an image.[7]

Livy, Strabo's contemporary, agreed that the Jews "do not state to which deity pertains the temple at Jerusalem, nor is any image found there, since they do not think the God partakes of any figure."[8] Like Hecateus and

Varro before them, neither Livy nor Strabo associated Mosaic religion with the total absence of visual art.

Tacitus (mid–first century to early second century C.E.) was hardly sympathetic to Jews or Judaism. He nevertheless noted begrudgingly that, unlike the Egyptians who "worship many animals and monstrous images; the Jews conceive of one god only, and that with the mind only: they regard as impious those who make from perishable materials representations of gods in man's image; that supreme and eternal being is to them incapable of representation and without end. Therefore they set up no statues in their cities, still less in their temples; this flattery is not paid their kings, nor this honour given to the Caesars."[9] Tacitus acknowledged that Jewish culture did not sponsor sculptured representations of its kings, God, or Roman emperors. But he did not deduce from these ethnographic data that Jewish culture also prohibited all other forms of religious, royal, and secular art, including temples, flat paintings, frescoes, mosaics, engraved sarcophagi, and decorated houseware.

Neither did Cassius Dio, another Roman historian, who lived one century after Tacitus. Cassius Dio observed that the

> Jews . . . are distinguished from the rest of mankind in practically every detail of life, and especially by the fact that they do not honour any of the usual gods, but show extreme reverence for one particular divinity. They never had any statue of him even in Jerusalem itself, but believing him to be unnamable and invisible, they worship him in the most extravagant fashion on earth. They built to him a temple that was extremely large and beautiful, except in so far as it was open and roofless.[10]

Cassius Dio's sparse remarks regarding Jewish monumental architecture coincide with the words of Josephus, the Greek writing, first-century Jewish historian of Judaism. *Antiquities*, for example, gives richly detailed descriptions of Solomon's lavishly decorated Temple and royal palaces, as well as those built and refurbished by Herod.[11] Josephus chastised Solomon for commissioning casts of oxen for the Temple and sculptured lions for his throne, and he lost no opportunity to excoriate Herod for placing politically inflammatory and unauthorized sculptures of living things within the Temple's precincts.[12] But nowhere did Josephus indicate that tradition disallowed *all* forms of domestic, secular, and religious visual art.[13] Philo, the first-century Jewish philosopher who lived in the cosmopolitan setting of Hellenistic Alexandria, agreed. Although in one passage he declared that Moses "banished from his own commonwealth painting and sculpture . . . because their crafts belie the nature of truth and work deception and illusions through the eyes to souls that are ready to be seduced," it is not obvious that Philo was referring to anything more than Moses' specific prohibition against artifactual representations of God.

Moreover, as H. A. Wolfson has shown, there are philological grounds for concluding that Philo did not believe "that the painting of images was prohibited by the Mosaic law." Wolfson argued that the "condemnation of images . . . is not of painted images but rather of statues painted with color."[14]

Greco-Roman Gentiles and Late Antique Hellenistic Jews therefore agreed. According to Hecateus of Abdera, Varro, Strabo of Amaseia, Livy, Tacitus, Cassius Dio, Josephus, and Philo, Judaism was renowned for abiding by a specific prohibition against sculptural representations of God. They did not report that Judaism was equally renowned or notorious for categorically opposing all painting, sculpture, and architecture. They did not stereotype the Jews as persons lacking visual talent. They did not understand Jewish artifacts to be the heterodox residue of foreign influence. Unlike nineteenth- and twentieth-century intellectuals, they did not ascribe to Judaism a comprehensive aversion to *all* visual images.[15]

An overview of early rabbinic Jewish law reveals a similar profile.[15] Pondering Scripture with customary acuity, one sage was troubled by the apparent contradiction between Exodus 20:4 that seems to prohibit the making of any "graven image" and Exodus 25:18 that demands the construction of two golden cherubs to surmount the ark of the covenant. He resolved the apparent contradiction by distinguishing legitimate and forbidden religious sculpture. He defined the religious status of sculpture heteronomously. In his view, God's revealed will constitutes the only rule governing Jewish art, including the spectacular ceremonial items located in the Tabernacle and the Temple. Objects are therefore not intrinsically idolatrous. What God explicitly commands, according to the rabbinic interpretation of that command, constitutes legitimate art; what God specifically prohibits, according to the rabbinic interpretation of that prohibition, constitutes forbidden art.[16] The rabbinic sage did not derive the distinction from a priori theological principles equating all possible forms of visual art with idolatry.[17] Unlike modern intellectuals, he drew no anthropological contrasts between culture-bound sensoria: He did not describe Jews as "auditory" and Gentiles as "visual." He articulated no theory of Jewish attempts to "deconsecrate" or "disenchant" the material world in the name of divine transcendence.[18] Neither did he weigh the aesthetic values of beauty against the ascetic virtues of spirituality, and decide in favor of spirit.

As the Mishnah reports, Rabban Gamliel also assumed that God's will did not comprehensively and automatically equate all artifacts with forbidden idolatry, especially artifacts whose similarity to pagan practice was particularly striking. Rabban Gamliel pragmatically allowed himself to bathe in pools dedicated to and adorned by a statue of the goddess

Aphrodite. He also used lunar charts or models in the round of the moon's phases in examining the eyewitnesses who had come to testify regarding the onset of the new month.[19]

These forensically useful models depicting the celestial realm, merely decorative Greco-Roman statues, and divinely sanctioned cultic cherubs constitute persuasive evidence. They indicate that early rabbinic Judaism subscribed to the restrictive but not the comprehensive understanding of biblical law.

Rabbinic aggadic Midrash, part biblical exegesis and part homiletic legend, also displays the restrictive understanding of biblical laws regulating visual images. Rabbinic legend has it that when God commanded Moses to make the golden, seven-branched menorah, or candelabrum, for the Tabernacle, Moses asked God how it was to be made. God told him to construct it out of a single, hammered clump of gold. Despite God's direct reply, Moses suffered technical difficulties, for when he descended he forgot the divine instructions. He reascended and asked, "My Master, how is the thing to be fashioned?" Perhaps assuming that His verbal instructions ought to have been sufficient for Moses, who apparently had no problem making any of the other components of the Tabernacle, God reiterated, "the menorah is to be made by hammer work" (Exodus 25:31, 36). Nevertheless, Moses suffered ongoing difficulties, for when he descended he again forgot how it was to be fashioned. He therefore reascended, saying, "My Master, I have forgotten it." This time around, God showed it to him, but Moses still had a hard time. Then God said to Moses, "Look, and make" (Exodus 25:40) while He took hold of a ball of heavenly fire and showed Moses the celestial model to be imitated. Moses was nevertheless still stumped. God therefore said to him, "Go to Bezalel, and he will make the thing." No sooner had Moses said a single word to Bezalel, and the thing was made. Moses was astonished. "As for me," he said, "the Holy One Blessed be He showed it to me any number of times, but I had a hard time making it. But you, you never saw it, yet you fashioned it with your own skillful knowledge."[20]

The contrast between this legend and modern Germanophone speculations is striking.[21] Heinrich Heine and Hermann Cohen boasted that Moses was adroit. He crafted a monumentally moral people, but not artifacts. In premodern rabbinic Judaism, it was possible to imagine Moses being a master artisan who took private lessons in God's celestial atelier. Perhaps nourished by the biblical tale in Numbers 21:4–9, which credits Moses personally with designing and casting a divinely sanctioned serpent in bronze "so that whoever looked at it would live," the rabbinic imagination was untroubled by the thought that, except for the menorah, the productive skills of Moses were virtuoso. Nothing in the handful of Late

Antique Greco-Roman texts already surveyed indicates that this imaginative possibility was restricted to the Talmudic sages. They all acknowledged that Jews were forbidden to imitate specified cultic practices contaminated by association with paganism. Jews were also prohibited from representing their God sculpturally within the sacred precincts of the Tabernacle or the Temple. The deduction was not made that Jews were therefore also forbidden or unable to produce and enjoy all other forms of visual art in every other possible location, public and private, religious, royal, or secular. When Jews produced or enjoyed the visual arts, according to this phase of the premodern consensus, they were not circumventing a comprehensive interdiction.

Medieval Jewish authorities followed suit. A thirteenth-century compendium of anti-Christian polemics recapitulated the Talmudic emphasis on divine heteronomy. Should a Christian antagonist raise the objection that Moses ought not to have fashioned the copper serpent because of the biblical prohibition against making "a sculptured image or any likeness" (Exodus 20:4), the compendium suggested the following tactical response.

> Answer him: The mouth which prohibited is the same mouth that permitted. Similarly, with regard to the prohibitions on the sabbath, it is written, "You shall kindle no fire" [Exodus 35:3], yet it is also written, "On the sabbath day: two lambs . . . the burnt offering" [Numbers 28:9–10]. Thus, one should not scrutinize the commandments of the Creator, blessed be he, on the basis of human reason; rather, what he prohibited is prohibited and what he permitted is permitted. . . . This is also what you should say regarding the cherubim, for that is what Scripture intended in saying, "You shall not make for yourself" [Exodus 20:4], i.e., on your own authority, but on my authority you may.[22]

Since the rabbinic principle of heteronomy was apparently restricted in jurisdiction to the realm of cultic practice, the number of permissible images in realms unrelated to the cult approached infinity. And even within the realm of forbidden ritual images, the number of artifacts explicitly proscribed by God's will was relatively small. These quantitative considerations imply that the scales of rabbinic theology and law were heavily weighted in favor of the visual arts.

The rabbinic interpretation of the biblical law was therefore permissively liberal. It allowed ample room for the production and enjoyment of a wide array of legitimate visual artifacts. So ample and legitimate, in fact, that yet another medieval Jewish intellectual was theoretically empowered to exploit the positive valence of the arts. He transformed architecture, weaving, sculpture, and interior decorating into a cosmogonic metaphor. Building upon the prestige of visual art in medieval Jewish culture, he celebrated God's creation of the universe by likening God to "someone who sets about building a palace; he beautifies it and lays it out, and hangs its walls with embroideries, and afterwards sweeps the house, and adorns it with tapestries and woodcarvings."[23] Similar examples of admiration for the visual arts are plentiful in medieval Jewish literature. Many of them are featured in the subsequent chapters of this book. Taken together, these examples add medieval Judaism to the consensus formed by Greco-Roman and Late Antique rabbinic opinion.

The same consensus prevailed in early medieval Christian thought and practice. Throughout the eighth and ninth centuries, Byzantine iconophiles and iconoclasts clashed over the ecclesiastical propriety of sacred images. Speaking for the iconophiles, John of Damascus (ca. 675–749) repeatedly invoked the biblical precedents of Tabernacle and Temple, especially the cherubs, to prohibit the worship but legitimate the veneration of icons and mosaics depicting Christ, Mary, the angels, the apostles, the martyrs, and the saints that adorned both public and private spaces. The iconoclasts refused the distinction between permissible veneration and forbidden worship. The iconoclasts objected to sacred images, declaring them idolatrous. The iconoclasts nevertheless promoted a religious and secular art of their own. Claiming adherence to the strict meaning of biblical injunctions, the iconoclasts sanctioned imperial portraits and "scenes in which the emperor, his court or his profane world in general appear"; they also reintroduced "representations of animals, plants, and ornaments" in their church decorations.[24] The iconoclasts and iconophiles therefore agreed that the components of the Mosaic law still binding on Christians only forbade worshiping representations of divine entities. Typical of the premodern consensus, they also agreed that the Mosaic law unequivocally sanctioned certain forms of religious art and permitted a wide range of secular art, including the representation of the human form. Like the Islamic culture with which it interacted, Byzantine Christianity in both its iconoclastic and iconophilic modalities allowed the visual arts to flourish under religious auspices.[25]

If the ascetic St. Bernard of Clairvaux (1091–1153) is a reliable witness to medieval Christian perceptions in the West, then Judaism was not associated with austere aniconism in the twelfth century. Offended by the newfangled and ostentatious monumental architecture of his day, the monastic Bernard sternly voiced his displeasure to William, Abbot of St. Thierry: "I say nothing of the vast height of your churches, their immoderate length, their superfluous breadth, the costly polishings, the curious carvings and paintings which attract the worshipper's gaze and hinder his attention, and seem to me in some way to imitate/revive/showcase the ancient Jewish rite [*et mihi quodammodo repraesentant antiquum ritum Judaeorum*]."[26] Bernard was presumably thinking of Old Testament passages regulating the construction and decoration of Tabernacle and Temple, the very same biblical passages that the *Catholic Encyclopedia* would cite eight hundred years later in 1910 to prove that authentically biblical Judaism and Christianity were anything but comprehensively aniconic.[27]

Even as late as the sixteenth century, it was still possible for the leading Protestant reformers to associate Judaism positively with the visual arts and to interpret the Second Commandment more liberally than Kaufmann Kohler was able to do in 1902. Recall that for Kohler "plastic art in general was discouraged by the Law; the prohibition of idols in the Decalogue being in olden times applied to all images, whether they were made objects of worship or not." By contrast, despite the fury of iconoclastic passion unleashed by the Reformation, the early Reformers encouraged all sorts of "distinctly Protestant . . . art and architecture of both a secular and a religious nature."[28] Belonging to the premodern consensus, Protestant Christianity shared with the Byzantine iconoclasts and Islamic culture what Barasch classified as the restrictive ban against visual images.

In 1524, Martin Luther reminded his iconoclastic opponent, Andreas Bodenstein von Karlstadt, that the "law of Moses" permits and forbids images. It forbids visual images of God that are objects of worship, but it permits altars and religious images like those of the "crucifix or Mary [Marienbild] . . . and the saints [Heiligenbilder]" as long as those images are not worshiped but are held as a "memorial and witness [Gedächtnis und Zeugen]."[29] Confessing that he was unable to hear or read God's deeds without forming their corresponding mental images, Luther reasoned that since it was no sin "to have the image of Christ in [his] heart," it was also no sin to behold those images with his eyes.[30] He insisted that the strictest bounds of the Mosaic law permit one to handle coins with engraved images and to read the Bible from illustrated books.[31] Luther also proclaimed that it was far "better to paint pictures on walls of how God created the world, how Noah built the ark, and whatever other good stories there may be than to paint shameless worldly things"; he therefore prayed that God might enable him to persuade "the rich and mighty" to have "the whole Bible painted on houses, on the inside and outside, so that all can see it."[32]

Uldrich Zwingli (1484–1531), leader of the iconoclastic Reformation in Zurich, would never have agreed to Luther's exuberant proposal that the walls of his city be transformed into murals illustrating the Bible. Fearful that ecclesiastical and liturgical art too easily becomes the object of forbidden worship and idolatrous veneration, thus interfering with imageless interiorized meditation on God alone, Zwingli was convinced that the biblical prohibitions outlawed public and private displays of religious art. He nevertheless believed that Scripture did not include all types of art among its proscriptions. He cautiously affirmed that, according to the strict meaning of Scripture, religious paintings depicting biblical narratives or historical events (*geschichteswyss*) may legitimately be placed "out-side the churches . . . as long as they do not give rise to reverence."[33]

According to John Calvin (1509–1564), the Second Commandment "consists of two parts. The former curbs the licentious daring which would subject the incomprehensible God to our senses, or to represent him under any visual shape. The latter forbids the worship of images, on any religious ground," whether those images be of God or the saints.[34] Calvin acknowledged that the Old Testament enjoined the now abrogated construction of religious sculptures in the form of cherubs, but he did not conclude, as did Kohler, that "plastic art in general was discouraged" in antiquity. Like Luther and Zwingli, Calvin did not assert, as did Kohler, that the prohibition against images of God was originally "applied to all images, whether they were made objects of worship or not."[35]

Among the objects that Calvin believed "may be lawfully enjoyed" with proper restraint are "gold and silver, ivory and marble . . . and painted pictures" for their sheer beauty.[36] Regarding the permissibility of visual art, Calvin explicitly declared that he was

> not, however, so superstitious as to think that all visible representations of every kind are unlawful. But as sculpture and painting are gifts of God, what I insist for is, that both shall be used purely and lawfully. . . . The only things, therefore, which ought to be painted or sculptured, are things which can be presented to the eye; the majesty of God . . . must not be dishonoured by unbecoming representations. Visible representations are of two classes—viz. historical, which give a representation of events, and pictorial, which merely exhibit bodily shapes and figures. The former are of some use for instruction or admonition. The latter . . . are only fitted for amusement.[37]

This restrictive approval of the visual arts is the background that makes salient Calvin's refusal to consider the Old Testament cherubs a normative precedent for contemporary Christian practice. In Calvin's retrospective view, the cherubs are excessively and sinfully iconic. They signal ancient Judaism's resemblance to the cultic errors of Roman Catholicism: puerile overindulgence in "superstitious rites" and the multiplication of "carnal frivolous observances which our stupid minds are wont to devise after forming some gross idea of the divine nature."[38] Calvin was nevertheless an exponent of the affirmative premodern consensus. He neither under-stood the biblical ban to be comprehensive nor perceived Judaism to be aniconic.

Calvin's Geneva hardly resembled Cosimo De Medici's Florence. They agreed, however, on the restrictive interpretation of the biblical law and its corollary, the divinely sanctioned status of visual art in Christian life and ancient Jewish culture. In 1550 and again in 1568, Giorgio Vasari, author of the famed *Lives of the Most Eminent Painters Sculptors and Archi-*

tects, used texts from Genesis and Exodus to prove indirectly that, prior to the pinnacle achieved by Greek artists, the "Babylonians had learned to make images of their deities" and the Egyptians were "making sculptures and paintings." In the course of his brief survey of antiquity, Vasari paused to explain why Moses had forbidden "under pain of death the making of images of God." Moses was appalled by the sin of people who worshiped the golden calf as if it were a god, but he was not offended by the golden calf because it was a statue. That Mosaic law generously encouraged the visual arts was obvious: "The art of design and sculpture, not only in marble but in all kinds of metal, was given by the mouth of God to Bezalel . . . and Oholiab . . . who fashioned the two golden cherubs, the candelabra, the veil, the borders of the priestly vestments, and so many other beautiful castings for the Tabernacle, for no other purpose than to induce people to contemplate and adore them."[39] Vasari too, then, belonged to the premodern consensus. Like the Greco-Roman authorities, the Late Antique and medieval rabbis, the medieval and Reformation Christian theologians, Giorgio Vasari, art historian of the Renaissance, confirmed Judaism's intimate association with the visual arts.

Two hundred years after Vasari, the premodern consensus was still vigorous, but it was beginning to show the signs of age. François-Marie Arouet, Voltaire (1694–1778), the quintessential *philosophe* and implacable foe of "infamous" revealed religion, and Johann Joachim Winckelmann (1717–1768), the great art historian and champion of Greek antiquity, introduced the changes. Voltaire did not contest the fact that ancient Jews practiced the full range of visual arts; he only disputed the original source and moral purity of their practices. He vilified the Jews, describing them as a motley collection of idolatrous "vagabonds" and leprous "brigands" who, "always lacking the arts" (*toujours privé des arts*), stole everything they had from the more advanced cultures surrounding them.[40] Voltaire's condemnation approximates the comprehensive denial of native Jewish art that was to prevail after the French Revolution. Ninteenth- and twentieth-century anti-Semites would adopt and refine Voltaire's opinions, sharpening his barbs. Opponents of anti-Semitism blunted or deflected Voltaire's barbs. The Jewish defendants exchanged the criminal vocabulary of theft for the scientific terminology of "influence" and the more polite discourse of "imitation." With the help of Kant and Hegel, they rationalized the absence of an indigenous Jewish art by invoking the chaste spirit of universal Hebraic morality. Voltaire himself, however, belonged to the premodern consensus. He never read Kant or Hegel, and he never claimed that Jewish culture disparaged the visual arts or represented itself as aniconic. He only denied that ancient Jews possessed original artistic talent.

Unlike Voltaire, Winckelmann neither debased the Jews nor questioned the origin of their art. He nevertheless deviated slightly from the premodern consensus. He wavered on the general status of the various arts in ancient Judaism, and he suggested that Israelite achievements in sculpture were minimal. Two considerations led Winckelmann to the tentative conclusion that ancient Jews considered the "fine arts" (*schönen Künste*) to be "superfluous [*überflüssig*] in human life" and therefore neglected their practice. The two considerations were Israelite reliance upon Phoenician artisans and Mosaic laws forbidding sculptural representations of God. The counterevidence, however, was more compelling. Winckelmann had read and personally noticed that Jews were physically beautiful. Like the Phoenicians and Greeks, the ancient Jews therefore possessed one of the environmental prerequisites for the production of beauty in art. He also relied on biblical texts reporting the unusually large number of artisans carried way from Jerusalem into the Babylonian Exile.[41] Winckelmann therefore concluded that except for sculpture (*Bildhauerei*) and despite the "poor opinion" (*schlechten Begriffe*) of the arts among the ancient Israelites, "drawing [*Zeichnung*] and artistic work (*künstlicher Arbeit*) must have reached a high level of achievement" in Israel.[42] Winckelmann's qualified praise is a far cry from the comprehensive denials of Jewish art that were to prevail in the nineteenth and twentieth centuries.

By the end of the nineteenth century, the premodern consensus no longer held sway: Judaism was generally understood to be aniconic by Jew and Gentile alike; the comprehensive understanding of the biblical ban— a relative latecomer to the history of ideas—was becoming the well-entrenched conventional wisdom. The specific biblical laws against sculptural representations of God in the Tabernacle or the Temple, together with the rabbinic elaborations of the laws against idolatry, were generalized by Germanophone and Anglo-American intellectuals to entail an absolute renunciation of all forms of representational art. The premodern notion of an indigenous Jewish art stemming from God and transmitted at Sinai by Moses, the inspired lawgiver and master craftsman, was forgotten and replaced by assertions of Jewish antipathy to almost all forms of visual art and Jewish reliance on the work of others to nourish what art there was in Jewish life. The affirmative premodern consensus was eclipsed by "no such thing as Jewish art."

Recall that for Harold Rosenberg in 1966 lecturing at the Jewish Museum in New York City, there are two answers to the question of Jewish art, "a Gentile answer and a Jewish answer. The Gentile answer is: Yes, there is a Jewish art, and No, there is no Jewish art. The Jewish answer is: What do you mean by Jewish art?" The historical record shows that Rosenberg was partially correct: The question indeed hinges on what people mean by the protean terms "Jewish" and "art." The historical record shows that Rosenberg was also partially mistaken: The two answers to the question of Jewish art do not stem from timeless and anonymous Gentiles and Jews inhabiting Harold Rosenberg's impressive wit. Diverse answers to the question of Jewish art are strictly chronological: premodern and modern. The premodern answer was uniform: It presupposed the restrictive understanding of the biblical law. It affirmed Jewish art. The modern answer is multiple. Its variety is forged in political and metaphysical quarrels between advocates of "no such thing as Jewish art" and partisans of "some sort of art." Advocates of Jewish aniconism paradoxically include both Jews and Gentiles. They tend to be Jewish integrationists, liberal friends, and anti-Semitic foes. Partisans of Jewish art also include Jews and Gentiles. They tend to be Roman Catholics, Jewish nationalists, Jewish integrationists in the Diaspora who cherish ceremonial artifacts or secular abstractions, and art historians who are persuaded by theories and artifacts that Jewish art of "some sort" exists.

The principles of Jewish aniconism are therefore unreliable guides to premodern Jewish culture. Synchronic products of the modernity they reflexively seek to explain, they fail to account for themselves and for the diversity of modern opinion. They impose anachronistic readings on ancient Near Eastern, Hellenistic, medieval, and early modern civilizations. Forming a Procrustean bed, the dogmatic assumptions of Jewish aniconism blind us to the affirmative premodern consensus and its recent overturning. Used judiciously as a foil, however, the assumptions of Jewish aniconism make it possible to envision a less distorted, more fully embodied, polychromatic portrait of premodern Judaism.

Four

The Well-Tempered Medieval Sensorium

I

Reconnaissance of sixteenth-century French literature convinced Lucien Febvre that "like their acute hearing and sharp sense of smell, the men of that time doubtless had keen sight. But that was just it. They had not yet set it apart from the other senses." He wittily concluded that "there was no Hotel Fairview in the sixteenth century, nor any Prospect Hotel. . . . The Renaissance continued to put up [*à descendre*] at the Rose, the Wild Man, or the Golden Lion, refugees from heraldry that had stumbled into the hotel business." Taking a cue from Febvre's search for the "sensory underpinnings of thought in different periods,"[1] historians of Judaism might ask: What are the aesthetic doctrines of Jewish thought? Where, for example, did medieval Jewish philosophers "put up"? Was their hearing acute, their sense of smell sharp, and their sense of sight keen? Did they set vision apart from the other senses?

Conventional answers to these questions were articulated by Martin Buber and David Kaufmann. Buber represents the legions of modernists who differentiate Judaism from mainstream Western culture. He emphasized the superiority of hearing. In 1951, Buber declared that "the Greeks established the hegemony of the sense of sight over the other senses, thus making the optical world into *the* world. . . . Philosophy is grounded on the presupposition that one see the absolutes in universals. In opposition to this . . . the religious communication of a content of being takes place in paradox. It is not a demonstrable assertion . . . but a pointing toward the hidden realm of existence of the hearing man himself."[2] Earlier, in 1903, he named that hearing man, declaring that "the Jew of antiquity was more acoustically oriented [*Ohrmensch*] than visually [*Augenmensch*], and more temporally oriented [*Zeitmensch*] than spatially [*Raummensch*]. Of all his senses he relied most heavily upon his hearing when forming his picture of the universe."[3]

David Kaufmann (1852–1899) was a pioneer in the scientific study of Jewish art and a distinguished historian of medieval philosophy. He represents the opposing legions of modernists who prefer to align Judaism with Western culture. Unlike Buber, these modernists celebrate rationalism.

They champion both hearing and sight. In 1884, Kaufmann argued that premodern Jewish philosophers ranked the senses hierarchically: They devalued touch, taste, and smell because these senses were nonintellectual and too bodily. They privileged hearing and sight because these senses played leading roles in the formation of scientific concepts, speculative theory, and abstract ideas. To support these claims, Kaufmann quoted Joseph Albo, a fifteenth-century Jewish theologian in Spain, who remarked that

> this is why we find that man has a stronger desire for the sensibilia of sight and hearing than for those of smell and taste. Nature has put in us a stronger desire for the former because we are more apt through them to acquire theoretical knowledge, upon which human perfection depends. The other sensibilia, on the other hand, bear a closer relationship to bodily feelings and desires, which are far away from the specific perfection of man. Man has them only for the maintenance of his body, like the other animals.[4]

The exclusion and degradation of touch, smell, and taste compose the common denominator in these conventional portraits of premodern Jewish psychology. Despite the common denominator, the portraits are antithetical. Buber deplored rationalist philosophy; Kaufmann embraced it. Even their shared inclusion of hearing points in divergent directions. Buber associated hearing with paradox, mystery, temporality, and engaged interaction with the particulars of concrete life. Kaufmann associated hearing with the acquisition of abstract theoretical generalizations.

The combination of agreement and divergence between Buber and Kaufmann is not coincidental. It stems from their common immersion in nineteenth-century Hegelian philosophic culture. Buber read Judaism against the grain of Hegelian idealism; Kaufmann read Judaism with that grain. When Kaufmann cited Albo's text, he was standing on familiar and congenial grounds. Using language remarkably similar to Albo's, Hegel had declared that "the sensuous aspect of art is related only to the two theoretical senses of sight and hearing, while smell, taste, and touch have to do with matter as such and its immediately sensible qualities. . . . What is agreeable for these senses is not the beauty of art. Thus art on its sensuous side deliberately produces only a shadow-world of shapes, sounds, and sight."[5]

As for Buber, he was thinking of Plato, Plotinus, and Hegel when he proclaimed that "philosophy is grounded on the presupposition that one see the absolutes in universals." Regarding Hegel's concepts of God and human perfection, Buber was dismayed. The following passage proves that Buber's rejection of Hegel was unequivocal:

> The radical abstraction, with which philosophizing begins for Hegel, ignores the existential reality of the I and of the Thou, together with that of everything

else. According to Hegel, the absolute—universal reason, the Idea, i.e., "God"—uses everything that exists and develops in nature and in history, including everything that exists in man, as an instrument of its, i.e., God's, self-realization and perfect self-awareness; but God never enters into a living, direct relation to us, nor does He vouchsafe us such a relation to Him.[6]

Just as the contradiction between Buber and Kaufmann discloses a common immersion in nineteenth-century Hegelianism, their agreement marks a shared participation in nineteenth-century Jewish apologetics. Buber advocated auditory spirituality; Kaufmann promoted auditory-visual rationalism. But they both excluded touch, taste, and smell from the "aesthetics" or sensory underpinnings of premodern Jewish thought.[7] Their assertions and exclusions belong to the postemancipation, Germanophone Jewish arsenal. Arguments endorsing one sense and excluding other senses were stockpiled by Jewish intellectuals in the war against modern anti-Semitism. Their polemics elevated Jewish spirit and intellect at the expense of body and space. Their arguments were designed to combat Feuerbachian-Marxist critiques of Jewish corporeality and materialism.[8] Their arguments assumed validity for premodern Judaism, as well. The praise of spirit or intellect and the disparagement of body were the templates used by Buber and Kaufmann to outline the conventional portraits of medieval Jewish psychology. Over time, however, even the best of portraits risk becoming dated when canons of representation change.

Steeped in late nineteenth- and early twentieth-century cultural politics, Buber and Kaufmann are poignant witnesses to the immediate past. They inhabited and worked a modernist landscape that once made their scholarly arguments lively and compelling. In more contemporary landscapes, defined by different social and intellectual features, their arguments seem outmoded. Kaufmann's book on medieval psychology was published in 1884. Now, more than one hundred years later, in the midst of late capitalist postmodernity, the book's wide-ranging collection of medieval evidence remains unsurpassed. The book's evidence is still authentically medieval, but its Hegelian arguments have become moribund. The once powerful arguments were casualties of mutinies and revolts against idealism instigated by "Marxism, positivism, British analytic philosophy, pragmatism, and existentialism."[9] Buber fought with the existentialist rebels, but his metaphysics are scorned by contemporary positivists and analytic philosophers. His devaluation of taste, smell, touch, and sight has also withered. It languishes in contemporary landscapes that demand "giving the body its due."[10] Like Kaufmann's tendentious exclusion of taste, smell, and touch, Buber's tendentious infatuation with hearing has outlived its credibility.[11] Nowadays, portraits of premodern Jewish psychology that deterritorialize and disembody Jewish culture in order to exalt Jewish spirit risk becoming false representations. The conventional portraits risk being as distorting as the conventional wisdom that mistakenly affirms premodern Jewish aniconism.[12]

II

That premodern Jewish culture was not aniconic is certain. That premodern Jewish philosophers did not advocate human perfection at the expense of a fully engaged sensorium needs proof. The following proof incurs minimal debts to Hegel, avoids fighting old battles with anti-Semitism, and honors the demand that bodies be given their due. The proof assumes that Buber and Kaufmann erred when they indulged in the dreadful pseudo-biological practice "of enlisting nature in our causes and crusades."[13] The proof begins to crystallize with hints supplied by two twelfth-century Aristotelians: Moses Maimonides and Ibn Rushd. In his ethical writings, Maimonides insisted upon a fundamental distinction between animals and humans. Animals and humans are rightfully described as seeing or hearing, as having sensation, but "sensation" is an equivocal term, a homonym, suggesting identity where none exists. Because human sensation is related to the categorically unique human soul and animal sensation is related to the categorically unique animal soul, their sensations differ categorically.[14] To post-Darwinians, this is similar to saying that microphones and rabbit ears "experience sound" differently. To pre-Darwinians, Maimonides's distinction implied that the difference between human sensation and animal sensation far outweighs the difference between human sensations of seeing and touch. Ibn Rushd clarified the implied difference: Humans can know abstract ideas, animals can only know particular, discrete things. In his own words, Ibn Rushd distinguished humans from animals by observing that "in man, [the senses of touch, smell, taste, hearing, and sight] perceive the differences in objects and the particular ideas represented by them. . . . Any one of of these senses in man can lead to the primary notions . . . especially the senses of hearing and sight."[15] Ibn Rushd, unlike Hegel and his disciples, extolled hearing and sight without disparaging touch, smell, and taste. Medieval Aristotelians did not exclude touch, smell, and taste from the privileged precincts of intellectual activity. Joseph Albo declared that hearing and sight are more apt than smell and taste to induce intellectual perfection. He did not assert that smell and taste are altogether incapable of perfecting human intellect.

Joseph Albo was fully aware of the medieval psychology articulated by Maimonides and Ibn Rushd. Albo's restatement of their principles introduce the quotation cited by David Kaufmann. Kaufmann decontextualized the passage to prove that medieval Jewish philosophers devalued touch, taste, and smell because these senses were nonintellectual while they privileged hearing and sight because these senses played exclusive roles in the perfection of human intellect.[16] In the light of Albo's immersion in Aristotelian psychology, which allowed each of the five senses serving the human soul access to abstract truth, Kaufmann's antisomatic, Hegelian interpretation is untenable. Even more fatal to Kaufmann's interpretation is Albo's explicit rejection of the philosophic ideal. The literary context of Kaufmann's quotation was Albo's impartial summary of doctrines endorsed by many philosophers.[17] The chapters immediately following this summary contain Albo's elaborate defense of bodily activity and his equally elaborate polemic against the philosophic claim that human perfection consists of acquiring abstract truth. Albo declared that the philosophic claim "is absurd in itself and in disagreement with the divine Torah."[18] He also declared that "man, being a material being, can not attain human perfection through intellectual contemplation alone without practical activity."[19] Practical activity involves all the bodily senses. If the fifteenth-century Joseph Albo was no Hegelian, neither was he a proleptic disciple of Buber. Buber found heteronomy and strict observance of rabbinic law uncongenial. Albo concluded that human perfection requires serving God's will. "In other words, man must do whatever he does with the intention of pleasing God and not for his own pleasure or any other purpose."[20]

By itself, the example of Joseph Albo does not prove that medieval Jewish philosophers tuned life to a well-tempered sensorium and a nuanced array of affective response. The example merely indicates what might be true. In the discussion to follow, Moses Maimonides and Profiat Duran (ca.1360–ca.1414) will speak for all the medieval Jewish philosophers. Two figures are needed because medieval Jewish philosophy unfolded in two chronologically and culturally distinct phases: an earlier phase within the orbit of Islamicate empires and a later phase within Christian Europe. Furthermore, two vastly different "epistemes,"[21] "paradigms,"[22] or "mentalities"[23] are discernible across the lines of all medieval Arabic, Hebrew, and Latin philosophy. Epistemes are the cultural templates that construct reality and make knowledge possible. Epistemes consist of the "interpreting skills one happens to possess, the categories, the model patterns and the habits of inference and analogy; in short what we may call . . . *cognitive style*."[24] Because of epistemes, philosophic discourse is intelligible and disagreement inevitable. The medieval epistemes are conventionally tagged Augustinian and Thomist.[25] The one belongs to the family of Platonisms and the other to various Aristotelian empiricisms. M.-D. Chenu named them "symbolist mentality" and protoscientific "nature"-ism.[26] When medieval intellectuals used the Platonic episteme to experience reality, they declared it a universe and searched it for spiritual affinities, correspondences, and analogies; when they used the Aristotelian episteme, they also declared reality to be a universe but searched it for impersonal structures, materialist regularities, and corporeal causation. Viewed historically, epistemes flourish, compete, and undergo change because they originate in living societies whose circumstances they reflect and whose needs they serve. Viewed critically, "epistemes," "paradigms," and "mentalities" are scholarly constructs to be used and inhabited with extreme care.[27]

In this fresh search for the sensory underpinnings of premodern Jewish thought, Maimonides, that redoubtable rationalist and towering presence in medieval Jewish intellectual history, speaks for an Islamicate "nature"-ist and Duran for the return to a "symbolist mentality" that challenged Maimonideanism and flourished among Jews in fifteenth-century, anti-Jewish, Christian Spain.

III

In the *Guide of the Perplexed* (2:25) Maimonides prefaced his interpretation of Judaism's laws by dividing all possible behavior, including God's, into four possible categories: futile, frivolous, vain, and good and excellent actions. He defined a frivolous act as one that aims low: "I mean to say that something unnecessary and not very useful is aimed at therein, as when one dances not for exercise or as when one does things in order to make people laugh about those things."[28] Maimonides explicitly emphasized that actions are not intrinsically frivolous and that their evaluation depends on the needs of the agent and the nobility of the intention behind the act. As doctors know well, "the different kinds of bodily exercise are necessary for the preservation of health."[29] In fact physical exercise is to bodily health what scribal skills are to the scholar. As the one kinesthetic act prepares the material implements needed for writing, so too the other conditions the body for thinking. Both actions equally command our respect: "Thus those who accomplish acts exercising their body in the wish to be healthy, engaging in ball games, wrestling, boxing, and controlling the breath, or those who engage in actions that are done with a view to writing, as for instance the cutting of reed pens and the making of paper, are in the opinion of the ignorant engaged in frivolous actions, whereas they are not frivolous according to the learned."[30] The argument on behalf of the body continues in 3:27. Somatic health is a noble aim because it is prerequisite for and subordinate only to spiritual-intellectual health: "For a man cannot represent to himself an intelligible . . . if he is in pain or is very hungry or is thirsty or is hot or is very cold."[31]

Readiness for intellectual activity, according to Maimonides, is also contingent upon the emotions. In the explicitly antiascetic chapter of his introduction to the Mishnaic treatise 'Abot (the so-called *Ethics of the Fathers*), known to posterity as *The Eight Chapters*, he affirmed that

man needs to subordinate all the powers of his soul to thought . . . and to set his sight on a single goal: perception of God. . . . On the basis of this reasoning, he would not aim at pleasure alone, choosing the most pleasant food and drink . . . rather he would aim at what is most useful. If it happens to be pleasant, so be it; and if it happens to be repugnant, so be it. Or he may aim at the pleasant in the fashion of medical science, like the person whose appetite for food has weakened is stimulated by well-seasoned and tasty dishes which man's soul desires or like someone afflicted with melancholy who dispels it by listening to music and various kinds of song, by strolling in gardens, by experiencing beautiful buildings, by associating with beautiful pictures, and similar sorts of things which broaden the soul, and thereby rids himself of the melancholy. The purpose in all this is to heal the body. And the purpose of the goal of healing the body is the acquisition of science. . . .

If a man sets this notion as his goal, he will discontinue many of his actions and greatly diminish his conversation. For someone who adheres to this goal will not be moved to decorate walls with gold or to put a gold border on his garment—unless he intends thereby to give delight to his soul for the sake of its health and to drive sickness from it, so that it will be clear and pure to receive the sciences. Thus they said: "An attractive wife, attractive utensils, and a bed prepared for the scholar" [B. Tal. *Shabbat* 133a]. For the soul becomes weary and the mind dull by continuous reflection upon difficult matters, just as the body becomes exhausted from undertaking toilsome occupations until it relaxes and rests and then returns to equilibrium. In a similar manner, the soul needs to rest and to do what relaxes the senses, such as looking at beautiful decorations and objects, so that weariness be removed from it. . . . Now it is doubtful that when done for this purpose, these are bad or futile, I mean decorating and adorning buildings, vessels, and garments.[32]

A striking parallel to this early, exoteric, antiascetic, halakhic passage is found in the later, esoteric, speculative context of the *Guide,* in which Maimonides addressed the law of the beautiful captive woman (Deut. 21:10–14). Unlike the passage from the *Commentary to the Mishnah,* it does not legitimate emotions solely because they are means to intellectual ends, but it does show Maimonides's esteem for the considerable powers of affect. To explain why her captor must not forbid her to grieve, to be disheveled, and to weep, he noted that "those who grieve find solace in weeping . . . until their bodily forces are too tired to bear this affection of the soul; just as those who rejoice find solace in all kinds of play"(*la'b, sehoq).*[33] Another illustration of this principle is found in Maimonides's discussion of the Temple cult. Because he recognized that abstract philos-

ophizing is no match for slaughterhouse odors and without insisting that
there be an immediate intellectual goal in sight, he explained that incense
was burned twice daily "in order to improve its smell and the smell of the
clothes of all who served there . . . for the soul is greatly solaced and attracted by pleasant smells and shrinks from stench and avoids it."[34]

Taken together, all of these passages dealing with nonverbal aesthetic
or emotional experience reveal the strong side of utilitarian hedonism
within the "multifaceted dialectical diversity" of Maimonidean thought,
which both repudiates and encourages ascetic austerity.[35] They show that
Maimonides used different criteria when he assessed texts and nonverbal
artifacts. He approved of secular and religious poetry regardless of its rhetorical form, as long as its thematic content encourages virtuous conduct
and inculcates true opinions.[36] He understood that scriptural and rabbinic
texts are allegories, parables, and integuments, whose use is pedagogically
legitimated because they protect complex philosophic notions while con-
veying them to the masses in popular form; but he did not insist that
nonverbal artifacts meet the same rigorous standards. According to Maimonides, paintings, architecture, music, tasty food, and perfumes, together with the emotional responses they elicit, are not shadowy cogni-
tions judged to be inferior when compared to the logical rigor and clarity
typifying the demonstrative proofs of philosophic discourse. Gardens do
not have to be allegories. He would have preferred that ball games, yoga-
like breathing exercises, paintings, decorated walls, music, and tasty foods
lead directly to philosophizing; but he was apparently willing to concede
that for certain people in certain circumstances it is appropriate to settle
for nonphilosophic yet salutary effects on somatic and emotional life.[37]

For Maimonides, then, each of the so-called five external senses was
given its due: the eye gazing upon a painting, the ear hearing music, the
nose smelling blossoms while strolling in the garden, the tastebuds savoring picquant cuisine, the body enclosed in architectural space, and the
sense of touch delighting in an attractive wife and a well-made bed were
all understood to be equally powerful in promoting emotional tranquility.
Each was also deemed capable of preparing the mind for philosophy.

Maimonides's appreciation of the egalitarian potential of the sensorium
is consonant with his metaphors of choice for intellectual perfection. As
to be expected, he favored light and vision. The introduction to part 1 of
the *Guide* characteristically teaches that the truths of physics, metaphysics,
and theology strike us like bolts of lightning, sometimes intermittently,
other times continuously, but always against the dark sky of ignorance.[38]
But he seems to have been equally fond of gastronomics. *Guide* 1:30 is a
lexicographic chapter devoted to the term "eating," which is construed as
a figure of speech signifying "knowledge, learning, and in general, the
intellectual apprehensions through which the permanence of the human

form (i.e., intellect) endures in the most perfect of states, just as the body endures in most of its states."[39] *Guide* 1:32 exploits the superficial resemblance between the cognitive limits of human reason and gastric distress.[40] The first half of the chapter appeals to the physiological reflex of temporary visual impairment caused by such actions as forcing the eye to gaze upon "very minute writing or miniature drawings"; the second half develops the simile of indigestion and vomiting caused by overindulgent consumption of honey.[41] Similarly, *Guide* 1:33 likens the premature introduction of theology and metaphysics into the curriculum to "someone feeding a nursing child with wheaten bread and meat and giving him wine to drink. He would undoubtedly kill him, not because these aliments are bad or unnatural for man, but because the child . . . is too weak to digest them so as to derive a benefit from them."[42]

Even the sense of touch supplies Maimonides with a metaphor of intellection. In *Guide* 3:50 the kiss of God, alluded to in the biblical Song of Songs, is construed to mean that Moses, Aaron, and Miriam died pleasantly in a "state of intense and passionate love" due to the perfection of their intellectual grasp of God.[43] This is all the more remarkable since Maimonides concurred with the proto-ascetic and Aristotelian notion that the sense of touch "is a disgrace to us"[44] insofar as it misleads us into excessive eating, drinking, and copulation, thus competing unfairly with the less sensational allure of philosophic contemplation.

Another indication of Maimonides's attitude toward the somatic can be extracted from his analysis of divine attributes and anthropomorphisms. Religious philosophers in the tradition of Xenophanes have long debated the propriety of ascribing certain qualities to God.[45] In *Guide* 1:47 Maimonides sought to explain why "hearing, sight and the sense of smell are figuratively ascribed" to God by the prophets, "whereas the sense of taste and that of touch are not."[46] He believed that God was perfectly incorporeal, so that strictly speaking, either all five of the senses should equally be ascribable to God in a metaphorical sense, or none of the senses—including hearing, sight, and smell—should ever be ascribed to God, even metaphorically. Maimonides resolved the inconsistency by noting that even common people understand that touch and taste require direct physical contact between perceiver and perceived, whereas the other three senses operate at a distance. Therefore no pedagogic harm is done by attributing sight, audition, and smell to God. In contrast the predicates of taste and touch, if applied to God, would demean Him in the minds of the masses. But to apprehend God appropriately, Maimonides argued, the masses must also come to understand that He no more sees, hears, or smells, as we do corporeally, than He either touches or tastes, even metaphorically.

If Graetz were correct in asserting that "the entire structure of Judaism attests to" the contrast between pagan sights and Judaic sounds, then Maimonides would paradoxically have to be excluded from the structure of Judaism. According to Maimonides, God is no more appropriately perceived in the "alternatingly loud and soft sounds of the movement of the waves, in the rhythm of word sounds" than He is made manifest in visions born in prophetic imagination[47] or fairly represented in the objects encountered when "strolling in gardens, experiencing beautiful buildings, associating with beautiful pictures, or similar sorts of things which broaden the soul." Adhering to the rabbinic legal tradition, Maimonides forbade the making of idolatrous paintings and various three dimensional forms,[48] but proscribing production ought not to be confused with forbidding the enjoyment of what others have created. With the notable exceptions of listening to particularly lusty secular music[49] or gazing upon idolatrous objects like those found in Christian places of worship,[50] he apparently set no limits on aesthetic experience. He forbade looking at nature in the form "of a woman who is prohibited to us, even to look at such a woman with a view to pleasure . . . and birds and beasts when they copulate,"[51] but he permitted almost unrestricted gazing upon crafted artifacts. This liberal attitude toward the arts coincides with his principle that no natural or artifactual object can serve to represent God. To expedite the intellectual cognition of the God concept within the confines of Jewish law regulating diet, sexuality, and aesthetic-somatic experience, Maimonides granted an egalitarian measure of hygienic, stabilizing freedom to all of the body's kinaesthetic, sensory, and emotive faculties. No one of them was privileged over the others.

Because Maimonides distinguished God over all other beings and processes, he also sharply differentiated human intellection of God from propaedeutic sensory experience.[52] Aesthetic-somatic freedom could be allowed only in partnership with constant reminders that, except for the human capacity for abstract intellection and purposive behavior in governance, there is no mythopoeic resemblance between God, human society, and nature.[53] He conceded the pedagogic necessity of using the analogies and metaphors belonging to what Chenu called the "symbolist mentality." That Maimonides possessed talent for composing a parable is evident in the well-known castle motif of *Guide* 3:51, but no correspondence between God, society, and nature is allowed to go unchecked. No sooner is an analogy offered than it is crushed under the weight of myriad qualifications.[54]

His distrust of symbols is neatly illustrated by the rough handling of the symbolists' favorite metaphor: man, the microcosm. Midway through *Guide* 1:72, after systematically weaving the cosmological parallels made obvious by this metaphor, he suddenly shifts tactics and proceeds systematically to unravel it:

This whole comparison can be consistently applied to every individual animal that has perfect limbs; but you never hear that one of the ancients has said that an ass or a horse is a small world. This is because of that which is a proprium of man only, namely the rational faculty—I mean the intellect, which is the hylic intellect. . . . Know that it behooved us to compare the relation obtaining between God, may He be exalted, and the world to that obtaining between the acquired intellect and man. . . . We should have compared, on the other hand, the rational faculty to the intellects of the heavens, which are in bodies.[55]

Of all the rich implications of the microcosm metaphor, only one remains standing after this Maimonidean critique: a drastically attenuated and obscure similarity between the perfected human intellect and the mysterious cognitive entities which cause celestial bodies to move.

Confident that nothing sensory or even humanly intellectual is capable of representing God, but realistic about the somatic underpinnings of all human behavior, Maimonides was able to appreciate the sensory. He indulgently granted almost total freedom to the need for aesthetic experience. As long as the people were warned not to let inferences from the natural and the cultural mislead them into forming idolatrous notions regarding God, and as long as people needed somatic-aesthetic weapons in their fight against physical weariness and emotional imbalance, he was not reluctant to prescribe a healthy dose of multisensory stimulation. He cautioned them, however, not to confuse somatic delight with spiritual pleasure. One prepares for the other, one superficially resembles the other, but the two have nothing else in common. The ultimate incommensurability of the somatic and the spiritual is forcefully stated in the introduction to his *Commentary on Mishnah: Sanhedrin*, chapter 10 (Pereq Heleq):

Know that just as the blind man cannot imagine color, as the deaf person cannot experience sounds, and as the eunuch cannot feel sexual desire, so bodies cannot attain spiritual delights. Like fish, who do not know what the element of fire is, because they live upon its opposite, the element of water, so are the delights of the spiritual world unknown in this material world. . . . We enjoy only bodily pleasures which come to us through our physical senses, such as the pleasures of eating, drinking, and sexual intercourse. Other levels of delight are not present to our experience. We neither recognize nor grasp them at first thought. They come to us only after great searching. It could hardly be otherwise, since we live in a material world and are, therefore, able to achieve only inferior and discontinuous delights. Spiritual delights are eternal. They last forever; they never break off. Between these two kinds of delight there is no similarity of any sort.[56]

This is precisely the strategy used by Maimonides in his interpretation of Job to differentiate human and divine activity: "Our act does not resemble His act; and the two are not comprised in one and the same definition.

Just as natural acts differ from those of craftsmanship, so too the divine governance of, the divine providence . . . differ from our human governance of, providence for . . . the things we govern, we provide for, and we purpose."[57]

This exploration of sensory underpinnings has shown that Maimonides likened philosophic speculation to the scribal arts. Bodies, like quills and paper, must first and always be kept sharpened and prepared. He declared that to think correctly, bodily appetites must first be satisfied, depression removed, and emotions balanced. Without sensation there is no thought; without thought firmly anchored in sensation and tempered by the Aristotelian sciences there is no access to the divine. Correct thinking about God, however, means approaching the quasi-ascetic ideal of pure "intellectual worship," described in *Guide* 3:51, in which human intellect is instructed to detach itself from its sensory underpinnings. Intellect might then oscillate mysteriously in the interstices between corporeality and incorporeality, contemplating silently the otherwise unknowable divine.

IV

The philosophy of Maimonides did not go unchallenged. Throughout the thirteenth and fourteenth centuries Kabbalists contested its principles, Aristotelians and Averroists questioned its conclusions, and Maimonidean defenders eliminated or modified its more radical claims.[58] In late fourteenth- and early fifteenth-century Spain, where Jewish intellectuals were contending with violent anti-Jewish riots and the spectacle of forced mass conversions to Christianity,[59] Hasdai Crescas synthesized all three of these strategies and mounted a devastating attack against the entire Maimonidean program.[60] Isaac ben Moses Levi, otherwise known by the Catalan Profiat (Profayt) Duran or by the punning Hebrew acronym Efodi, traveled in Crescas's circle.[61] Duran, a moderate Maimonidean, composed a straightforward commentary on the *Guide of the Perplexed* and incorporated numerous citations from the rest of the Maimonidean corpus within his own writings. He salvaged Maimonidean bric-a-brac and used the disconnected fragments for building blocks in his own non-Maimonidean ideology of the aesthetic.

By 1403, when Duran was composing the introduction to *Ma'aseh Efod*, his grammar of biblical Hebrew,[62] he had probably reverted to Judaism after a forced conversion to Christianity. He was taking to task the Talmudists, the philosophers, the Kabbalists, and the general populace for neglecting the conscientious study of Scripture.[63] Duran disputed the adequacy of the Maimonidean position. Agreeing with Maimonides, he taught that Scripture conveys its ideas in rhetorical forms and that its legislation is meant to guide the ascent of human intellect after first securing the socioeconomic order. Disagreeing with Maimonides, he asserted that Scripture is also an artifact whose aesthetic or sensational properties do more than merely convey ideas and govern society. To make his point, Duran likened the artifactual Bible to the art of medicine. "Just as some medications work when consumed as food and drink, while others work by touch, some by smell, and also by gazing—as with eyeglasses for the weak sighted,[64] so too with respect to this sacred Book. For the effects resulting from its property vary. It also works, in some way, by being gazed upon and by being pronounced and recited."[65] Two aspects of this passage deserve immediate comment: like Maimonides, Duran respected the sheer power of somatic experience. Like the Arabophone Maimonides and the sixteenth-century intellectuals and poets of Febvre's France, Duran was typical of post–1391 Spanish Jews who "doubtless had keen sight. But that was just it; they had not yet set it apart from the other senses."

The unqualified rhetorical richness of the Scripture-as-medical-treatment analogy indicates that Duran's thought was anchored in anti-Maimonidean principles. Maimonidean intellectualism and ambivalence toward symbols never survived intact the arduous journey from the relative tranquility of twelfth-century Islamicate Egypt to the persecutions of fifteenth-century Christian Spain. Where a Maimonidean would have insisted that the resemblance between Scripture and medication is suggestive but, strictly speaking, a resemblance in name only, Duran unapologetically asserted that Scripture is druglike and is itself "in some way" a drug.

Duran's penchant for symbols and resemblances belongs to an episteme that played a decisive role in Western culture until the end of the sixteenth century. According to Foucault, the operative terms in this mode of thinking were *convenientia, aemulatio, analogia, sympathy,* and *antipathy.* The *similitude* between things "must be indicated on the surface of things; there must be visible marks for the invisible analogies." To the question, what does something mean, the answer must take the form of "bring[ing] to light a resemblance."[66] This is precisely the operation performed by Duran when he argued that Scripture is an artifact which is somatically sensational and therapeutically effective.

Duran's notion of artifactual power is the key to understanding his pedagogic instructions for biblical study. He was attending to the manifest appearance of Scripture rather than to its latent content when he suggested that it is best studied from texts written in "square, block script inasmuch [as] this script, owing to its loveliness and beauty, will leave its impress on the common sense and in the imagination, on account of which it will be better preserved in memory."[67] He urged that one ought to consult only those books whose script inclines to the "thick and heavy, rather than to the delicate," both for its salutary effect on memory and for its greater legibility in old age when vision degenerates.[68] He also recommended that Scripture be studied in pleasantly decorated schoolrooms. His best-known prescription decrees that Scripture be read from gorgeously decorated, beautifully illuminated, and lavishly bound manuscripts since "the contemplation and study of pleasing forms, beautiful images and drawings broaden and stimulate the soul. They strengthen its faculties."[69]

Duran's attentiveness to somatic effects and aesthetic considerations reveals terminological and conceptual debts to Maimonidean, psychoeducational utilitarianism. But the Scripture-as-medicine simile indicates that his principles were not purely Maimonidean. In Duran's view the manifest appearance of Scripture is a catalytic agent equal in power to Scripture's ideas because Scripture is also a physical artifact equivalent to Temple. Scripture formally recapitulates sacred, architectural space; Scripture and Temple are physically and materially isomorphic. Alluding to the traditional tripartite division and sequential ordering of the Masoretic Bible, i.e., Pentateuch, Prophets, and Writings,[70] Duran declared that "because this sacred Book is equal in its properties to the Temple, it was originally divided into three sections just as was the arrangement of the Temple. In it were the Holy of Holies, the place of the Ark containing the Torah; the Sanctuary, the place of the Table, the Candelabrum, and the Golden Altar; and the Gathering Place or Courtyard in which there was the Altar for Burnt Offerings."[71] The iconographic resemblance between Scripture and Temple was nothing new to Duran's contemporaries. Scholars would have recognized it as a familiar rabbinic tradition.[72] People with access to expensively produced, illuminated manuscripts would have recognized it in the opening pages of their Bibles. Cultivating a practice that originated not later than the thirteenth century, Spanish Jews were fond of decorating their biblical manuscripts with lavishly painted pictures of Temple ornaments, structures, and implements. The material evidence, comprising some twenty illuminated manuscripts of Spanish provenance,[73] is reflected in Duran's sardonic but equally apologetic report that

> in every generation, highly esteemed wealthy people exerted great efforts to have beautiful compilations written and numerous books produced, even though for most of them, it was a matter of self-glorification, thinking that placing them in their treasure chests was the same as preserving them in their minds. Nonetheless, there is merit to their actions, since, in some way, they cause the Torah to be exalted and beautified. And even if they are not worthy of it, they bequeath a blessing to their children and to those who succeed them.[74]

Duran's willingness to assign merit to the mere physical possession of beautifully illustrated manuscripts stems from his notion of Scripture as artifact and indicates his discomfort with Maimonidean intellectualism.

Because the symbolist mentality delights in constructing chains of correspondences and resemblances,[75] Duran joined Scripture-as-Temple to the medieval, hierarchical great chain of being: "All of this is a symbol and similitude for the three divisions of reality which are the intelligible world of the God of Israel and the holy angels; the world of heaven and those pure bodies; and this lower world, the world of generation and corruption."[76] This is Duran's innovative combination of two venerable traditions: the Temple-as-cosmos motif[77] and the familiar medieval trope of the Book. The trope's claim that God is an author exerted a profound influence in governing the common methods for reading the spatiotemporal Book of Scripture and the polysemous literary *Book of Nature*.[78]

Duran also extended the unifying chain of Scripture-Temple-cosmos by linking it with revelation as differentiated in Maimonidean prophetology[79] and rabbinic tradition. The three divisions of Scripture were ordered from high to low in the scale of sanctity and authority:

> So too with respect to this sacred Book. It contains the divine Torah which is God's Torah, emanating from Him, may He be blessed, to our Master Moses, peace be upon him, prince of all prophets whose prophecy is distinguished from all other prophets in that God communicated with him face to face. The second division is the Prophets which originated with God even though it was through the mediation of the angel emanated from the heavenly movers. . . . The third division are those Writings uttered through the Holy Spirit inasmuch as this rank is lower than the rank of prophecy. . . . And as a consequence of all this, how well he did who called the name of this great Book the Temple of God, made by His hands. "The tablets were the work of God; the writing, the writing of God" [Exodus 32:16].[80]

Duran then took a familiar page from the *Eight Chapters* of Maimonides, combined it with the established "fact" of the spatial Scripture-Temple-cosmos-revelation isomorph, and concluded that it was legitimate both to produce and to study from the opulent scriptural artifacts favored by his contemporaries. He argued that these were legitimate practices because they imitated God's instructions for the beautification of the Temple in Jerusalem.

> The [talmudic rabbis] declared that "three things prolong a man's life: an attractive wife, beautiful furnishings, a pleasant dwelling [B. Tal. *Berakhoth* 57]." And in this respect it is permitted to make decorations and pictures on buildings, furnishings, and clothing. For the soul grows weary and thought passes away [becomes ugly?] in seeing always ugly things. Just as the body grows weary from doing heavy work until such time as it is able to rest and be restored, its constitution reverting then to its equilibrium, so too must the soul occupy itself in the restorative pacification of the senses by beholding decorations and beauti-

ful things so that its weariness be removed. . . . This matter is also appropriate and required, I mean to beautify the Books of God and purposefully to attend to their beauty, adornment, and loveliness. For just as God desired to beautify the place of His Temple with gold, silver, precious stones, and material delights, so too is it appropriate [to beautify] His sacred books, and especially this sacred Book which is the Temple of God made by His own hands, in such a manner that they resemble the most noble of all corporeally existent objects, namely the celestial body in which He included that which He did from among the comely and the beautiful.[81]

Duran's pedagogic recommendations for lavishly produced and visually attractive textbooks testify eloquently to the religious and aesthetic sensibility of early fifteenth-century Spanish Jewry. His ideological or political motives emerge when his recommendations are read against the social background of a struggle for survival. Between 1391 and 1415 the Church was bent on destroying Spain's Jews. In Duran's utterances his contemporaries heard a rationalization for the venerable custom of using illuminated Bibles, prayerbooks, Passover Haggadahs, and general texts. But they also heard, in a period of extreme adversity, a stabilizing reaffirmation of life conducted according to the norms of rabbinic Judaism. Duran assured them that their suffering was not irremediable, that they were not helpless victims. He urged them to channel their financial and intellectual resources toward the Bible. For them, illuminated manuscripts ostentatiously displayed wealth, improved memory, and delighted the eye.[82] But if Duran was right, illuminated manuscripts also showed that their life was legitimated by and sheltered under the sacred, but equally beautiful, "canopy"[83] of God's tripartite universe. Just as the world was made beautiful, so too was the Temple made lavishly spectacular. In Duran's way of seeing, it was therefore only "natural" for them to find refuge in cosmic patterns. Duran encouraged them to defend themselves by imitating God's style in their use of books that mirrored the structure and celestial radiance of cosmos and Temple.

Duran was convinced that Scripture possesses sensational properties and that, as a visual artifact, its manifest appearance must imitate the Temple. Using similar arguments, he also argued that biblical and rabbinic texts resemble sacred *libretti* whose musical settings must emulate Temple practice:

It is particularly appropriate that studying and being engaged with Scripture be conducted with song and melodies, for these increase yearning and desire in the one engaged with it. Stimulation of one's faculties and their being strengthened also improves the faculty of memory, because, within the length of time of the singer's phrasing, there are movements, sounds, rests, and pauses. Simultaneously, understanding of and attentiveness to the phrase are perfected during the length of time in which it is sung. This is the reason for praying with pleasant voices and sweetly in synagogues so that proper attention in prayer be perfected. This was done to perfection in the Temple singers and instruments. It was considered by them to be a major science. And it is appropriate that, to the extent possible, this sacred Book resemble it, the Temple of God made by His hands, inasmuch as the true meaning of this science is absent from us nowadays.

The philosophers have said that belonging to this science, which is the practical division of the science of music, there is an efficient cause which moves the faculties and brings into equilibrium one's natural constitution to the extent that it is restored to its health when it has departed. Furthermore, it too belongs to that which brings one to rejoicing and mourning, as well as to the other accidental states of the soul. I think that this is the reason why "To the Conquering Leader [La-Menatztzeah]" is inscribed in several of the Psalms, since the tune that was particular to that Psalm belonged to that which caused one or more of the soul's faculties to prevail by restoring them to a proper level [yosher] and corrected state [tikkun]. David was great among the experts in this science and with the special instruments which powerfully aided in this. . . .

It also belongs to its property to arouse the faculty of prophecy. As for the special melody with which we sing the phrases of this sacred Book, the rank of its properties is not that of the one just mentioned. Nevertheless, it has a virtue and rank beyond any of the melodies used by the nations in singing their utterances and prayers, for by itself it almost provides the meaning intended by the phrases.[84]

The similarities between this passage and those relating to the visual, artistic appearance of Scripture are obvious. Sacred texts are understood to be reenactments of the Temple cult and audiovisual aids affecting cognitive memory and emotional response. But the difference in Duran's treatment of the auditory is significant: He claimed no resemblance between scriptural cantillation and cosmic, Pythagorean music. This deviates from his claim that the visual appearance of Scripture reflects the tripartite structure of the cosmos. In all likelihood Duran did not invoke *musica mundana* because he was siding with Maimonides who had endorsed Aristotle's notion of a silent heaven.[85] Duran's enthusiasm for composing runs of symbolic correspondences was apparently moderated by intellectual commitments to the comparatively sober Maimonidean cosmology.

Duran was also loyal to Maimonidean psychology. He excluded the soul from both the visual Scripture-Temple-cosmos-revelation isomorph and the auditory parallel between the Temple cult and the musical setting of religious texts. Like Maimonides, Duran did not subscribe to theories regarding *musica humana*. They conceded that visual art and *musica instrumentalis* affect the soul, but they did not ground this claim in any formal or substantive resemblance between the arts and the soul. Unlike other medieval theoreticians of music, they drew no correspondences between biological pulsations and musical rhythms or between physiological structures and musical instruments. Duran seems to have agreed with Maimonides in implying that man is a microcosm in only the most restricted, abstractly intellective sense of the term.

His Maimonidean principles also surface in the denial of music's contemporary power to induce prophecy. If Duran was aware of contemporary mystical techniques, then his denial may be read as a direct repudiation of Abulafian practice with its claims to mantic, ecstatic, unitive prophecy.[86] For Duran music was laudable only insofar as it balanced the emotions, imitated Temple practice, unified the community, and aided the cognitive tasks of memorization and comprehension.

Duran's assimilation of the Book to the Temple transformed textual study into artistic performance, both visual and musical. For him, these structural affinities and aesthetic resemblances signified equivalent functions. Sacred books became the cultic surrogate for the Temple. He argued that textual study as *imitatio dei* is performative because

> He [God] said, "I am their quasi-Temple [*miqdash*] in the lands to which they came" (Ezekiel II:16). Just as the Temple was the cause of the dwelling of God's Presence [*shekhinah*] in the midst of the people Israel, so too is this sacred Book that on account of which divine Providence is upon the people through the frequent reading of it with acceptable intention and the investigation of the pearls of its statements. . . . Furthermore, just as those mighty rituals performed in the Temple are the cause on account of which God forgives the sins of the people in their trespassing on His commandments, may He be blessed, so too being occupied with the sacred Book with acceptable intention—remembering it and observing it in the heart—is the cause on account of which God forgives the iniquities of the people and its sins.[87]

These formal and structural correspondences between artifactual Scripture and recollected Temple disclose the full significance of Duran's Scripture-as-therapy metaphor. Following the precedent of Maimonides, which he invoked by referring his reader to *Guide* 3:51, 21, Duran also attributed to the study of Scripture a decisive role in launching intellect on its contemplative ascent to theoretical, rational enlightenment regarding an ultimately unknowable God. Inspired by Maimonidean utilitarianism, Duran stressed that proper textual study aesthetically prepares the body and frees the mind from all emotional distractions, thereby enabling mind to concentrate on God when engaged with Scripture in worship or study.

Unlike Maimonides, Duran venerated religious texts as quasi-sacramental artifacts and was therefore particularly stringent regarding their outer appearance and musical setting. In keeping with his principles, Duran also attached quasi-theurgic and unequivocal penitential potency to the simple acts of "merely being occupied with, pronouncing and reciting"[88] sacred texts. "Merely being occupied with" apparently means merely possessing illuminated manuscripts; merely commissioning their abundant production; merely storing them away in treasure chests; merely handling the texts, gazing upon their jewel-studded bindings, beholding their decorative and narrative illuminations; merely chanting their words with appropriate melodies; and even the uncomprehending, merely mechanical recitation of young children in elementary schools.[89] For Duran sheer aesthetic experience with sacred texts is sufficiently potent to produce cultic, soteriological effects even in the absence of logocentric, cognitive comprehension. This was the explicitly anti-Maimonidean upshot of his medical metaphor.

Duran's radical aestheticizing empiricism did not go uncontested. Ironically, his Scripture-as-medical-treatment metaphor aroused the opposition of the equally empiricist Maimonideans. Duran was a gifted polemicist. He was either anticipating the battle or reporting one that had already occurred when he formulated their trenchant rationalist arguments fairly and forcefully:

> One might object and say that all this is merely speculation and the product of uncontrolled thinking. It is fine for credulous believers who live by their faith, but who do not seek proof for it. All these are merely words uttered without their corresponding to reality outside of the soul. Science requires that one not look to the sensory for agreement with whatever is conceived in the soul, but to let reality accord with true opinions, in addition to making public its difference. It is the work of those who mislead, inasmuch as logic decrees nothing at all regarding it. Neither does it belong to that which intellect, by its nature, predisposes and convinces.[90]

Duran defended himself against the paired charges of irrationalism and unscientific reasoning by succinctly articulating the empiricist case for the profound limits of reason and the inadequacy of the philosophic sciences:

> I say that the forces of existing things including their properties are not grasped by syllogistic logic and theoretical speculation. They possess nothing which intellect decrees. On the contrary, everything known is known through sensation and experience. Then it is possible to supply things with a cause inasmuch as they are things which are consequent to the universal form which cannot be apprehended. For despite all of their investigation, the philosophers are unable to grasp the form of the smallest plants and other existing things. Similarly with regard to this sacred Book: What the Israelites grasped with respect to that property, they grasped through direct experience and from those who reliably reported it.[91]

This appeal to "sensation and experience" indicates that Duran, like so many of his contemporaries who were appalled by the mass of forced defections to the Church, was attracted to the anti-Aristotelian, historicizing thought of Judah Halevi.[92] Duran was dissatisfied with the Maimonidean version of Judaism because it favored philosophic sciences over biblical studies and seemed to offer nothing more than setting the somatic and emotional stage for abstract intellection.

He remained, nevertheless, a moderate Maimonidean. As a moderate, Duran's cosmic aestheticizing of sacred Hebrew texts fell short of a similar transformation of the entire Law in theurgic-theosophical Kabbalah,[93] just as it fell short of Crescas's distaste for Aristotelian rationalism. For Duran, the Law continued to be a Maimonidean vehicle on which Jews ascended to dazzling heights of contemplative meditation. But Duran required of the Law that it also bring God to earth. To save Spanish Jewry from extinction, the Law would have to be charged with more power than Maimonides had been willing to grant. With Duran's help, the aesthetic pleasures and pedagogic benefits of Hebrew texts were enhanced. Sacred books became densely packed artifactual symbols in which the natural order was morphologically recapitulated. Illuminated manuscripts became sacramental instruments by which Jewish history was soteriologically reenacted. Duran was therefore anything but indifferent to both the manifest visual appearance and the musical rendition of religious texts.

I cannot claim that the ardent biblicism of Duran and the austere intellectualism of Maimonides were typical of popular medieval Jewish culture. Because medieval philosophers were an elitist minority, the light they shed on medieval culture is partial and subdued. Aristotelianism was unacceptable to the ascetics, and even moderate Maimonideanism was outmatched by the traditional sway of Talmudism, the popularity of folk religion, and the growing allure of Kabbalah. But who exceeds the ascetic in acknowledging the sensory underpinnings of pietistic discipline?[94] And who exceeds the Talmudist or the Kabbalist in imposing religious significance on the entire sensorium? Because Maimonides and Duran proposed comparatively moderate ideologies of the aesthetic, they provide us with a conservative estimate of medieval Jewish attitudes toward the sensory, the sensuous, and the sensual.

The lingering influence of late nineteenth-century apologetics would have us believe that medieval Jewish culture devalued the body, privileged one or two of the senses—usually hearing—over all the others, and lacked appreciation for the visual arts. I have used Duran and Maimonides to prove otherwise. Duran's sacramentalization of beautifully illuminated manuscripts suggests that medieval Jewry was anything but aniconic. His notion of Scripture as artifact is imbued with Maimonidean respect for the sheer power of somatic-aesthetic experience. Duran's Maimonideanism and debt to Judah Halevi indicate that the sensory underpinnings of medieval Jewish culture did not conform to nineteenth-century ideals. Duran and Maimonides confronted diverse social circumstances. Their philosophic loyalties differed, but neither of them argued that human eyes and ears should be valued solely because they were vital to physical survival, hedonism, or abstract intellection. To the contrary, they both urged their contemporaries, for different purposes, to enjoy the multiple aesthetic benefits of a fully engaged, well-tempered sensorium.

Five

Medieval Beauty and Cultural Relativism

MEDIEVAL JEWS were familiar with all sorts of beauty. For earthy types, consider this poetic testimonial: "Encircle the breasts of a beautiful woman at night, kiss the lips of a good looking woman by day . . . there is no life except in the company of beauty's offspring. . . . Plunge your heart into pleasures, be merry, drink out of wine-skins by the riverside to the sound of lyres, doves, and swifts; dance and rejoice; clap your hands; get drunk; and knock on the door of a fair maiden."[1] So wrote Moses ibn Ezra, the tenth- and eleventh-century Hebrew poet who lived in Spain, proving that at least one medieval Jew had the usual reasons for noticing beauty. Another Hebrew poet, this one a warrior-diplomat as well, was sufficiently intimate with erotic beauty and murderous battle to incorporate their sensations in a sardonic metaphor: "War, in its beginning, resembles a beautiful woman with whom every man desires to frolic, but in its end, is like a repulsive hag, her suitors all weep, turning cholic."[2] So wrote Samuel Hanagid (993–1056), who commanded the armies of Granada. Even for less outgoing Jews, beauty was inescapable. Sacred literature was replete with it and sacred literature demanded bookish scrutiny.

Why, for example, did Potiphar's wife recklessly invite Joseph to share the sinful pleasures of her lusty bed? Genesis 39:16 alludes to a partial answer; it reports that Joseph was "beautifully shaped and beautiful in appearance [*yefeh-to'ar ve-yefeh-mar'eh*]." Fascinated by the odd rhetoric of this biblical phrase, if not by beauty itself, ancient and medieval Jewish commentators repeatedly sought to embellish its charms, inventing its meaning or extracting its implications.[3] One twelfth-century exegete from northern France, Rabbi Josef Bekhor Shor, noted that Joseph's original beauty was diminished by various misfortunes. Joseph's beauty was restored after he was elevated to power in his master's household. The promotion caused Joseph to forget his former troubles and native land. Only then did he attract the attention of Potiphar's wife, her love for him being "inflamed" because the Egyptians were closely related to Ethiopian stock and therefore unfamiliar with Joseph's exotic beauty.[4] Other twelfth-century commentators ignored the interplay of economic status and ethnic identity in the psychodynamics of sexual attraction. Abraham ibn Ezra, for example, the Spanish-born "poet, grammarian, biblical exegete, philosopher, astronomer, astrologer and physician,"[5] used the biblical phrase to expound genetic theory. He elliptically noted that Joseph's beauty was an inherited trait, for Joseph "took after his mother."[6] Adept in the art of intertextual literary criticism, Ibn Ezra was apparently referring to Genesis 29:17, where the same idiom describes Rachel, Joseph's mother, as "beautifully shaped and beautiful in appearance [*yefat-to'ar ve-yefat-mar'eh*]."

Like other medieval Jewish commentators, Ibn Ezra understood the phrase "beautifully shaped" to mean the pleasing physical contours of Rachel's face (her "eyes, nose, and mouth") and the phrase "beautiful in appearance" to mean the effect on the enchanted observer of her combined physical attributes. In *The Book of the Honeycomb's Flow*, a fifteenth-century Hebrew treatise on rhetoric composed in Italy by Renaissance polymath Rabbi Judah Messer Leon, these biblical phrases describing Rachel were adduced to prove that bodily excellence in women is twofold: "proper proportion of the limbs and [overall] appearance."[7] Sixteenth-century Italian commentator and philosopher Rabbi Ovadiah Sforno understood the phrase "beautiful in appearance" to be an allusion to the pleasing Ciceronian colors of Rachel's complexion.[8]

Moses Maimonides was also familiar with the biblical report of Joseph's beauty. In the first chapter of the *Guide of the Perplexed*, he cited it to prove, as did Abraham ibn Ezra, that the Hebrew term *to'ar* designates the "shape and configuration" of something physical.[9] For Maimonides, this semantic fact explained why the Bible never applies the term *to'ar* to God, since God is altogether incorporeal. It also explained why the Bible uses the term *tzelem* (translated as image and meaning something like an Aristotelian formal cause or substance) in such phrases as "in the image of God created He him." As for the related Hebrew term *demut* (meaning resemblance or likeness), Maimonides explained that it "signifies likeness in respect of a notion" or a concept, but not likeness in the sense of an exact physical replica. To illustrate the point that two things may resemble one another in some respects without being absolutely identical in all respects, Maimonides invoked the biblical example of Ezekiel 31, which likened the villainous and doomed kingdom of Egypt to a magnificent cedar tree in Lebanon. Regarding verse 8, "the cedars in the garden of God could not rival it . . . no tree in the garden of God was like it in beauty," Maimonides glossed that the intended likeness was not likeness with respect to such features as trunk size or leaf pattern but "likeness with respect to the notion of beauty" (in the original Arabic, *ma'ani al-hasan*, and in Samuel ibn Tibbon's medieval Hebrew translation, *'inyan ha-yofi*, the notion or concept of beauty).

This evidence suggests that, for Maimonides, beauty was something associated with physical bodies. What more did the Maimonidean notion of beauty entail? Unlike Plotinus before him and Kant after him, Maimonides did not say, at least not in so many words. When he did use the term, he activated the venerable ambiguities lurking behind the Greek *kalos*, the Latin *pulcher*, the Arabic *jamil*, and the Hebrew *yafeh*. In all of these terms, as in the confounding English term *good*, aesthetic and ethical connotations mingle indiscriminately.[10] But with help coming from an admittedly anachronistic quarter, David Hume, elements of the Maimonidean concept can be cautiously extrapolated from scattered remarks and then pieced together to form a relatively coherent account of one influential, and ultimately controversial, medieval Jewish philosophical account of beauty. In arguing that there is a Maimonidean aesthetics, I take issue with those who insist that, with the possible exception of Leone Ebreo's sixteenth-century *Dialoghi D'Amore*, premodern Jewish thought did not speculate on beauty.[11] In turning to the skeptical Hume for heuristic purchase on Maimonidean turf, I follow the lead of Shlomo Pines, for whom Maimonidean theology and metaphysics operate with Kantian-like critiques of pure reason.[12]

Reverting to the Maimonidean passages already cited and the preliminary conclusions that I drew from them, it is apparent that Maimonides conceded the sheer existence of beauty and that he understood earthly beauty to be something superficially associated with the class of physical things. Confirmation that Maimonidean beauty resides close to the surface of corporeality is found, for example, in chapter 24 of his medical compendium, *Pirqe Mosheh*, in which the following prescription is reported in the name of Galen: "I have heard from the ancients that someone who wanted to have a beautiful child commissioned from a most famous artist a painted portrait of the image of a beautiful child. Then he insisted that his wife gaze on the portrait, without blinking or moving her eyes either to the right or the left, during sexual intercourse. And so it happened; she gave birth to a beautiful child who resembled not the image of his father but that of the painting."[13]

Another example confirming the initial impression that Maimonidean beauty never went much deeper than the skin is found in the *Guide* 3:45. To explain why priests were obliged to wear "the most splendid . . . beautiful garments" and why blemished or deformed priests were ineligible for service, Maimonides referred to the lamentable popular prejudice that confuses truly virtuous stature with handsome physiques and beautiful clothes. Because the law wanted everyone to consider the Temple and its servants great, it exploited popular opinion by insisting on handsome priests garbed in impressive, resplendent attire. As Maimonides codified it, the law also requires that the kings of Israel honor their office and inculcate respect for it by attending carefully to their physical appearance, having their hair cut daily, and adorning themselves with "pleasant and beautifully decorated clothing."[14]

These examples suggest that superficial Maimonidean beauty was also strictly utilitarian. To corroborate the hypothesis that Maimonides was a functionalist who stressed the pragmatic effect of beautiful things on human behavior,[15] we might reconsider the explicitly antiascetic remarks of the fifth chapter of his *Commentary on the Mishnah Avot*, known to posterity as the *Eight Chapters*. Maimonides argued that "The soul needs to rest and to do what relaxes the senses, such as looking at beautiful decorations and objects, so that weariness be removed from it. . . . Now it is doubtful that when done for this purpose, these are bad or futile, I mean decorating and adorning buildings, vessels, and garments."[16] That Maimonides recognized the sociopolitical and therapeutic potential of beauty should now be apparent.

That he also considered the ultimate origin of beauty something fundamentally human needs to be made equally apparent. Starting from different empiricist and epistemological premises, David Hume concluded that beauty originates exclusively in human minds. In his 1757 essay, "Of the Standard of Taste," Hume declared that "beauty is no quality in things themselves: it exists merely in the mind which contemplates them; and each mind perceives a different beauty."[17] Anticipating the results of the following discussion, one might say that, according to Maimonides, earthly beauty has no transcendental analog and therefore reflects no metaphysical archetype; that beauty is not an intrinsic property belonging to physical things; that theoretical intellect plays no role in the recognition of beauty; that beauty is a popular or conventional response to physical things; that, unlike scientific knowledge, beauty is culturally bound and historically variable; and, finally, that beauty made its first appearance in the world with Adam's sin in the Garden of Eden.[18]

These conclusions emerge more or less clearly whenever Maimonidean discussions of ethics, logic, epistemology, and metaphysics pivot on the difference between impersonal philosophic truth and all-too personal, unenlightened human opinion. Maimonidean aesthetics can be detected, for example, in the *Guide* 3:22–24, where the interpretation of the book of Job is framed by an extensive analysis of divine providence. Apparently thinking of the biblical phrase that describes Job as a "blameless and upright man who fears God and turns away from evil" (Job 1:1, 8), Maimonides proposed that "the most marvellous and extraordinary thing about this story is the fact that knowledge is not attributed in it to Job. He is not said to be a wise or a comprehending or an intelligent man. Only moral virtue and righteousness in action are ascribed to him. For if he had been wise, his situation would not have been obscure for him."[19] Had Job been wise and therefore immune to false imaginings and egocentric, wishful projections, Maimonides proceeded to argue, Job would have known better than to complain about his fate and to assume mistakenly

that God's "knowledge is like our knowledge or that [God's] purpose and
[God's] providence and [God's] governance are like our purpose and our
providence and our governance."

The categorical distinction between theoretical, philosophic discourse
and moral or aesthetic discourse surfaces frequently in Maimonidean literature. In chapter 8 of his youthful *Treatise on Logic*, Maimonides distinguished four types of propositions: reports of sensory perceptions; evoca-
tions of the primary axioms of logic; declarations of popularly held
opinions; and assertions of traditional lore. Maimonides illustrated the
class of sensory reports with such examples as "when we know this is black,
this is white, this is sweet, and this is hot." Examples illustrating the third
class of popularly held opinions or conventions "are such sentences as
when we know that uncovering the genitals is repugnant, and that com-
pensating a benefactor is lovely or honorable." Regarding "sensations,"
Maimonides declared, all people with healthy constitutions experience the
same thing and there is no disagreement among them over truth and fal-
sity. "Conventions," by contrast, are not universal; they are marked by
diverse opinions and cultural disagreements.[20]

Shame caused by exposed genitalia, the example used to illustrate
"conventions" in the *Treatise on Logic*, resurfaces in the *Guide* 2:2, which
interprets the fall of Adam. Maimonides's interpretation presupposes that
aesthetic and moral judgments belong to the class of "conventional" propositions.[21] His interpretation also provides a psychogenetic answer to the
question of where aesthetic judgments originate.[22] Calling attention to
the biblical phrase "the eyes of them both were opened, and they knew
that they were naked" (Genesis 3:7), Maimonides remarked that the Bible
used the verb *knew* rather than *saw* to describe the discovery of their na-
kedness because "what was seen previously was exactly that which was seen
afterwards," except that now, after the sin had been committed, Adam
"entered upon another state in which he considered as repulsive things
that he had not seen in that light before." Before the sin, Adam could not
have known that his exposed genitals were shameful because the only faculty of the soul that he exercised was intellect, and

> through the intellect one distinguishes between truth and falsehood. Beauty
> and repugnance (*al-hasan wa-al-qabih; ha-na'eh ve-ha-meguneh*), on the other
> hand, belong to conventions, to things generally accepted, but not to things
> cognized by the intellect. For one does not say: it is beautiful that heaven is
> spherical, and it is repugnant that the earth is flat; rather one says true and false
> with regard to these assertions. . . . Now man in virtue of his intellect knows
> truth from falsehood; and this holds for all intelligible things. Accordingly when
> man [or Adam] was in his most perfect and excellent state . . . he had no faculty
> that was engaged in any way in the consideration of conventions, of generally

accepted things, of popular opinion, and he did not apprehend them. So among these generally accepted things even that which is most manifestly bad, namely, uncovering the genitals, was not bad according to him, and he did not apprehend that it was bad. However, when he disobeyed and inclined toward his desires of the imagination and the pleasures of his corporeal senses . . . he was punished by being deprived of that intellectual apprehension.

In his thirteenth-century commentary to the *Guide*, Shem Tov ben Joseph Falaqera sought to clarify Maimonides's argument by identifying the faculty of the soul that considers conventional things and passes judgment on their goodness and evil with Ibn Sina's version of Aristotle's practical intellect.[23] Whether we take Falaqera's word for it that Maimonides assigned aesthetic judgments to the practical intellect or rely on Maimonides's explicit reference to the non- or subintellectual domain of sense experience, imagination, and appetite, the consequence for Maimonidean aesthetics is the same: beauty originates exclusively in the mental state of the imperfect human observer.

Like Hume, then, Maimonides located "beauty in the mind that contemplates"; and more precisely in that part of the mind that Hume distinguished from reason and referred to as "taste" or "sentiment." As if echoing the Maimonidean distinction between intellect that discovers truth and imagination that invents beauty, Hume summed up his conclusions in appendix 1 of the *Enquiry Concerning the Principles of Morals* by asserting that "the distinct boundaries and offices of *reason* and of *taste* are easily ascertained." Like Maimonides, Hume believed that reason "conveys the knowledge of truth and falsehood" and that taste "gives the sentiment of beauty and deformity, vice and virtue." Like Maimonides, Hume believed that reason "discovers objects as they really stand in nature" and that taste "has a productive faculty, and gilding or staining all natural objects with the colours, borrowed from internal sentiment, raises in a manner a new creation." Like Maimonides, who followed the lead of Aristotle for whom scientific knowledge pertains to the invariable and the necessary,[24] Hume argued that "the standard of [reason], being founded on the nature of things, is eternal and inflexible, even by the will of the Supreme Being."[25]

But the twelfth-century Arabophone, Moses Maimonides, and the eighteenth-century Scotsman, David Hume, cannot be expected altogether to have seen eye to eye regarding beauty. At least four differences are worth noting. First, when Hume alluded to the "finer arts,"[26] he was presupposing a hierarchical ranking of the various arts and crafts that was unknown to the medieval Maimonides. In the twelfth century, painting, sculpture, architecture, music, and poetry had yet to emerge as a distinct class of elite cultural objects unified by a transcendental principle known as the beautiful or the sublime.[27] In agreement with Lucien Febvre, who cautioned historians against assuming "that all intellectual attitudes are possible in all periods,"[28] it must be noted that Maimonides was as unaware of the eighteenth-century distinction between the arts and the "finer arts" as he was untroubled by the modern problems of quantum mechanics and statistical induction.[29]

Second, when Hume concluded that the standard of taste, "arising from the eternal frame and constitution of animals, is ultimately derived from that Supreme Will, which bestowed on each being its peculiar nature,"[30] he parted both historical and philosophic company from Maimonides, since, for Maimonides, Adam's prelapsarian inability to invent beauty proves that an aptitude for beauty is neither an essential feature of human nature nor does it belong to the divine plan for the most excellent human being. Third, although Hume conceded that utility had something to do with the ultimate causality of pleasure,[31] Maimonides did not consider the pleasure and happiness produced by beauty to be ends in themselves. Maimonides countenanced sensory pleasure deriving from beautiful things because he saw that pleasure was useful in attaining bodily health (*tikkun ha-guf*), which itself is a prerequisite for reaching the supreme goal of disinterested intellectual perfection (*tikkun ha-nefesh*), namely, the acquisition of correct opinions regarding God.[32]

The fourth difference between Maimonides and Hume is implicit in the title of Hume's essay, "Of the Standard of Taste," and it is alluded to in Hume's phrase the "finer arts." The phrase suggests that, for Hume, there are gradations among the various objects of art and differing degrees of beauty to be discerned by discriminating critics. The title neatly announces Hume's dissatisfaction with parochial prejudices in art criticism and his search for "general rules of art" and "those qualities in objects which are fitted by nature" to evoke the sentiments of pleasure or disgust that mark beauty and ugliness.[33] One such universal quality discussed by Hume in the *Enquiry Concerning the Principles of Morals* is the timeless virtue of "just proportions" in nature. Horses, for example, have always been considered beautiful because "of the advantage they reap from the particular structure of their limbs and members, suitably to the particular manner of life, to which they are by nature destined."[34] Another such universal criterion for beauty in artifacts is compatibility with human nature. Hume argued that since "all men are equally liable" to physical injuries, "there is no rule in painting or statuary more indispensible than that of balancing the figures. . . . A figure which is not justly balanced is ugly; because it conveys the disagreeable ideas of fall, harm, and pain."[35] Hume therefore tempered the radical subjectivism of his assertion that "beauty exists merely in the mind which contemplates" when he undertook the search for standardized rules and universal, objective criteria that play a partial role in the discovery or invention of beauty.

In sharp contrast to Hume, Maimonides did not temper the radical subjectivism of his aesthetics by introducing objective criteria for experiencing beauty. We have already sampled evidence showing that Maimonides emphasized the social and personal benefits to be gained from beautiful priests, beautifully attired kings, beautiful clothes, beautiful trees, beautiful children portrayed in paintings, beautiful monuments, beautiful paintings, beautiful household utensils, beautiful wall decorations, and beautiful things in general. But nowhere did Maimonides specify what the formal criteria of beauty might be. He also never argued that reason played a significant role in experiencing beauty.

Hume did. In sharp contrast to Maimonides, Hume qualified the radical subjectivism and irrationalism of his view that beauty originates in feelings of pleasure when he acknowledged that reason often lends a helping hand in ferreting out beauty, especially when beauty is made so obscure by prejudicial critics and the newfangled "finer arts." In the *Enquiry*, for example, Hume proposed that "in many orders of beauty, particularly those of the finer arts, it is requisite to employ much reasoning, in order to feel the proper sentiment." As in the scientific study of nature, so too in the study of art, Hume argued, "it is often necessary . . . that much reasoning should precede, that nice distinctions be made, just conclusions drawn, distant comparisons formed, complicated relations examined, and general facts fixed and ascertained."[36]

These are the sorts of concessions to beauty that Maimonides never made. Perhaps Maimonides never assigned reason a role in discovering beauty because he was persuaded that the experience of beauty was not the product of theoretical intellect but rather an affective response stemming from the always nonintellectual and potentially anti-intellectual domain of desire-ridden imagination and pleasure-seeking sensoria. Perhaps he bypassed the search for objective criteria that timelessly mark beauty because he was no ethnographer interested in cataloging the vast array of culture-bound popular conventions but a philosopher whose Aristotelian conviction it was that variable things are not subject to scientific knowledge. It is also likely that Maimonides never considered the topic of beauty to be on a par with either the philosophic study of nature or the rigorous investigation of the divine law. He therefore would not have encouraged his disciples to squander intellectual capital on the close investigation of beautiful things. Maimonides may have adopted all of these philosophic and religious attitudes because beauty made fewer demands on the intelligentsia of the twelfth-century Maghreb than it was to make on cultivated folk in eighteenth-century Europe.[37] Judging from Maimonides's remarks, one might say that he was spared Hume's confrontation with beauty made obscure by the "finer arts." Apparently, for a twelfth-century Jewish Aristotelian living in the Maghreb, it was still possible for beauty to be as self-evident as Joseph's physique and as obvious as the enchanting nose on Mother Rachel's face.

In stressing once again that twelfth-century cultural realities had something to do with Maimonidean notions of beauty, I bid a reluctant farewell to Hume and anachronistic comparisons. Allowing Maimonides and Hume to rub shoulders on my keyboard is a philosopher's ploy for roughing out the figure of Maimonidean aesthetics. The comparison is also useful in suggesting links between the history of aesthetic concepts and the history of art, but it does not help in understanding how Maimonidean notions of beauty related to other trends in medieval Jewish thought.

We have already seen, for example, that Maimonides was silent on the question of objective criteria. Was his silence intentional or inadvertent? To answer this question without committing yet another anachronism, I am obliged to ignore the ancient Stoics, who typically stressed the objective criterion of "just proportions," and Plotinus, who criticized the Stoics for doing so.[38] It is therefore useful to know that Yosef ben Yehudah ibn Aqnin was familiar enough with the equation of "just proportions" and beauty to employ it in his combined philological, midrashic, and philosophic commentary on the Song of Songs.[39] This literary fact assures us that Maimonides was not silent with respect to objective criteria because of what Febvre classified as intellectual impossibilites, for Yosef ben Yehudah ibn Aqnin, who may once have met Maimonides, also lived in the twelfth-century Maghreb, and he too was a Jewish Aristotelian steeped in rabbinic lore. It may be, then, that Maimonides was silent with regard to objective criteria because he was tacitly negating what other scholars had affirmed.

We have also already seen that Maimonides restricted beauty to physical things. Merely to hint at the enormous significance of this restriction, it may be useful to consider Solomon ibn Gabirol's eleventh-century Hebrew poem, "The Royal Crown" (*Kether Malkhuth*), in which the realm of divine presence and celestial light to which the human spirit returns is vividly depicted as "the World-to-Come . . . where the souls see and are seen by the Lord's face . . . and where goodness and beauty have no end."[40] Our familiarity with this passage raises the suspicion that when Maimonides restricted beauty to physical things, he was again rebuking the garrulous poets whose indulgent excesses included the error of anthropomorphism and the incoherent ascription to God of positive, essential attributes.[41] The guilty parties, among whom Solomon ibn Gabirol must be counted, were Neoplatonists inspired by late rabbinic Merkabah mysticism.[42] Driving home his points that God "cannot be apprehended by the intellect, and that none but He Himself can apprehend what He is, and that apprehension of Him consists in the inability to attain the ultimate term in apprehending Him," Maimonides invoked the anonymous collective of "all philosophers" and allowed himself a polemicizmg oblique allusion to a metaphysical beauty associated with God: "Thus all the philosophers say: We are dazzled by His beauty [*ubharna bi-jamalihi*], and He is hidden from us because of the intensity with which He becomes manifest, just as the sun is hidden to eyes that are too weak to apprehend it."[43]

Book 1:10 of Bahya ibn Paquda's *Book of Guidance to the Duties of the Heart* came to similar conclusions regarding sunlight, human limits, and God's essential unknowability, but it was probably the Aristotelian tradition represented by Al-Farabi and Ibn Sina (Avicenna) that Maimonides had in mind when he referred to "all philosophers." Al-Farabi's discussion in *The Principles of the Views of the Citizens of the Virtuous City (Al-Madina al-Fadila)* regarding the First Cause and its "dazzling" beauty is typical. According to Al-Farabi, "it is difficult and hard for us to apprehend [the First Cause] because of the weakness of our intellectual faculties, mixed as they are with matter and non-being. . . . The overwhelming perfection [of the First Cause] dazzles us [*kamalahu tabaharana*]. . . . The more perfect and the more powerful a visible is, the weaker is our visual apprehension of it . . . the perfection of its splendor dazzles our sight so that our eyes are bewildered. Thus are our minds in relation to the First Cause, the First Intellect and the First Living." Several paragraphs later, Al-Farabi defined "beauty" as synonymous with anything in a state of "ultimate perfection." He therefore concluded that "since the First is in the most excellent state of existence, its beauty surpasses the beauty of every other beautiful existent" by virtue of its essence and by virtue of its self-intellection. Therefore, unlike human beings and other existents who possess beauty as a result of "accidental qualities . . . the beautiful [*al-jamil*] and the beauty [*al-jamal*] in the First are nothing but one essence."[44]

Perhaps wary of Al-Farabi's equation of perfection and beauty, which sounds suspiciously like an objective criterion, and preferring contemplative silence to even negative attributes, Maimonides distanced himself from Al-Farabi's typical exposition by attributing it to "all the philosophers" instead of claiming it as his own opinion. Consistent with his reading of Job, which denied any similarity between human activities and divine behavior, Maimonides nevertheless embraced Al-Farabi's notion that God's beauty is sui generis and therefore only a homonym with respect to earthly beauty. Disagreeing with Ibn Gabirol, Maimonides also exploited Al-Farabi in affirming that declarations of God's beauty were synonymous with the ultimate negation of all essential divine attributes. For Maimonides, then, poets like Ibn Gabirol betrayed their ignorance when, without all due qualification, they ascribed beauty to God's realm, since, philosophically speaking, beauty is an apophatic homonym paradoxically signifying the absolute unknowability of God's unity and essence.

Having skimmed the mere surface of Al-Farabi, Bahya ibn Paquda, Solomon ibn Gabirol, and Yosef ben Yehudah ibn Aqnin in order to clarify Maimonidean aesthetics, I reluctantly abandon them, as I did David Hume. Maimonides's notions of beauty originated as a response to the ideas of his predecessors and contemporaries,[45] but his notions were also explicitly incorporated, reworked, and made controversial in late medieval Jewish thought. Surveying the afterlife of Maimonidean beauty is the task now at hand.

In fifteenth-century North Africa, Maimonides was put to good use by Rabbi Solomon ben Simon Zemah Duran, who had been asked to adjudicate the propriety of an ordinance forbidding people to wear shoes during worship in the synagogue. Rabbi Solomon began his formal reply with a legal reminder that "synagogues must be beautified, exalted, and honored," adding, however, that what "truly constitutes honor [kavod] and disrespect [bizzayon] depends on what people think and on local custom." Integrating Maimonidean philosophic notions with legal reasoning, Rabbi Solomon also reminded his petitioners that honor and dishonor, respect and disrespect reside in the "soul" (nefesh). He explained that they are judgments which vary from place to place, not intrinsic qualities belonging to actions or objects. To illustrate his point, he contrasted the dress codes of Christian and Islamic lands. In Christian Europe, shoes are not considered to be a sign of disrespect; they are worn in the presence of royalty. Therefore, it is no disgrace for Jews living in Christian lands to wear shoes in the synagogue. In Islamic domains, "where it is an insult to wear shoes in the presence of dignitaries, especially so in the presence of royalty," it is no disgrace to enter the synagogue barefooted. Making explicit reference to authoritative legal precedents, Rabbi Solomon then invoked the ruling of Maimonides obliging people to attire themselves beautifully before they enter a synagogue and warning them against worshiping with "bared heads or bared feet in those locales where the fashion is that people stand with covered feet in the presence of dignitaries."[46] In the light of these considerations, Rabbi Solomon decided to affirm the propriety of the local ordinance forbidding people to enter the synagogue with shoes on their feet.

The wholesale incorporation of twelfth-century Maimonidean rulings and philosophic principles in Rabbi Solomon's fifteenth-century responsum alerts us to a perennial feature of medieval Judaism that taxed the legislative ingenuity and diplomatic skill of the rabbinate: quasi-autonomous, decentralized, culturally diverse communities with marked differences in ritual practice.[47] As Rabbi Solomon's responsum indicates, both he and Maimonides preferred to respect these regional differences rather than impose universal adherence to a uniform practice.[48] Viewed retrospectively in the light of Rabbi Solomon's responsum regarding shoes in the synagogue, the cultural relativism of Maimonidean aesthetics appears to owe as much to the historical factor of medieval Jewish subcultural diversity as it does to the fine points of Aristotelian logic and epistemology. Furthermore, given the historical constant of medieval Jewish diversity, it is no wonder that the cultural relativism of Maimonidean aesthetics retained its appeal throughout the Middle Ages. At the very least, Maimonidean aesthetics was unavoidable. Regarding the question of synagogue attire, as in so many other aspects of the law codified in the *Mishneh Torah*, the most prestigious and widely read legal compendium in medieval Jewish literature, Maimonides wove a seamless web of philosophy and rabbinics.[49]

Maimonidean aesthetics was also unavoidably controversial. Like the philosophy of which it was so integral a part, it became all the more controversial as Christian Europe transformed itself into a "persecuting society" and its Jews into an "alienated minority."[50] Caught between church and state, Jewish life was made untenable by an increasingly aggressive and hostile array of socioeconomic and religious forces.[51] Gaining momentum from the late twelfth century and on, these antagonistic forces typically spent their energy in explosive anti-Jewish crusades, like the one in Spain that lasted from 1391 to 1415 and culminated in the final trauma of expulsion in the woeful summer of 1492.[52] Bloody anti-Jewish riots; the spectacle of mass conversions, forced and otherwise; and the catastrophes of 1492 exacerbated the already truculent antiphilosophic sentiment that had first crystallized among Jewish traditionalists and mystics in the thirteenth century. Particularly irksome was the way in which Maimonidean apophatic theology seemed to deny that God was passionately engaged with human life. No less exasperating was the way in which Maimonidean historicism, utilitarianism, and subjective aesthetics seemed to rob Jewish ritual practice of theocentric import and intrinsic meaning. Like Joseph in Potiphar's Egypt, the cosmos was about to recover its lost beauty in late medieval Jewish Spain. Theologians and philosophic moderates would settle for positive divine attributes, abstract metaphysical beauty, and intellect's affinity with the beautiful. The Kabbalists were more demanding. They insisted on restoring to God and the cosmos an interlocking, mythopoeic, sacramental beauty. Kabbalists, theologians, and philosophic moderates all agreed, however, that beauty was not merely contingent on the vagaries of human sentiment and imagination.

Rabbi Isaac ben Moses Arama (1420–1494), communal rabbi in Spain and a famed preacher, was therefore not alone when he blamed philosophy for sapping Jewish faith and undermining obedience to the law.[53] He railed against those Maimonideans who lumped the commandments with generally known things and conventions, arguing that if the laws regulating good and evil were conventions, nothing more than mere aesthetic preference, their origin would have to be, as Maimonides suggested in his reading of the fall of Adam, human imagination and sensory appetite. But if the laws originated in human imagination, then they could not be the product of divine revelation, and neither God nor the angelic intelligences who move the heavenly spheres would be capable of knowing the law, lacking as they do the human faculties of particularized imagination.[54]

Answering Arama's objections in order to defend Maimonides, the moderate Don Isaac Abravanel (born in Lisbon, 1437; died in Venice, 1508), yet another distinguished exile from Spain, conceded that if the Law were conventional and derived from imagination, it would indeed follow that neither God nor the celestial intelligences could know the Law.[55] But since, according to Abravanel, just as for Falaqera before him, Maimonides had located the source of judgment regarding good and evil, beauty and ugliness in the practical intellect, then, God's intellect being altogether superior to human intellect, God does know the Law in the way he can know opposites simultaneously, both of which are epistemological feats impossible for mere mortals. Regardless of their differences, then, both Arama and Abravanel agreed that the Law is certified by cosmic and divine authority. In their view, the Law, including its many regulations regarding beauty and goodness, is legitimated by metaphysical warrants.[56] Beauty is therefore a proper thought in God's mind, and therefore a cosmic absolute rather than a culture-bound, popular convention.

Abravanel's son, Judah, known to the West as Leone Ebreo or Leo Hebraeus (c. 1460–c. 1523), developed this line of reasoning in his famed *Dialoghi D'Amore*. Having been instructed by Philo that there are degrees of beauty, ranging from the utter perfection of the idea of beauty "in the mind of the Creator and true architect of the world" to the earthly "beauty of lower natural and artificial bodies," Sophia asks, "How are the eyes of our soul and intellect thus fitted [*si proporzionano*] for perception of the spiritual beauties [*le bellezze spirituali*]?"[57] She is told that "our rational soul" is the "image [*immagine*] of the soul of the world" and that the "pure intellect which shines forth in us is likewise a facsimile [*similmente immagine*] of the pure divine intellect." With the venerable principles of microcosm/macrocosm and "like knows like" operating behind the scenes of his argument, Philo concludes that "we may behold in one intuition the highest beauty of the first intellect and of the divine ideas."[58] Eventually, Sophia is also made to understand that beauty is a correlate of God's wisdom, which explains why "we can easily pass from the knowledge of corporeal beauty to the beauty of our own intellect and of the world soul, and by means of our pure intellect to the knowledge of the highest beauty of the first divine intellect."[59] Nothing could be further removed from Maimonidean notions of God's unknowability and beauty's noncosmic superficiality than the philosophic arguments advanced by Leone Ebreo.[60]

Other echoes of fifteenth-century Iberian anti-Maimonideanism reverberate in the specifically religious, or Mosaic, aspects of Ebreo's *Dialoghi*.[61] Discussing beauty and "pleasure [*dilettazione*] in the divine intellect," Philo invokes Psalm 104 ("God rejoices in His works") and treats Sophia to a lesson in biblical exegesis. He reminds her that "divine pleasure is the perfect union of the image of God with Himself, and of His created universe with Himself as Creator." He also reminds her that God "is the highest pleasure of the universe" and that "the highest pleasure must reside in Him, proceed from Him, and be directed towards Him. Therefore, the ancient Hebrews used to say . . . 'Blessed be He in whose habitation there is joy.' Pleasure in Him is identical with the one who experiences pleasure [*dilettante*] and with that which causes pleasure [*diletta*]."[62]

Ebreo's biblical exegesis and theology replicate patterns of thought developed in fifteenth-century Spain by Hasdai Crescas (d. 1412) and popularized by Crescas's disciple, Joseph Albo (d. 1444).[63] Discussing God's attributes, Albo defined joy as

the perception of the agreeableness of a pleasant and appropriate thing. It is without doubt an emotional affect. The Bible attributes it to God in declaring, "God rejoices in His works." And the Men of the Great Synagogue established in the liturgical order of benedictions [the phrase] "in whose habitation there is joy." . . . This benediction is used in the marriage ceremony because joy in every case is the result of duration and permanence. . . . It is possible, too, that the expression, "in whose habitation is joy," alludes to something more profound, namely as the philosophers say, that God rejoices with His own essence, because He has beauty and majesty and perfection in Himself and needs no one else, while all things are influenced by Him and need Him, having no duration except through Him. . . . The joy of God is inherent in His essence. All existing things emanate from Him by a chain of causation, and by comprehending the activities which flow from His loving-kindness [*hasdo*]. . . . [People] derive wonderful pleasure [*ta'anug nifl'a*] and satisfaction, namely, in the world of souls.[64]

Maimonides too had associated human intellectual knowledge of God with a transcendental type of human pleasure and human love for God.[65] But unlike Crescas, Albo, and Leone Ebreo, who allowed God a self-contained enjoyment of his essential beauty, Maimonides refused to see in divine beauty anything more than a synonym for God's utter unknowability.

Coupling this late medieval, Spanish, and non-Maimonidean preference for transcendental, cosmic beauty with Maimonidean utilitarian aesthetics, Isaac ben Moses Levi, otherwise known as Profiat Duran, encouraged

fifteenth-century Jews to spend their wealth on handsome books, especially Scripture. He counseled them to study in pleasantly decorated
schoolrooms. He also insisted that the Bible be studied from gorgeously
decorated, beautifully illuminated, and lavishly bound manuscripts because "the contemplation and study of pleasing forms, beautiful images
and drawings broaden and stimulate the soul. They strengthen its faculties." For Duran, then, and very much unlike Maimonides, who ignored
objective criteria, beautifully illuminated biblical manuscripts became sac-
ramentally charged artifacts whose layout and design symbolically and
iconographically recapitulate the physical structure and beauty of the
Temple. The Temple, in turn, was understood by Duran to reflect the
beauty of the universe created by God, for whom beauty was a fundamental
architectural principle. To study Scripture from beautiful manuscripts was
therefore a pedagogic practice well founded in the science of human psychology. But more importantly for fifteenth-century Spanish Jews, who
were contending with a hostile society bent on destroying them, studying
from beautiful manuscripts was also a reassuring sacramental act with cosmic implications. It reinforced patterns of communal value by defining
them as imitations of God.[66]

As for fifteenth-century Spanish Kabbalists, they were heirs to theurgic
and theosophic traditions that had crystallized almost simultaneously with
the first appearance of Maimonideanism on the stage of Jewish life in
Christian Europe. According to these mystical traditions, not only the
Bible but every Jewish ritual practice was obligatory because it was a cosmic
signifier, a symbolic and iconographic recapitulation of divine archetypes
and intradeical processes.[67] From the very beginning, the Kabbalists had
known that beauty was at home in the mysterious depths of God's being
and that beauty was therefore suffused throughout the universe. They were
familiar with the ancient *Sefer Yezirah* (Book of Creation) according to
which the alphabetic elements of God's mysterious, creative wisdom generated the cosmic polarity of "beauty and ugliness."[68] They were conver-
sant with the prophet Isaiah, who had admonished them "to see the King
in His beauty" (Isaiah 33:17). They were therefore inspired by an ecstatic
religious practice that produced numinous hymns like this: "Lovely face,
majestic face, face of beauty, face of flame, the face of the Lord God of
Israel. . . . His beauty surpasses the beauty of the aged . . . whoever
glimpses His beauty is spilled out like a pitcher."[69] The late medieval Kabbalists also knew the twelfth-century *Sefer ha-Bahir (Book of Dazzlement)*,
which was was filled with references to God as the "beautiful vessel" or
the "beautiful matrona" or the "beautiful and precious stones."[70]

The late thirteenth-century *Zohar*, the most authoritative and influential of all the books in the Jewish mystical library, taught that one of the
symbolic names of divine beauty in its masculine modality was "Joseph."

The *Zohar* explained that the earthly Joseph was "beautiful in shape and beautiful in appearance" and that he resembled the earthly beauty of Jerusalem because both Joseph and Jerusalem were terrestrial manifestations of the same divine archetype of beauty.[71] In fact, the *Zohar* luxuriated in mythopoeic descriptions of intradeical beauty whenever it touched upon the dynamics of sacred union between divine masculinity and femininity. For example, this astonishing, but typical, passage describing intradeical *hieros gamos* in mythological terms inspired by two verses in the Song of Songs:

> "I am black, but beautiful, daughters of Jerusalem. Do not look upon me for I am black [1:5–6]." When she is feeling great love for her beloved, because of the straining need for love which she is unable to bear, she reduces herself to such a small size that all that remains of her is the smallness of one letter, namely *yod*. Thereupon she immediately hides herself from all her hosts and regiments, saying, "I am black," for in this letter there is none of the whiteness which exists in the other letters. . . . Therefore she says, "Do not look upon me," do not gaze upon me at all, since I am merely a miniscule point. What do her mighty champions and regiments do? They roar like powerful lions. . . . Listening from above to these sounds and mighty roars . . . the lover knows that his beloved is as much in love with him as he is in love with her, so much so that neither her iconic image nor her beauty is visible. Then, with the help of those sounds and roars uttered by her powerful champions, her beloved lover goes forth from his palace laden with gifts and offerings, with perfumes and spices, coming upon her and finding her black and miniscule, without any iconic image and beauty. He approaches her, embraces and kisses her, until she is slowly aroused by the perfumes and spices. And with the joy she experiences in the company of her lover, she is built up and restored to her ornaments, her iconic image, and her beauty, becoming the letter *heh*, as in the beginning. . . . Similarly in the lower world, when there are evil ones in a generation, she hides herself, reducing herself until the only thing visible of her iconic image is a single point, but when the truly righteous appear, they make this word, as it were, and she slowly begins to glow, her iconic image and beauty being restored, a *heh*, as at the beginning.[72]

Savoring this chivalrously romantic, Kabbalistic meditation on the physical shape of letters, the amorous power of animal sounds, the size and color of God's beauty lost and restored by the earthly deeds of righteous people, we seem to have circled back to the sensuously erotic language of Moses ibn Ezra with which this survey of medieval Jewish beauty began. It is ironic that the author of the *Zohar*, Moses de Leon, like Moses ibn Ezra before him, attended to such objective criteria for beauty as size, shape, appearance, and color, but Maimonides, the so-called Aristotelian, did not. For it is the sacramental theology of the *Zohar*, and not Maimonidean aesthetics, that echoed Aristotle's empiricist com-

ments in the *Poetics* 7: "Beauty is a matter of size and therefore impossible
. . . in a very minute creature, since our perception becomes indistinct as
it approaches instantaneity."

Given the historical crisis they faced, it is no wonder that late medieval
Jewish intellectuals renounced the strictly psychological, relativistic, and
antimetaphysical foundations of Maimonidean aesthetics. Like Joseph
Albo, Don Isaac Abravanel, and his son, Leone Ebreo, many of these intellectuals thought well enough of beauty to consider it a necessary and
proper thought in God's transcendental mind. Like Profiat Duran, many
of them thought well enough of this transcendental concept in God's
mind to recommend the making of earthly beauty as a sacramental imitation of God's cosmic creativity. Inspired by the *Zohar*, increasing numbers
of them were persuaded that cosmic beauty originates within the mysterious depths of God's being and that it was within their power to arouse that
beauty, theurgically preventing its extinction. Moses ibn Ezra imagined
earthly beauty and incited others to make love; the theurgic Kabbalah
imagined divine beauty and obliged others to make God. No wonder then
that Maimonidean aesthetics excited so little enthusiasm among late medieval Jewish thinkers. No wonder too that Maimonidean aesthetics is
nevertheless still able to capture the attention of a historian of Jewish
thought living in the late twentieth century, whose philosophic climate is
antimetaphysical and whose social reality is culturally plural.

Six

Twelfth-Century Pilgrims, Golden Calves, and Religious Polemics

I

Medieval Jewish philosophers and mystics had good reason to ponder visual images and imagery. Engaged in the systematic analysis of physical sensation and eager to understand human attraction to beauty of all sorts, they necessarily touched upon the psychology, aesthetic properties, and metaphysical implications of visual experience. Reading and writing books, they reflexively cherished sight. Practitioners of scholarship, they embodied the "implications of literacy."[1] Not all medieval Jews, however, were sophisticated philosophers or virtuoso mystics. Not all medieval Jews authored books. Medieval Jews were nevertheless spectators, keenly observing the world. They were not immune to the power of visual and visionary images. They craved the visible, the spectacular, and the "picturesque."[2] Their lives and livelihoods depended upon sight. Many were artisans, producers of the various crafts, secular and religious.[3] They specialized in precious metals and textiles. Some were doctors examining patients and surgeons performing cures.[4] Some were astrologers who read the heavens; others navigated ships at sea.[5] Many were merchants and moneylenders whose discerning eyes sought fashionable, unusual, or valuable objects.[6] Medieval Jews also traveled, by necessity or choice. Some resembled impressionable tourists, taking in various sights and sounds, remarking beauty and exotic oddities. Others were intrepid pilgrims, piously devoted to sacred geography, regardless of location. In the late twelfth century, the age of the Crusades, Benjamin of Tudela and Petahiah of Ratisbon (Regensburg) were two of the many adventurous and well-funded Jews who went far out of their way to become tourists and pilgrims.[7]

In all likelihood, Benjamin was a traditionally educated, successful merchant in Spain, and Petahiah was a learned Talmudist living in Bohemia. Neither of them was a mystic or a philosopher. More closely resembling the vast majority of medieval Jews, Christians, and Muslims, they nevertheless attended mindfully to the visual. During their travels, Bejamin and Petahiah noticed all sorts of landmarks, flora, and fauna. They were fascinated by all sorts of Jewish and Gentile shrines. They examined architectural monuments, sculptures, paintings, and crafted artifacts. They acknowledged beauty without making it an end unto itself. They knew that beauty aroused desire and marked wealth and power. They were amazed by technological expertise whenever it confronted them, and they were awed by sacrality wherever its miraculous presence was felt. Benjamin and Petahiah knew that crafted objects were intentional, that sites preserved worthy memories of the historical past and conveyed significant messages for the present. To a modern reader, their travelogues indicate that even the most pious medieval Jews were neither indifferent nor hostile to the visual arts. Benjamin and Petahiah challenge widespread modern assumptions that Jews lack visual sensibilities and that Judaism timelessly equates all images with forbidden idolatry.

Benjamin's travelogue reports that he began his journey in Saragossa.[8] On his way from there to Tortosa and on to "small and beautiful" Barcelona, he passed through Tarragona, situated on the coast of the Mediterranean. Benjamin observed that Tarragona was "ancient," containing gigantic stone structures left there by the "Greeks." Revealing his connoisseurship, Benjamin noted that similar structures "existed nowhere else in all the lands of Spain." His interest in uniqueness, construction materials, and patronage remained constant throughout his travels. In Rome, he saw "more buildings and interesting sights than a person could count," many of which struck him as "different than any building in the world," including the "immense church [*bamah*] of St. Peter's, the large palace of Julius Caesar . . . the palace of Titus . . . the hall of the palace of Vespasian, and a gold-covered bronze statue of Constantine with his horse." Benjamin was particularly intrigued by one palace hall that "contained three hundred sixty windows, corresponding to the days of the year." Benjamin added that a battle was once fought on the site of the palace and that the king memorialized it in a marble sculpture didactically portraying "army against army, the men, their horses, and their battle-weapons." Turning his attention to Jewish history and artifacts, Benjamin referred to the church, which contained "two copper pillars made by King Solomon on each of which was inscribed 'Solomon, son of David.' " He also reported the presence, at the exterior of another church, of a "sculpted representation of Samson with a stone ball (or lance) in its hand, as well as one of Absalom, the son of David."[9]

From Rome, Benjamin eventually made it to the "large capital-city of Constantinople." His attention was captured by "Hagia Sophia, the church of the Pope of the Greeks, containing as many altars as the days of the year and great wealth beyond counting, the sort of riches not found in all the churches of the world. Inside the church, there are golden and silver pillars, as well as more golden and silver lamps than a person could count." Benjamin also gathered information regarding annual celebrations sponsored by the emperor at the richly decorated Hippodrome.

These celebrations featured an international gathering of performers and
animal fights "the likes of which appear nowhere else in the world." Benjamin's most lavish descriptions were reserved for the large palace built on
the seashore by King Emannuel, who "covered the pillars and capitals with
sterling gold and silver, depicting upon them sculptured images of all the
wars of the ancients who preceded him as well as the wars he himself
undertook. He placed there his throne made of gold and precious stones.
A golden crown hanging from a golden chain is suspended over the throne
. . . this golden crown being studded with jewels whose value no one can
estimate. At night, no candles are necessary, for everyone is able to see by
the light of those jewels whose brightness is so exceedingly intense. In that
place, there are interesting curiosities that no one can describe." Benjamin
concluded that the "opulence and buildings" of Constantinople "are un-
equalled anywhere in the world."[10]

Visiting Jerusalem, Benjamin pondered the walls, gates, waterworks,
tombs, and architectural history of the city. He noted the Tower of David,
whose "foundation [stones] are the remnants of the ancient structure built
by our ancestors, the rest being a construction of the Ishmaelites," two
Crusader "Hospitals," and "the immense church which they call the Sepulchre, the tomb of "that man [Jesus], to which all the wayward pilgrims
go." Benjamin also remarked the Temple Mount. His travelogue mentions
the "Templum Domini, located on the site of the Temple, upon which
Omar ben Al-Khattab built a large and exceedingly beautiful cupola. The
Gentiles do not bring into it any statue [tzelem] or painted image [temu-
nah]. They come only to offer their prayers." The travelogue also refers to
the site of Solomon's stables, allowing Benjamin a rare chance to boast an
unparalleled Jewish architectural feat: "Solomon, using immense stones,
built an exceedingly strong structure. A building similar to it is not to be
seen anywhere in the land."[11]

Regarding Damascus, "a large and exceedingly beautiful city," Benjamin's travelogue conveys admiration for the "Mosque" [kenisah], a building unmatched in all the land." One of its wonders was a "glass wall in
which they made as many apertures as the number of days in the solar
year. The sun enters each and every one of them, descending by twelve
steps that correspond to the hours of the day, thereby allowing people to
recognize daily the hourly time." In close quarters with this palatial
mosque, "there are structures made of gold and silver, shaped like a tub
and large enough to allow almost three persons to enter and bathe."[12]

The travelogue entry for Baghdad is extensive. The grounds of the ca-
liph's palace are described as including "many large buildings, golden and
silver pillars, hiding places, and every kind of precious stone." The entry
also refers to twenty-eight synagogues in the metropolitan area, singling
out the opulent interior of the "Exilarch's immense synagogue [kenisah]

which contains multi-colored marble columns covered over with gold and silver. On the columns, there are verses from The Book of Psalms in gold letters. There are some ten marble steps leading up to the Ark."[13]

Benjamin visited other synagogues in the region, as well. In Babylon, where he noted "the ruins of Nebuchadnezzar's palace," Benjamin reported on the synagogue "built in antiquity by Daniel himself and constructed out of dressed stones and bricks."[14] From there, approximately one day's travel down the Euphrates and passing the remnants of the biblical Tower of Babel, Benjamin arrived at the site of the prophet "Ezekiel's Synagogue [*keneset*]." The travelogue pauses here to luxuriate in empirical observation and historical recollection: "Sixty towers front the synagogue, and between each and every tower there is a synagogue. In the courtyard of [Ezekiel's] Synagogue, there is an Ark, and behind the Synagogue, Ezekiel's tomb on top of which there is a large dome and an exceedingly beautiful building constructed by King Jekhoniah of Judah and the thirty-five thousand Jews who accompanied him. . . . Jekhoniah and all those who came with him are engraved on the wall, Jekhoniah at the top and Ezekiel at the end. To this very day, that place is a 'quasi-Temple,' people coming from afar to pray there between the New Year and the Day of Atonement, performing a joyous celebration."[15] Still in Mesopotamia, Benjamin stopped in the town of Shaf Yativ, where he reported on a synagogue "built by the Jews and constructed out of the soil and stones of Jerusalem."[16] Later, during his tour of Persia, Benjamin came upon the "grave of Ezra the scribe and the priest . . . in front of which the Jews built a large synagogue . . . and the Ishmaelites a Mosque [*bet tefillah*], owing to their affection for him. They love the Jews."[17]

On his return home, Benjamin traveled across Egypt, where he apparently experienced the pyramids, "platform structures [*'amudim*], built magically, the likes of which are not to be seen in all the land or in any place. They are constructed out of plaster and stones, forming an exceedingly strong structure." He also reported on remnants of "Joseph's numerous granaries" and the synagogue of "Moses, our teacher." In Rameses, his eye registered ruins and "something like towers made out of brick" which his mind's eye saw as the remnants of "the building which our ancestors constructed." On the seashore of Alexandria, Benjamin observed "a marble sepulchre on which were depicted all sorts of birds and animals. Everything is written in the script of the ancients, and no one is able to decipher that script."[18] Covering Sicily, Benjamin's travelogue describes the royal property in Palermo: "The King's boats are covered in silver and gold. . . . In the garden, there is a large palace. The surface of the walls are colored with images and covered in gold and silver. The [mosaic] pavement on the floors is composed of marble stones depicting all sorts of images in the world. In all that land, there is nothing like that building to be seen."[19]

Wherever he went, Benjamin was particularly eager to list or visit the tombs of his rabbinic ancestors. The entry for Rome refers to a "cave on the banks of the river Tiber where those righteous ones of blessed memory, the 'Ten Martyrs Slain for God's Kingdom,' are buried." The entries covering the land of Israel, including Sepphoris, Tiberias, and Meron, detail the Talmudic sages interred there. The entries for Babylonia list scores of rabbinic burial places. The laconic entry for Hillah, a town several miles away from Babylon, is typical: "Its population numbers approximately ten thousand Jews, and it contains four synagogues. One of them is associated with Rabbi Meir who is buried in front of it. . . . Jews pray there daily."[20]

Petahiah of Ratisbon, the other twelfth-century pilgrim, was equally interested in tombs and synagogues memorializing his biblical and rabbinic forebearers. Like Benjamin of Tudela, Petahiah also never missed an opportunity to associate architectural structures with a venerable Jewish patron or artisan. In Nisibis, he visited "the synagogue [*bet ha-keneset*] built by Ezra," the scribe.[21] In Hebron, outside of Jerusalem, where the patriarchs are buried in a cave, Petahiah's travelogue alludes to "an immense palace hall [*hekhal*] built by Abraham, our Father."[22] Touring the "mountains of the upper Gallilee," Petahiah reconnoitered the burial sites of the Mishnaic sage, Nittai the Arbelite, and the biblical figures of Joshua, Caleb, Obadiah and Jonah. Petahiah's travelogue reports that there are "beautiful structures built near . . . [or] over the graves" and that the structures here, like "all buildings in the Land of Israel, are made of stone."[23] In Baghdad, Petahiah met Rabbi Samuel, the exilarch, who provided him with an authoritative pass of safe conduct allowing him ready access to "the burial place of rabbinic sages and righteous men (*tzaddiqim*)."[24] One day's travel out of Baghdad, Pethahiah approached the fringes of a town called "Polos" where he found "a grave with a beautiful building upon it." He learned that it was the burial site of a Jew named "Berozaq," a childless Judean who accompanied King Jekhoniah into the Babylonian Exile. Berozaq eventually appeared in a dream to a wealthy and childless man, informing him that if he "were to build a beautiful house over [Berozaq's] grave," the wealthy man "would have children. He built the house, and he had children."[25]

Petahiah's dual fascination with the material reality of tombs and the fabulous rewards for pious devotion associated with them surfaces in the detailed entry describing the prophet Ezekiel's grave. The travelogue estimates that, on the holiday of Tabernacles [*sukkot*], some "sixty to eighty thousand Jews, in addition to the Ishmaelites" gather in the courtyard surrounding the tomb. They worship, "making vows and offerings at his grave. Men and women who are barren, or whose animal is barren, make vows and pray." To substantiate the efficacy of these gravesite devotions, Petahiah's travelogue narrates the miraculous tale of Ezekiel's intercession on behalf of a reneging trickster who unsuccessfully tried cheating the prophet out of his due after the trickster's barren animal gave birth to an expensive and "handsome foal." As for Ezekiel's tomb itself, the travelogue declares that "whoever has not seen the structure of the large palace over his grave, has never seen a beautiful building. The interior is covered in gold. The stucco [sic] on top of the sepulchre reaches as high as a man. The stuccowork is surrounded and topped by a gilded, cedar wood structure. The eye has never seen such a thing. It has apertures into which people place their heads and pray. Above, there is a large and golden cupola surrounded inside with beautiful tapestries. Inside, there are also exceedingly beautiful glass vessels. Thirty lamps, burning olive oil, flicker day and night."[26] Such detailed visual inventories are rare in Petahiah's travelogue. The few that exist nevertheless reveal what was noteworthy and visually unproblematic to a pious rabbinic pilgrim.

Whether sparse or generous in visual detail, not all the entries in Petahiah's travelogue pertain exclusively to tombs as places of worship. Like Benjamin, Petahiah also had an eye for secular art and opulence, especially when they were saturated with Jewish historical significance. The entry for Baghdad describes the city's gates, giving their measurements ("one hundred cubits long and ten cubits wide"), evoking their crafted magnificence, and establishing their authentic provenance: The gates "are constructed out of smoothly burnished bronze, and ornamented with images the likeness of which no man knows how to make. A boss [masmer] fell out, and no artisan has been able to refasten it. Originally, horses used to stagger backwards, because the clear brightness of the bronze made it seem as if [other] horses were running after them, forcing them to flee. So people took vinegar, boiled it, and poured it over the gates, thereby doing away with the golden luster of the smooth burnish in order to allow the horses to enter. High up, where they did not pour the vinegar, [the original] is partially visible." To account for such astonishing phenomena, especially to credit the original Israelite patrons and craftsmen with more skill than his contemporaries in Baghdad could muster, Petahiah furnished an historical explanation. He observed that "these gates belong to the gates of Jerusalem."[27]

The entries for Rachel's tomb in Bethlehem and the Temple Mount in Jerusalem are perhaps the most telling examples of Petahiah's preoccupation with historical meditations. The entries reveal that Petahiah saw archaeological remains as if they were persons. He infused monuments with the attributes of live Jewish and Christian bodies locked in social conflict. He was convinced that Jewish artifacts and architectural space are ineradicably and authentically Jewish, that they categorically differ from idolatry and miraculously resist its illicit presence. Rachel's tomb is said to contain a stack of "ten marble stones," the uppermost and largest of which is Jacob's, bearing his engraved name. Petahiah's travelogue reports that [Christian] "priests [komerim]" repeatedly took Jacob's stone, fixing it in an idolatrous structure [binyan 'avodah zarah]. On the following day, they discovered [the stone] over [Rachel's] tomb, where it was originally. After several attempts, they gave up trying to take it."[28] Regarding the Temple Mount, Petahiah's travelogue describes one building, "a beautiful palace [hekhal na'eh] which the Ishamelites built in olden days when Jerusalem was under [their] control," and another building, presumably the exquisite Dome of the Rock, constructed on the exact site of the ancient Temple. He reports that the site was reserved exclusively for Jewish worship by the Muslim ruler who was motivated by gratitude and love for the Jews. The travelogue calls this second structure "a marble palace, a beautiful palace [hekhal na'eh] whose marble stones were red, green, and all sorts of colors." Eventually, this palace fell into the hand of the Gentiles [goyyim], presumably Christians, "who placed within it idolatrous statues [tzelamim] that kept toppling over. So they embedded the statue in the thickness of the walls. Within the precincts of the Holy of Holies, however, the statue was unable to remain upright."[29] Added to his comments regarding simultaneous Muslim and Jewish worship at Ezekiel's tomb, the passages regarding Rachel's Tomb and the Temple Mount indicate that Petahiah considered the material culture of Muslim and Jewish shrines to be ritually unproblematic and Christian shrines to be idolatrous.

Benjamin of Tudela, a Spanish Jew, was either more tolerant or more circumspect. His travelogue never explicitly applies the technical rabbinic term 'avodah zarah (idolatry) to Christian monuments. Instead, it allusively uses the biblical term bamah to designate churches and martyria, bamah being a pejorative term naming idolatrous "high places."[30] Bamah is also the term Benjamin used when describing polytheistic or pagan shrines encountered along his way.[31] Mosques and synagogues, by contrast, are designated by the interchangeable and neutral term, kenisah, literally meaning assembly or gathering place. The terminology suggests that Benjamin classified Judaism and Islam in one category and Christianity in another. The nuanced terminology also suggests that Benjamin was as reluctant to apply the technical term for idolatry to Christian monuments, as he was unwilling to declare an Israelite structure idolatrous. On the road to Damascus, Benjamin passed the site of King Jereboam's "altar [mizbeah]" to "the golden calf."[32] Benjamin's description of the site is brief and noncommittal. It uses neither bamah nor 'avodah zarah. Although the argument is based on silence, it is intriguing to think that Benjamin considered the golden calf to be no more an example of idolatry than a church.

Regardless of Benjamin's cautious or liberal view of Christianity, he shared Petahiah's unambiguous opinions regarding Judaism. Benjamin and Petahiah affirmed the respectability of Jewish artifacts and architectural monuments. They basked in the historically saturated significance of Jewish spaces and objects. They savored their beneficent power, and they enjoyed their unproblematic beauty. They were astonished by all sorts of richly decorated objects. Untroubled by the modern ideals of a purely spiritual and totally imageless religion, Benjamin and Petahiah embraced the visual. They acknowledged its power to stimulate pious devotion. They did not equate all artifacts and monuments with forbidden idolatry. They were astute observers, and their Judaism was neither aniconic nor disembodied. It was intimately associated with the visual arts. No wonder that Benjamin and Petahiah went so far out of their way to behold a vast array of legitimate sights, to worship in their sacred presence, and to record their visual impressions so faithfully.

II

In many respects, these two medieval Jewish pilgrims were atypical. They were among the adventurous few who enjoyed the expensive benefits of visiting far-flung sites and shrines. Made cosmopolitan by their travels, they were more visually sophisticated than the vast majority of their contemporaries. They were not, however, the only medievals or Jews to crave visual excitement, admire a stunning image, or recoil from a repugnant scene. Pilgrims, moreover, do not originate in cultural vacuums. The pilgrim's eye is not a tabula rasa. Long before Benjamin of Tudela and Petahiah of Ratisbon ever dreamed of traveling abroad, they were equipped with customized habits of sight. Their native cultures prepared them with tastes, concepts, and expectations to which the world would conform. The travelogues suggest that the pilgrims were conditioned to be visually attentive. They were taught to distinguish neutral or legitimate images from forbidden idolatry. The travelogues indicate that the pilgrims were overwhelmed by Jewish sights, astonished and relatively untroubled by Islamic monuments, and impressed but aggrieved by Christian images. The travelogues imply that these aesthetic predispositions were securely lodged within the pilgrims long before they ever left home.

As children and adults, the future pilgrims studied Scripture. The lessons they learned are preserved in the corpus of twelfth-century medieval biblical commentaries. The commentaries explicate what the travelogues merely imply. The commentaries and travelogues corroborate the conclusions drawn in the previous two chapters regarding aesthetics and beauty. The commentaries and travelogues verify that medieval Jews were neither

iconoclasts nor indifferent to visual experience. Medieval Jews were instructed by their native cultures to seek the multiple benefits of visual
images. They were taught to abhor idolatry. They learned that Jewish artifacts are legitimate. They were drilled in the historical significance of Jewish monuments. These lessons were implanted and reinforced whenever
the homebodies and potential pilgrims studied the "copper serpent" mentioned in Numbers 21 and the "golden calves" described in Exodus 32,
Deuteronomy 9, 1 Kings 12, Psalms 109, and Nehemiah 9. The thorny
issue to be explored was the same theoretical and practical problem facing
all medieval Jews, Christians, and Muslims. They argued it among themselves and between each other: What differentiates lawful from unlawful
images? Within Christianity, the problem exploded dramatically during
the Byzantine Iconoclastic Controversy and the Protestant Reformation.
Within Islam, the problem recurred in twelfth-century Spain when the
invading "Almohads . . . were responsible for the destruction and white-
washing of Almoravid mosques, which [the Almohads] considered too
distracting and opulent in decoration."[33] For rabbinic Jews in the Latin
West, the problem of lawful images was framed by ancient rabbinic traditions and complicated by medieval realities.

The complex Talmudic traditions surrounding the golden calf were tai-
lored for medieval Jewry by Rabbi Solomon ben Isaac of Troyes (1040–
1105), the preeminent biblical and Talmudic commentator known by the
popular acronym, Rashi.[34] According to his elegantly concise retelling of
the narrative, the calf was not the result of a misguided attempt to symbol-
ize the one true God.[35] Instead, the calf was intended to be a polytheistic
idol representing multiple numbers of false deities. Reeking with polytheism, the egregious idol could not have originated with the Israelites. Aaron
tried his best to dissuade the people from the sin and defer the production
of the idol until Moses might return, but Aaron was no match for Satan,
who produced a replica of Moses ascending heaven. The replica convinced
the vulnerable and anxious Israelites that Moses had abandoned them.
Satan subsequently animated the calf with sound effects, thereby persuad-
ing the people that the idol was truly a god. Nor was it Aaron who actually
fashioned the calf. In all likelihood, according to Rashi, Aaron merely
collected the gold, wrapped it in scarves, and threw it into the fire. At
that moment, the opportunity was seized by the 'erev rav, the "mixed
multitude" of Egyptian Gentiles, converts, idolaters, and magicians who
had accompanied the Israelites on their escape to freedom. It was exclusively the Gentiles and converts who originated the idea of the idol, and
it was the idolatrous magicians who fashioned it using sorcery. Left to their
own devices, free from the corrupting influence of the "mixed multitude,"
the Israelites would never have resorted to idolatry. Had the Israelites been
guilty of either the thought of the idol or responsible for its actual produc-

tion, Scripture would have read, "these are *our* gods, O Israel, which brought *us* out of Egypt." Scripture reads, however, "these are *your* gods, O Israel, which brought *you* out of Egypt," proving that it was not the true Israelites who were guilty but the menacing Others, the "mixed multitude," the Egyptian Gentiles, converts, and magicians.

As for the innocent and victimized Israelites, Rashi reminded his audience that the entire tribe of Levi refused to participate in the idolatrous worship. Rashi also exonerated the true Israelites by shifting part of the blame to God Himself, for it was God who arranged "to shower them with so much gold and satisfy their desires," thereby weakening their resistance to sin. It was as if God were "a king who wined, dined, and adorned his son, hanging a purse around his neck and placing him at the doorway of a brothel. How could the son not have sinned?" No wonder that the Israelites succumbed to the idolatrous calf, and no wonder that God forgave them. Were it not for the people's innocent confusion over Moses's anticipated return, Satan's interventions, unfaithful converts, the magical powers of idolatrous sorcerers, and God's overabundant solicitude, the golden calf would never have happened. Having sinned, the people were nevertheless punished, as they are whenever they sin. Their covenant with God, however, remains everlasting and intact. God forgave the people and continues to do so.

Rashi's disgust over the golden calf was outweighed by his faith in the unbroken validity of the covenant. His disgust was also surpassed by the pleasure taken in elaborating upon the cultic furnishings of the ancient Tabernacle. Commenting on the allegorical significance of Song of Songs 1:13, he was reassured of God's eternal love for Israel, a love that was mediated by the symbolic artifacts of golden ritual. Rashi observed: " 'My beloved is my bundle of myrrh,' my beloved has become like one with a bundle of myrrh on his chest, saying, 'this bundle will exude a more pleasant aroma than the first one that you lost.' Similarly, the Holy One, Blessed be He, was lovingly reconciled with Israel regarding the episode of the calf. He found for them an atonement for their sin. He said, 'Donate generous offerings for the Tabernacle, and the gold for the Tabernacle will come and atone for the gold of the calf.' "[36] Rashi therefore did not revile the calf because it was made of gold. Neither did he revile it because it was a sculpture. In addition to the atoning powers of the Tabernacle and its furnishings, there was the divinely sanctioned copper serpent fashioned by Moses. Commenting on God's instructions to Moses for curing the plague of poisonous creatures described in Numbers 21: 8, "Make a serpent, and set it on a pole. Whoever is bitten and gazes upon it shall live," Rashi observed: "Our Rabbis have said, 'Is it really the serpent that kills or restores life? But when the Israelites lifted their gaze upward and subjugated their hearts to their Father in heaven, they were cured. If not, they

decayed.' "[37] These biblical interpretations reveal that Rashi was no iconoclast. He condemned idolatrous artifacts without repudiating images altogether and without undercutting reverence for the artifacts and sacred
spaces of Jewish practice.

The ancient copper serpent sustained Rashi's confidence in the efficacious power of worship related to legitimate images. The golden Tabernacle convinced him of God's unbroken love for Israel in antiquity. Regarding the present, contemporary Jewish institutions and structures reassured
him of the everlasting, mutual love between God and Israel. Commenting
on the allegorical significance of Song of Songs 1:5, "I am black and beautiful," Rashi reworked rabbinic traditions affirming that the ancient sin of
the calf was forever offset by ongoing Jewish subjugation to God and
heartfelt practice of Torah. He remarked: "The community of Israel says
to the nations, I am 'black' with respect to my deeds and 'beautiful' owing
to the deeds of my ancestors. Even among my own deeds, some are beautiful. Although the sin of the calf is mine, I have the merit of having received
the Torah.' " In Rashi's time and place, the Torah was continuously received, practiced, and housed within Jewish walls. His commentary on
Song of Songs is laced with praise for the "beautiful" and meritorious
"synagogues and houses of study" upon which God casts a loving gaze;
"the houses of study which are the headwaters of Torah"; "the synagogues
and houses of study in exilic lands within which God causes his presence,
the *shekhinah*, to dwell"; and "the synagogues and academies that nurse
Israel with words of Torah." Explicating the allegorical significance of
Song of Songs 8:13, "She who dwells in gardens, friends are listening to
your voice," Rashi heard God say to Israel. "You are scattered in exile,
grazing in the 'gardens' of others, 'dwelling' in synagogues and houses of
study. The ministering angels, your 'friends,' your divine counterparts,
'listen.' They come to hear 'your voice' in the synagogues, after which
they utter sanctification."

Rashi's profound veneration for contemporary synagogues and rabbinic
academies reverberates in the travelogues composed by the medieval Jewish pilgrims. Their veneration indicates that they were not disinterested
antiquarians gathering pleasurable lore about ancient texts, ancient rituals,
ancient sites, and ancient history. Rashi and the pilgrims were as responsive
to their present as they were to their past. The pilgrims sought eyewitness
proof for the global vitality of contemporary Jewish life; Rashi filled his
commentaries with references to contemporary Jewish practices and allusions to the "nations" of his own time and place, the corrupting Gentiles
and converts who seem forever eager to compel or lure Israel into surren-
dering its faith and embracing idolatry. His comments on Song of Songs
1:6 reiterate the past tense verbs employed in his glosses to Exodus 32.
The verbs blamed the ancient Egyptian "mixed multitude" for initiating

the sin of idolatry: "My mother's children snarled at me, they made me keeper of the vineyards, but my own vineyard I did not keep. The 'children' of Egypt who went out with me in a 'mixed multitude,' they are the ones who provoked me with their enticements and seductions, that is, they gave me the idolatrous worship of false gods. 'But my own garden,' mine from my ancestors, 'I did not keep.' " Commenting on Song of Songs 2:7 and 3:5, Rashi dropped the past tense. With verbs conjugated for the present and future, he openly threatened his contemporary enemies with extinction, and he defiantly announced his refusal to commit apostasy or join their fold: " 'I adjure you,' you nations, 'by the gazelles or the hinds of the fields,' you who will be ownerless prey like the deer and stag, 'that you neither disturb nor contest the love between me and my Lover, seeking to change it or replace it, demanding of me that I be seduced by you. . . . 'I adjure you' nations, today, during my exile in your midst, 'that you neither disturb nor contest' my love for my Beloved with seductions that I abandon Him and turn away from Him."

Rashi's historiography of the golden calf was therefore double hinged: He made the past coincide with the present and the present reenact the past.[38] His hostility toward the idolatrous "mixed multitude" of ancient Egyptians carried over and ran parallel to his hostility toward the seductive and increasingly oppressive Christianity of his own day.[39] Condemning one nation, he typologically condemned the other. Similarly, his veneration for the divinely sanctioned ancient Tabernacle carried over and ran parallel to his veneration for the divinely pleasing synagogues and Talmudic academies of his own day. Praising one sacred institution, he simultaneously praised the others. Denouncing the sinful idolatry of the ancient Egyptian calf and emphasizing God's everlasting forgiveness of the true Israel, Rashi was deliberately countering anti-Jewish tendencies in eleventh-century Christian biblical exegesis.

The golden calf had been a staple of Christian polemics ever since Paul alluded to it in 1 Corinthians 10:7, the apostle Stephen preached against it in Acts 7:39–43, and an uninterrupted string of apostolic, patristic, and medieval authorities elaborated its theological and political implications.[40] The early second-century *Epistle of Barnabas*, addressed to Christians, typically claimed that the Jews eternally forfeited their covenant with God when they worshiped the idolatrous calf: "Do not be like certain people, compounding your sins, by claiming that your covenant is irrevocably yours. But they lost it completely . . . when they turned to idols, they lost it. For the Lord speaks thus: Moses, Moses, descend immediately for your people . . . have sinned. And Moses understood, and he hurled the tablets from his hands. And the covenant was smashed to bits so that the covenant of Jesus, the Beloved One, might be sealed in our heart, in hope of his faith."[41] Similar claims were repeated and intensified by Christian theologians and exegetes in Rashi's hostile environment.[42] Responding to these claims, Rashi was unwilling to deny the facticity of the sin because his rabbinic authorities unequivocally affirmed it. He therefore conceded the sin and continued to follow his Talmudic precedents: He blamed the Gentiles and stressed God's everlasting forgiveness of the Jews as mediated by the ongoing practice of Torah in synagogues and academies. Christians understood the consequences of the sin to be the absolute termination of God's covenant with the Jews; Rashi was confident that the Christians were mistaken. Relying on God's perpetual covenant with the Jews, Rashi reversed the Christian argument. His biblical interpretations warned against ancient idolatry in its contemporary manifestation: seductively attractive, polemically contentious, and aggressively hostile Christianity. Jewish images and sacred monuments were religiously legitimate; Christian images and monuments were not. According to Rashi, contemporary Christianity reenacted the ancient sin of the golden calf.

Rashi's polemical interpretation of the golden calf neither silenced Christian commentators nor satisfied every Jewish intellectual. Medieval Christians persisted in condemning the sinful and "satanic synagogue."[43] Some Jews relied on the affirmation of ancient Israelite idolatry to rationalize the horrendous suffering endured by Jews during the First Crusade.[44] These traditionalists were slowly outnumbered by Jewish intellectuals who denied that the calf was idolatrous. Perhaps the first to know and deviate from Rashi's Talmud based interpretion was his grandson, disciple, and partner in scholarship, the accomplished talmudist and innovative biblical commentator, Rabbi Samuel ben Meir (1085–1174).[45] Rabbi Samuel agreed with his grandfather that Aaron's role in fashioning the calf was limited to gathering the gold, wrapping it in a garment, and casting it into the fire.[46] Unlike his grandfather, however, Rabbi Samuel did not ascribe the manufacture of the calf to the sleight of a sorcerer's hand. Rabbi Samuel preferred more naturalistic and technological explanations. He taught that "other men, following the practice of metalsmiths, shaped a mould out of clay and wax in the form of a calf. They poured the gold into the mould, and the calf was produced." Rabbi Samuel also deviated from his grandfather regarding Satan. In Rashi's commentary, Satan is prominent. He devilishly misleads the vulnerable Israelites in two ways: Satan creates a replica of Moses ascending heaven, and Satan animates the calf with lifelike sounds. In Rabbi Samuel's commentary, Satan is altogether absent.

No less significant is Rabbi Samuel's radical departure from his grandfather's understanding of the sin and assignment of guilt. Rashi defined the sin as outright idolatry. He traced it to the "mixed multitude" of corrupting Egyptians, faithless converts, and sorcerers. Rabbi Samuel disagreed. In his opinion, the "mixed multitude" was not involved in the episode of the calf and the sin was not idolatry because the Israelites never intended the calf to be an object of worship misrepresenting the one true God. After all, Rabbi Samuel argued, the people were not "fools who might not have known that a calf born on that day could not have brought them out of Egypt." Fearing that Moses would never return to lead them, the people demanded of Aaron "something like the sort of divination figurines [*teraphim*], made by sorcery, which would tell them what they needed to know." Rabbi Samuel explained that such figurines were able to speak and therefore simulated true prophets. The Israelites therefore "committed the mistake of likening the figurines which spoke by virtue of an impure spirit to true prophets who speak by virtue of the holy spirit." The people erroneously assumed that the figurines spoke "by virtue of the holy spirit from on high." This error explains why they declared, "These are your 'divinely inspired spokesmen' [*elohim*] who brought you out of Egypt." To prove that it was God who made the figurine speak in order to test the people, and not Satan in order to mislead them, Rabbi Samuel cited for his proof text Deuteronomy 13:1–5, the biblical laws forbidding sorcery and divination: "for the Lord your God is testing you." According to Rabbi Samuel, the golden calf was an oracle, a forbidden image, a failed test of the ability to discriminate between true and false modes of prophetic divination, but it was not idolatrous.

These startling departures from the authoritative Midrashic traditions summarized in Rashi's version of the calf are partially explained by Rabbi Samuel's decision to compose a nontraditional commentary dedicated to discovering the philologically rigorous, "ordinary," "plain," "natural" (*lefi derekh 'eretz, secundum physicam*), or "literal sense" of Scripture.[47] This programmatic decision accounts for Rabbi Samuel's technological explanation of the waxen mold with which the calf was crafted, his use of intrabiblical lexicography to establish the nondivine referent of *'elohim* in verse 5 of Exodus 32, and his choice of texts from Deuteronomy to prove that it was God's test and not Satan's intervention that endowed the figurine with oracular speech.

There were other, equally compelling, reasons for Rabbi Samuel's thorough erasure of Satan from the scene at Sinai. Like his grandfather, Rabbi Samuel composed historiography that was intentionally double hinged. It was designed to open forward and back. It clarified the past in the light of the present and corrected the present in terms of the past. God was made the calf's ventriloquist and Satan was expunged from Sinai because Rabbi Samuel was vehemently opposed to the occult practices and beliefs of contemporary Jews and Christians in northern Europe.[48] Rabbi Samuel's relatively naturalistic worldview apparently included a belief in "impure spirits." He accepted their role in divination, but he did not recognize Satan as their ultimate source of power or authority. Rabbi Samuel

did not countenance Jewish resort to those "impure spirits" for the purposes of divination.[49] When he erased Satan, Rabbi Samuel was aware of
the intimate connection between visual artifacts, belief in the devil, de-
monology, and occult practices. Voicing his opposition to these beliefs and
practices, he declared that only God who "resides in heaven," the true
God worshiped by Jews, can endow inanimate images with speech.[50] He
therefore rebuked contemporary Jews and Christians alike for their credu-
lous belief in Satan's powers and their misguided practice of relying on
ungodly images to foretell history.

Other aspects of his rebuke were directed at Christianity alone. In Rabbi
Samuel's opinion, the divinely sanctioned and mysterious Urim and
Thummim worn by the priests of ancient Israel were legitimate images
and proper instruments of prophetic divination.[51] Ancient images like the
golden calf were not. Neither were the "living," weeping, bleeding, fly-
ing, and speaking icons and sculptures of contemporary Christian piety,
worship, and drama.[52] Rabbi Samuel's familiarity with these Christian devotional practices facilitated his understanding of Scripture and made his
interpretations plausible to his Jewish contemporaries. In turn, Scripture
provided him with the authority to condemn Christian devotional practices without his having to name Christianity explicitly. Interpreting
the biblical tale of a golden calf, Rabbi Samuel insinuated that the "living"
images of Christian practice were contemporary reenactments of an ancient transgression. Similarly, under the protective shield of his commentary on Exodus 20–24, the law requiring unadorned and earthen altars,
he alluded to the idolatrous Christian practice of surmounting crucifixes on altars that are decorated with all sorts of "images and sculptured
reliefs."[53]

Rabbi Samuel's thinly veiled attacks on Christianity were integral to
his announced intention of composing a biblical commentary that would
explain things "naturally and refute the heretics."[54] His erasure of Satan
from Sinai was another such refutation. Medieval Christians, inspired by
Augustine, who taught that the Jews had been transformed into satanized
bodies during the episode of the golden calf, identified "the Jew with the
devil."[55] Rabbi Samuel sought to defuse this charge by eliminating Satan
from the scene altogether and by insisting that it was God alone who made
the calf speak. And if, as Rabbi Samuel insisted, the sin of the calf was
improper divination but not idolatry, then the Christians were mistaken
when they concluded that the Jews were idolaters, the old covenant bro-
ken, and the new covenant with the Church firmly established. Like his
grandfather, but adopting different means, Rabbi Samuel used the episode
of the calf to reverse the tables on Christianity: Rabbi Samuel denied the
alleged connection between Judaism and idolatry. He simultaneously ar-

gued that Christian misreadings of the Bible are as obvious as the idolatry of Christian images and practices.

Similar conclusions regarding the golden calf were almost reached by Rabbi Samuel's younger contemporary, the twelfth-century French Talmudist and biblical scholar, Rabbi Joseph Bekhor Shor of Orleans.[56] Like Rabbi Samuel, Rabbi Joseph was committed to discovering the *peshat* or "literal" meaning of Scripture. In their biblical commentaries on Exodus 32, they deviated radically from Rashi's epitome of the Midrashic traditions. The two rabbis certainly shared Rashi's veneration for synagogues and houses of study. They certainly shared Rashi's faith in God's loving forgiveness and unbroken covenant with the Jews, but they refused to follow Rashi's lead in blaming Gentile culprits or highlighting Satan's magical interventions in the episode of the calf. Against the combined weight of rabbinic tradition and Christian exegesis, the two rabbis unequivocally denied that the ancient Israelites "ever intended to commit idolatry."[57] From there on, Rabbi Samuel and Rabbi Joseph parted company. Rabbi Samuel explained the calf by extricating it from the framework of biblical polemics against idolatry. He classified the golden calf with other examples of oracular divination in which the use of visual images is prominent and indispensable. Rabbi Joseph ignored the functional link between visual images and divination, perhaps because he feared that it would inadvertently reinforce Christian charges of Jewish sorcery, perhaps because he was not persuaded that the biblical text literally warranted Rabbi Samuel's hermeneutical moves, perhaps because he was more attentive than Rabbi Samuel to the intimate connection between visual images and politics.

In Rabbi Joseph's reconstruction of the biblical episode, the Israelites feared that Moses would never return to lead them on their desert journey. They therefore demanded of Aaron that he replace Moses with a new and earthly commander in chief, "an arbitrator, a judge, a leader, an intercessor." When the people asked Aaron for an *'elohim*, they were not seeking a deity. They were merely seeking a human figure to replace Moses. To prove his point, Rabbi Joseph invoked the parallel passages in Exodus 7:1—"I have made you a spokesman (*'elohim*) to Pharaoh"—and Exodus 22:7–8 —"the case of both parties shall come before the judges (*'elohim*)." Aaron therefore confronted a politician's dilemma: Regardless of his choice for a human successor to Moses, Aaron worried that the disappointed partisans of the failed candidates would initiate a bloody civil war. But if he were to refuse altogether to select a new leader, the various factions would seize the initiative, select their own leader, and the dreaded civic violence would erupt. And if he were to risk appointing himself, Moses would soon enough disapprove, finding Aaron's decision "difficult." Aaron therefore decided to bargain for time and "to preoccupy them with various matters until Moses might return. He made for them an object without any real substance," the golden calf. The people, however, mistook Aaron's intentions. Relying on Aaron's capacity to perform miracles, the people assumed that the calf was meant to be the replacement for Moses and that Aaron would be able to endow the image with speech. Aaron sensed danger. He "feared that the people might consider the matter and say, 'how could such a thing save us?' and choose for themselves a [human] leader." Aaron therefore bargained for more time. He "misled" the Israelites by deferring the coronation ceremony of the calf until "the next day" as part of a celebration dedicated to God.

Rabbi Joseph supported these claims intrabiblically. To prove that it was Moses, but not God, whom the Israelites wanted to replace, Rabbi Joseph cited Psalms 106:20: "They exchanged their glory for the image of an ox that eats grass." Rabbi Joseph understood "their glory" to be an allusion to "Moses, their glory, by whose hand God performed miracles and wonders." Rabbi Joseph explained that the people "replaced Moses with the image of the ox. They bowed down to the molten image in order to honor it but not to worship it idolatrously." To prove incontestably that the episode of the calf was steeped in politics and that the religious celebration was not idolatrous, Rabbi Joseph invoked the parallel case of 1 Samuel 11:15, which describes the altar and legitimate offerings made by King Saul when his royal dominion was renewed. In both cases, Rabbi Joseph asserted, the sacrifices and offerings were respectable acts of piety. Regarding the golden calf, he declared, the "people intended things only for the sake of heaven, bowing down to it in a gesture of honor [*kavod*], but not idolatrously." Innocent of idolatry, the Israelites nevertheless sinned. They betrayed an utter lack of confidence in Moses, "rebelling against" him, and "even though they intended no idolatry" they trespassed on the Second Commandment prohibiting them from making and using in worship any cultic image not explicitly commanded by God. The Israelites thereby condemned their descendants to the ridicule of "nations who mock us by saying, 'you made the calf.' "

By "nations who mock," Rabbi Joseph meant the Christians. Living in their midst, reading their books, and conversing with them personally, Rabbi Joseph knew the Christians well. He reacted to them throughout his biblical commentaries and specifically to their "mockery" involving the calf in his glosses to Exodus 32.[58] Like Rabbi Samuel, he defended Judaism by denying the major premise of the Christian argument: The Israelites rebelled against Moses and sinned by making an unauthorized image, but they neither intended nor actually committed idolatry. Christian exegetes were therefore mistaken when they used the calf episode to prove that God had rejected the Jews and replaced them with the Church.

Rabbi Joseph's polemical strategy also called for aggressive counterattacks. He returned Christian fire over ancient Jewish satanic idolatry with Jewish fire over the Eucharist: "The nations revile us for drinking the water [in which Moses dissolved the pulverized ashes of the calf]. But the allusion here is to the god that they eat and drink. There is nothing real about him, but they eat the flesh of their idolatry and drink his blood every year."[59] His counterattacks also included blasts of ironic sarcasm and charges of Christian hypocrisy: "The nations ridicule us because of a single calf made by our ancestors. But, every day, they make heaps of statues whose number has no end." Rabbi Joseph worked his way toward this conclusion by relating the parable of "a man who had an exceedingly beautiful wife. She had maidservants who used to say, 'our master will divorce our mistress and marry us.' They were asked, why? [They replied:] 'Yesterday, when our master returned from the market, he saw a spot of dirt on her hand which had touched some charcoal. He was repulsed, and will divorce her.' Fools. What are you babbling? Will he set aside his beautiful wife on account of the charcoal mark on her hand, and marry you? You are so filthy with smears and charcoal stains from the pots and pans you wash that even your noses and mouths are invisible."[60] The caustic parable implied that if the Christians were right that God had rejected the Jews because of a single act of idolatry, then how much more so must it be true that God rejects the Christians for their unceasing and multiple acts of idolatry. The parable also taught that God was no more likely to have rejected the Jews and replaced them with Christians than a man would divorce his beautiful wife on the basis of an isolated peccadillo and replace her with lowly servants made unlovely by the never ending refuse of a scullery.

"Manipulating the arsenal of the enemy against him,"[61] Rabbi Joseph's intelligence also allowed him to mount a surprise attack against Christian strongholds. He exonerated the ancient Israelites by repeatedly insisting that the acts of worship associated with the calf were merely gestures of *kavod*, "honor," but not tokens of idolatry. This was precisely the technical distinction made by Christian theologians in their defense against internal accusations of idol worship. Polished during the Byzantine Iconoclastic Controversy, the vocabulary of *latria, dulia, hyperdulia, adoratio,* and *honor* was continually used to justify the use in worship of icons, paintings, and statues depicting God, Jesus, Mary, angels, martyrs, and saints.[62] St. Thomas Aquinas put the permissive vocabulary of *honor, latria,* and *dulia* to good use in the thirteenth century, and Rabbi Joseph put it to equally good use in the twelfth.[63] He imported it from Christian theological discourse into Jewish biblical hermeneutics in order to persuade Christians, on their own terms, that Israelite worship associated with the image of the golden calf was qualitatively no more idolatrous and quantitatively far less improper than ordinary Christian practice. The argument was shrewd: It exploited Christian reverence for religious images to silence Christian allegations of Jewish idolatry.

Rabbi Joseph's glosses on Exodus 32 contain no hint that his dialectically keen argument led him to abandon Jewish allegations of Christian idolatry, adopt a neutral stance regarding Christian images, or cultivate an enlightened appreciation of Christian ritual.[64] He vindicated ancient Israelites by insisting that their devotions at Sinai were theoretically as unproblematic as King Saul's religious celebration. He also insisted that Israelite intentions inolving the calf were godly and their devotions mere acts of *kavod* (honor). Rabbi Joseph might therefore have conceded that Christian theologians cogently refute his arguments and successfully defend Christian image worship when they invoke biblical precedents, posit godly intentions, and make crucial distinctions between outright idolatry and proper gestures of *latria, veneratio, adoratio, dulia,* or *honor.* Nothing in the glosses suggests that Rabbi Joseph drew these self-critical, tolerant conclusions. Because his biblical commentary was a monologue intended for a Jewish audience rather than the protocol of actual or imagined debate meant for wider distribution, neither do his glosses report on the Christian response to his arguments.

Gilbert Crispin's widely read *Disputatio Iudei et Christiani* preserves how some late eleventh- and early twelfth-century Benedictine intellectuals in northern Europe actually reacted to similar Jewish arguments.[65] Gilbert's "Jew" uninhibitedly avows that "Christians adore [*adorant*] sculptures and take delight in their idols," that Christians egregiously disobey God's law by "carving effigies, making and painting them, adoring and worshiping them wherever they can." Gilbert's "Christian" responds to these accusations by reminding the Jew of the numerous objects used in the Tabernacle and Temple, including the sculptured cherubs and the ark of the covenant. They were mandated by God for proper worship and are therefore beyond the suspicion of idolatry. Drawing conclusions that create common ground between Christians and Jews, Gilbert's "Christian" says:

> God prohibits the making of graven images and yet as we read graven images have been made on the Lord's command. . . . Excluding therefore the idolatry of false worship, sculptured images were made by [the Jews] and can also be made by us. In God's honor we make carvings, in God's honor we also make graven images. But we do not adore [*adoramus*] them or worship [*colimus*] them as if they were divine. For even the cross itself, which we call holy, we regard as wood and not as God and we hold that in itself and by itself it holds no virtue. And after it has been sanctified by the priest's blessing in the memory of the

Lord's passion we still receive, tend, and venerate it not with divine worship but with the worship of true veneration, as it is said in the Psalms: "Adore his footstool, for it is holy."[66]

Gilbert's "Christian," if not Gilbert himself, has the last word. The response of the "Jew" is not recorded, if there were any response from his lively interlocutor. It is unlikely, however, that the "Jew" was any more persuaded by Gilbert's reasonable "Christian" that Christian images are not idolatrous than Christians were persuaded by Rabbi Joseph's arguments that Jews are innocent of idolatry. Defending themselves against similar charges, twelfth-century Jews and Christians resorted to identical answers: Rabbi Joseph claimed that the ancient Israelites were merely "honoring" the calf, not worshiping it as if it were an idol pretending to be God. Benedictine intellectuals similarly claimed that contemporary Christians merely "honor" the cross, not worshipping it as if it were an idol simulating God. Christians and Jews both cited the same biblical precedents to support their claims. Christians nevertheless persisted in labeling Judaism idolatrous, and Jews persisted in describing Christian images as idolatry. In reviling one another's images, they dialectically reinforced their profound attachment to their own.

In their biblical commentaries, Rabbi Joseph, Rabbi Samuel, and Rashi invoked Midrashic traditions and designed new arguments to defend Judaism against Christian allegations. The rabbis invented the complex richness of medieval Jewish visual culture in the course of denouncing Christian images as idolatrous. The hostile rabbinic rejection of Christian images was the inevitable expression of an overall hostility to French and German Christianity in the eleventh and twelfth centuries. Jewish hostility smoldered prior to the First Crusade in 1096. The hostility flared in the gruesome aftermath of martyrdom and forced conversions, as Jewish memory nursed its wounds and northwestern Europe increasingly became a "persecuting society."[67] Jewish hostility pervaded "all types of Jewish literature throughout the Middle Ages," including historical chronicles, synagogue liturgies, pietistic treatises, legal works, polemics, and biblical commentaries.[68] Petahiah of Regensburg grew up with this literature. It supplied him with reasons to adore Jewish artifacts and scholastic explanations for his abhorrence of Christian spaces and images. He also grew up in a city with more than a bookish investment in comparative Jewish-Christian aesthetics. In 1096, the Crusaders had entered Regensburg. They forced the entire Jewish community to the riverbanks, "made the evil sign in the water, the cross, and baptized them all simultaneously in that river. . . . [The Jews] also returned immediately to the Lord after the enemies of the Lord passed through. They repented greatly, for what they had done they had done under great duress."[69] Less than one hundred years later, Petahiah embarked on his pilgrimage. No wonder he was so fascinated and reassured by Jewish sites. No wonder he was so repelled by Christian images and monuments that he explicitly declared them 'avodah zarah, idolatry. No wonder he was so amazed to find Jews and Muslims congenially praying together at the same shrines. Such "interfaith sociability" was "uncharacteristic . . . of the Christian milieu from which [he] hailed."[70]

III

Petahiah hailed from twelfth-century Ashkenaz, the Jewish settlement in northern France and Germanic Europe. Benjamin of Tudela hailed from twelfth-century Sepharad, the Jewish settlement in Spain. Ashkenaz and Sepharad were distinctive medieval Jewish "subcultures."[71] They absorbed and helped define "the main division . . . between North and South: between the lands which felt the pull of the Mediterranean, which had formed the core of the Roman Empire . . . and those lands which were separated from the Mediterranean by the heights of Auvergne or a journey through the appalling Alps."[72] Sepharad, the South, was profoundly differentiated from Ashkenaz by its prolonged participation in multiethnic, relatively tolerant "Islamdom" and "Islamicate cultural traditions" as well as by its fateful experience of the Christian *Reconquista* of the Iberian peninsula.[73] The dynamic combination of geography, Roman heritage, Arabic culture, and Muslim-Christian political interaction in Spain was decisive for the Jews of Sepharad. It determined every aspect of their lives: legal status, range of economic activity, place in the social hierarchy, degree of religious tolerance, and extent of religious persecution.[74] By 1391, the social, political, and religious gaps between Sepharad and Ashkenaz began to close as Spain intensified its thirteenth-century efforts to follow northern European leads in first destabilizing Jewish life, then outlawing Judaism, and ultimately expelling the Jews from Christendom.[75] In 1119, Alfonso I of Aragon captured Tudela from the Muslims.[76] Almost fifty years later, in 1165, Benjamin embarked on his journeys. In twelfth-century Tudela, unlike twelfth-century Regensburg, it was still possible to produce a pilgrim like Benjamin who delighted in Jewish monuments, lavished praise on Islamic architecture, and admired Christian monuments without explicitly labeling them 'avodah zarah, idolatry.[77] He acquired these visual tastes in cosmopolitan Sepharad, where the locals may have given special attention to treatises and biblical commentaries composed by two of Tudela's most distinguished natives, Judah Halevi (1075–1140) and Abraham ibn Ezra (1089–1164). Their comments on Exodus 32, the episode of the golden calf, are telltale signs of commonality and difference between Ashkenaz in the age of Crusades and Sepharad in the early period of *Reconquista*. Their comments indicate that Benjamin's visual tastes were not idiosyncratically liberal.

Judah Halevi and Abraham ibn Ezra denied that the golden calf was idolatrous. Halevi's arguments were twofold: historical and aesthetic. In the historical argument, Halevi affirmed that reverence for visual images is a timeless constant in religion, but he also acknowledged that the choice of specific images varies in accordance with historical context. Lacking this historical perspective, Halevi's contemporaries harshly misjudged the Israelites. Halevi sought to correct this misunderstanding. He explained that in antiquity "all nations used to engage in worship related to visual images"; even the most metaphysically inclined philosophers "were unable to dispense with a visual image, teaching their people and the masses that the divine presence was attached to that image which was distinguished by some wondrously marvelous power."[78] To prove that fashions in religious imagery change over time, Halevi appealed to his contemporaries' familiarity with religious architecture. His reference to religious buildings was generic, perhaps suggesting that he intended to include the majority of religious shrines and all mosques, synagogues, and churches. Halevi remarked that freestanding, theriomorphic ritual monuments like the calf were no longer popular: "Nowadays, these visual objects for worship have been eliminated by the majority of nations." Nowadays, most nations prefer "autonomously to construct buildings, take pride in them, and feel blessed by them. We sometimes say that God dwells in them and that His angels surround them." Clarifying his historical argument, Halevi reasoned that his contemporaries would deem the sin of the calf less repugnant had the Israelites behaved more like later generations in "building a house of their own choosing for worship, using it to orient themselves, offering sacrifices in it, and honoring it" instead of fashioning the golden calf. Of course, Halevi concluded, such behavior would have been an anachronistic impossibility in an era when images like the calf were fashionable and the Israelites, like all other nations, were merely conforming to local custom.

In the argument based on aesthetics, Halevi presupposed that images are not successful mimetic representations. He knew that "statues made of marble and plaster, endowed with heads, eyes, ears, and all limbs" are vastly inferior to the person portrayed. No matter how accurate the statues might be, they always lack the spirit of life, "they are only imitations [*tashbih wa-taswir*] of men, not men in reality."[79] True for secular images, the principle of nonrepresentation is no less true for ritual images. They never seek to depict the divine. Their function is less ambitious. Understanding this principle, the ancient Israelites knew better than to confuse material images with spiritual realities or to mistake the calf for the divine itself. They merely "demanded an object of worship [*ma'budan*] towards which they could turn, like the other nations, without denying [*yajhadu*] the exclusive sovereignty of the One who took them out of Egypt."[80] Halevi insisted that the calf was not intended to be an idolatrous representation of God. It was merely a *qiblah*, an object resembling an architectural feature of mosques, a specially marked niche or *mihrab* that spatially oriented worshipers to God alone.[81] The calf was therefore intended to be no different from all the other visible objects that signaled God's will and presence. *Qiblahs* occasioned prayer and aligned the worshipers in God's direction. These visual signs, or *qiblahs*, included the pillar of cloud and the pillar of fire that had accompanied the Israelites ever since their departure from Egypt; the cloud that hovered over Moses while God spoke with him; the cherubs in the Tabernacle and Temple; the two tablets of the Law; and their container, "the ark towards which [the people] should direct their gaze during their devotions." Once his contemporaries understood that the calf was an innocuous *qiblah* rather than a repugnant idol, Halevi must have hoped that misguided defamation of Judaism would be silenced and replaced by sympathetic understanding, if not praise.

Although Halevi exculpated the Israelites from idolatry, he did not consider them blameless. They sinned by relying on their own judgment instead of obeying the law that forbids ritual images not explicitly sanctioned by God: "They should have waited [for Moses to return] and not have created for themselves an object of worship, arranging an altar and sacrifices." The people were misled by autonomous, freethinking "astrologers and makers of talismans" who initiated the idea of a calf. Aaron and the nobles who actually fashioned the calf "sinned in causing what was only a sin of intention to be a sin in deed." Having specified the sin and the sinners, Halevi numbered them and stated their punishment. He deduced that the sin was not widespread. Of the 600,000 Israelites, "slightly less than three thousand" commited one sin only: They worshiped with a divinely unauthorized ritual image; they were punished by death.[82] For the people at large, there were no other negative consequences: Manna continued to fall, the cloud still shaded them, the pillar of fire still guided them, prophecy flourished, and they lost nothing that had been given them. "Their sin was forgiven." Rabbinic Judaism had come to the same conclusion, and Halevi was merely reiterating a conventional truth. Christians disagreed. They claimed that God had abandoned the Jews because of their sins. Halevi contradicted this Christian claim. His ally was Islam. He was certainly thinking of mosques, *qiblah*, and *mihrab* when he interpreted Exodus 32, and he may have been alluding to the Qur'an when he marshaled the evidence of God's forgiveness. Describing the aftermath of the sin of the calf, the Qur'an declares: "We pardoned you that you might be thankful. . . . We revived you after your death that you might be thankful. We shaded you with clouds, and We sent down to you the manna and quails."[83]

Unlike Benjamin of Tudela, Halevi took a harder line with King Jereboam. As reported in 1 Kings 12, Jereboam "made two golden calves . . . placing one in Bethel and the other in Dan." According to Halevi, the royal action amounted to outright *'avodah zarah*, idolatry.[84] The calf at Sinai did not. In one crucial respect, however, Jereboam and his followers were as praiseworthy as the Israelites at Sinai. Jereboam's party piously "acknowledged the God of Israel who delivered them from Egypt." Because they acknowledged God, their sin was not worse than the one committed at Sinai: They worshiped with an unauthorized visual image. Their sin also exceeded the one at Sinai because they mistook the material image of Jereboam's calves for the spiritual reality of God. Jereboam's calves were not relatively innocuous statues that functioned as *qiblahs* directing the people away from Jerusalem and toward Dan and Bethel. The golden calves were idols because they were meant to represent God.

This line of reasoning led Halevi to conclude that Jereboam's version of Judaism was superior to humanistic religions based on philosophic speculation but inferior to contemporary religions that "have done away with [idolatrous] visual images." Halevi was presumably alluding to Islam and Christianity. Monotheistic in their beliefs and moderately nonidolatrous in some of their practices, Christianity and Islam were almost on par with Judaism, as Halevi understood them. He nevertheless measured the "distance" between the apogee of Judaism and the lower rank of the other monotheisms in units of ritual behavior: "[Christianity and Islam] altered the direction of prayer [*qiblah*] and sought the divine presence where it is not to be found, to say nothing of their deviating from most of [Judaism's] ritual laws."[85] But they were not unequivocally idolatrous.[86] In twelfth-century Ashkenaz, these conclusions were unthinkable.[87] The golden calves compelled Jewish intellectuals in Ashkenaz to defend Judaism against vituperative allegations of idolatry. The Jews of Ashkenaz also counterattacked: They objected to Christian interpretations of the Bible. They challenged the premises of Christian theology, and they condemned Christian visual culture. In twelfth-century Sepharad, the golden calves also occasioned Judah Halevi's defense of rabbinic Judaism. They prompted him to articulate the unsurpassed significance of Jewish sacred space and monuments, but they did not lead him to accuse Christians of outright idolatry.

Halevi was not the only Jew in twelfth-century Sepharad to reach these conclusions. They are embodied in Benjamin of Tudela's travelogue and they reverberate in Abraham ibn Ezra's biblical commentaries. Ibn Ezra composed his commentaries during the last twenty-five years of his life. He spent those remarkably productive years in self-imposed exile seeking patrons and students among the Jewish communities of Christian-dominated Italy, France, and England.[88] Despite his immediate and prolonged contact with Christian Europe, he seldom referred to Christianity in his commentaries. They include strenuous objections to Christological readings of Isaiah and Christian spiritualizations of biblical law, but they generally ignore Christianity and avoid condemning it for being idolatrous.[89] According to Ibn Ezra, idolatry (*'avodah zarah*) is slack monotheism. It consists of thoughts, verbal utterances, or ritual practices that acknowledge God together with another force equal to or greater than God.[90] This definition privileges strict monotheism. It also bypasses Christianity. Commenting on the Ten Commandments, Ibn Ezra explained that

> the sin of someone who does not believe in the Name [of God] is greater than the sin of one who worships idolatrously. There are many who believe in the Name [of God] but who offer sacrifices and fumigate incense to something idolatrous. They resemble those who fumigate incense to the celestial world thinking that it will do them some good. They say, 'ever since we stopped fumigating incense to the celestial world we have lacked everything.' Scripture states: "So they feared [the Name of] God but worshipped their deities" [2 Kings: 17:33]. That is precisely what Na'aman did when he bowed down at Bet Rimmon [2 Kings 5:17–18]. These people acknowledge the Name [of God], but they polytheistically associate something else with It.[91]

This excerpt indicates that Ibn Ezra did more than bypass Christianity in framing his definition of idolatry. The example of Na'aman does not evoke Christianity. It conveys Ibn Ezra's recognition that idolatry is pocked with religious syncretism. The example of astrologers wafting incense heavenward neither alludes to nor specifies Christianity. It depicts a slack monotheism steeped in the arcane beliefs and Hermetic rituals of theurgic magic. Taken together, these examples indicate that Ibn Ezra excluded Christianity from the class of idolatrous religions. Christianity is conspicuously absent from Ibn Ezra's discussion of idolatry. Astrology and Hermetic theurgy are conspicuously present.

Ibn Ezra's polemic against magic and astrology included a comparative analysis of visual images. Commenting on Exodus 20:4, "You shall not make a graven image or the shape [*temunah*] of anything in the heaven above," he remarked that "regardless of the craft, one is forbidden to make a shape of any heavenly body. . . . The shapes in heaven number only forty-eight forms (*tzurot*). Skilled theurgists (*hakhme ha-tzurot*) produce things that don't conform [to heavenly realities]. Their productions approximate idolatry."[92] Commenting on Exodus 20:5, "You shall not worship them or serve them," Ibn Ezra explained that these prohibitions are directed against people "like the skilled theurgists (*hakhme ha-tzurot*) who think that they are able to force the power from the upper worlds to descend downward for the need of some individual."[93] Ibn Ezra faulted some of the sacramental means whereby the theurgists sought their goals, but not the theurgic goals themselves. He affirmed that the ambition to draw down the heavenly flux was perfected in Jewish practice. Introducing his extensive commentary on the Tabernacle and its sculptured furnishings, Ibn Ezra proposed a general rule: "Every cherub was produced in order to receive power from the upper worlds."[94] He acknowledged the existence of additional artifacts that were crafted "to receive power from the upper worlds." These artifacts were neither restricted to the Tabernacle nor were they specifically Jewish. Commenting on Genesis 31:19, "Rachel stole her father's *teraphim*," Ibn Ezra explained that some authorities understand *teraphim* to mean chronometers

> made out of bronze and designed to determine the various divisions of the hour. Others say that astrologers [*hakhme ha-mazalot*] have the capacity of making an image [*tzurah*] at certain times so that the image speaks. Their supporting evidence is "the *teraphim* speak wrongdoing" [Zechariah 10:3]. But the interpretation of the verse is not so. It seems to me that the *teraphim* take the form [*tzurat*] of human beings; this form is produced in order to receive a power belonging to the upper worlds. But I cannot explain. Evidence that this is what the *teraphim* are [comes from] the *teraphim* that Michal, the daughter of Saul, placed in the bed with the result that the guards thought it to be David [1 Samuel 19:13–17]. . . . Some say that Rachel stole them in order to suspend her father's idolatry. If this were so, however, why did she carry them with her instead of hiding them somewhere along her way? It seems that her father knew the constellations. She was afraid that her father would gaze at the constellations in order to know which way they fled.[95]

These passages, and countless more like them scattered across his biblical commentaries and treatises, corroborate the inference that Ibn Ezra rejected "the facile, indiscriminate use of astrological concepts in the interpretation of Scripture. [He did] not regard Scripture as an *arcanum* that is to be decoded by means of astrology. . . . On the other hand, in his opinion, certain rites and events may find their correct explanation within an astrological framework. . . . Religious structures such as the Tabernacle may be interpreted symbolically, as a representation of the structure of the cosmos."[96]

The passages assembled in the previous paragraphs also show that Ibn Ezra recognized formalistic and functional similarities between idolatrous and legitimate images: Both categories of images symbolically replicate natural entities—either human or astronomical—and both categories of images operate theurgically as conductors or mediums drawing down energy or information from the upper world. Like the *teraphim*, the cherubs were shaped to imitate human beings.[97] Ibn Ezra nevertheless declared the cherubs and *teraphim* to be proper images, contrasting them to images made by "skilled theurgists" and "astrologers" that he deemed either idolatrous or "close to idolatry." On what grounds did he draw the distinction? Historical fact and legend affirm that, before his self-imposed exile from Andalusia, Ibn Ezra and Judah Halevi were close friends and colleagues. It is not impossible that they discussed the difference between legitimate and idolatrous artifacts.[98] Halevi would have carped against the naturalistic implications of astrology and argued that only divinely authorized images are legitimate, all other ritual images risk being idolatrous.[99]

Ibn Ezra might have been less insistent on the principle of heteronomy. He might have claimed that accuracy in representation is the more decisive factor. Images that do not conform to reality border on idolatry. He might then have emphasized that even the most accurate depiction of a natural figure would amount to idolatry if the artifact was not understood to be a gesture of honor addressed to the utterly transcendent, unmediated, and solitary power of God. Anticipating what he would eventually write in his commentary on Exodus 20:20, Ibn Ezra might have reminded Halevi that the same image can mean different things to different people. Regarding the "calf" at Sinai, Aaron and the Israelites understood that it was an object meant "to receive power from the upper worlds." The people and Aaron nevertheless entertained divergent perceptions. Unlike Aaron, who "made the image for the glory of God [alone]," the Israelites mistakenly thought that the calf image, like all the other theurgic receptacles of God's power, signified "the intermediaries between" God and the people. But God "needs no intermediaries." Knowing that the people would make images, God forbade the making of gold and silver "gods" in order to foreclose the possibility that the people might mistakenly affirm intermediary powers.[100] Summing up his argument, Ibn Ezra might have said: Images are indispensable to astrology, theurgy, and Judaism. Images are not idolatrous if they are understood to honor God alone. Images made by the "skilled theurgists" and "astrologers" are idolatrous whenever they ascribe autonomous power to the heavenly bodies and worship them. The essential difference between legitimate and illegitimate images is neither formal nor functional. It is psychologically interior, residing in the beliefs and intentions of the worshiper.

Ibn Ezra revisited and refined these arguments when his commentarial enterprise reached the golden calf of Exodus 32. Anxious to defend Aaron's reputation against unfounded or ludicrous charges, Ibn Ezra defied the classical Midrashic authorities and the later rabbinic commentators who conceded that a widespread sin had occurred. He insisted that "it is a forbidden desecration [to think that] Aaron committed idolatry. Furthermore, the Israelites did not seek idolatry. They merely thought that Moses had died" from starvation on Sinai. They consequently sought an artifactual surrogate for the personal guidance of Moses. They requested another *'elohim*, another "bodily form on which God's glory settles," something similar to the divinely angelic "pillar of cloud" that guided them on the first leg of their journey in the desert. As verse 5 indicates, Aaron commissioned the calf solely for the "glorification of the Name [of God]." As verse 6 affirms, the people obeyed Aaron's commands and offered proper sacrifices to God alone. The calf was therefore a legitimate image; it was "produced for honoring the Name [of God]." The relatively benign aftermath of the episode proves that the actions of Aaron and the vast majority of the people were praiseworthy. Less than three thousand people, a mere "one-half of one one-hundreth" of the population of 600,000, were found guilty and penalized with death. They were the Israelites who had been corrupted by the idolatrous "mixed multitude" (*'erev rav*). These Israelites "were the scant few who considered [the calf] to be an idol. They brought sacrifices, bowed down to it, and declared, 'This is your deity [*'elohim*], O Israel.' " The majority of Israelites used exactly the same words in their declaration, except that for them it meant, "This is your [earthly receptacle and medium of] divine [power] [*'elohim*], O Israel."[101] Ibn Ezran idolatry, like Maimonidean beauty, is subjective. It resides in the mind of the beholder.

In developing his notion that the calf was a legitmate medium manifesting divine power, Ibn Ezra cited an earlier authority, "the Gaon," presumably Saadia, who suggested that the decision to replicate a calf's shape can be explained by referring to "people in India who think that the shape is conducive to receiving supernal power." Ibn Ezra seems to have rejected the Gaon's proposal of an Indian precedent; he certainly agreed with the Gaon's suggestion that the calf was an earthly medium for divine presence.[102] Astrological considerations supplied Ibn Ezra with other explanations for why the medium was cast in the shape of the calf. In one commentary, he elliptically remarked that "one who understands the secret of the heavenly world will know why the shape of a calf," but he did not clarify what he meant.[103] In the parallel commentary, he was less enigmatic: "The astrologers [*hakhme ha-mazalot*] have said that the major conjunction of the two upper [planets, Saturn and Jupiter] was happening in the sign of Taurus [*shor*]. This is wrong, for [the conjunction] was happening only in the sign of Aquarius. According to astrological science, [Aquarius] is the sign of Israel."[104] Considered together, these passages suggest that Ibn Ezra rejected the specific proposal that the calf was an astrological symbol for Taurus, the Bull. Because ibn Ezra suggested no alternative to Taurus, these passages might also suggest that he was unsure of the calf's specific astrological significance. Like Rabbi Samuel ben Meir, Rabbi Joseph Bekhor Shor, and Judah Halevi, Abraham ibn Ezra was convinced that the calf was not idolatrous. Whether he thought that the calf was "intended to imitate an astral form" remains an open question.[105]

IV

Nestled geographically between the established communities of Sepharad and the relatively newer settlements in Ashkenaz, the Jews of southern France—Provence, Languedoc, or the Midi—developed a rich and distinctive culture. Some of their major settlements were "Aix, Argentière, Avignon, Bagnols, Beaucaire, Béziers, Bordeaux, Carcassonne, Carpentras, Cavaillon, Lunel, Marseille, Montepellier, Narbonne, Nimes, Orange, Perpignan, Salon, Tarascon, Toulouse, Trinquetaille."[106] Eastbound, Benjamin of Tudela visited "Narbonne . . . Béziers . . . Montepellier . . . Lunel . . . Beaucaire . . . Bourg de St. Gilles, a Gentile pilgrimage site . . . Arles . . . and Marseilles."[107] Regarding visual images, what might Benjamin have learned from Jewish scholars residing in late twelfth-century, Christian dominated, southern France?

Straddling Sepharad and Ashkenaz, southern France was ideally situated to become a center of translation where Arabic texts were rendered into Hebrew. Jacob ben Reuben, born probably in 1136, fled his native Spain in 1148 and settled in southern France. He may have been the scholar who translated an Arabic polemic into the Hebrew text known to posterity as *Nestor the Priest*.[108] He certainly knew the text in one version or another, as did some of his predecessors and contemporaries in Sēpharad and southern France. Originally composed midway through the ninth century by a Jew living in an Arabophone society, the polemical treatise probably began its new life as a Hebrew in the twelfth century.[109] The Arabic polemic and its Hebrew versions rail against several Christian practices: ringing bells, burying the dead in churches, baptizing the impure, making relics of saints' bones, and "worshipping the cross made of silver and gold" or "buying a rotten tree and making from it an image from which there is no benefit . . . a practice not found in the Gospel."[110] Such antagonism was more typical of twelfth-century Ashkenaz and southern France than it was of contemporary Sepharad.

Other facets of the Arabic polemic were comparatively more universal. These facets would have been welcome wherever twelfth-century Jewish scholars pondered the golden calf of Exodus 32. Building its case against Christianity, whose sins far exceed those of Israel, the Arabic version of the text asks a rhetorical question: "Do you not know that when the Israelites strayed while Moses tarried, they made for themselves a golden calf? They deluded themselves into thinking that it can replace the prophet and that it is an intermediary between themselves and their Creator."[111] This passage might have been welcome because it insisted that the Israelites were not guilty of premeditated idolatry. It understood the calf to be a surrogate for Moses and an intermediary for God, but itself neither an idol nor a false god. To those who never considered the possibility, the notion that the calf was not intentionally idolatrous might have suggested a useful line of thought. To those who had come independently to similar conclusions, the text offered reinforcement. To those who knew their Judah Halevi or Abraham ibn Ezra, the text sounded familiar and true. Both its denial of premeditated Jewish idolatry and its fascination with the complex significance of visual artifacts were commonplace in twelfth-century Jewish travelogues, biblical commentaries, and polemical treatises.

It is unlikely but not impossible that Jacob ben Reuben translated *Nestor the Priest*. There is no doubt, however, regarding his other literary activities. Between 1160 and 1170, he composed *Sefer Milhamot Ha-Shem* (*The Book of the Lord's Wars*), one of the first and most widely cited Hebrew treatises directed against Christianity and the text of the New Testament.[112] Cast in the form of a dialogue, the treatise pits Christian against Jew, the "denier" (*mekahed*) against "the champion of God's unity" (*meyahed*). In one passage, the "denier" reminds the Jew that God's law categorically forbids making and worshiping images. Casuistically, the "denier" then springs an apparent contradiction on the "champion," citing Numbers 21:8, "God said to Moses, 'Make a fiery serpent, place it on a pole, and whoever looks at it will live.' " What Scripture forbids in one verse, it seems to enjoin in another. The Christian argues that the contradiction between these verses signals "an exceedingly profound secret, lessons that do not appear at first glance in Scripture." The secret is this: The serpent allegorically represents mortality, "and no medical doctor is able to cure that bite, for it is unlike ordinary poisons in a human body." Doctors are no match for this serpent, but "Jesus, our Messiah" outmatches death. Thus, when God commanded Moses to make the serpent and suspend it from a pole, God was "allusively making it known that whoever gazes upward with a full heart at that figure. . . . Who was destined to be crucified on account of [the serpent] and, resembling it, suspended on a pole in His death, shall live forever." According to Jacob ben Reuben's Christian, the "denier," death, is the serpent against which Jesus alone is the antidote.[113]

Unfazed by the Christological homily, the "champion of God's unity" replies with four arguments. He refutes the Christian's premises, logic, and conclusion. The first argument challenges the misreading of Scripture and uses the apparent contradiction to clarify the legal status of images:

> The question you raised against me concerns two verses. You claimed that in one
> of the verses the Creator forbade us even to make a graven image or a picture; in

the other verse, the Creator commanded Moses to make the fiery serpent. On this scriptural basis, you claimed that your messiah resembles the serpent. See now the many ways in which you incorrectly raised the question. Our Creator, may He be praised, never forbade the production of statues and pictures. He only forbade them with respect to worship and service. As it is written, "You shall not have other gods before Me; Do not make a graven image or any figure" for the purpose of divinity. So too, the end [of the verse] proves the point, because it declares "do not bow down and do not worship them." But Scripture never forbade the making of images or the act of beautifying some work or building. This is precisely what Solomon did when he had numerous images made for the Temple. Furthermore, this is precisely what Moses, our Master, did when he himself fashioned the two golden cherubs as part of the building of the Tabernacle.[114]

The attack and response are familiar: Charged with being blind to Scripture's true meaning, the Jews countered with dazzling displays of dialectical acuity. Challenged with allegations of idol worship, Jews and Christians justified their visual habits by appealing to precedents established by Moses and Solomon.

Jacob ben Reuben's Christian, however, did not intend to raise the issue of idolatry. Being a literary prop in *The Book of the Lord's Wars*, he was satisfied with contesting Jewish understandings of Scripture. The Christian was allowed to fault the Jews for overlooking a rhetorically sophisticated Christological allusion to the ritual significance of the crucifix. Outmaneuvered by his ventriloquist, the Christian only succeeded in evoking truculent formulations of a major trend in twelfth-century Jewish polemics. In Ashkenaz, the consensus held that the crucifix and other Christian images were idolatrous. Evidence culled from Benjamin of Tudela, Judah Halevi, and Abraham ibn Ezra indicates that a similar consensus did not prevail in twelfth-century Sepharad. Jacob ben Reuben's *Wars* suggests that Jews in contemporary southern France aligned with Ashkenaz. His "champion" scolds Christians for their sinful ways: "You make the image of Adam (*tzurat 'adam*) and the shape of a man (*tavnit 'ish*), and you bow down to him, even though you cunningly claim that 'we do not not worship the essence of the tree, for we certainly know that it lacks power. We only worship the God who is depicted in that form.' Hence, you revile and blaspheme."[115] Being the ventriloquist, Jacob ben Reuben allowed his "champion" the last word. Familiar with the classical Christian responses to this attack, he refused to moot religious symbols. He lambasted Christian devotion to the crucifix and silenced the "denier."[116]

Although not all twelfth-century Jews agreed that Christian artifacts were unequivocally idolatrous, the Jews of Ashkenaz, Sepharad, and southern France unanimously affirmed the legitimacy of Jewish visual images. Jacob ben Reuben voiced that consensual affirmation with emphatic

references to Moses and Solomon in his rejoinder to the Christian "denier." The same affirmation pervades twelfth-century Jewish literature, in
travelogues, biblical commentaries, and polemical treatises. Halevi
adopted the golden calf into the family of praiseworthy *qiblahs*, ibn Ezra
placed it in a good home with the family of efficacious, theurgic, astrological media. In the framework of medieval Jewish culture, Scripture is not
an iconoclast's manifesto. Neither does it inculcate indifference to the
visual arts. Medieval Jews understood that Scripture categorically forbids
idolatry; but Scripture does not classify all statues, paintings, and architectural structures as idols. Twelfth-century Jewish Scripture specifically or-
dains the production and beautification of particular ritual artifacts, and it
generically permits the production and beautification of countless others.

Seven

The Power and Regulation of Images in Late Medieval Jewish Society

BETWEEN the thirteenth and sixteenth centuries, traditional Jewish regard for visual experience remained constant. It also became more elaborate. Twelfth-century authorities became late medieval classics. Arguments developed by Maimonides, Rashi, Rabbi Samuel ben Meir, Rabbi Joseph Bekhor Shor, Judah Halevi, Abraham ibn Ezra, and Rabbi Jacob ben Reuben were combined, challenged, and augmented by a host of scholars. Polemicists sustained the attack against Christian images. Biblical commentators continued to interpret golden calves, ritual objects, secular images, and sacred architecture. Kabbalists enriched the discussions by elaborating the iconographic complexities of theosophic symbolism. Talmudic scholars remained vigilant in guarding the border between permitted images and forbidden idolatry. None of these communal leaders harbored iconoclastic or aniconic tendencies. Their affirmative theories of the visual complemented late medieval Jewish practice: pilgrims continued to be astounded by artifacts and monuments;[1] patrons continued to construct and decorate synagogues; artisans continued to illuminate prayerbooks, manuscripts, and marriage contracts; engrave tombstones; sculpt statues; install stained glass windows; devise amulets and talismans; manufacture decorated ceramic bowls and plates; embroider needlework; weave tapestries; cast metal pointers, boxes, lamps, and Torah crowns; carve wooden containers; fashion cups; and design all sorts of jewelry. What the artisans produced, people traded and used. Artifacts and visual images were ubiquitous, indispensable, and occasionally troublesome in late medieval Jewish society.

I

Late medieval Jews were a persecuted minority. Oppressed by the Church, they did not encounter Christian images and behold them as artistic masterpieces displayed in a museum. The grandeur and sanctity of Christian monuments were invisible to medieval Jewish eyes. Unlike hegemonic medieval Christian intellectuals who were able to discover "beauty" in ancient polytheistic shrines, vanquished medieval Jews were unable to "neutralize" Christian artifacts, aestheticize them, and experience them as "art."[2]

Christian regulations prohibited Jews from entering churches and cathedrals. Defying these regulations, some Jews nevertheless became familiar with ecclesiastical interiors when they walked through them to use their spaces for safekeeping money and valuables.[3] Barred from the streets on Sundays and holidays, especially during Holy Week, some Jews must have caught a furtive glance at the sacred statues and crucifixes that accompanied the passing processions.[4] To the dismay of church authorities, Jewish moneylenders persisted in receiving from impecunious clergy "ecclesiastical books, vestments, and other ornaments as security pledges."[5] Throughout the thirteenth century, Jews were repeatedly reminded that the boom in Gothic architecture dominating the landscapes of their towns and cities meant bearing the oppressive burden of additional taxes and "tithes."[6] In late medieval Jewish consciousness, Christian images and monuments embodied alien Christian spirituality. They proclaimed oppressive Christian hegemony, served as essential props in anti-Jewish campaigns, and evoked Jewish terror. The traces of this terror and its corollary, Jewish condemnation of Christian images and monuments, are recorded in late medieval polemics.

A typical Hebrew text captures the fundamental difference between Jewish and Christian responses to "the living theater of medieval art."[7] *Nizzahon Vetus* describes a newly constructed church in Speyer as "ugly." Christians experienced the church otherwise. The text reports the Christian king's boastful challenge to a rabbinic scholar: "In what way was the building of [Solomon's] Temple greater than this?" To which the Rabbi replied, regarding the case of Solomon's Temple, "Priests were unable to stand and minister because of the cloud, for the glory of the Lord had filled the house of God.' In this case, however, if one were to load a donkey with vomit and filth and lead it through the church, [the donkey] would remain unharmed."[8] Another passage in the same *Nizzahon Vetus* demonstrates that Jews could be more temperate. Occasionally, the Jews were aware that the direct objects of Christian worship were sacramental symbols, that Christians claimed to "honor" and "pray to . . . the one in whose image and likeness" the wooden crucifixes "were made" without idolatrously worshiping the wood and image itself. Late medieval Jews were nevertheless convinced that Christian devotions were sinful and futile.[9] The Jewish disputants routinely declared that "the uncircumcised [Christians] who make images and bow down before them transgress, for they too were commanded against idolatry."[10]

The Jewish polemical texts also record Christian responses to Jewish charges of Christian idolatry. According to *The Book of Joseph the Zealous*, a thirteenth-century Hebrew compilation of disputes conducted in northern France, the standard Christian defense rested upon Old Testament precedents. When the Jews cited Exodus 20:4, "You shall make no graven images," as proof that Christian devotional practice was forbidden, the Christian interlocutors "licentiously raised an objection" (*poqrim*). They reminded the Jews of the biblically sanctioned cherubs. The logical force of the Christian reminder was dialectically subtle and twofold: If Exodus 20:4 forbids all statues, then the Jews are as guilty of idolatry because of the cherubs as the Christians are guilty because of Christian images. If, however, Exodus 20:4 permits selected sculptures, then Christian devotional images are as legitimate as the Israelite cherubs. Since the cherubs were indeed biblically sanctioned "sculptures" (*tzelamim*), then the Jewish charge of Christian idolatry is both logically inconsistent and doctrinally unfounded. The thirteenth-century Jewish reply was equally subtle and dialectical. It interpreted the biblical prohibition to mean that only exact mimetic replicas of anything "in the heavens above, the earth below, and the waters below" are forbidden. The shape (*dugma*) of the cherubs, however, did not replicate anything that actually exists in the universe, since their only features were "faces and wings." The cherubs therefore do not legitimate Christian practices that represent the entire body of Jesus and the other saints. Rabbi Joseph ben Nathan Official, the compiler of *The Book of Joseph the Zealous*, listed two additional arguments for good measure. First, unlike the Christian images, the cherubs were not displayed publicly. "They were placed where no one entered except for the High Priest once a year." Second, unlike the Christian images, the cherubs were not direct objects of worship. To clinch the argument for the permissibility of images not meant for worship, thereby denouncing Christian practice and affirming the legitimacy of Jewish images, Rabbi Joseph alluded to 1 Kings 10:19–20. They describe the fourteen sculptured lions commissioned by King Solomon to decorate his throne.[11]

Because Christian pressures against the Jews persisted throughout the late Middle Ages, Jewish allegations of Christian idolatry were recurrent. The fight over images was as prominent and unavoidable as arguments over the True Israel, the divinity of Jesus, and the status of ceremonial law.[12] It is no surprise, therefore, that the perennially contentious topic of images also surfaced in late fifteenth-century Italy. In response to a Franciscan friar's claim that Christians faithfully "maintain the Ten Commandments" despite the general abrogation of Old Testament laws, Elijah Hayyim ben Benjamin of Genazzano, the Jewish interlocutor, insisted that such claims are "unacceptable." He implied that Christians are not true monotheists. He declared that Christians "err with respect to the First Commandment and altogether uproot it. Scripture commands that 'you shall make neither graven image nor likeness,' but you [Christians] nevertheless make all sorts of images (*tzurot*) for your houses of worship. And the worship of images belongs to the category of 'worshipping other gods.' "[13]

The ongoing debate with Christians kept reminding medieval Jews that religious images and monuments exude sociopolitical significance. The articulation of that significance required speculative theory, scholastic dialectics, and biblical justification. Within their biblical framework, the Jews attacked Christian artifacts and defended their own. These attacks and defensive maneuvers drew upon twelfth-century precedents, intensifying an already heightened medieval Jewish sensitivity to the convergence of biblical texts and visual images. The convergence was inescapable at Exodus 32, the epsiode of the golden calf at Sinai, the same calf that had attracted so much Jewish and Christian exegetical attention in the twelfth century. Commenting on the episode, one thirteenth-century Hebrew polemicist seized the opportunity to vilify the Christian dogma of Incarnation: He conceded that the Israelites had sinned when they mistakenly assumed that the golden calf was a "pure and clean" receptacle for the holy "spirit of God." He also conceded that the Israelites were punished for their sin. He then put his concessions to work, dialectically: "An *a fortiori* conclusion applies here: [The Israelites] erred in worshipping a clean thing like gold, and yet their iniquity was marked before God. . . . Certainly, then, you who err in saying that something holy entered into a woman in that stinking place—for there is nothing in the world as disgusting as a woman's belly [*beten*], which is filled with feces and urine, which emits discharge and menstrual blood and serves as the receptacle for man's semen—you will certainly be consumed by a 'fire not blown" [Job 20:26] and descend to deepest hell."[14]

The golden calf elicited other sorts of polemics, as well. The belligerent debate with Christianity demanded Jewish interest in visual experience. Kabbalah, Jewish mysticism, enlivened that interest. In the thirteenth century, Rabbi Moses ben Nahman (1194–1270), known to the West as Nahmanides, critically engaged the opinions of his predecessors in Ashkenaz and Sepharad. In accordance with the mainstream of twelfth-century opinion that deviated from Rashi's epitome of Talmudic tradition, Nahmanides denied that the Israelites originally intended the calf to be an idolatrous representation of a false deity. Agreeing with his predecessors, Nahmanides explained that the Israelites innocently sought a surrogate leader (*'elohim*) for Moses, whom they feared had died. Explicitly rejecting Abraham ibn Ezra's Hermetic interpretations, Nahmanides denied that Aaron had decided upon the figure of a calf because of its theurgic potential for drawing down the "glory" of celestial power. According to Nahmanides, the calf was not a Hermetic medium and conductor but a legitimate and Kabbalistically inspired iconographic representation of one of the ten sephirotic, divine powers reflected in the four beasts of Ezekiel's vision of the mystical chariot, the ox, man, lion, and eagle. Had the Israelites not confused this one power with the totality of God's complex or-ganism and had they not worshiped that one power to the exclusion of all the others, the actual production of the calf would not have been a sin. To support this contention, Nahmanides shrewdly observed that the people merely demanded of Aaron that he make them some sort of an unspecified "leader" (*'elohim*). It was Aaron himself, a master of Kabbalistic lore, who knew that the only appropriate figure for the ominous circumstances of the desert was that of a protective and symbolic "ox" or calf.[15] Like all Kabbalists devoted to theurgic-theosophical speculation, Nahmanides was adept at combining formalist analysis and symbolic hermeneutics in the interpretation of visual artifacts.[16]

In the fourteenth century, the golden calf continued to attract scholarly attention. Bahya ben Asher (died 1340) addressed the problem in his widely read biblical commentary.[17] In his comments on the calf, he juxtaposed the Kabbalistic opinions of Nahmanides and the astrological suggestions of Abraham ibn Ezra. Typifying the growing prestige of mysticism in late medieval society, Bahya unequivocally sided with the Kabbalistic traditions that legitimated the golden calf by associating it with the divine sephirotic powers of stern justice. He also followed Nahmanides and his predecessors in exonerating Aaron and the vast majority of the Israelites from the sin of idolatry: "Their intention was not to make the calf the object of idolatrous worship. . . . They did not want it to serve as a deity, but to function as a leader [*manhig*]."[18] Levi ben Gershom (Gersonides, 1288–1344), the independent-minded Aristotelian philosopher and biblical commentator from the region of Provence, also commented upon the golden calf. He argued that the vast majority of Israelites did not intend the calf to be an idol but rather an instrumental "talisman possessing the supernal power to inform them of the future. It would serve only until a [human] replacement for Moses" might be appointed. Gersonides attributed this request "to their being caught up in the false beliefs of the Egyptians who made similar images [*tzurot*] on the mistaken assumption current in those days that such images possess supernal power." He also argued that Aaron was fully aware of the people's persistent and misguided attachment to Egyptian culture. This explains why Aaron decided personally to sculpt the bull rather than the ram that was so intimately associated with Egyptian cultic practice. Invoking the arcana of astrological lore, Rabbi Levi observed that Aaron, bargaining for time until Moses might return, was cleverly trying to wean the people away from their belief in Egyptian deities: "The constellation that ascends after Aries the Ram is Taurus the Bull. Aaron sagaciously fashioned the figure of Taurus in order that [the Israelites] might have more confidence in it [than in Aries]."[19] The divergent opinions of Gersonides and Bahya presage the competition between mysticism and philosophy in late medieval

Jewish society. Some scholars specialized in one or the other; most sought to harmonize or combine them.[20]

Among eclectic commentators in late-fifteenth-century Spain, the golden calf was still a lively topic. Rabbi Isaac Arama (c. 1420–1494), justifiably famed as "the preacher's preacher," composed an elaborate interpretive essay weaving scores of classical rabbinic traditions together with the diverse opinions articulated by Rashi, Abraham ibn Ezra, Moses ben Nahman, and Levi ben Gershom.[21] For the section of the essay revolving around Exodus 32:11, "O Lord, why are you angry," Arama invented the oration with which Moses appeased God:

> You are God, supreme deity and ruler of rulers, the truth of whose greatness is obvious and well-known to all the world. Why then should You be angry if this nation seeks and wants to test whether the Lord is in their midst or not, even though because of their foolish ignorance a few of them have bowed down before [the calf] and offered it sacrifices? Truthfully, they have performed a vain and futile act. But is it not so that a brave hero is only jealous of another brave hero, one sage [jealous] of another sage, and a wealthy person [jealous] of another wealthy person?

As Arama explained the meaning of this rhetoric, Moses was suggesting to God that divine anger over the calf was disproportionate to the minor severity of the act itself. The anger was therefore beneath God's dignity. The calf, after all, was merely a golden artifact, lacking all "potency and dynamism." Compared to God, the calf was a "nothing." Arama then offered a parable likening the calf to a sex toy: The episode of the calf resembles the example of a "woman who makes statues of men, using wood, stone, silver, or gold, and commits adultery with them. Because [making love to statues] is a ridiculous act of immense bestiality, it is proper that her husband remove her from them and chastise her. But it is unworthy of her husband to be jealously angry with her because of it."[22] In addition to proving that Arama belongs to the mainstream of medieval Jewish commentators who mitigated the sin of the calf, this passage suggests that Arama and his audience in late fifteenth-century Spain were prudishly scandalized but not prudishly unfamiliar with the venerable connection between sexual activity and crafted artifacts.

Don Isaac Abravanel (1437–1508) was another major figure in late fifteenth-century Spanish Jewry who answered the challenge of the golden calf.[23] Conscientiously and scholastically sifting through the diverse opinions of his predecessors, Abravanel chided the traditionalists who mistakenly insisted upon defining the act as "absolute idolatry." Oblivious to subtle Kabbalistic allusions, Abravanel also disagreed with Nahmanides, who had suggested unreasonably that the calf was a nonidolatrous, apotropaic instrument designed to protect the Israelites from demonic dangers lurking in the desert.[24] Abravanel declared that he found a satisfying solution to the problem of the calf in an eclectic combination of views advanced by Abraham ibn Ezra, Judah Halevi, and Levi ben Gershom. From the fact that Aaron was not included among the three thousand non-Israelites (the "mixed multitude") who were punished for their sin, Abravanel deduced that neither Aaron nor the true Israelites had committed idolatry. He also deduced that the calf itself was not intrinsically sinful. It never "occurred to [the Israelites] that the calf was the Cause of Causes, may It be blessed, the Creator of heaven and earth." The calf was intended to be a "talisman," an inert and transportable device, modeled after Egyptian prototypes, "possessing supernal powers for predicting the future, by means of which miracles and signs could be performed, and replacing Moses to lead and inform them of coming events." Abravanel explained that the Israelites insisted on a fabricated piece of subservient technology to replace Moses because they were weary of being led by a mortal being with a mind of his own. Like Moses, another mortal was liable to wander off, abandoning them to their fate. The Israelites preferred the dependability of impersonal artifacts to the vagaries of personal presence, and many of them wrongly believed that Moses himself had used such a talisman in accomplishing his many deeds.

Abravanel left open the question of who selected the figure of a bull: Aware of the bull's astrological significance and certain that Moses had exploited its powers to vanquish the Egyptian Aries, the people might have specified the sign of Taurus. Alternatively, the people may have been ignorant of astrology and the exact source of Mosaic power. They therefore would have relied upon Aaron's judgment and artistic skill in fashioning the appropriate image. Regardless of who initiated the idea of the bull, according to Abravanel, Aaron is to be credited with "stalling [the people] until Moses's return" and for using every means at his disposal "to show the people their foolishness, since the talisman they sought was ineffective [hevel] and without spirit in its midst." Aaron was also to be credited with possessing equal measures of practical wisdom regarding social psychology and practical skill regarding artistic production. Aaron knew how to design an image, collect appropriate raw materials, and melt gold. He also knew how to handle a sculptor's tools. Painstakingly and accurately, he used the tools to shape the calf.[25]

Aaron's golden calf was not the only statue that intrigued Don Isaac Abravanel. Reading the tale of Jereboam's calves in the light of commentaries written by his predecessors, Abravanel brought to bear on Scripture the diplomatic experience that made him intimately familiar with court politics. He was fully aware of royal tastes in monumental art. He concluded that his predecessors had misjudged Jereboam's intentions and actions. According to Abravanel, Jereboam's "calves were not idolatrous.

They were not meant for divine worship." Jereboam needed to consolidate his schismatic northern kingdom of Israel. One of his royal strategies was to provide the population with an acceptable substitute for Solomon's Temple in Jerusalem. Jereboam therefore constructed the two calves as competitors imitating the two pillars placed at the entry to the Temple in Jerusalem. The two pillars were intended to represent Solomon and his father, King David. Seeking a "heraldic icon [*zekher ve-siman*] for his own dynasty [*malkhuto*]," Jereboam chose the image of the ox. Abravanel remarked that Jereboam's choice of the ox was no allusion to the calf at Sinai. The true iconographic significance of Jereboam's ox was to be found in the explicit reference to oxen in the ancient blessing bestowed by Moses upon Jereboam's tribe, Joseph. To account for Jereboam's decision to render the ox in gold, Abravanel reconstructed the king's thought processes. He observed that "gold signifies the permanence and stability of [Jereboam's] dynasty, as well as the glory of its excellence. [Gold] suggests that the icon of the King of Judah is a bronze pillar, but the icon of the King of Israel is made of pure gold formed in the shape of the best and most useful animal, the ox." It was Jereboam's hope that the people would be duly impressed and their loyalty to his regime assured by the spectacular sight of the golden calves. The people would "travel to see them," for the "masses are more profoundly moved by something sensory [*muhash*] than by something abstractly conceptual [*muskal*]."[26] Abravanel's keen interest in the sensory components of governmentally sponsored monuments and public works also surfaces in his technical discussion of the architecture of Solomon's Temple and palace, a discussion based upon his close study of the Christian commentators and his direct familiarity with building practices and financing in late fifteenth-century Spain, Portugal, and Italy.[27]

II

Abravanel was not the only medieval Jewish commentator to explore the political and sensory dimension of artifacts, and Isaac Arama was not the only one who understood the powerful links between visual artifacts and sexuality. The thirteenth-century author of the *Zohar*, the canonical text of Jewish mysticism, pondered Genesis 12:14–15: "When Abram entered Egypt the Egyptians saw that [Sarai] was very beautiful. When the princes of *Pharaoh* saw her, they praised her to *Pharaoh*. So the woman was taken into *Pharaoh's* house." Our midrashically attuned thirteenth-century author noticed that the word "Pharaoh" appears three times in the passage. He concluded that the verbal repetition denotes three distinct Pharaohs: one was the contemporary of Abram and Sarai, another was the contemporary of Joseph, and the third was the contemporary of Moses. The first Pharoah was so infatuated with Sarai's beauty that he commanded his artisans to paint her portrait on the walls of his bedroom. Unsatisfied with the portrait, he commissioned a wooden effigy of her. "When he got into bed, he took her with him." Subsequent Pharaohs did the same, taking delight in her image and frolicking in its presence. When they got into bed, they took her with them, procuring their lascivious pleasure with that image.[28]

As in chemical reactions, so too with visual images: Some compounds are catalysts that remain unchanged by the processes they trigger, whereas others are reagents that are transformed by the processes they affect. Some paintings and sculptures remain signs or symbols. They merely represent objects or persons and arouse desire in us for them. Others images arouse and become the object of desire itself.[29] Arama's parable of the woman who fashioned male statues in order to copulate with them suggests that medieval Jews understood the power of images to arouse, become, and satisfy desire in women. The *Zohar's* exegesis of Pharaonic behavior suggests that medieval Jews also understood that paintings and sculptures exert similar powers over men. Medieval Jews understood that visual images, in simulating reality, stimulate human behavior. Parallel assumptions regarding the capacity of images to become active reagents underlay the contemporary plausibility of several medieval Jewish interpretations of the golden calf. Classified as a talisman, a dynamic receptacle for astrologically or Kabbalistically defined energy, the calf could reasonably be understood as a potent artifactual surrogate for the personal presence and leadership of Moses. In the diverse frameworks of medieval Jewish thought, statues of men, wooden effigies of beautiful women, and golden calves all belonged to the same ontological category. The images were all received as efficacious living powers, some of them erotic or political, some of them scandalous, some of them not. Regardless of their moral status, images were understood to be powerful.

The notion that images, colors, and shapes can modify behavior helped some commentators make the perplexing episode of Jacob's breeding rods less of a mystery. As reported in Genesis 30:31–43, in order to increase his flocks, assure his wealth, and outsmart his stingy father-in-law and employer, "Jacob took himself moist rods of poplar and almond and plane-tree, and peeled white stripes in them, laying bare the white on the rods. And he stood the rods he had peeled in the troughs . . . opposite the flocks, which went into heat when they came to drink. And the flocks went into heat at the rods and the flocks bore brindled, spotted, and speckled young."[30] Levi ben Gershom explained Jacob's behavior naturalistically, in accordance with the principles of "medical science." Jacob must have known that "the color of offpsring is generally determined by the color of their immediate progenitors and ancestral lineage." Laban, Jacob's father-in-law, had removed from Jacob's flocks all the striped and speckled goats and thus Jacob's wages were restricted to multicolored animals. Realizing that no wages would be forthcoming unless he could induce the flocks to breed speckled offspring, Jacob resorted to artificial means. He peeled strips of bark from fresh branches, creating rods with contrasting bands of white wood and "dark bark." He placed the rods where the goats gathered to breed. "When they were in heat and mated, the he-goats and she-goats gazed upon the rods, and the various colors [of the rods] affected their biological constitution [*mezeg*] so that the resulting traits [*tev'a*] of their offspring appeared as if they had derived from [actually] striped and speckled flocks, for colors affect the bodily humors. After all, do you not observe that gazing upon red things arouses the blood and fortifies it and that gazing upon dark things arouses black bile and fortifies it?"[31] Other scholars took a less physiological approach to the problem, preferring instead to stress psychological explanations that acknowledged the mediating affects of imagination. Rabbi Ovadiah Sforno (ca. 1470–1550), Italian commentator and philosopher, explained that "the image [of the speckled rods] would be impressed on imagination at the moment of conception, for images formed in the imaginative power at the moment of conception usually result in offspring resembling that same image."[32]

The motifs relating to the power of images—Jacob's flocks, sexual desire, inherited traits, psychological or physiological explanations—coalesced in a late medieval text composed by Shi'mon ben Zemah Duran (1366–1444), a physician, philosopher, and commentator who left Spain after the massacres of 1391 and migrated to Algiers, where he was appointed chief rabbi in 1408.[33] After reviewing the strictly anatomical and physiological reasons for why offspring do not always physically resemble their progenitors, Rabbi Shim'on turned his attention to the considerations of psychology and the legitimate, popular use of visual images in daily life.

> It has to do with the agency of imagination, for at the moment the fetus comes into being, it assumes the shape imagined by the male or the female. . . . Accordingly, when the child resembles the father, it is because the female desires the male more than the male the female. But when the child resembles the mother, the opposite is true. And when the child resembles them both equally, it is because their desire for one another is equal. As for the case of a child resembling an individual other than them, it has to do with what they were imagining while engaged in intercourse. This is the reason why the sages of Israel sanctify themselves at the time of intercourse so that they might not think about other women. Rabbi Yohanan made it a practice to stand at the gates of the ritual bath-house so that on their way out women would experience a powerful desire

for male offspring during their intimacies. They would form an efficacious mental image, with the result that their offspring would be as handsome as [Rabbi Yohanan]. They were also careful, after their ritual immersion, to avoid encountering an unpleasant form. Moreover, let us not neglect the episode of the colored rods fashioned by Jacob . . . from which episode Rabbi Aqiva deduced the answer he gave to the Arab King who asked: "I am dark and my wife is dark, but my children are white?" Rabbi Aqiva inquired about the colors of the walls in his home. [The King] replied: "They are white." Similarly, the Romans used to gaze upon beautiful pictures while engaged in sexual intercourse.[34]

Similar beliefs regarding the affective power of external images entering the mind's eye were widespread in late medieval Jewish thought and practice. The therapeutic power of paintings and sculptures was widely recognized. In late fourteenth-century Spain, for example, Rabbi Solomon ibn Adret permitted the manufacture and use of "lion-shaped metallic figurines" to cure disease. He defended the practice on the basis of precedents established by Moses Nahmanides and on a thorough review of Talmudic sources allowing the use of magical amulets and talismans for medicinal purposes.[35] Throughout the Middle Ages, philosophic and scientific investigation of the means by which images exert their power constituted a central topic in numerous treatises and commentaries devoted to Aristotle's *De Anima* and *Parva Naturalia*.[36] Recognition of the power of images also surfaced in compendia of anti-Christian polemics. Challenged to account for the difference in physical appearance between "dark" Jews and "fair-skinned" Gentiles, the Jewish disputant invoked differences in cultural practice. With scorn, he observed "that Gentiles are incontinent and have sexual relations during the day, at a time when they see the faces on attractive pictures; therefore they give birth to children who resemble those pictures, as it is written, "And the sheep conceived when they came to drink before [Jacob's] rods."[37]

Beliefs honoring the power of visual images were also prominent in Judah Halevi's regimen for achieving Jewish perfection. He declared that "the pious man . . . commands imagination to produce, with the assistance of memory, the most splendid pictures possible, in order to resemble the divine things sought after, for example, the scene at Sinai, the scene of Abraham and Isaac at Mount Moriah, the Tabernacle of Moses, the Temple service, the presence of God's glory in the sanctuary, and all the many other [similar images]."[38] Halevi's regimen would not be incompatible with the habit of looking at sculptures, illuminated manuscripts, portraits, and decorated monuments. Among premodern Jews, as among practioners of Ignatius of Loyola's "spiritual exercises," Halevi's regimen may even have encouraged and rationalized the production and edifying enjoyment of such beneficial images.[39]

Medieval Jews were fully aware that visual images exude power. In theological debates with Christians, Jewish polemicists argued the scriptural warrants and devotional significance of that power. In treatises and commentaries, philosophers and Kabbalists investigated the pragmatic benefits, actual dangers, and theoretical implications of that power. Medieval Jews also regulated that power. Many of the polemicists, philosophers, and Kabbalists were also Talmudists, legal authorities, and communal rabbis.[40] The leading examples include Maimonides, Moses Nahmanides, Solomon ibn Adret, and Shi'mon ben Zemah Duran. It was their legislative and judicial responsibility not only to understand but to govern the production and use of images. Their rulings are contained in scores of late medieval responsa and Talmudic commentaries whose conclusions were summarized in authoritative law codes. In turn, the codes prompted subsequent rounds of renewed halakhic inquiry, clarification, and decision.[41]

The medieval halakhic authorities were not iconoclasts.[42] Talmudists and codifiers were obliged to forbid idolatry, not visual art. Prizing the salutary power of visual images and sharing the premodern consensus that affirmed the restrictive interpretation of the Second Commandment, the halakhic authorities kept the scales of rabbinic law heavily weighted in favor of the production and utilization of a vast array of paintings, sculptures, decorations, and architectural forms.[43] The halakhic authorities tended to be slightly more cautious with engravings and sculptures representing things actually existing in nature than they were with flat representations of anything at all. Boaz Cohen, a modern legal expert, remarked that "the formulation of the law concerning visual representations by the three greatest Jewish codifiers, Maimonides, R[abbi] Jacob ben Asher, and R[abbi] Joseph Caro," generally adopts the late Talmudic, permissive consensus. The consensus was permissive because it (1) "took no exception to the introduction of mosaics in the synagogues . . . (2) permitted sculpture of all living things except that of the combination of the four beings of the heavenly chariot [ox, man, lion, and eagle] . . . [and] (3) forbade the use of a signet ring with a human figure on it in relief, even if made by a Gentile, lest suspicion arise that the the Jew made it himself." Cohen also observed that "French-Jewish scholars of the twelfth century" were even more lenient. They "permitted statuary of the incomplete human figure."[44] Even a cursory review of the halakhic literature reveals that medieval rabbinic opposition to images was sporadic and restricted to questions involving public worship. There were occasional differences of opinion among the rabbis regarding the propriety of a particular representational painting, tapestry, or sculpture whose architectural setting was the synagogue.[45] In other spatial settings, the same images were fundamentally unproblematic.

The permissive scope of medieval rabbinic legislation is succinctly captured in several rulings codified by Rabbi Joseph Caro in the still authoritative sixteenth-century *Shulhan 'Arukh* (The prepared table).[46] To paraphrase Rabbi Joseph's terse formulations: The law "forbids the making of decorative images [*tzurot*]" representing either angels or the human figure, as long as those images are made "in relief." It permits the making of images representing angels or the human figure as long as the images are "intaglio, woven into a garment, for example, or painted with pigments on walls." It "forbids the making of images representing the sun, moon, or stars, whether those images are in relief or intaglio." It nevertheless permits images representing the sun, moon, or stars, "either in relief or intaglio, if they serve instructional or forensic purposes." It permits images, both in relief and intaglio, representing "domestic stock, beasts, birds, and fish, as well as images of trees, grasses, and similar things." It permits images representing the human figure as long as the figure is incomplete. It specifically permits human "busts and torsos."

No one familiar with these legal provisions can deduce that medieval Jewish society favored aniconism, harbored iconoclastic beliefs, or discouraged its members from becoming artists. Far from condemning the artists and their craft, medieval Jewish law protected them by generously and precisely defining the realm of permissible production. In protecting the artists and their craft, the law concurred with generations of pilgrims, polemicists, biblical commentators, philosophers, and mystics who acknowledged the power of images and found them worthy of critical attention. At no time and in no corner of medieval Jewish society were Jewish eyes otiose or the visual arts taboo.

Notes

Introduction

1. Freedberg, *Power of Images*, 54.
2. Carmilly-Weinberger, *Fear of Art*, 4.
3. Chagall, *Marc Chagall and the Jewish Theater*, 176. The speaker was Marc Chagall, whose original Yiddish text was edited by Benjamin Harshav and translated by Benjamin and Barbara Harshav.
4. Brenner, *Renaissance of Jewish Culture*, 153.
5. Breslin, *Mark Rothko*, 57.
6. Ong, *Presence of the Word*, 3. First published in 1967, Ong's book originated as the renowned Terry Lectures in 1964. See also Auerbach, "Odysseus's Scar," 3–23.
7. Wolfson, *Through a Speculum That Shines*, 13.
8. Gay, "Social History of Ideas," 120. Gay's admonition and programmatic manifesto deserve to be quoted in full: "All ideas have this much in common: all of them are, in Freud's word, overdetermined; all of them, we might say, have more reasons for existing than they need. And all coexist in several realms at once: all are at least touched by the unconscious, with its crude distortions and insatiable need for gratification; by the stylistic tradition of which it is an expression or against which it is in rebellion; by social, economic, political pressures which lend it its particular urgency and its unique shape. The relative weight of these factors will differ from time to time and place to place, but they are all present, and it is to them that the social historian of ideas must address himself—or leave his assignment unfinished."
9. Richard I. Cohen, *Jewish Icons*, 3.
10. By "critical theory," I mean the line of thought anchored in Marx's historicist dictum, "the forming [*Bildung*] of the five senses is a labor [*Arbeit*] of the entire history of the world down to the present," and elaborated by Max Horkheimer: "A conception is needed which overcomes the onesidedness that necessarily arises when limited intellectual processes are detached from their matrix in the total activity of society. . . . The facts which our senses present to us are socially preformed in two ways: through the historical character of the object perceived and through the historical character of the perceiving organ. Both are not simply natural; they are shaped by human activity, and yet the individual perceives himself as receptive and passive in the act of perception. . . . Human production also always has an element of planning to it. . . . The perceived fact is therefore co-determined by human ideas and concepts, even before its conscious theoretical elaboration by the knowing individual. . . . In this context the proposition that tools are prolongations of human organs can be inverted to state that organs are the prolongations of the tools. In the higher stages of civilization conscious human action uncon-

sciously determines not only the subjective side of perception but in larger degree the object as well." For the citation, see Horkheimer, *Critical Theory*, 199–201. For the passage in Marx, see *Karl Marx Friedrich Engels Gesamtausgabe (MEGA)*, 1: 2, 270, and the translation, *Economic and Philosophic Manuscripts of 1844 by Karl Marx*, 141. For the connection between Marx and Horkheimer, see the editor's comments in Levin, *Sites of Vision*, 1.

11. For "ways of seeing," I relied upon Joseph Alsop, *Rare Art Traditions*, 4–7, passim. By synchronic and diachronic, I follow Carl E. Schorske, who described a "field where two lines intersect. One line is vertical, or diachronic, by which [the historian] establishes the relation of a text or system of thought to previous expressions in the same branch of cultural activity (painting, politics, etc.). The other is horizontal, or synchronic; by it [the historian] assesses the relation of the content of the intellectual object to what is appearing in other branches or aspects of a culture at the same time. The diachronic thread is the warp, the synchronic one is the woof in the fabric of intellectual history." Schorske, *Fin-De-Siècle Vienna*, xxi–xxii.

12. Guttmann, *Philosophies of Judaism*, 3.

13. Danto, *Transfiguration of the Commonplace*, 54.

14. For the notion of "scopic regime," see Jay, "Scopic Regimes of Modernity," 1–27.

15. Let one example suffice: "Pagans project their consciousness of God into a visible image or associate Him with a phenomenon of nature, with a thing in space. In the Ten Commandments, the Creator of the universe identifies Himself by an event in history, by an event in time, the liberation of the people from Egypt, and proclaims, 'Thou shalt not make unto thee any graven image or any likeness of any thing that is in the heaven above, or that is in the earth, or that is in the water under the earth.' " Heschel, "Epilogue," in *The Earth Is the Lord's*, 95. Heschel's *The Sabbath* was originally published separately in 1951.

16. The shopworn strains of "Hebraism vs. Hellenism" are widespread and persistent. In literary criticism, see, for example, Auerbach, *Mimesis*, 3–23. In theologically steeped biblical studies, see, for example, Boman, *Hebrew Thought Compared with Greek*. In political science, see, for example, Kohn, *Idea of Nationalism*, 27–34. In philosophy, see, for example, Barrett, *Irrational Man*, 69–91. For a wide-ranging investigation of the ubiquitous Hebraic versus Hellenic trope in modern Jewish intellectual history, see Shavit, *Athens in Jerusalem*. Shavit's exclamation is an incontrovertible understatement: "The number of texts in which I have found an explicit or implict reference to the antimony between the visual culture and the auditory culture is astonishing" (p. 261).

17. For a persuasive anthropological discussion, see Goody, *Domestication of the Savage Mind*.

18. On the intermingling of sensation, I was convinced by John Dewey, who argued that "nothing is perceived except when different senses work in relation with one another . . . and then new modes of motor responses are incited which in turn stir up new sensory activities. Unless these various sensory-motor energies are coordinated with one another there is no perceived scene or object. But equally there is none when—by a condition impossible to fulfill in fact—a single sense alone is operative. If the eye is the organ primarily active, then the color quality is

affected by qualities of other senses overtly active in earlier experiences." Dewey, *Art as Experience*, 175.

19. Plato, *Republic* 1. 327b–328c. For the requirement of "keen eyesight," see 2.368d.

20. Plato, *Republic*, 10. 601c–605c.

21. Moses Maimonides, *Guide of the Perplexed*, 7. Hereinafter *Guide*

22. For the terms of the dispute, see Reines, *Maimonides and Abrabanel.*

23. For just one of the recent monographic attempts to describe and interpret the work of the medieval Jewish artisans, with abundant references to current scholarship, see Epstein, *Dreams of Subversion*. For recent encylopedic coverage of the artisans and artifacts, see Sed-Rajna, *Jewish Art.*

24. For a pungent and picquant summary of this argument, see Staniszewski, *Believing Is Seeing*. Marxist foundations for the argument were laid by Benjamin, "Work of Art in the Age of Mechanical Reproduction," 217–252.

25. For a persuasive argument distinguishing modern "art" from medieval images, see Belting, *Likeness and Presence*, xxi–xxii.

26. For a discussion of Gombrich's critique of the "innocent eye" and the related notion of "essential copy," see Bryson, *Vision and Painting*, 1–35; and Mitchell, *Iconology*, 37–38, 118–119.

27. Husik, *History of Mediaeval Jewish Philosophy*, xi–xii.

28. See Novick, *That Noble Dream.*

29. See Himmelfarb, "Postmodernist History," in *On Looking into the Abyss*, 131–135. For a fictional account of the impossibility of historiographical "objectivity," see Borges, "Pierre Menard, Author of the *Quixote*," in *Labyrinths*, 36–44. For a philosopher's account of subjective mischief in all epistemologies, see Goodman, *Ways of Worldmaking*, 1–22.

30. Husik, *History of Medieval Jewish Philosophy*, xiii.

31. Nochlin, "Why Have There Been No Great Women Artists?" 1–39; Wallace, "Afterword: 'Why Are There No Great Black Artists?' " 333–346. See also bell hooks, *Black Looks*, and idem, *Art on My Mind*. For a thoughtful review of the festering issues, see Powell, *Black Art and Culture*, 7–40.

32. Her private comments entered the public domain: Wharton, *Refiguring the Post Classical City.*

33. Richard I. Cohen, *Jewish Icons*, 263 n. 25.

Chapter One

1. For further discussion and a slightly different translation, see Amishai-Maisels, "Chagall and the Jewish Revival," 71–100. Reading Chagall's statement, Arthur A. Cohen concluded that he intended "a weak affirmation of [Jewish art's] possibility." See Arthur A. Cohen, "From Eastern Europe to Paris and Beyond," 62. For further discussion regarding the Eastern European matrix of Chagall's attitudes, see Kampf, *Jewish Experience*, passim.

2. Goodenough, *Jewish Symbols in the Greco-Roman Period*, 1: 27–28.

3. See Exodus 20:3–6 and its parallel in Deuteronomy 5:7–10. For additional legislation, see Deuteronomy 4:9–18. For the difference between Jewish and Roman Catholic–Lutheran traditions in numbering the anti-idolatry command-

ment, see Sarna, *JPS Torah Commentary: Exodus*, 108. For an informative discussion of the tension in biblical literature between "seeing" and "hearing" God, see Weinfeld, *Deuteronomy* 38, 198–208.

4. See, for example, Rosenberg, "Is There a Jewish Art?" *Commentary* 42 (1966): 58–59. Referring to "silver menorahs and drinking goblets, embroidered Torah coverings, [and] word carvings," Rosenberg concluded "that this priestly work is not art in the sense in which the word is used in the 20th century." For the standard complaint against critics who "ignore the existence of Jewish ritualistic art," see Kayser, "Defining Jewish Art," 457. Kayser was director of the Jewish Museum in New York City. For analysis of the cultural politics involved in ascribing aesthetic value to diverse artifacts, see Clifford, *Predicament of Culture*, 220–230. This issue is more fully explored in chapter 2 of the present volume.

5. *Jewish Encyclopedia*, 2: 142.

6. Fortescu, "Images," in *Catholic Encyclopedia*, 7: 664–665.

7. For Kohler's leadership at the 1885 conference in Pittsburgh, see Meyer, *Response to Modernity*, 267–270. For the text of the declaration, see p. 388: "We consider ourselves no longer a nation, but a religious community, and therefore, expect neither a return to Palestine, nor a sacrificial worship under the sons of Aaron, nor the restoration of any of the laws concerning the Jewish state."

8. For the notion of a causal nexus between national groups and the arts, see Haskell, *History and Its Images*, 217–235; and Williams, *Culture and Society*, 130–158 ("Art and Society: A. W. Pugin, John Ruskin, William Morris"), 265–285 ("Marxism and Culture").

9. Focusing on racism and anti-Semitism, I follow the lead of Baron, *Jewish Community*, 2: 137; and Rosenberg, "Is There a Jewish Art?" 58. Marshall G. S. Hodgson identified similar ideological motives in scholarship regarding the visual arts in Islam; see *Venture of Islam*, 2: 503 n. 3. To Hodgson's list of "silly . . . Western racialism," one may add Schwarz, *Juden in der Kunst*, 199. Schwarz claimed that the Jewish spirit tends to the abstract in intellectual matters but to color rather than sculpture in the visual arts. He believed that fascination with color and discomfort with sculpture are typical of all "Orientals."

10. As I seek to prove in chapter 3, the nineteenth-century Germanophone intellectuals did more than articulate the doctrine of Jewish aniconism. They invented and perfected it.

11. For the panorama of Zionism's diversity, see Hertzberg, *Zionist Idea*.

12. Kant, *Critique of Judgment*, trans. Werner S. Pluhar, 135.

13. Hegel, *Aesthetics*, 1: 70. For Hegel's earlier speculations, see "Spirit of Christianity," 182–205. For discussion of these earlier speculations, see Olin, "C[lement] Hardesh [Greenberg] and Company," 43. For additional discussion of Hegel's complex evaluation of Judaism, see Yovel, *Dark Riddle*, 1–101.

14. Kant, *Religion within the Limits of Reason Alone*, 116–118. For discussion, see Rose, *German Question*, 91–97.

15. For the German philosophic landscape in which Jewish intellectuals thoroughly ethicized Judaism, see Guttmann, *Philosophies of Judaism*, 327–451; Rotenstreich, *Jewish Philosophy in Modern Times*, 1–218; and Schweid, *History of Jewish Thought*, 122–151, 216–272; 281–328. For the "gist of Kant's and Hegel's analy-

sis of Judaism" with which the German Jewish intellectuals had to contend, see Rotenstreich, *Jews and German Philosophy*, 3–7.

16. Formstecher, *Religion des Geistes*, 68.

17. Ibid., 71

18. Ibid., 69

19. Ibid., 68–69.

20. *Heine*, "Geständnisse," 12: 70–71. 12: 70–71. The English translation is taken, with some minor modifications, from Prawer, *Heine's Jewish Comedy*, 620–621. For biographical details and additional literary studies of Heine's various works, see Sammons, *Heinrich Heine*. For the topos of Moses in modern German Jewish thought, see Goldstein, *Reinscribing Moses*, esp. 26–36.

21. For the original text, see Hermann Cohen, *Religion der Vernunft*. It was first published in 1919. For an English translation, see Hermann Cohen, *Religion of Reason*. For philosophic discussion, see the histories of Julius Guttman, Nathan Rotenstreich, Eliezer Schweid, and the comments of Hans Liebeschütz, "Hermann Cohen," 3–33. See also Gay, "Encounter with Modernism," esp. 114–121. For Cohen's familiarity and sympathy with Heine, see his 1867 essay "Heinrich Heine und das Judentum," 2: 2–44. Other references to Heine are scattered throughout Cohen's writings, especially in connection with Spinoza and the problems of pantheism and the affinity between German and Jewish spiritual outlooks. For the persistent influence of Spinoza, see Yovel, *Spinoza and Other Heretics*.

22. For an account of the debate, see Meyer, *Response to Modernity*, 10–224.

23. Cohen, *Religion der Vernunft*, 427–429; *Religion of Reason*, 368–369.

24. Cohen, *Religion der Vernunft*, 484–486; *Religion of Reason*, 417–419.

25. Cohen, *Religion der Vernunft*, 43–44; *Religion of Reason*, 37.

26. Cohen, *Religion der Vernunft*, 63; *Religion of Reason*, 54.

27. Cohen, *Religion der Vernunft*, 62; *Religion of Reason*, 53.

28. Cohen, *Religion der Vernunft*, 64; *Religion of Reason*, 55.

29. For illustrations and analysis, see Hammer-Schenk, *Synagogen in Deutschland*; *Synagogen in Berlin*; Hammer-Schenk, "Die Architektur der Synagogue," 157–286; and Krinsky, *Synagogues of Europe*. I am grateful to my colleague Professor Annabel J. Wharton for these references.

30. Cohen, *Religion der Vernunft*, 66; *Religion of Reason*, 57. For an art historian who placed Cohen's approval of religious architecture at the heart of a systematic study of Jewish art, see Rosenau, *Short History of Jewish Art*.

31. Cohen, *Religion der Vernunft*, 447; *Religion of Reason*, 384.

32. For Cohen's inconclusive remarks regarding visual representations of the human being, see *Religion der Vernunft*, 66–67; *Religion of Reason*, 57–58. The implication seems to be that for Cohen, visual depictions of the human are as aversive to the spirit of Judaism's ethical monotheism as are the visual images of God.

33. For Heine's profound appreciation of biblical literature, see Prawer, *Heine's Jewish Comedy*, esp. 609–623. For the persistence and cultural significance of the trope "portable homeland," see Ezrahi, "Our Homeland, the Text," 463–497.

34. Rosenzweig, *Star of Redemption*, 245–246. The argument of behalf of the superiority of poetry among the arts is intensified on pages 370–371: "Thus it

remained for the poetic arts to emerge as the arts of the whole man over and beyond the fine arts and music." The translation is based on the second edition, published in 1930. Rosenzweig completed the book in 1919. For his conceptual relationship to Hermann Cohen, see Derrida, "Interpretation at War," 39–95.

35. Cohen, *Religion der Vernunft*, 67; *Religion of Reason*, 58.

36. Kant, *Critique of Judgment*, 196–198.

37. Hegel, *Aesthetics*, 1: 88–90.

38. Cited in Schelling, *Philosophy of Art*, 291. For the Kantian dilemmas facing modern poets in their ambivalent reliance on visuality, see Hartman, *Unmediated Vision*.

39. Steinheim, *Die Offenbarung*, 2: 428–429. For discussion, see the histories of Guttmann, Rotenstreich, and Schweid. See also Shear-Yashuv, *Theology of Salomon Ludwig Steinheim*, 56; and Shear-Yashuv, ed., and *Salomon Ludwig Steinheim*.

40. Steinheim, *Offenbarung*, 2: 433. For a discussion of this distinction and its relevance to Buber, Bergson, Proust, and Freud, see Kern, *Culture of Time and Space*, 50–51. The afterlife of Steinheim's distinction can be traced in the widely read and deeply flawed, tendentious monograph by Thorlief Boman, *Das hebräische Denken*. Boman's arguments loom large in Handelman, *Slayers of Moses*, 33–37. I discuss Handelman's synthesis of these older arguments and postmodernism in chapter 2.

41. *Offenbarung*, 2: 433.

42. Ibid., 2: 434.

43. Ibid., 2: 436.

44. Ibid., 2: 445.

45. Ibid., 2: 446.

46. See Graetz, *Structure of Jewish History*, 68–69. This passage was cited and its point developed, uncritically, by Faur, *Golden Doves with Silver Dots*, 29–49. Elliot R. Wolfson too seems to agree with Graetz. Wolfson assures his readers that "there can be no doubt that the view that became normative in the history of Judaism is one that favored auditory over visual images," and he uses ideas developed by Derrida to validate "the ancient preference reflected in the Deuteronomic author [that] it is more appropriate to speak of a voice of God rather than a visible form." It is against the background of this "normative" aniconism and funicular preference for the auditory that Wolfson's researches in the phenomenology of Jewish mysticism yield such stunning and corrective results. See Wolfson, *Through a Speculum That Shines*, 13–16. I elaborate upon these themes in chapter 2.

47. Graetz, *Structure of Jewish History*, 174–183.

48. See Arnold, *Culture and Anarchy*, 163–175 and passim. For Arnold's debt to Heine, see Super's comments on pages 435–436.

49. *Structure of Jewish History*, 301. The essay was originally published in two installments in *Jewish Quarterly Review*: 1 (1889): 4–13 and 2 (1890): 257–269. The passage cited is found on page 269.

50. *Structure of Jewish History*, 233. For the biography, work, and critical reception of Hans Makart (1840–1884), the Austrian artist whose paintings Graetz reviled, see Gallwitz, ed., *Makart*, and Heinzl, *Hans Makart*.

51. *Structure of Jewish History*, 236.

52. See Prawer, *Heine's Jewish Comedy*, 621. For further discussion of Heine's distinction between the "Greek" and the "Hebraic," see Lambropoulos, *Rise of Eurocentrism*, 175–176. For the echoes of Heine in Matthew Arnold's famous distinction between "Hebraism and Hellenism," see Arnold, *Culture and Anarchy*, 86–96. Arnold cited Heine explicitly on page 87. For nineteenth-century racial and ethnic typologies, see Olender, *Languages of Paradise*.

53. For discussion, see Yerushalmi, *Freud's Moses*, and Goldstein, *Reinscribing Moses*, 66–136.

54. Freud, *Moses and Monotheism*, 144–152. In the *Standard Edition of the Complete Psychological Works of Sigmund Freud*, vol. 23, the relevant passages are found on pages 112–119. For the original German text, I consulted Sigmund Freud, *Der Mann Moses und die monotheistische Religion*, 200–210.

55. For the original German text on which my modifications of the English translation are based, I consulted *Das Wesen des Christenthums*, 6: 136–137. For a critical discussion of Feuerbach's proclamations, see Fackenheim, *Encounters between Judaism and Modern Philosophy* 79–169, esp. 134–152. See also Rose, *German Question/Jewish Question*, 253–255; and Traverso, *The Marxists and the Jewish Question*, 18–19.

56. See Kant, *Anthropology from a Pragmatic Point of View*, 101–102. For the German original, see *Kants Gesammelte Schriften*, Konglich Preussischen Akademie der Wissenschaften 7: 205–206, corresponding to book 1, section 46 of the *Anthropologie in pragmatischer Hinsicht*.

57. Cited in *The Jew in the Modern World*, ed. Mendes-Flohr and Reinharz, 324–327, from the translation prepared by Helen Lederer. For the German original, see *Karl Marx / Friedrich Engels Gesamtausgabe*, ed. Dlubek, 141–169. The passages cited are found on pages 164 (30–33); 166 (35–36); 169 (9–16). For discussion, see Rose, *German Question / Jewish Question*, 296–305.

58. For Wagner's niche in the history of modern anti-Semitism, see Jacob Katz, *From Prejudice to Destruction*, 184–194.

59. *Richard Wagner Gesammelte Schriften und Dichtungen*, 3: 144–145. For the standard English translation, see Ellis, trans., *Richard Wagner's Prose Works*, 1: 177, 179.

60. Wagner, "*Das Judenthum in der Musik*," 72–73 (facsimile reproduction of the original 1888 edition published in Leipzig). For discussion and bibliographic references to the immense literature surrounding this essay and Wagner's anti-Semitism, see Katz, *The Darker Side of Genius*; and Rose, *Wagner*, esp. 78–88. For an alternate, apologetic view that did not profit from Jacob Katz's discussion and overlooks the racist language and revolutionary politics stressed by Rose, see Rather, *Reading Wagner*, 114–178.

61. See Richard I. Cohen, "An Introductory Essay"; and Berkowitz, "Art in Zionist Popular Culture," 3–42; Richard I. Cohen, "Self-Image through Objects," 203–242; and Gutmann, "Is There a Jewish Art?" 1–19. For the other defensive reactions of Germanophone Jews, see the discussions in Reinharz, ed., *Living with Antisemitism*, 3–208. See also Meyer, *Origins of the Modern Jew*; and Sorkin, *Transformation of German Jewry*.

62. For an overview of Buber's struggle against anti-Semitism, see Mendes-Flohr, "Buber and the Metaphysicians of Contempt," 133–164.

63. See Buber, ed., *Juedischer Kuenstler*, 1–6.

64. In a monograph written in 1946, Buber modified his opinion regarding the total absence of visual art in biblical Israel. See his *Moses*, 115–118, 125–127. "The fight against [images of God] is not a fight against art, which would certainly contrast with the report of Moses' initiative in carving the images of the cherubim; it is a fight to subdue the revolt of fantasy against faith." (p. 127). For Buber's earlier denials of Jewish art at the Fifth Zionist Congress in Basel in 1901 and in an article published in 1902, see Kampf, *Jewish Experience*, 15, 203.

65. For discussion of Buber's dialogic religious existentialism, see Stahmer, "*Speak That I May See Thee*," 183–215. For a critique of Buber's typological distinction between Hebraic ears and Hellenic eyes, see Lambropoulos, *Rise of Eurocentrism*, 304–311.

66. For the persistence of these antirabbinic themes in Buber's thought, see the so-called early addresses (1909–1918) collected in Glatzer, ed., *On Judaism*, 3–107. For Buber's fascination with Hasidism, see Mendes-Flohr, "*Fin-de-Siècle* Orientalism," 96–139. For a critique of Buber's rendition of Hasidism, see Scholem, "Martin Buber's Interpretation of Hasidism," 228–250.

67. For a scathing parody of racist stereotypes regarding Jewish bodies and Jewish art, see Harold Rosenberg, "Is There a Jewish Art?" 57–58. "And if there is such a thing as looking like a Jew, does it not follow that the art Jews produce must also have a look of its own—that this art must look like Jewish art? In that case, there is a Jewish style—for in art the look is the thing." Rosenberg, of course, denied that there was a distinctive style or "look" to the art produced by Jews.

68. Herlitz and Kirschner, 3: 934–938.

69. See the comments of Susan L. Braunstein in "Sigmund Freud's Jewish Heritage," 13.

70. For the modern controversy regarding the relation of Jewish culture to its host societies, see Ahad Ha-'Am (Asher Ginzberg), "Imitation and Assimilation," 107–138. For the original Hebrew, see Ahad Ha-'Am, *'Al Parashat Derakhim*, 1: 162–173. See also Gerson D. Cohen, "The Blessing of Assimilation in Jewish History."

71. For the complexities of racism, see the useful collection of essays edited by David Theo Goldberg, *Anatomy of Racism*. For specific applications to the Jews, see Gilman, "The Jewish Body"; and Geller, "(G)nos(e)ology, 223–282. See also Gilman, *The Jew's Body*.

72. Baur, Fischer, and Lenz, *Human Heredity*, 246, 264, 272, 294, 336, 351, 354, 358, 402, 404, 418, 423–424, 437, 439, 446, 454 (hysteria), and 644ff. for the behavioral implications, including Jewish aptitude for music, shrewd commercial instincts, poor visual skills, and their incapacity for the visual arts. Lenz is the author of all the cited passages.

73. For the politics of cultural anthropology, see, for example, Asad, *Genealogies of Religion*; and Goody, *Domestication of the Savage Mind*, esp. 146–162.

74. For an exploration of anti-Semitism and its ambiguities in the perspective of art history, see Nochlin, "Starting with the Self," 7–19.

75. Sombart, *Die Juden und das Wirtschaftsleben*, 242–245. For the English translation, see Sombert, *Jews and Modern Capitalism*, 205–209.

76. In a frequently cited study of Judaism's positive attitude toward visual art, J. B. Frey ruminated on the claims that Jews prompted the destruction of Christian images by both iconoclast emperors and Muslims. Frey concluded that the Jews had indeed lapsed into iconoclasm. He blamed their anti-Christian motives. Invoking Tertullian, Frey emphatically agreed that "the Jewish synagogues are the source of persecutions [*Synagogue Iudaeorum fontes persecutionnum*]." See Frey, "La Question des images," 265–300. For the historical implausibility of effective Jewish influence on the iconclastic emperors, see Ladner, "Origin and Significance of the Byzantine Iconoclastic Controversy," 37–47.

77. For the general historical context, see the references in note 1 above; Mendelsohn, *Jews of East Central Europe between the World Wars*; Mendelsohn, *On Modern Jewish Politics*; and the essays by Michael Stanislawski ("The Jews and Russian Culture and Politics"), Susan Tumarkin Goodman ("Alienation and Adaptation of Jewish Artists in Russia"), John E. Bolt ("Jewish Artists and the Russian Silver Age"), and Ziva Amishai-Maisels ("The Jewish Awakening: A Search for National Identity") in Goodman, ed., *Russian Jewish Artists in a Century of Change*. See also the illustrations and essays accompanying *Semyon An-Sky*. For original texts in translation, see *Jew in the Modern World*, 372–448; and Dawidowicz, *Golden Tradition*. For parallel claims regarding distinctive "non-Western conceptions of national identity . . . [that] sprang up . . . in Eastern Europe and Asia" that explain "why lexicographers, philologists and folklorists have played a central role in the early nationalism of Eastern Europe and Asia," see Smith, *National Identity*, 10–11.

78. See Kampf, *Jewish Experience*, 15–47. For the subsequent fate of Jewish art and artists in Russia, see the essays by Alexandra Shatskikh ("Jewish Artists in the Russian Avant-Garde"), Boris Groys ("From Internationalism to Cosmopolitanism"), and Viktor Misiano ("Choosing to Be Jewish") in *Russian Jewish Artists in a Century of Change*.

79. See prefatory comments by Jacob B. Agus in *Abraham Isaac Kook*, xi. See also *Hertzberg*, ed., *The Zionist Idea*, 416–431. For a sketch of the salient lines in the "East European school of mystical theology" to which Rabbi Kook seems to belong, see Green, "New Directions in Jewish Theology in America."

80. For the Hebrew original, see Kook, *Letters*. 1: 203–206. For the English translation that I cite and modify in the following paragraphs, see Feldman, trans., *Rav A. Y. Kook*, 190–198.

81. For a collection of essays exploring the present-day legal and cultural implications of Rabbi Kook's letter, see Cassuto, ed., *Judaism and Art*. In Hebrew.

82. Mann, "Icons and Iconoclasts," 32. I am grateful to Professor Mann for providing me with a copy of the dissertation and for calling my attention to Manne's essays and visual poetics.

83. Manne, "The Jewish Painter, Oppenheim," 39–60. In Hebrew. For critical discussion of Oppenheim himself and a catalogue of the paintings that have so moved so many observers, including Manne, see Elisheva Cohen, *Moritz Oppenheim*.

84. For an overview of the practice and ideology of art as they actually unfolded in the modern state of Israel, see Kampf, *Jewish Experience*, 144–175.

Chapter Two

1. Kaufmann, "Art in the Synagogue," 254–269. Kaufmann also published the article in German in Vienna in 1897 under the title "Zur Geschichte der Kunst in den Synagogen." For Kaufmann's place in the emergence of Jewish art history as an academic discipline, see Joseph Gutmann, "Jewish Art," 193–211; and idem, "Is There a Jewish Art?" 1–5. For more recent scholarship on the Jewish arts in Italy, see Mann, ed., *Gardens and Ghettos.*

2. Solomon, "Art and Judaism," 553–556.

3. For a striking parallel to Solomon's critique of Roman Catholicism and his praise for the moral, intellectual, and cultural achievements wrought by the Protestant Reformation led by Martin Luther, see Heine, *Religion and Philosophy in Germany,* 45–58. See, for example, page 47: "Praise to Luther! Eternal praise to the dear man whom we have to thank for the deliverance of our most precious possessions, and on whose benefits our life still depends."

4. Howarth, "Jewish Art and the Fear of the Image," 142.

5. See Naomi W. Cohen, *Not Free to Desist,* 10, 263–264.

6. Rosenberg, "Is There a Jewish Art?" 57–60.

7. See Berenson, *Aesthetics and History in the Visual Arts,* 162–164. For the genesis of the book, its critical reception, and its place in Berenson's thought, see Samuels, *Bernard Berenson,* 440–441, 464, 498, 503–507.

8. Hartman, "Religious Literacy," 28–29. For the rabbinic legends recounting Abraham's iconoclastic streak, see Ginzberg, *Legends of the Jews,* 1: 195–198, 209–215. For Hartman's sponsorship of rabbinic literature, see Hartman and Budick, eds., *Midrash and Literature.* For another panorama of what rabbinic literature yields to literary studies, see the collection of essays edited by Michael Fishbane, *The Midrashic Imagination.*

9. Ozick, "Previsions of the Demise of the Dancing Dog," 278.

10. Rand, "Torah's Incipient Esthetics," 25 n. 15.

11. For analysis of the cultural politics involved in ascribing aesthetic value to diverse artifacts, see Clifford, *Predicament of Culture,* 220–230.

12. For the history and politics of museums in general, see Bennet, *Birth of the Museum.*

13. The chief of the Department of Medieval Antiquities, Dr. Angela Franco, was kind enough to inform me of plans to correct this deficiency. See Ángela Franco Mata, "Antigüedades Medievales Judías En El Arqueológico Nacional," 103–114.

14. Dimont, *Jews, God, and History,* 49. On pages 83 and 122, Dimont used the murals of Dura-Europos to boast that the Jews "were originators of an art form heretofore thought of as strictly Christian" and that "it was a Jewish touch which created the Byzantine school of painting." Seventy-two pages later, however, as if suffering from amnesia, Dimont reverted to the dogma of Jewish aniconism: "The Jews . . . produced a Golden Age . . . in every area of human endeavor except art, which the Jews did not enter until the Modern Age." In early 1995, the publishers claimed that 1.5 million copies of Dimont's book were in print.

15. Dimont, *The Indestructible Jews,* 49. "It is regrettable that overzealous rabbis, who saw their duty and overdid it, interpreted the Second Commandment to

include not only a ban on making images of God but a ban on all pictorial art. . . . For several centuries before and after Jesus, the Jews circumvented the rabbinic interpretations of the place of art in Jewish life, carrying their paintings, mosaics, and objets d'art not only into their homes but even into their synagogues and cemeteries. But after the destruction of the Temple, with the Diaspora, art as a medium of expression of the Jewish soul died. It was not resurrected until the nineteenth century A.D., when avant-garde intellectual Jews rebelling against the authority of the Talmud, defied the rabbinic bans on art."

16. Janson, *History of Art*, 252.

17. *Gardner's Art through the Ages*, 265.

18. See Kraeling, *The Synagogue*.

19. Ong, *Presence of the Word*, 3. I discussed Graetz and Buber in chapter 1. For additional discussion by Buber, see "Spirit of the Orient and Judaism," 56–62, and "Religion and Philosophy" in Buber, *Eclipse of God*, 40–44. For a compelling critique of Buber's tendentious distinctions between the "Oriental man of pronounced motor faculties" and the "Occidental type . . . whose sensory faculties are greater than his motor" and between "Greek . . . opticizing of thought" and the "religious existence . . . of the hearing man," see Lampropoulos, *Rise of Eurocentrism*, 306–311 and passim.

20. Faur, *Golden Doves with Silver Dots*, 29–30 n. 6. Oddly enough, Faur cites and disregards the counterevidence indicating that the rabbinic tradition was not "offended" by visual experiences and expressions of God's presence. See page 30 n. 7.

21. Habermas, "The German Idealism of the Jewish Philosophers," 21–43. The passages cited appear on pages 21–24. For the German original, see idem, "Der deutsche Idealismus der jüdischen Philosophen," 37–66. For Habermas's close connection to the Frankfurt School and the significance of the passages cited, see Jay, *Dialectical Imagination*, 34 and passim. See also idem, *Downcast Eyes*, 265, where Jay remarked: "Even Marxists like the members of the Frankfurt School appreciated [that] the force of the taboo on images [*Bildverbot*] explicitly derived from the ancient Jewish interdiction but implicitly in accordance with a long standing German inclination."

22. Arendt, *Life of Mind*, 111, 119. "Thinking" appeared in the *New Yorker* 53 (1977): 41–42. For the biographical background, see Young-Bruehl, *Hannah Arendt*, 448–460. For Heidegger's influential notions of visuality, see the nuanced discussion in Jay, *Downcast Eyes*, 265–275. For the essay by Hans Jonas, the close friend to whom Arendt was so deeply indebted, see "Nobility of Sight" in Jonas, *Phenomenon of Life*, 135–156. For the current debate over the cultural contexts and metaphoric implications of visuality, see the useful collection of essays edited by David M. Levin, *Modernity and the Hegemony of Vision*. Levin correctly calls special attention to the important study by Ezrahi, *Descent of Icarus*. Also useful are the essays edited by Hal Foster, *Vision and Visuality*; Bryson, Holly, and Maxey, eds., *Visual Theory*; Jenks, ed.; *Visual Culture*; Brennan and Jay, eds., *Vision in Context*; and Levin, ed., *Sites of Vision*.

23. Handelman, *Slayers of Moses*, 34.

24. Jay, *Downcast Eyes*, 546, 555. See also 23–24 and 33–36. Jay, however, is cautious in affirming the proposition that Judaism is monolithically antiocular;

see page 549. As Jay notes, Derrida (*Truth in Painting*, 134) is to be credited for attending to the echoes of Kant in this celebration of the biblical prohibition against visual images of God; see p. 590. For the source in Levinas cited by Jay, see Hand, ed., *Levinas Reader*, 141 ("Reality and Its Shadow"). For additional discussion of the Greek-Hebrew dichotomy in Levinas, see Robbins, *Prodigal Son/Elder Brother*, 104–132.

25. Baudrillard, *Simulacra and Simulation*, 4–6. For discussion of the "faddish figure of Baudrillard," see Jay, *Downcast Eyes*, 544–545.

26. Breslin, *Mark Rothko*, 57. For a discussion of the "frail" tradition of Jewish art in Eastern Europe and its possible impact on budding Jewish artists in New York's Lower East Side, see Howe, *World of Our Fathers*, 573–585. For a corrective to Howe, see Heyd and Mendelsohn, " 'Jewish' Art? 194–211; and Kampf, *Jewish Experience*, 14–48.

27. Mayer, *Bibliography of Jewish Art*.

28. Baron, *A Social and Religious History of the Jews*, 1: 210–212, 2: 330.

29. Baron, *Jewish Community*, 2: 137–138.

30. Kayser, "Defining Jewish Art," 457.

31. Joseph Gutmann, "The 'Second Commandment' and the Image in Judaism," in Gutmann, *No Graven Images*, 16. The essay originally appeared in *Hebrew Union College Annual* 32 (1961): 161–174.

32. Roth, ed., *Jewish Art*, 30.

33. For a concise survey of historical scholarship that posited Jewish prototypes for Christian art, including the contributions of Joseph Strzygowski, Kurt Weitzman, and Bezalel Narkiss, see Sed-Rajna, *Hebrew Bible in Medieval Illuminated Manuscripts*, 7–8. *Hebrew Bible* appeared simultaneously in French in 1987.

34. Roth, ed., *Jewish Art*, 19, 22.

35. Avi-Yonah, "Jewish Art," 888–900.

36. Kaplan, *Judaism as a Civilization*, 203–204.

37. Patai, *Jewish Mind*, 355–357.

38. Speaking to the World Conference of the Jewish Scientific Institute (YIVO) convened in Vilna, Chagall argued that "the Torah, which gave us the ten Commandments, snuck in an eleventh commandment too: 'Thou shalt not make unto thee any graven image.' Our monotheism was dearly bought—and, because of that, Judaism had to give up observation of nature with our *eyes*, and not just with our soul. On religious grounds, Judaism struggled with ancient idolatry, whose remnants are displayed today in all museums of the world, so that it remained with no share in the treasures of graphic art. We left nothing behind us in the world's museums except for Torah scrolls and the abandoned synagogues that are no longer attended. But we, the new Jews, have revolted against this, we no longer want to recognize such a state of affairs, we want to be be not just the People of the Book, but also a people of art." Quoted in *Marc Chagall and the Jewish Theater*, 176. The original Yiddish text was edited by Benjamin Harshav and translated by Benjamin and Barbara Harshav.

39. Baron, *Jewish Community*, 2: 137–138. Baron credited Krautheimer in 3: 146–147 n. 15.

40. Krautheimer, *Mittelalterliche Synagogen*, 18–20. For an updated Hebrew translation, see Goren, trans., *Batte Keneset Bime Ha-Benayyim*, 3–12. In 1987,

Krautheimer retrospectively remarked that *Mittelalterliche Synagogen* was "not a good book and valuable only because of the catalogue of buildings, most of them demolished during the Third Reich." See his autobiographical sketch "And Gladly Did He Learn and Gladly Teach," 97.

41. Baron, *Jewish Community*, 147.

42. The text of the responsum is readily accessible in all printed editions of the "Vilna" Babylonian Talmud. See the entry "Keruvim" in the *Tosaphot* for *Yoma* 54a–b. It also appears in all editions of Rabbi Meir's Responsa. See, for example, *She'eloth ve-Teshuvot* (Venice, 1515), 14–16. For a complete English translation of the responsum, see Bland "Defending, Enjoying, and Regulating the Visual," in *Judaism in Practice*, ed. Larry Fine (Princeton: Princeton University Press, forthcoming).

43. See Roth, *Jewish Art*, 22, and Joseph Gutmann, *No Graven Images*, xix–xx. Roth described Rabbi Meir as "object[ing]" to but not forbidding the illuminations. Gutmann described Rabbi Meir as "inveigh[ing] against" but not forbidding the illuminations. Jacob Leveen used Rabbi Meir's lenient responsum to suggest that prayerbooks, but not Bibles, were the first medieval Hebrew texts to be illuminated. See Leveen, *Hebrew Bible in Art*, 84–85; and Wischnitzer, "Judaism and Art," 1335.

44. For art "in the European sense [that] was forbidden in the Jewish tradition," see Harshav, "Chagall," in *Marc Chagall and the Jewish Theater*, 15.

45. Laity with strong institutional loyalties and ritual practice also embraced ceremonial art. See, for example, Kanof, *Jewish Ceremonial Art*; and Kanof, idem, *Jewish Symbolic Art*. See also Kanof's introductory remarks to the facsimile edition of the pioneering work of Bernard Picart (1673–1733), *Ceremonies of the Jews*.

46. See Rabbi Finkelstein's remarks in the foreword to Kayser, *Jewish Ceremonial Art*, 6.

47. Spero, "Towards a Torah Esthetic," 53–66.

48. For the 1937 Columbus Platform, which challenged Reform Jews to cultivate the visual arts in ritual, and the 1885 Pittsburgh Platform, which passed over the visual arts in telling aniconic silence, see Mayer, *Response to Modernity*, 387–391.

49. For the history and institutional philosophy of the museum, which boasts one of the world's most extensive collections of ritual objects, see Vivian B. Mann with Emily Bilsky, *The Jewish Museum New York*. Serving a different constituency, the Israel Museum in Jerusalem devotes distinct space to Judaica, Jewish ethnography, Israeli art, and historical archaeology. For an overview, see Lewitt, ed., *The Israel Museum*.

50. Kellner, ed., *Pursuit of the Ideal*, 1.

51. Schwarzschild, "Aesthetics," 1–6.

52. Similar arguments were advanced by other scholars as well. José Faur, for example, argued that Judaism considers "the outer aspect of things [to be] unimportant. Neither Scripture nor the rabbis gave visual descriptions of things or people. . . . The more 'objective' descriptions found in the Song of Songs . . . intend to convey pathos rather than visual sensation, much like impressionist paintings. (Without knowing it, the Pizarro brothers, Modigliani, and Pascin were

projecting a visual modality peculiar to their own tradition.)" See Faur, *Golden Doves with Silver Dots*, 30.

53. Similar arguments were made by other philosophically inclined American Jewish intellectuals. See, for example, Arthur A. Cohen, "From Eastern Europe to Paris and Beyond," 61–62. For similar, philosophically inclined discussions of the link between idolatry and aniconism, see Halbertal and Margalit, *Idolatry*, 37–66, 180–213; and Kochan, *Beyond the Graven Image*.

54. Kampf, *Jewish Experience*, 197. In addition to Schwarzschild, the membership of this group seems to include Kampf himself, Leo Steinberg, Hermann Cohen, and Rachel Wischnitzer. In stressing the "lack of . . . tactile details" in modernism, Kampf seems to have absorbed Heinrich Wölfflin's formalistic distinction between the "linear" and the "painterly" modalities in art. Wölfflin considered the shift from "tactile picture" to "visual picture" the "most decisive revolution which art history knows." According to Wölfflin, however, this shift occurred long before modernism. See Wölfflin, *Principles of Art History*, 18–23.

55. Rose, ed., *Art-as-Art*, 190.

56. For the explicit critique of Kampf, see Rosenberg, "Jews in Art," in idem *Art, and Other Serious Matters*, 258–269. The essay originally appeared in the *New Yorker*, 22 December 1975.

57. These themes were also explored by Rosenberg in other essays. See, for example, "Being Outside" and "Metaphysical Feelings in Modern Art," both of which are collected in *Art and Other Serious Matters*, 270–277, 306–317.

58. Rosenberg, "Is There a Jewish Art?" 60.

59. For a structurally similar appreciation of Chagall's "postmodernism," which left room for figural representations, see Benjamin Harshav, "Chagall," in *Marc Chagall and the Jewish Theater*, 15–60.

60. Rosenberg, *Der Mythus des 20. Jahrhunderts*. For the excerpted translation, see Harrison and Wood, eds., *Art in Theory, 1900–1990*, 393–395. For Nazi attitudes and Alfred Rosenberg's role in shaping them, see Petropoulos, *Art as Politics in the Third Reich*, 3–99.

61. See Margaret Olin, "C[lement] Hardesh [Greenberg] and Company," 39–59. For further discussion, see Kaplan, "Reframing the Self-Criticism," and Kuspit, "Meyer Schapiro's Jewish Unconscious" in Soussleff, ed., *Jewish Identity in Modern Art History*, 180–199, 200–217. For a political reading of the apolitical formalist tendencies in modern art and art criticism, see Guilbaut, *How New York Stole the Idea of Modern Art*. Guilbaut's analysis is compelling. He correlates modernism's abstractions with a repudiation of Stalinist Communism, especially its propagandistic control of the visual arts and its attacks against artistic individualism or creativity. It is astonishing, however, that unlike Olin, Kaplan, and Kuspit, Guibart evades altogether the Jewish identity of so many of the artists and critics he discusses.

62. Greenberg, *Art and Culture*, 92, 95. The essay "Marc Chagall" was originally published in 1946.

63. Kampf, *Jewish Experience*, 197.

64. Greenberg, *Collected Essays and Criticism*, 3: 104. The essay "Feeling Is All" first appeared in 1952.

65. Newman, *Selected Writings and Interviews*, 178. Newman wrote the statement for his first one-man show in New York City in 1950. For Newman's antimetaphysical and profeeling response to Clement Greenberg's criticisms, see pp. 161–163, 202–204.

66. Margoliouth, "Hebrew Illuminated Mss," 118–144. A similar denial of a distinctive Jewish style in illuminated manuscripts is found in Joseph Gutmann, *Hebrew Manuscript Painting*, 9–15. For a partisan summary of this major trend in Jewish art history, see Strauss, "Jewish Art as a Minority Problem," 147–171.

67. See Stassoff and Gunzburg, *L'ornement hébreu*. This pioneering work in the scientific study of Jewish art was judiciously reviewed and its conclusions were challenged. See George Margaliouth's critically negative review in *Jewish Quarterly Review* 19 (1906): 761–767. In contrast to Margaliouth, advocates of Jewish art applaud Stassoff and Gunzburg. See, for example, Ernest Namyeni, *Essence of Jewish Art*, ix–x. Originally published in French (*L'esprit de l'art Juif*), Namyeni's monograph argued that the "essence" of Jewish art is the mechanism of "continuous narrative" that conveys the dynamic "becoming" rather than the static "being" of God's will. See pp. 7–8.

68. For the classic discussion, see Kuhn, *Structure of Scientific Revolutions*.

69. See Gregory, *Eye and Brain*, 2–22, 141–233. For the classical example of the line drawing that appears now as a duck and then as a rabbit made famous by Wittgenstein, see Kuhn, *Structure of Scientific Revolutions*, 126–127.

70. Goodman, *Ways of Worldmaking*, 6. For a sustained and elegant argument that vision is existentially engaged and thoroughly personal rather than mindlessly automatic and neutrally mechanical, see Elkins, *The Object Stares Back*.

71. Danto, *Embodied Meanings*, 7.

72. See Bourdieu, "Outline of a Sociological Theory of Art Perception" and "The Historical Genesis of a Pure Aesthetic" in Johnson, ed., *Field of Cultural Production*, 215–237, 254–266. "Outline" first appeared in French in 1968; "Historical Genesis" in 1987.

73. Mitchell, *Iconology*, 119. See also Bryson, *Vision and Painting*, 31. "Perception is therefore an historically determined process, never yielding direct access between consciousness and the outer world but instead disclosing the limited version of that outer reality which the given stage of evolution in the schemata permits." Mitchell and Bryson may be seen as following the lead of Karl Marx, who proposed that "the formation [*die Bildung*] of the five senses is a labor [*Arbeit*] of the entire history of the world down to the present." See Karl Marx, *Economic and Philosophic Manuscripts of 1844*, 141. For the German original, see *Karl Marx Friedrich Engels Gesamtausgabe (MEGA)*, 270. Not less historically minded but more attuned to the history of scientific technology is Jonathan Crary, *Techniques of the Observer*. For twentieth-century technological developments, see Virilio, *Vision Machine*, first published in French in 1988. For pungent, politically aware, and persuasive arguments on behalf of the historically determined perception of art, see Berger, *Ways of Seeing*, and Staniszewski, *Believing Is Seeing*.

74. See Jay, *Downcast Eyes*.

75. For a compelling discussion of the social environment necessary to produce art and artists, see Burke, *Italian Renaissance*, 43–123.

76. Eagleton, *Ideology*, 1–2.

77. Dewey, *Art as Experience*, 5–10.

78. Ibid., 8–9. For another perspective on the emergence of "art for art's sake," see Abrams, "Art as Such," in *Doing Things with Texts*, 135–158.

79. For methodological reflections on the limits of historical scholarship, see Bloch, *Historian's Craft*, 138–144 ("Judging or Understanding?"). For a slightly different formulation of the historian's limits, see Haskell, *History and Its Images*, 9. "The historian of medicine is not expected to be able to cure a stomach ache: should the historian of a particular historical method be required to solve the problems raised by its use?" Stomachaches presumably have a cure, so that in principle a clinically trained historian of medicine might indeed be able to cure that ache. In principle, however, circles cannot be squared. The problems raised by the questions of Jewish art more closely resemble those of the circle to be squared than the stomachache to be cured. Following Marc Bloch's advice, I therefore leave the resolution of the problem of Jewish art to those who are empowered to invent it.

80. Schorske, *Fin-De-Siècle Vienna*, xxii.

Chapter Three

1. Barasch, *Icons*, 13, 15–18.

2. See Febvre, *Problem of Unbelief*, 6, where historians are warned against assuming that "all intellectual attitudes are [equally] possible in all periods."

3. Richard I. Cohen, *Jewish Icons*, especially chapter 2 ("Ceremonial Art, Patronage, and Taste") and chapter 3 ("The Rabbi as Icon").

4. Stern, ed., *Greek and Latin Authors on Jews and Judaism*, 1:26, 28.

5. For a summary of the empirical evidence, see Prigent, *Le Judaïsme et l'image*.

6. Stern, ed., *Greek and Latin Authors on Jews and Judaism*, 1: 209. For St. Augustine's reference to Varro and a provocative discussion of the cultural significance reverberating in the "myth of aniconism," see Freedberg, *Power of Images*, 62.

7. Stern, ed., *Greek and Latin Authors on Jews and Judaism*, 1:294, 299,–300; and Stern's notes on 306.

8. Ibid., 1: 330.

9. Ibid., 2:19, 26. See also Gager, *Moses in Greco-Roman paganism*, 82–86, for Tacitus, and passim for the other Greek and Latin authors who considered Moses.

10. Stern, ed., *Greek and Latin Authors on Jews and Judaism*, 2:, 349–351.

11. Josephus, *Antiquities of the Jews* 7.3–5; 15.11.

12. Ibid., 7.7; 17.

13. My colleague Professor Erich Gruen kindly called my attention to *Antiquities* 18.3, which refers to images of Caesar placed and eventually removed from Jerusalem by Pilate, and *Wars of the Jews* 2: 10, which describes images of Caesar placed by Petronius. Josephus notes that these images offended Jewish sensibilities and practices. These passages support the contention that Josephus lost no opportunity to excoriate officials, whether Jewish or Gentile, for placing politically inflammatory images in sacred precincts. The passages also support the

contention that Josephus entertained the restrictive but not the comprehensive view of the Second Commandment.

14. See Philo, *On the Giants*, 475; and Wolfson, *Philo*, 1: 29–30 n. 22.

15. For a thorough review of rabbinic legislation, see Urbach, "Rabbinical Laws of Idolatry," 149–265, 228–245. The complete Hebrew version of this article is in *Eretz-Israel* 5 (1958): 94–96, 189–205. For a more recent summary, see Stern, "Figurative Art and *Halakha*," 397–419. In Hebrew.

16. Cited from *Midrash 'Aggadah* in *Torah Shelemah*, 34.

17. For a philosophically and historically nuanced discussion of idolatry that draws deeply on the stores of Jewish literature, see Halbertal and Margalit, *Idolatry.*

18. For a modern attempt to construct this interpretation of rabbinic Judaism, see Lionel Kochan, *Beyond the Graven Image*, 24–29. Kochan's argument for "disenchantment" is anchored on pages 7–10, 81–86, 106–111, 159–170 with an elaborate defense of the difference between musically inclined, logocentric Hebraic ears and epistemologically inadequate Greek eyes.

19. For Aphrodite's bathhouse, see *Mishnah 'Avodah Zarah* 3:4; for the controversial lunar models, see *Mishnah Rosh ha-Shanah* 2:8.

20. *Ba-Midbar Rabbah* (*Numbers Rabbah*) 15:6. For a convenient narrative summary of the rabbinic materials clustered around Moses the craftsman, and Bezalel the craftsman, see Ginzberg, *Legends of the Jews*, 3: 148–173 and the accompanying notes in 6: 62–69.

21. For the telling evidence from silence that modernity has overlooked Moses, the gifted craftsman, see Silver, *Images of Moses*, and Goldstein, *Reinscribing Moses.*

22. Berger, *Jewish-Christian Debate*, 72–73 (English), 32–33 (Hebrew), 260–261 (notes).

23. *The Ethical Treatises of Berachya Son of Rabbi Natronai ha-Nakdan*, 239 (English), 117 (Hebrew). The author seems fond of these architectural metaphors for God; see also 41 and 242 English.

24. See Ladner, "Origin and Significance of the Byzantine Iconoclastic Controversy," 51. For the biblical precedents, especially the cherub motif, according to John of Damascus, see *On the Divine Images*, 21–22, 24–28, 56–57, 61–62, 66, 78–79, 87. For additional texts and discussion, see Mango, *Art of the Byzantine Empire*, esp. 149–199; and Belting, *Likeness and Presence*, esp. 144–183. For an extraordinarily informative collection of papers, see Bryer and Herrin, eds., *Iconoclasm.*

25. For a corrective to the popular misconception of Islamic antipathy to the visual arts that is alleged to have influenced the Christian iconoclasts, see Grabar, "Islam and Iconoclasm" in Bryer and Herrin, *Iconoclasm*, 45–52. I have also found the following helpful in correcting my own misunderstanding of Islamic attitudes toward the visual arts: Humphreys, *Islamic History*, 59–65, 151–153, 249–254; Terry, *Five Essays on Islamic Art*; Ettinghaus and Grabar, *Art and Architecture of Islam*; Mitchell, ed., *Architecture of the Islamic World*; Hodgson, *Venture of Islam*, 1:246–247, 368–369, 469–472; 2:325–328, 497, 501–531; Grabar, *Formation of Islamic Art*; and Arnold, *Painting in Islam.*

26. For texts, translations, and discussion, see Migne, *Patrologiae Cursus Completus, Series Latina*, 182: 914; Holt, *Documentary History of Art*, 1:19; Panofsky,

Abbot Suger, 10–16, 25–26; Schapiro, "On the Aesthetic Attitude," 5–10; and Rudolph, *"Things of Greater Importance."*

27. See, for example, Exodus 25–31:11; 1 Kings 6:14–7:37; 2 Chronicles 3:10–4:22; and Ezekiel 40–42.

28. Kaufmann, *Court, Cloister, and City,* 128. In addition to Kaufmann's monograph, I have also found the following texts a powerful corrective to my own egregious misperceptions of the Protestant attitudes to the visual arts: Christensen, *Art and the Reformation in Germany;* Eire, *War against the Idols;* Freedberg, *Power of Images,* 368–369, 378–440; Duffy, *The Stripping of the Altars;* Belting, *Likeness and Presence;* as well as the still useful Crouch, *Puritanism and Art;* and Coulton, *Art and the Reformation.*

29. See Bergendoff, ed., 40:88–91. For the German original, I consulted Martin Luther, *Ausgewählte Werke,* 4: 78–81. For specific information regarding Luther's relationship to the Cranach family of painters and illustrators, see Schade, *Cranach,* 71–77; and Cook, "Picturing Theology," 22–39.

30. *Luther's Works,* 40: 99–100; *Ausgewählte Werke,* 4: 88.

31. *Luther's Works,* 40: 88, 96, 99; *Ausgewählte Werke,* 4: 78, 84–85, 87.

32. *Luther's Works,* 40: 99; *Ausgewählte Werke,* 4: 88.

33. For Zwingli's texts and a historical analysis of his views, see Garside, *Zwingli and the Arts,* 76–183.

34. Calvin, *Institutes.* 1.11–12; 2.7. I have cited the English translation of the 1559 edition published by Henry Beveridge (Grand Rapids: Eerdmans, 1989), 1: 90–107, 330.

35. For Calvin's polemics with Roman Catholics over the normative precedent suggested by the cherubs, see *Institutes* 1.11.3.3. In Beveridge's translation, 1: 92–93.

36. *Institutes* 3.10.2–3; in Beveridge, 2: 32–33.

37. *Institutes* 1.11.12; in Beveridge, 1: 100. For discussion of Calvin's antiasceticism, see Bouwsma, *John Calvin,* 134–135.

38. *Institutes* 2.7; Beveridge, 330.

39. For the Italian original, I consulted Giorgio Vasari, *Le Vite de Più Eccellenti Pittori Scultori e Architettori, Volume primo,* 166–167. "Da le quali statue appresero per avventura I Caldei fare le immagini de loro dii; poiche centocinquanta anni dopo, Rachel, nell fuggire di mesopotamia insieme con Iacob suo marito, furò gli idoli di Laban suo padre, come apertamente racconta il Genesi. Né furono però soli I Caldei a fare sculture e pitture, ma le fecero ancora gli Egizii . . . quanto arguisce il severo comandamento fatto da Mosè . . . cioè che sotto pena della morte non si facessero a Dio imagini alcune. Costui nello scendere di sul monte, avendo trovato fabricato il vitello dell'oro et adorato solennemente dalle sue genti . . . che avevano commessa quella idolatria. Ma perché non il lavorare le statue, ma l'adorarle era peccato sceleratissimo, si legge nell'Esodo, che l'arte del disegno e delle statue, non solamente di marmo, ma di tutte le sorte di metallo, fu donato per bocca di Dio a Beseleel . . . et ad Oliab . . . che furono que' che fecero i due cherubini d'oro e candellieri e 'l velo e le fimbrie delle veste sacerdotali e tante altre bellissime cose di getto nel tabernacolo, non per altro che per indurvi le genti a contemplarle et adorarle." For the English translation, I consulted Vasari, *Lives of the Most Eminent Painters, Sculptors, and Architects,* xxxviii–xxxix.

40. Voltaire, "Abraham," in *The Complete Works of Voltaire*, 35: 298. For these recurring themes in Voltaire's writings, especially his views regarding the extent of visual art and its idolatrous character, see the treatise *"Dieu et les hommes"* (69: 334–364). For parallel passages in English translation, see Voltaire, *Treatise on Toleration and Other Essays*, 193–196; and *Voltaire on Religion, Selected Writings*, 108–117. For a provocative discussion of the ideological framework of Voltaire's remarks regarding the status of visual art in ancient Israelite culture, see Hertzberg, *French Enlightenment and the Jews*, 280–313.

41. Winckelmann was apparently thinking of 2 Kings 24:16. "Seven thousand warriors and one thousand artisans . . . the King of Babylon took them to exile in Babylonia."

42. Winckelmann, *Geschichte der Kunst des Altherthums*, 60–61 (bk. 1, chap. 2, sec. 2 ("Art among the Phoenicians and Persians"), para. 1). For an English version based on the earlier and original German edition, see Winckelmann, *History of Ancient Art*, 212–213.

Chapter Four

1. Febvre, *Problem of Unbelief in the Sixteenth Century*, 423–442, especially the section "underdevelopment of sight" (436–37), from which the direct quotations are drawn. Traditionally, aesthetics is the branch of philosophy dealing with theories of sensation. The term was later expanded in the eighteenth century to denote speculative investigations of beauty.

2. Buber, *Eclipse of God*, 40–43.

3. Buber, *Juedischer Kuenstler*, 7–12.

4. Albo, *Sefer Ha-'Ikkarim*, 3.2.16. This passage was cited by Kaufmann, *Die Sinne*, 139. This exhaustively documented monograph was arranged thematically. Each of the five senses, for example, was discussed in its own section. Passages were therefore detached from literary and historical contexts. A true Hegelian, Kaufmann was convinced that the history of ideas is the most noble (if not the true) history of humanity ("wenn nicht die wahre Geschichte, so doch das edelste Capitel in der Geschichte der Menschheit," p. 2).

5. Hegel, *Introduction to Aesthetics*, 38–39.

6. Buber, *Eclipse of God*, 19.

7. For the versatility of the term "aesthetic" and its political implications, see Eagleton, *Ideology of the Aesthetic*, 1–30.

8. For the details, see chapter 1.

9. Barrett, "Twentieth Century in Its Philosophy," in Barrett and Aiken, eds., *Philosophy in the Twentieth Century*, 27.

10. See, for example, the essays collected Sheets-Johnstone, ed., in *Giving the Body Its Due*; the essays and annotated bibliography, "A Repertory of Body History" in Feher, ed., *Fragments for a History of the Human Body*; Scarry, *The Body in Pain*; Bynum, *Resurrection of the Body*; Butler, *Bodies That Matter*; and Steinberg, *Sexuality of Christ*. For examples of the impact of "body studies" on Judaic scholarship, see Eilberg-Schwartz, *People of the Body*.

11. For Buber's comparatively moderate but nevertheless ambivalent approval of the somatic and his (questionable) distinction between "sensory-type" and

"motor-type," see Buber, *On Judaism*, 56–68, and idem, "The Way of Man according to the Teachings of Hasidism" in Kaufmann, ed., *Religion from Tolstoy to Camus*, 425–441.

12. For the details, see chapters 3, 6–7.

13. Mitchell, *Iconology*, 119.

14. Maimondes, *Eight Chapters*, chapter 1.

15. Averroes, *Epitome of the Parva Naturalia*, 20–21.

16. Albo, *Sefer ha-'Ikkarim*, 3.1. 1–9.

17. For evidence of this widespread endorsement, see, for example, Levi ben Gershom (Gersonides), *Commentary on Song of Songs*, 21, 45. I am grateful to my colleague Professor Kellner for calling this passage to my attention.

18. Albo, *Sefer ha-'Ikkarim*, 3.3.24.

19. Ibid., 3.4. 39–40.

20. Ibid., 3.5. 40–50.

21. See Foucault, *Archaeology of Knowledge*, passim.

22. For the many senses of this term, see Kuhn, *Structure of Scientific Revolutions*.

23. For the general sense made popular by anthropology, see Levi-Strauss, *Savage Mind*, and his critics, Goody, *Domestication of the Savage Mind*, and Lloyd, *Demystifying Mentalities*.

24. Baxandall, *Painting and Experience*, 30.

25. See Eco, *Aesthetics of Thomas Aquinas*.

26. See *Nature, Man, and Society*, 1–48, 99–145.

27. For an overview of historiographic distortions latent in "episteme" and its kindred terminology, see the warnings issued by Burke, *Varieties of Cultural History* 162–212, and Danton, *The Kiss of Lamourette*, 191–292.

28. Maimonides, 502–503. *Guide of the Perplexed*, hereafter *Guide*.

29. Ibid. For similar notions in the context of his medical writings, see "Moses Maimonides' Two Treatises on the Regimen of Health," esp. 17–18, 38; and *Medical Aphorisms of Moses Maimonides*, 281–283.

30. Ibid., 502–503.

31. Ibid., 511.

32. I have combined two translations from the Arabic original: Goodman, *Rambam*, 234–237, and Weiss with Butterworth, *Ethical Writings of Maimonides*, 75–78.

33. See *Guide* 3:42 (567).

34. Ibid., 3:45 (580–581). This chapter also contains aestheticizing explanations for why priests had to be physically handsome and their garments beautiful, why Levites were disqualified from service if their voices were unpleasant, and why the Temple was so lavishly decorated. He also noted the pedagogic utility implicit in the formal requirement that there be two, rather than one, cherubic sculptures over the ark. For his aestheticizing explanation of why sacrificial offerings consisted mainly in "meat, wine, and song," see *Guide* 3:47 (591–592). Western philosophic reflections on the sense of smell are surveyed in Le Guérer, *Scent*, 141–203.

35. See Twersky, *Introduction to the Code of Maimonides*, 405, 459–68.

36. For translations of the original Arabic text, see Twersky, *Maimonides Reader*, 390–393; or Roth, *Maimonides*, 52–56. For further references and

discussion, see Twersky, *Introduction to the Code of Maimonides*, 250–251; Scheindlin, *Wine, Women, and Death*, 21; and Brann, *The Compunctious Poet*, 77, 193–196, passim.

37. Harvey, "Ethics and Meta-Ethics, Aesthetics and Meta-Aesthetics in Maimonides," 131–138.

38. *Guide*, 6–8.

39. Ibid., 63.

40. See Pines, "The Limitations of Human Knowledge," 82–109; and Altmann, "Maimonides on the Intellect" in Altmann, ed., *Von der mittelalterlichen zur modernen Aufklärung*, 60–129. For references, see Lachterman, "Maimonidean Studies," 197–216.

41. *Guide*, 68–69.

42. Ibid., 71.

43. Ibid., 627–28.

44. Ibid., 2:36, 371; 3:8, 432; and 3:49, 608. For discussion, see *Die Sinne*, 188–191 and the supplementary note in Malter, "Shem Tob ben Joseph Palquera," 480–481.

45. Jaeger, *Theology of the Early Greek Philosophers*, 49ff.

46. *Guide*, 104.

47. See ibid., 2:32–47.

48. See *Mishneh Torah, Laws of Idolatry* 3:10–11. "(10) It is forbidden to make images merely for decoration even though it is not for the sake of idolatry . . . so that one might not be mislead by them and imagine that they are intended for idolatry. It is only forbidden to form, for the sake of decoration, the shape of a person . . . if the shape is in relief. But if the form is flat . . . like those which are woven in a tapestry, such are permitted. (11) . . . it is also forbidden to form the shape of the sun, moon, stars, constellations, and angels . . . even on a flat surface. It is permitted to form the shapes of animals and other living things, with the exception of a person, and the shapes of trees, grasses, and the like, even if the shape is in relief." The implicit contrast between making and viewing is reiterated in the *Book of Commandments* (negative, no. 4): "We are forbidden to make figures of human beings out of metal, stone, wood, and the like, even if they are not made for the purposes of worship. The purpose of this is to deter us from making images altogether, so that we should not think, as the masses do, that they contain supernatural powers. . . . Exodus 20:20." See *Sefer ha-Mitzvoth of Maimonides*, 2: 2–5.

49. For his responsum on music, see Werner and Sonne, "Philosophy and Theory of Music," 16:313–315, 17:539ff.1; also Boaz Cohen, "Responsum of Maimonides Concerning Music," 167–182; and Adler, *Hebrew Writings Concerning Music*, 240–241.

50. For texts and discussion, see Twersky, *Introduction to the Code of Maimonides*, 452–53; and Novak, *Jewish-Christian Dialogue*, 57–64.

51. See *Guide*, 3:49 (608) and the explicit cross reference to the "Laws of Forbidden Intercourse: XXI" in his *Mishneh Torah*.

52. See especially ibid., 3: 8–9.

53. See Fishbane, "Israel and the 'Mothers,' "28–47; and Frankfort et al., *Before Philosophy*, 11–36, 237–763.

54. Ambivalence toward myths, metaphors, and symbols is deeply rooted in the Greek philosophic tradition to which Maimonides was heir. For a useful discussion of the ancient precedents, see Lloyd, *Revolutions of Wisdom*, 172–214.

55. *Guide*, 190–193.

56. Twersky, *Maimonides Reader*, 410.

57. Ibid., 496–497.

58. See, for example, J. Guttman, *Philosophies of Judaism*, 207–301; and Sirat, *History of Jewish Philosophy*, 205–412. For the struggle over Maimonidean studies, see Sarachek, *Faith and Reason*; Silver, *Maimonidean Criticism*; and Scholem, *Origins of the Kabbalah*.

59. See Baer, *History of the Jews in Christian Spain*. For developments in the earlier centuries, see Chazan, *Daggers of Faith*. For the iconic record, see Blumenkranz, *Le Juif médiéval*; and Camille, *Gothic Idol*, esp. 165–94. See also Baron, *Social and Religious History of the Jews*, 10: 118–219.

60. For the texts and analysis, see Wolfson, *Crescas' Critique of Aristotle*; R. Hasdai Crecas, *Sefer Or Hashem*; and Ravitzky, *Crescas' Sermon on the Passover*, with English summary, v–x. For discussion of the mystical thread in Crescas, see Harvey, "Kabbalistic Elements in Crescas' Light of the Lord," 75–109; English summary, ix–xi.

61. For the meager biographical data, see Baer, *History*, 2: 150–158; Sirat, *History of Jewish Philosophy*, 352–357; Talmage, *Polemical Writings of Profiat Duran*, 9–15 (in Hebrew); and Emery, "New Light on Profayt Duran," 328–337.

62. See the Hebrew edition by Friedländer and Kohn, *Maase Efod*, hereafter cited as *Efod*.

63. For discussion, see Twersky, "Religion and Law," 69–82.

64. Translating the Hebrew *mar'oth* as eyeglasses is philologically unproblematic; it is demanded by context and supported by the popularity of metal-framed corrective lenses (*oculares*) in fifteenth-century Spain after their invention in late thirteenth-century northern Italy. See the useful comments of Turner and Baumann in *Spectacle of Spectacles*. The Hebrew adjective *sigith* baffles me. Is it a misprint? Does it transliterate the Arabic *siga*, meaning fashioned by a metal smith? Or the Spanish *soga*, meaning attached by a string?

65. *Efod*, 13.

66. See Foucault, *Order of Things*, 17–26, 29. "Up to the end of the sixteenth century, resemblance played a constructive role in the knowledge of Western culture . . . organized the play of symbols, made possible knowledge of things visible and invisible, and controlled the art of representing them" (17).

67. *Efod*, 21. The association between visual aids and memorization has been explored by Frances A. Yates in *Giordano Bruno and the Hermetic Tradition*, 190–202, 325–337, and in *Art of Memory*. See also Carruthers, *Book of Memory*. For samples of square and cursive scripts and their history, see Birnbaum, *Hebrew Scripts*, 126–190, 259–277, and the accompanying plates in vol. 2 (1954–1957).

68. *Efod*, 21.

69. *Efod*, 19. J. Gutmann called this passage to attention in his *No Graven Images*, xvii, citing it to illustrate the positive impact of Spanish royal and religious art on Latinate-European Jewry.

70. See Moore, *Judaism in the First Centuries of the Christian Era*, 1: 239–47; Kieval, *High Holy Days*, 229–230; Urbach, *The Sages*, 287, 309; and Wieder, "Sanctuary as a Metaphor," 166–67.

71. *Efod*, 11.

72. For the philological history of this equation reaching back to the Dead Sea Scrolls and a discussion of Duran's most likely medieval sources, see Wieder, " 'Sanctuary' as a Metaphor," 165–175.

73. For the most complete scholarly analysis, based on twenty illuminated manuscripts of Spanish provenance, see Joseph Gutmann, "The Messianic Temple in Spanish Medieval Hebrew Manuscripts," 125–145. For additional color reproductions of Temple implements and discussion of the visual arts popular in Duran's Spain, see B. Narkiss, *Hebrew Illuminated Manuscripts*, 50–82; J. Gutmann, *Hebrew Manuscript Painting*, 17–21, 50–57; and Sed-Rajna, *Jewish Art*, 169–73. For a succinct and useful introduction to the topic, see Evelyn M. Cohen, "Decoration of Medieval Hebrew Manuscripts," 47–60.

74. *Efod*, 20.

75. When asked by his younger colleague Meir Crescas for an explanation of why the number seven is so prominent in biblical law, Duran replied correlating the mathematical qualities of seven with a wide variety of cosmological, anthropomorphic, and cultic resemblances; see *Efod*, 313–317.

76. *Efod*, 11.

77. See, for example, Patai, *Man and Temple*; Eliade, *Myth of the Eternal Return*, 3–11; or Eliade, *The Sacred and the Profane*, 8–65.

78. See Gellrich, *Idea of the Book in the Middle Ages*, 29–80; and Curtius, *European Literature*, 302–347.

79. See *Guide*, 11:36. For a discussion of the uniqueness of the Mosaic rank, see Bland, "Moses and the Law According to Maimonides," 49–66.

80. *Efod*, 11

81. *Efod*, 19.

82. Even a cursory glance at the richly painted, densely ornamented medieval Hebrew illuminated manuscripts reveals that the secular, aesthetic values of Romanesque art described by Meyer Schapiro ("spontaneity, individual fantasy, delight in color and movement, and the expression of feeling that anticipate modern art") continued to thrive in late fourteenth- and fifteenth-century Jewish life in Spain. See Schapiro, *Romanesque Art*, 1–28.

83. See Berger, *Sacred Canopy*, 3–101, 175–77, for a synopsis of Marxian, Weberian, and Durkheimian social theory, which emphasize the legitimizing and stabilizing functions of projection or externalization in religious systems.

84. *Efod*, 20, and Adler, *Hebrew Writings*, 128. For texts and studies related to the history of Jewish music, see the references cited *supra* n. 37 and the still useful classic, Idelsohn, *Jewish Music in its Historical Development*.

85. See *Guide* 2:5 (259–260) and 2:8 (267). In his comments to 2:8 Duran only took issue with Maimonides's explanation for the celestial mechanism whereby sound might be produced, but not with Maimonides's contention that the heavenly bodies, in fact, produce no sound.

86. For a discussion of the three types of music made famous by Boethius, see Wemer and Sonne, "Philosophy and Theory of Music," 253. For texts and useful comments on the theory of music in medieval Jewish thought, see Adler, *Hebrew Writings concerning Music*; and Judith Cohen, "Jubal in the Middle Ages," 83–99. For a discussion of Abulafian techniques and the possible target of Duran's polemic, see Idel, "Music and Prophetic Kabbalah," 151–169.

87. *Efod*, 11.

88. *Efod*, 13.

89. *Efod*, 14.

90. *Efod*, 13.

91. *Efod*, 13.

92. See *Kitab al Khazari* and *Book of Refutation* for the texts. For discussion, see Silman, *Thinker and Seer*.

93. See Idel, *Kabbalah*, 74–199; Scholem, *On the Kabbalah*, 118–157; and Tishby, *Wisdom of the Zohar*, vol. 3 ("Sacred Worship" and "Practical Life").

94. See Dan, *Jewish Mysticism and Jewish Ethics*, esp. 45–103.

Chapter Five

1. See Carmi, ed., *Penguin Book of Hebrew Verse*, 324. Cf. H. Schirmann, *Ha-Shirah ha-ivrit*, 1.2: 370–371. For more samples and discussion of his poetry, see Scheindlin, *Wine, Women, and Death*; and Brann, *Compunctious Poet*. For English translations of brief excerpts from his Arabic rhetoric, see Rosenthal, *Classical Tradition in Islam* 18, 19, 43–44. For the rhetoric itself, see Halkin, ed., *Kitab al-Muhadara wal-Mudhakara*.

2. Carmi, ed., *Penguin Book of Hebrew Verse*, 291. For discussion, see the references to Scheindlin and Brann in note 1 above.

3. See Kugel, *In Potiphar's House*, 28–124.

4. *Commentary to the Pentateuch by R. Joseph Bechor Shor*, 64.

5. See Sirat, *History of Jewish Philosophy in the Middle Ages*, 104.

6. Ibn Ezra, *Long Commentary on the Pentateuch*, Genesis 39:6, ad loc.

7. See Rabinowitz, ed., *Book of the Honeycomb's Flow*, 293. For recent discussions of the historical context of his thought, see Ruderman, *World of a Renaissance Jew*; Tirosh-Rothschild, *Between Worlds*; Bonfil, *Jewish Life in Renaissance Italy*; and idem, *Rabbis and Jewish Communities in Renaissance Italy*.

8. See Gottlied, ed., *Be'ur 'al ha-Torah le-Rabbi 'Ovadiah Sforno*, 73. For Cicero's emphasis on color, see *Tusculan Disputations*: "Et ut corporis est quaedam apta figura membrorum cum coloris quadam suavitate eaque dicitur pulcritude, sic in animo . . . pulcritudo vocatur" (4:13). For discussion of the Renaissance equation of beauty and symmetrical relations "between the parts of a whole," see Kristeller, *Philosophy of Marsilio Ficino*, 265–269. For the classical background, see the typical discussion in Curtius, *European Literature and the Latin Middle Ages*, 180–182.

9. Maimonides, *Guide*, 21–22.

10. See Black, *Logic and Aristotle's "Rhetoric" and "Poetics,"* 140.

11. See, for example, Schwarzschild, "Aesthetics," 1; and Levy, "Status of Aesthetics," 83–102. For Judah Abravanel, see Ebreo (Giuda Abarbanel), *Dialoghi D'Amore*, and the discussion to follow.

12. See "Limitations of Human Knowledge," 82–109. For the opposing view, see Altmann, "Maimonides on the Intellect," 60–129.

13. For the Hebrew text, see Ben Maimon, *Medical Aphorisms of Moses*, par. 26b, 307. For comments on the translator into Hebrew, Nathan ha-Me'ati, see Shatzmiller, *Jews, Medicine, and Medieval Society*, 46–47, 49.

14. *Mishneh Torah*, "Laws of Kings," 2:5.

15. For functionalist trajectories in Maimonidean ethics, see Twersky, *Introduction to the Code of Maimonides*, 458; and Harvey, "Ethics and Meta-Ethics," 131–138.

16. This passage was also discussed in chapter 4. For the original Arabic text of chapter 5, see the edition of Gorfinkle, *The Eight Chapters*, or Ben Maimon, *Acht Kapitel*, 16–19. For the English translations on which I based my own, see Goodman, *Rambam*, 234–237 and Weiss with Butterworth, *Ethical Writings*, 75–78. Cf. Al-Farabi, *Fusul al-Madani*, sec. 70 (Eng., 60–61; Arabic, 151). For discussion of Maimonidean dependence on al-Farabi, see Davidson, "Maimonides' *Shemonah Peraqim*," 33–50; and Kraemer, "Alfarabi's *Opinions of the Virtuous* City." Thirteenth-century philosopher Badr-ad-din ibn Muzaffar echoed the same views articulated by Maimonides: "All physicians, philosophers and respectable men agree that the contemplation of artistic and beautiful pictures gladdens and delights the soul, removes melancholy thoughts and hallucinations from it" (see Rosenthal, *Classical Heritage in Islam*, 265–266).

17. See Hume, "Of the Standard of Taste," in *Selected Essays*, 136. In understanding Hume's aesthetics, I have found the following useful: Jones, "Hume's Literary and Aesthetic Theory," 255–280; and Norton, *David Hume*, esp. 124–125.

18. For the sake of comparison with the Latin Scholastic tradition, see Eco, *Aesthetics of Thomas Aquinas*. For an important corrective, see Schapiro, "On the Aesthetic Attitude in Romanesque Art," esp. 23–35. "When [Aquinas] speaks of art, he has nothing to say about the beautiful; art is for him skilled work of any kind, whether of the carpenter or logician or surgeon, and its perfection lies in the achievement of a practical end."

19. *Guide* 3:22, p. 417.

20. See Efros, "Maimonides' *Treatise on Logic*," 47–48. For additional discussion of "conventions" (*mefursamot, mashurat*) see Black, *Logic and Aristotle's "Rhetoric" and "Poetics,"* 141–43.

21. Similar ideas made themselves known in such fourteenth-century Hebrew philosophical texts as Samuel ben Judah of Marseilles's translation of Ibn Rushd's (Averroes) commentary to Plato's *Republic*. See *Averroes' Commentary on Plato's Republic*, 185–86 (Heb. 66–67), where the contrast is drawn between the theologians' "beauty," which is identified heteronomically as God's decree, and the philosophic and religious "beauty," which is defined functionally: That "which leads to the end is good and beautiful, whereas everything that impedes it is evil and ugly" (185). Except for the universalizing implication that the same thing is

beautiful for all persons at all times, Maimonides's opinion aligns with the functionalism of the philosophers. For discussion of the translator, see Berman, "Greek into Hebrew," 289–320. For a refutation of the view that "beauty is no more than a conventional term coined by man," see the Arabic version of Galen's *Ethics* translated into English in Rosenthal, *Classical Heritage in Islam*, 93.

22. For a psychogenetic and anthropocentric explanation of beauty that differs sharply from the Maimonidean view, see the fourteenth-century arguments of Ibn Khaldun: "If an object of vision is harmonious in the forms and lines given to it in accordance with the matter from which it is made, so that the requirements of its particular matter as to perfect harmony and arrangement are not disregarded— that being the meaning of beauty and loveliness . . . that [object of vision] is then in harmony with the soul that perceives it, and the soul, thus, feels pleasure as a result of perceiving something that is agreeable to it. . . . In another sense, the meaning of it is that existence is shared by all existent things, as the philosophers say. Therefore, [existent things] love to commingle with something in which they observe perfection, in order to become one with it. The object that is most suited to man and in which he is most likely to perceive perfect harmony, is the human form. Therefore, it is most congenial to him to perceive beauty and loveliness in the lines and sounds of the human form. Thus, every man desires beauty in the objects of vision and hearing, as a requirement of his nature [*fitrah*]" (Ibn Khaldun, The Muqaddimah, 329. For the Arabic original, I have consulted *Muqaddimat Ibn Khaldun* 424–25. Ibn Khaldun considered the human form to be the most natural place to experience beauty; Maimonides did not. Ibn Khaldun argued that the psychological impetus to experience beauty is innate and inevitable; Maimonides affirmed that the capacity for experiencing beauty is innate but he denied that it is inevitable, as his discussion of Adam's sin and its implications of human perfection will indicate.

23. See Shem Tov Falaqera, *Moreh ha-Moreh*, 11–12. For texts and studies related to Falaqera, see Harvey, *Falaquera's "Epistle of the Debate"*; and Jospe, *Torah and Sophia*, esp. 235–337, 345. In his commentary to the *Guide*, ad loc., Don Isaac Abravanel (1437–1508) also assumed that Maimonides was referring to the practical intellect.

24. *Nicomachean Ethics*, 6.1,1139a., 5–15; 6.3.

25. See Hume, *Enquiries concerning the Human Understanding*, 285–294.

26. Ibid., 173.

27. See Kristeller, "Modern System of the Arts," 163–227; and Dewey, *Art as Experience*, 5–10. In the fourteenth century, the sociologically minded Arab historian Ibn Khaldun distinguished the "necessary crafts of agriculture, architecture, tailoring, carpentry, and weaving" from the "noble" crafts of "midwivery, the art of writing, book production, singing, and medicine," which are "noble" because they "call for contact with great rulers in their privacy [*halawatihim*] and at their intimate parties [*majalis unsihim*]. Thus they have nobility [*sharaf*] that other crafts do not have." (See Ibn Khaldun, The Muqaddimah, 319; for the Arabic text see *Muqaddimat Ibn Khaldun*, 405–406). But there is no evidence that the twelfth-century Maimonides was aware of such a ranking of the arts and crafts.

28. Febvre, *Problem of Unbelief*, 6.

29. See Hacking, *Emergence of Probability*, esp. 1–48.

30. Hume, *Enquiry concerning the Principles of Morals*, 194; and cf. *Treatise of Human Nature*, 547.

31. Ibid., 576.

32. *Guide*, 3:27.

33. Hume, *Selected Essays*, 138, 141.

34. *Enquiries*, 244; cf. "it is on the proportion, relation, and position of parts, that all natural beauty depends" (291).

35. Ibid., 245.

36. Ibid., 173. For discussion of Hume's dispute with the irrationalists and his tempering of aesthetic subjectivism with the search for objective criteria and the role of reason, see Cassirer, *Philosophy of the Enlightenment*, 297–309.

37. Regarding the premodern philosopher's indifference to the sheer beauty of artifacts valued for their usefulness, see Schapiro, "On the Aesthetic Attitude," 23.

38. See the still useful Krakowski, *L'esthetique de Plotin*, esp. 164–184; and the discussions of Cicero in Summers, *The Judgment of Sense*. For Plotinus's critique of the Stoic doctrines, see the *Enneads* 1:6, 1–5.

39. See Yosef ben Yehudab ibn Aqnin, *Divulgatio Mysteriorum Luminumque Apparentia*. Page 176, for example, interprets the verse, "your lips are like a scarlet thread, your mouth is lovely, your cheeks are like the rind of the pomegranate behind your veil" (4:3) by noting that it alludes to three conditions of beauty: "softness [*lin*], delicateness [*riqqa*], and coloration [*laun*]." Similar examples abound throughout the commentary. For general background on Ibn Aqnin, see Sirat, *History of Jewish Philosophy*, 206, 207–209.

40. See Solomon ibn Gabirol, *Kingly Crown*, verse 27: "[In] the World-to-Come are stations and vistas for the standing souls . . . seeing and being seen by the face of the Lord. This is the rest and the inheritance whose goodness and beauty have no end." (See Davidson, ed., *Selected Religions Poems of Solomon ibn Gabirol*, 103.

41. For the Maimonidean critique of misguided liturgical poetry, see *Guide* 1:59, which is framed by the discussion of attributes in general (1:50–60). For further discussion of his attitudes toward poetry, see Twersky, *Code of Maimonides*, 250–251; Brann, *Compunctious Poet*, 77, 193–196, passim; and Scheindlin, "Hebrew Poetry in Medieval Iberia," 39–59, esp. 51 n. 8.

42. For Gabirol's dependence on rabbinic mysticism, see Liebes, "Rabbi Solomon Ibn Gabirol's Use of the *Sefer Yesira*, 73–123; for a Maimonidean repudiation of Neoplatonists, mystics, and their anthropomorphism, see *Guide* 2:26; and Altmann, "Moses Narboni's Epistle," 231–232; for a typical Merkabah hymn ascribing beauty to God's face, see note 68.

43. *Guide* 1:52. For a judicious discussion of this passage stressing the parallel with Plotinus and bringing Ibn Bajja into view, see Altmann, "Maimonides on the Intellect," 122. Munk called attention to the close parallel between this passage and book 1:10 of Bahya ibn Paquda's Arabic classic, *Duties of the Heart*. Standing behind all of these traditions, perhaps, is Plato's discussion in the *Republic*, esp. 6. 506e–509c, and 7. 514–519.

44. See Walzer, *Al-Farabi on the Perfect State*, 79–81, 83–85. Cf. Samuel ibn Tibbon's Hebrew translation of the parallel text of the *Siyasa al-Madiniya* (The political regime) published by Z. Philipowski, *Sefer he-Asif* (Leipzig: K. F. Köhler,

1849), esp. 12–13; and Steinschneider, *Die Hebraeischen übersetzungen des Mittel-alters* 290–292. On the essential identity of beauty and the beautiful in the Neopla-tonic One, cf. *Pseudo-Dionysius*, 76 ("But do not make a distinction between 'beautiful' and 'beauty' as applied to the Cause which gathers all into one" [*Divine Names*, 701c]). Maimonides also knew Ibn Sina's *Hayy Ibn Yaqzan*, who was also intimate with God's beauty. See Corbin, *Avicenna and the Visionary Recital*, esp. 149–150, where speaking of the "King," Ibn Sina wrote: "Let none, then, be so bold as to compare Him to anything whatsoever. . . . He is all a face by His beauty, and His beauty obliterates the vestiges of all other beauty. When one of those who surround His immensity undertakes to meditate on Him, his eye blinks with stu-por and he comes away dazzled. Indeed, his eyes are almost ravished from him. . . . It would seem that His beauty is the veil of his beauty. . . . Even so it is by veiling itself a little that the sun can be better contemplated. . . . Whoever perceives a trace of his beauty fixes his contemplation upon it forever." For the Arabic text, see Avicenna, *Traites Mystiques d'Abou Ali al-Hosain b. Abdallah b. Sina*, 20–21. Ibn Sina also discussed God's perfection, beauty, and unknowability in the various versions of his *Metaphysics*. For example, in the *Najat*, the chapter which follows the discussion of "the Necessary Existent and Intellect, Intelligence, and Intelligi-ble" is titled: "That in Itself, It is the Beloved and the Lover, The Object of Plea-sure and the Subject of Pleasure, and that Pleasure is the Perception of the Good and the Proper[ly Proportioned]." (See Avicenna, *An-Najat fi-al-Mantiq wa-l-Ilahiyat*, 99–102). See also Fackenheim, "A Treatise on Love by Ibn Sina," 208–228, in which Avicenna's emanationist cosmology leads him to assert that the "rational soul recognizes that the closer a thing is to the First Object of love, the more steadfast it is in its order, and the more beautiful in its harmony" (220). It is also no surprise that Ibn Tufayl's *Hayy* was familiar with God's beauty (see Gau-thier, *Hayy Ben Yaqdhan*, 89–96, 127). Ibn Rushd and al-Ghazzali also referred to God's perfection, beauty, and unknowability. See, for example, the fifth discus-sion in *Tahafut Al Tahafut*: "When it is said that He is the lover and the beloved, the enjoyer and the enjoyed, it means that He is every beauty and splendour and perfection. . . . But the First possesses the most perfect splendour and the most complete beauty, since all perfection is possible to him . . . and he perceives this beatity. . . . All these concepts refer to His essence and to his perception and to His knowledge of His essence . . . for He is pure intellect, and all this leads back to one single notion" (*Averroes' Tahafut Al-Tahafut*, 1:184–185 and Al-Ghazali, *Incoherence of the Philosophers*, 95). These texts were known in their Hebrew trans-lations and commented upon by medieval Jewish authors, including Abraham ibn Ezra and Moses Narboni. I hope in another context to trace Maimonides's refer-ence to "all the philosophers" and to investigate the impact of these Islamic no-tions on medieval Jewish thought.

45. See the comments of Shlomo Pines in Maimonides, *Guide*, cxxxii–cxxxiv; and Twersky, "Did R. Abraham ibn Ezra Influence Maimonides?" 21–48.

46. See *Mishneh Torah*, "Laws of Prayer," 2:5. For a partial English translation of Rabbi Solomon's responsum (no. 285), see Finkel, *Responsa Anthology*, 38. For the Hebrew original, see Solomon ben Zemah Duran, *Sefer HaRashbash*, 53r-v.

47. See, for example, Zimmels, *Ashkenazim and Sephardim*. For an overview of medieval communal structure and governance, see Baron, *Jewish Community*, and idem, *Social and Religious History of the Jews*, 2:172–214, 396–407.

48. For a comparative discussion of the historical impact of Jewish mysticism on Jewish law, see Katz, *Halakhah and Kabbalah*.

49. See Twerky, "Some Non-Halakic Aspects of the *Mishneh Torah*," 95–118.

50. See Moore, *Formation of Persecuting Society*, and Stow, *Alienated Minority*. For historiographical information and comparative study, see Mark R. Cohen, *Under Crescent and Cross*.

51. For discussion and English translations of the important primary sources, see Chazan, *Church, State, and the Jew*.

52. See Baer, *History of the Jews in Christian Spain*.

53. For the historical context of Arama's polemics against philosophy, see Baer, *History of the Jews*, 2:253–259. See also Sirat, *History of Jewish Philosophy*, 389–392. For discussions of his thought from the perspective of his preaching, see Bettan, *Studies in Jewish Preaching*, 130–191; and Saperstein, *Jewish Preaching*, 17–18, 74–77, 392–393. For monographic treatment of his religious thought, see Wilensky, *Philosophy of Isaac Arama*. For the struggle over philosophy in late-fourteenth- and fifteenth-century Spain, see Guttmann, *Philosophies of Judaism*, 254–291.

54. See Arama, *'Aqedat Yizhaq*, 1:98–100.

55. In addition to the discussions of Baer, Sirat, and Guttmann mentioned in note 53, see Netanyahu, *Don Isaac Abravanel*. Netanyahu's scholarship is surpassed by Lawee, "Inheritance of the Fathers."

56. See Abravanel, *Commentary to the Guide*, 1:2.

57. Leone Ebreo, 387–389 (English); 325–326 (Italian).

58. Leone Ebreo, 389 (English); 326 (Italian).

59. Leone Ebreo, *Dialoghi*, 393 (English); 329 (Italian).

60. For Maimonides's insistence that human intellect and divine intellect radically differ, see the critique of the microcosm motif in the *Guide*, 1:72, and esp. 192–193. The unknowability of God's essence is stressed in the *Guide*, 1:54.

61. For Leone Ebreo's self-declared Jewish identity, see *Dialoghi* 418 (English: "Since I am a follower of Moses [*mosaico*] in matters relating to theology; 351 (Italian).

62. Leone Ebreo *Dialoghi*, 456 (English); 382 (Italian).

63. For Crescas's diplomatic struggles and Albo's communal responsibilities, see Baer, *History of the Jews*, vol. 2. For general discussions of Crescas's thought, see Guttmann, *Philosophies of Judaism*, 256–274; Sirat, *History of Jewish Philosophy*, 357–370; and Wolfson, *Crescas' Critique of Aristotle*. For general discussion of Albo's thought, see Guttmann, *Philosophies of Judaism*, 281–286; and Sirat, *History of Jewish Philosophy*, 374–381. For a nuanced discussion of resonance between Crescas and Leone Ehreo, see Guttmann, *Philosophies of Judaism*, 294–299. The relation between Leone Ebreo and medieval Jewish-Islamic philosophy has heen widely discussed; see, for example, the suggestions and the bibliographic references offered by Davidson, "Medieval Jewish Philosophy in the Sixteenth Century," 125–130; Ivry, "Remnants of Jewish Averroism in the Rennaissance," 246–250; and Pines, "Medieval Doctrines in Renaissance Garb?" 365–398, all three of

which appear in Cooperman, ed., *Jewish Thought in the Sixteenth Century.* See also Dethier, "Love and Intellect in Leone Ebreo," 353–386.

64. See Albo, *Sefer ha-'Ikkarim*, 2: 90–98 (=book 2:15). Cf. 3: 40–52 (book 3:5). For the passages from Crescas relating to intellectual perfection and God's cosmic goodness alluded to by Albo, see "The Light of the Lord," in Hyman and Walsh, *Philosophy in the Middle Ages*, 440–449. For discussion, see Harvey, "Crescas versus Maimonides on Knowledge and Pleasure," 113–123.

65. See the *Guide*, 3:51, esp. 627–628. For discussion, see Vajda, *L'amour de Dieu*, 118–140, 261–293.

66. For the sources and full discussion, see chapter 4.

67. For a typical late-medieval Kabbalist, see Goetschel, *Meir ibn Gabbay*, and Meir ibn Gabbai, *Sod ha-Shabbat.*

68. See *Sefer Yezirah*, chap. 4.I. Gruenwald, "A Preliminary Critical Edition of *Sefer Yezirah*," 156–157. For discussion, see Scholem, *Kabbalah*, 23–30; and *Origins of the Kabbalah*, 24–35. Cf. Idel, *Kabbalah*, passim.

69. See Carmi, ed., *Hebrew Verse*, 196 (n. 40). For parallel passages, see Schäfer, ed., *Konkordanz zur Hekhalot-Literatur*, 1:300 (*yofi*). For discussion of these ancient hymns, see Swartz, *Mystical Prayer in Ancient Judaism.*

70. See *Sefer ha-Bahir*, 54, 94, 96, 190, and passim. For discussion of the book and its imagery, see Scholem, *Kabbalah*, 312–316; and *Origins of the Kabbalah*, 49–198.

71. See *Zohar*, 1:206b; and Psalms 48:2. For discussion, see Wolfson, *Through a Speculum That Shines*, 85–86, 336–345, 357–368, 383–392, which trace the Kabbalistic equation of beauty (*yofi*) and the divine phallus. For an introduction to the symbolism of the *Zohar*, see Tishby, ed., *Wisdom of the Zohar*, 1: 230–255, 269–307, 371–387.

72. *Zohar* 3:191a.

Chapter Six

1. For the social and cognitive impact of visually based book learning on medieval Christian society, see Stock, *The Implications of Literacy.* Writing these medieval chapters, I was often mindful of Stock's provocative and useful proposition that "oral and written traditions made different demands on the human senses. The one emphasized the ear, the other the eye. The new complexity of the sensorium eventually altered the form and function of the visual and plastic arts" (p. 81). Already dependent on oral learning and bookishly complex, the medieval Jewish sensorium was visually well practiced. It was predisposed to experiencing and interpreting artifacts with as much complexity as it processed texts.

2. Abrahams, *Jewish Life in the Middle Ages*, 212.

3. For an overview and bibliographic guidance, see Baron, *Social and Religious History of the Jews*, 4: 150–227; Wischnitzer, *History of Jewish Crafts and Guilds*, 54–124; and Goitein, *A Mediterranean Society*, 1: 75–147. For an early attempt to summarize and tabulate these data, see Israel Abrahams, *Jewish Life in the Middle Ages*, 211–247. For updated, additional information and graphic evidence, see Metzger and Metzger, *Jewish Life in the Middle Ages*, 151–196; Roth, *Jewish Art*,

253–491. For a recent attempt to identify the names of medieval Jews who illuminated manuscripts, see Zirlin, "Celui qui se cache derrière l'image," 33–53.

4. See Shatzmiller, *Jews, Medicine, and Medieval Society.*

5. For travel and seafaring, see Goitein, *A Mediterranean Society,* 1: 273–352.

6. For an overview and bibliographic references to this vast domain of medieval Jewish activity, see Stow, *Alienated Minority,* 210–230; and Sasson, ed., *History of the Jewish People,* 390–392, 469–475, 565–567. For a representative selection of primary texts in English translation relating to the vexatious issue of usury, see Chazan, *Church, State, and Jew,* 197–220.

7. See Levanon, *Jewish Travellers.* The book features Benjamin, Petahiah, and Jacob ben Nathaniel ha-Cohen. It judiciously reviews various theories accounting for their travels, emphasizing messianic hopes and minimizing commercial interests. It stresses the continuous tradition of Jewish travelling. It overlooks parallel developments in medieval Christian society involving the traffic in relics and the phenomenology of pilgrimage.

8. For the Hebrew original, an English translation, extensive notes, and related essays, see Asher, ed., *Itinerary of Rabbi Benjamin of Tudela* (hereafter *Itinerary*). (All subsequent citations refer to this edition. Where necessary, I have modified the translation.) An abridged translation is also available in Adler, *Jewish Travellers,* 38–63.

9. *Itinerary,* 38–41 (English); 8–11 (Hebrew).

10. *Itinerary,* 50–56 (English); 19–24 (Hebrew).

11. *Itinerary,* 68–75 (English); 34–40 (Hebrew).

12. *Itinerary,* 83–86 (English); 46–48 (Hebrew).

13. *Itinerary,* 93–105 (English); 54–64 (Hebrew).

14. *Itinerary,* 106 (English); 65 (Hebrew).

15. *Itinerary,* 107–109 (English); 66–67 (Hebrew).

16. *Itinerary,* 111–112 (English); 69 (Hebrew).

17. *Itinerary,* 116–117 (English); 73 (Hebrew).

18. *Itinerary,* 153–158 (English); 102–107 (Hebrew).

19. *Itinerary,* 159–161 (English); 108–109 (Hebrew).

20. *Itinerary,* 106–107 (English); 65 (Hebrew).

21. For the annotated critical edition of the Hebrew text, see *Sibbuv Ha-Rav Petahiah mi-Regensburg.* (Hereafter cited as *Sibbuv.*) For a different English translation, see Adler, *Jewish Travellers in the Middle Ages,* 64–91. For the entry on Nisibis, see *Sibbuv,* 4–5 (English, 85).

22. *Sibbuv,* 33 (English 89).

23. *Sibbuv,* 31 (English 87).

24. *Sibbuv,* 12 (English 73).

25. *Sibbuv,* 12–13; (English 73).

26. *Sibbuv,* 13–17; English 74–76.

27. *Sibbuv,* 33 (English 89).

28. *Sibbuv,* 31–32 (English 88).

29. *Sibbuv,* 32–33 (English 88–89).

30. *Bamah* is also used for the monastery at Mt. Sinai; see *Itinerary,* 159 (English); 107 (Hebrew).

31. *Itinerary,* 140–141 (English); 92–93 (Hebrew).

32. *Itinerary,* 83 (English); 46 (Hebrew).

33. Dodds, "Mudejar Tradition and the Synagogues of Medieval Spain," 117.

34. Recent studies devoted to Rashi's life and works include two monographs by Avraham Grossman, *The Early Sages of Ashkenaz,* passim, and *The Early Sages of France,* 121–253 (Hebrew). For studies focused on his biblical commentary, see Kamin, *Rashi's Exegetical Categorization* (Hebrew); Gelles, *Peshat and Derash;* and Melammed, *Bible Commentators* 1: 353–447.

35. The text of Rashi's commentary to Exodus 32 is published in all editions of the rabbinic Bible. For a literal English translation and references to the immediate Talmudic sources of the commentary, which I condense and occasionally cite directly in these paragraphs, see *Pentateuch and Rashi's Commentary,* 399–413.

36. For a critical edition of Rashi's commentary, accompanied by useful references to the talmudic antecedents, see Rosenthal, "Rashi's Commentary on the *Song of Songs,*" 130–188. The English translations in these paragraphs are all based on Rosenthal's edition. For general comments regarding Rashi's methods, see Marcus, "The Song of Songs In German Hasidism and the School of Rashi, 265–272.

37. For the rabbinic tradition cited by Rashi, see *Mishnah: Rosh ha-Shanah* 3:3

38. For discussions of rabbinic and medieval Jewish typological historiography, see Yerushalmi, *Zakhor,* 5–52 and the opposing opinion espoused by Funkenstein, "Medieval Exegesis and Historical Consciousness" 88–130. See also Gerson D. Cohen, "Esau as Symbol in Early Medieval Thought," 19–48.

39. For a thorough study of the polemical motifs in Rashi's commentary, see Kamin, "Rashi's Commentary on *The Song of Songs,*" 218–248 (Hebrew); and Grossman, *Early Sages of France,* 477–479. See also Schreckenberg, *Die christlichen Adversus-Judaeos Texte (11.-13 Jh.),* 36–40. For the political and cultural background of Rashi's France, see Chazan, *Medieval Jewry in Northern France* and *European Jewry and the First Crusade.* For an overview of medieval Jewish attitudes toward Christianity, see Katz, *Exclusiveness and Tolerance.* Regarding the intensity and scope of medieval Jewish hostility toward Christianity, a lively scholarly debate was provoked by Yuval, "Vengeance and Damnation, 25–89 (Hebrew). For refutations and refinements of Yuval's arguments, see the related essays, rejoinders, and Yuval's response to his critics in *Zion* 59 (1994). In Hebrew; English summaries are found on pp. x–xx. The most recent critical survey of modern theories accounting for medieval Christian antisemitism against which the Jews reacted is Chazan, *Medieval Stereotypes.*

40. For a thumbnail sketch of early Christian readings of the golden calf, with useful bibliographic references to the patristic sources, see Smolar and Aberbach, "The Golden Calf in Postbiblical Literature," 93–95, 97–101. For a more complete and theologically nuanced review of the Christian sources, see Bori, *The Golden Calf.*

41. *The Apostolic Fathers,* 89–90. Epistle 4.

42. For recent discussions of the diverse medieval, Christian mystical, ecclesiastical, and Marian traditions and their dependence on patristic literature, especially Origen, see Matter, *Voice of My Beloved,* which stresses literary theory, and Astell, *Song of Songs,* which altogether ignores polemics against Judaism and stresses Jung-

ian archetypes. For the visual evidence regarding medieval Christian charges of Jewish idolatry and desecration of images, see Camille, *The Gothic Image*, 165–194.

43. In the early twelfth century, for example, Rupert of Deutz construed "my mother's children" (Song of Songs 1:6) to be an allusion to the pugnacious and deluded Jews, "children of the synagogue," the "satanic synagogues" ("Iudaei sunt, filii synagogae, immo qui se dicunt Iudaeos esse et non sunt, sed sunt synagoga Satanae") (*Commentaria in Canticum Canticorum*, 21, lines 407–410). In the same century, Honorius of Autun construed the same "mother's children" to be an allusion to the sinful "mother of the church," the "synagogue, the Judean children who attacked the church . . . by killing Christ, stoning Stephen" and persecuting Christians. ("Ecclesia . . . cujus mater erat Synagoga, ejusque filii Judaei, qui Ecclesiam multis modis impugnaverunt. Nam Christum occiderunt, Stephanum lapidaverunt, utrumque Jacobum interfecerunt, alios flagellaverunt, alios persecuti sunt.") Migne, *Patrologia Latina*, 176, c369. For overviews of Rupert and Honorious, see Schreckenberg, *Die christlichen Adversus-Judaeos Texte (11.-13 Jh.)*, 100–107 (Rupert), 114–116 (Honorius). On the motif of the satanic synagogue, see Trachtenberg, *The Devil and the Jews*.

44. See Chazan, *European Jewry and the First Crusade*, 161, 244, 329–330.

45. For a biographical sketch, see Urbach, *The Tosaphists*, 42–54 and passim. For monographic treatment of his biblical scholarship, see Japhet and Salters, *Commentary of R. Samuel Ben Meir (Rashbam)*; Gelles, *Peshat and Derash*, 123–127; and Melammed, *Bible Commentators*, 1: 449–513.

46. For the complete commentary and updated references to the scholarly literature it spawned, see Lockshin, ed., *Rashbam's Commentary on Exodus*.

47. See Rabbi Samuel's programmatic statement in his glosses to Genesis 37:2. A sufficiently reliable and annotated English translation is provided by Jacobs, *Jewish Biblical Exegesis*, 22–26. Using this text for the point of analytical departure, Kamin compared Rabbi Samuel and Hugh of St. Victor, thereby revealing the precise contours of Rabbi Samuel's commitment to the *sensus litteralis*. See Kamin, "Afinities between Jewish and Christian Exegesis," 141–155.

48. For descriptions of these northern European occult practices and beliefs, together with reports of widespread rabbinic ambivalence toward them, see Güdemann, *Geschichte des Erziehungswesens*, 199–227; Trachtenberg, *Jewish Magic and Superstition*, 11–68, 208–229; and Ta-Shma, *Early Franco-German Ritual and Custom*, 102–103 and passim.

49. Referring to the parallel comments on Exodus 28:30 and Deuteronomy 13:3, Martin Lockshin also concluded that Rabbi Samuel "clearly believe[d] that the forces of impurity do work for divination. Jews should refrain from using those forces despite the fact that they could provide accurate information about the future." See Lockshin, *Rashbam's Commentary on Exodus*, 365–366. A more complete review of this medieval rabbinic policy was made in the thirteenth century by Rabbi Moses ben Nahman (Nahmanides) in his extended comments to Deuteronomy 18:9. For the Hebrew text of Rabbi Moses' comments, see the annotated edition of *Perush ha-Torah le-Rabbenu Moshe ben Nahman*, 2: 426–428 and the English version, translated by Chavell, *Ramban (Nahmanides)*. Although Rabbi Moses represents Spanish Jewry, his teachers were northern Europeans whose tra-

ditions he preserved, including those related to divination. See Twersky, ed., *Rabbi Moses Nahmanides (Ramban)*.

50. For Rabbi Samuel's polemically motivated insistence on God's heavenly abode, see his comments on Exodus 32:4, in Lockshin, trans., *Rashbam's Commentary on Exodus*, 395.

51. See Rabbi's Samuel's comments on Exodus 28:30 and the explanation offered by M. Lockshin, *Rashbam's Commentary on Exodus*, 365–366.

52. For examples, historical context, and critical analysis, see Belting, *Likeness and Presence*, 261–296, 310, 351, and passim; and Freedberg, *Power of Images*, 283–316 and passim. The references assembled by Freedberg on p. 299 are particularly important, since they stem from Rabbi Samuel's immediate environment in twelfth-century northern Europe, thus supporting the contention that Rabbi Samuel was fully aware of these "living" Christian images and purposefully polemicizing against them.

53. For the English translation and notes registering no awareness of Rabbi Samuel's anti-Christian intentions, see Lockshin, *Rashbam's Commentary on Exodus*, 220–221.

54. See Rabbi Samuel's comments on Leviticus 11:34; 19:19; and Deuteronomy 22:6, which repeat the formula "*lefi derekh 'eretz uleteshuvat haminim.*" For the overall anti-Christian tenor and intention of his commentary, see Touitou, "*Peshat and Apologetics,*" 248–273. In Hebrew; English summary on p.v.

55. Smolar and Aberbach, "Golden Calf in Postbiblical Literature," 101. See Augustine's comments in his *Exposition of Psalms* 74:13.

56. For the scanty bibliographic data and an overview of his works, see Urbach, *Tosafists*, 113–120. For overviews and samples of his biblical exegesis, see Smalley, *Study of the Bible in the Middle Ages*, 151–156; and Krauss and Horby, *Jewish-Christian Controversy*, 85.

57. Regarding Exodus 32:1, Rabbi Joseph declared: "*has veshalom lo nitkavvnu le'avodah zarah.*" See also his comments on verse 8, "*shelo kivvnu le'avodah zarah.*" See, *Commentary to the Pentateuch*, 149–150. The summary and direct translations of his commentary in the following paragraphs are based on pages 149–151 in this edition. I also consulted the edition by Y. Nebo, *Perushe Rabbenu Yoseph Bekhor Shor 'al Hatorah*.

58. See Kamin, "Polemic against Allegory in the Commentary of Rabbi Joseph Bekhor Shor," in *Jews and Christians Interpret the Bible*, 367–392. In Hebrew; for an English summary, see *Jerusalem Studies in Jewish Thought* III-3 (1983/84), X–XI] and the section devoted to Rabbi Joseph in Grossman, "The Jewish-Christian Polemic and Jewish Biblical Exegesis in Twelfth-Century France," esp. 51–52. In Hebrew; English summary.

59. Commentary on Exodus 32:20. For debates and transformations in the celebration of the Eucharist in twelfth-century France of which Rabbi Joseph might have been aware, see Rubin, *Corpus Christi*. For other indications that Jews in northern Europe "were aware of the eucharistic sacrifice," see Marcus, *Rituals of Childhood*, 155 n. 89. For an overview of Jewish philosophical reactions to the doctrine of transubstantiation in the rite of the Eucharist, see Lasker, *Jewish Philosophical Polemics against Christianity* 140–151.

60. Commentary on Exodus 32:25. The parable may have been derived from an earlier Midrashic tradition directed against Greco-Roman cults or Christianity. See *The Midrash Rabbah—Song of Songs*, trans. Maurice Simon (London: Soncino, 1939), 9:58, 58 (*Shir Hashirim Rabbah* 1:6, 3 in the name of Rabbi Isaac).

61. Jeremy Cohen, "Towards a Functional Classification of Jewish anti-Christian Polemics," 113. Cohen's extraordinarily useful survey explicitly announces its debt to the equally useful classification suggested by Amos Funkenstein, "Changes in Christian Anti-Jewish Polemics," 172–201. Another attempt, using numerical scales, to bring conceptual order to the mass of medieval polemics is offered by Hanne Trautner-Kromann, *Sword and Shield*, 1–18.

62. For texts (*Libri Carolini*), references to the secondary literature, and historical discussion of the eighth-century contentious transition of this vocabulary to the Latin West from the Greek East, see Belting, *Likeness and Presence*, 6, 154, 158, 533–534. For additional discussion and original texts in translation, see Davis-Weyer, *Early Medieval Art*, 99–108.

63. See St. Thomas Aquinas, *Summa Theologica* 2.103; also 2.94 (*de idolatria*): "Neque in veteris legis tabernaculo seu templo, neque etaim nunc in ecclesia imagines instituuntur ut eis cultus latriae exhibeatur; sed ad quamdam significationem.") and 2.84 (*de adoratione*). For further discussion and references to the scholarly literature, see Camille, *Gothic Image*, 203–220. For textual evidence of this terminological distinction in the Byzantine Controversy, see Cyril Mango, *Art of the Byzantine Empire*, 169 and the excerpts from the influential John of Damascus, 169–172.

64. For a discussion of the medieval "exclusion of Christianity from the category of idolater," see Jacob Katz, *Exclusiveness and Tolerance*, 114–128.

65. For the most recent critical edition, references to the secondary literature, and analysis, see Gilbert Crispin, *Works of Gilbert Crispin*. For further references and discussion, see Schreckenberg, *Die christlichen Adversus-Judaeos-Texte (11.-13.th Jh.)*, 58–65; Krauss and Horbury, *Jewish-Christian Controversy*, 1: 72–73; Jeremy Cohen, "Towards a Functional Classification of Jewish anti-Christian Polemic," 102 n. 28; and Abulafia, "Christians Disputing Disbelief," 131–148. Universally acknowledged is the indispensable Bernhard Blumenkranz, *Les auteurs Chrétiens Latins*, 279–287.

66. Slightly modified and excerpted from Caecilia Davis-Weyer, *Early Christian Art*, 164–167. For the original Latin, see Gilbert Crispin, *Works of Gilbert Crispin*, 50–53. For further discussion, see Camille, *Gothic Image*, 175–178. The passage from Psalms is 98:5.

67. See Moore, *Formation of a Persecuting Society*. For a concise textbook overview of Jewish experience during the first two Crusades, see Stow, *Alienated Minority*, 102–120. For monographic treatment, see Robert Chazan, *European Jewry and the First Crusade*.

68. Abulafia, "Invectives against Christianity," 67. It is possible that Jewish literary invectives had their iconographic counterparts. See Marcus, *Rituals of Childhood*, 81–94.

69. Excerpted with slight modifications from the "long" Hebrew Chronicle composed by Solomon bar Simson and translated in Chazan, *European Jewry and the First Crusade*, 293. See also Eidelberg, *The Jews and the Crusades*, 67.

70. Mark. R. Cohen, *Under Crescent and Cross*, 135–136.

71. Marcus, *Rituals of Childhood*, 9.

72. Southern, *Making of the Middle Ages*, 20.

73. For the conceptual and terminological significance of "Islamdom" and "Islamicate" (society and culture "in which, of course, non-Mulims have always formed an integral, if subordinate, element") as opposed to "Islamic" (religion), see Hodgson, *Venture of Islam*, 1: 57–60. For Jewish history in Islamicate Spain, see Ashtor, *Jews of Moslem Spain*. For the impact of the Reconquista on Jewish life, see Baer, *History of the Jews in Christian Spain*.

74. See Mark R. Cohen, *Under Crescent and Cross*. Cohen defines the historiographical problems of drawing or overdrawing the contrasts between Jewish life in the "Latin West" and "Muslim East" in the introduction and chapter 1. He addresses comparative legal status in chapters 3–4, economics in chapter 5; social hierarchy in chapters 6–8; and religious factors in chapters 2, 9–10.

75. For the asymmetries between various region of Europe with respect to the persecution of minorities and the eventual closing of the gap between North and South, see Nirenberg, *Communities of Violence*.

76. See Baer, *History of the Jews in Christian Spain*, 1: 52–53 and passim. Baer dates the capture to 1115.

77. For the persistence of a notable Islamic presence in Navarre, particularly Tudela, after its control passed to the Christians, see Harvey, *Islamic Spain*, 138–150.

78. *Kuzari* 1:97. For a critical edition of the Arabic original, see *Book of Refutation and Proof on the Despised Faith*, 29–32. For a convenient collation of the Arabic original, Judah ibn Tibbon's Hebrew translation, and a relatively modern, annotated English translation, see Hirschfeld, *Kitab Al Khazari*, 46–53 (Arabic, Hebrew), 67–70 (English). See also *Jehuda Halevi: Kuzari Abridged Edition with an Introduction and a Commentary by Isaak Heinemann in Three Jewish Philosophers* (New York: Meridian Books, 1960), 47–49. Hirschfeld and Heinemann, among others, identically translated Halevi's opening line as if it were addressing idolatry rather than visual objects used in legitimate worship (*ma'budat*): "All nations were given to idolatry at that time." The translation is reasonable but insufficiently attentive to the context of *Kuzari* 1:97; 2:11, 74; and 4:13, where Halevi used the technical rabbinic term *'avodah zarah* when he meant to specify idolatry.

79. *Kuzari* 2:30. Halevi made the same point in *Kuzari* 4:25, which emphasizes the difference between drawing a human figure and producing a living person. In *Kuzari* 3:9, Halevi extended the concept of "imitation" to religious practice; referring to nations who replace the Jewish Sabbath with a different day of celebration, he declared: "Were they able to achieve a resemblance other than the one between the image of a statue and the image of a living person?"

80. *Kuzari* 1:97.

81. See *Juda Hallevi: Le Kuzari, Apologie de la Religion Meprisse*, 29. Touati's modern French translation and accompanying note also reflect the understanding that Halevi was drawing special attention to the Islamic denotations of *qiblah*. In their otherwise persuasive interpretation of *Kuzari* 1:97, M. Halbertal and A. Margalit overlooked the emphasis on calf as *qiblah*. They compromised their argument by describing the nonidolatrous calf as a "picture . . . that symbolized

God for [the Israelites] more than anything else" and which the Israelites "could address as a deity." If the calf were indeed "as a deity," it would not illustrate the point Halbertal and Margalit were seeking to draw. See Halbertal and Margalit, *Idolatry,* 186–187.

82. The figure of 600,000 excludes men under the age of twenty, all women, and all children. It rounds out the census variously recorded in Exodus 12:37 and Numbers 11:21 (600,000); Exodus 38:26 and Numbers 1:44 (603,550); and Numbers 26:51 (601,730). Halevi took the rough figure of three thousand slain sinners from Exodus 32:28.

83. Sura II ("The Cow"): 51–57. The *Qur'an* also refers to the calf in Sura 7 ("The Battlements") and 10 ("Ta Ha").

84. *Kuzari* 4:13.

85. For a thorough exposition of these architectonic *leitmotifs* in Halevi's thought, including the difference between philosophic religion and revealed religions, the unsurpassed significance of correct ritual behavior, and the distinctions between the three monotheistic religions, see Yohanan-Silman, *Thinker and Seer* (in Hebrew). For the English version, see Silman, *Philosopher and Prophet.* For the poetic counterpart to the *leitmotifs,* see Halevi's "To the Rivals" in Carmi, *Penguin Book of Hebrew Verse,* 335.

86. In the original version of this chapter, I had written that "they were not idolatrous." Persuaded by arguments generously offered in a private communication by my colleague Professor Barry S. Kogan, I modified that conclusion by inserting the qualifying term "unequivocally." Professor Kogan correctly directed my attention to *Kuzari* 4:11, where Halevi's rabbinic spokesman declares that Christians and Muslims "praise the place of prophecy in words, but they turn in praying to places of idolatry. . . . They retain the relics of ancient worship and feast days, changing nothing but this, that they have demolished the idols, without doing away with the rites connected with them. I might *almost* [emphasis added] say that the verse often repeated, "you will serve there other gods, wood and stone" [Deuteronomy 28:36, 64], alludes to those who worship the wood [Christians] and the stone [Muslims], towards which we incline daily more and more because of our sins. But it is true that they believe in God." Puzzling over Halevi's "almost," Professor Kogan is nevertheless convinced that Halevi was less tolerant in his views of the other monotheisms than my original formulation indicated. The language of *Kuzari* 1:97 supports the view of Halevi's unequivocal tolerance; the language of 4:11 supports the view of Halevi's more tentative, negative assessment. In the light of both these chapters and their divergent implications, I think it judicious to conclude that Halevi was either undecided on the issue or willing to grant Christianity and Islam a status higher than pure idolatry but lower than Judaism, especially with respect to ritual practice.

87. For the divergent attitudes between Sepharad and Ashkenaz toward Islam and Christianity, see Mark R. Cohen, *Under Crescent and Cross,* 141–143, 154–161, 174–194. For a reference to Jewish antipathy toward Christianity among the Jews of Sepharad, see Grossman, " 'Redemption By Conversion,' " 325–342. In Hebrew; English summary, xvi.

88. For the implications of the self-imposed exile on the content of Ibn Ezra's numerous and duplicative biblical commentaries, see Simon, "Abraham ibn-

Ezra," 23–42 (in Hebrew). For an overview of his biblical commentaries, see Friedlander, *Ibn Ezra Literature*, 4: 102–212; and Melammed, *Bible Commentators*, 2: 519–714.

89. See Friedlander, *Ibn Ezra Literature*, 4:121, 127, 144–145; and Simon, "Abraham ibn-Ezra," 39. For his critique of Christological interpretations, see *'Suffering Servant' of Isaiah*, 2: 43–49, and his comments on Genesis 49:10, Isaiah 7:14, and Isaiah 63:1. For his critique of Christian spiritualization of the law, see his methodological introduction to the commentary on the Pentateuch. In some versions of the introduction, the "first" class of interpreters refers to the "uncircumcised" Christians; in other versions, they are the "third" class. For an English translation of the introduction in which Christians constitute the "third class," see Jacobs, *Jewish Biblical Exegesis*, 13–14. It is unlikely that Jacobs was correct in identifying allegorists following Philo's lead as the target of Ibn Ezra's critique.

90. This summarizes Ibn Ezra's detailed excursus introducing Exodus 20:1–17, the Ten Commandments. See the "Long" commentary on Exodus 20:1 available in all rabbinic Bibles and in the facsimile edition of Vatican Manuscript Ebr. 38 published by Etan Levine, fols.44b–46b. By "a cosmic force equal to or greater than God," I mean what medieval Jewish philosophers writing in Hebrew called *shittuf* and what medieval Islamic and Jewish philosophers writing in Arabic called *shirk*. The two terms and their various derivatives literally mean partner or associate. For typical usage, see *Qur'an* 31:13; Saadia Gaon, *Book of Beliefs and Opinions*, 28; *Sefer ha-Nivhar be-'Emunot ve-De'ot*; and Bahya ibn Paquda, *Book of Direction to the Duties of the Heart*, 279 (*Hovot ha-Levavot* 5:5). Unlike Ibn Ezra, Bahya classified Christianity, along with dualism, naturalism, and foolish astrology, as "association" or polytheistic idolatry. For the Jewish critiques of Trinitarian doctrines, see Wolfson, *Repercussions of the Kalam in Jewish Philosophy*, 1–40.

91. "Long" commentary on Exodus 20:2 (Vatican Ebr. 38, fol. 46b). By the "Name [of God]," Ibn Ezra meant the tetragrammaton, YHVH. For further discussion, see Friedlander, *Essays on Ibn Ezra*, 4: 18–24.

92. "Long" commentary on Exodus 20:4. For the "forty-eight" heavenly shapes, see Levy and Contera, eds., *Beginning of Wisdom*, 153 (English), VI (Hebrew, *Sefer Reshit Hokhmah*).

93. "Long" commentary on Exodus 20:5.

94. "Long" commentary on Exodus 25:40 (Vatican Ebr. 38, fol. 56a).

95. "Long" commentary on Genesis 31:19 (Vatican Ebr, 38, fol. 15b). Where the printed editions read "image [*tzurah*] at certain times [*be-sh'aot yedu'ot*] so that the image speaks," Vatican Ebr. 38 reads, "*tzurah be-mazlot yedu'ot*," meaning "an image with [or of] certain constellations." Either reading conforms to astrological lore; both readings can easily be accounted as scribal misreadings.

96. Langermann, "Some Astrological Themes," 28–85. My direct quote is found on page 34. Langermann's finely nuanced article cites the relevant secondary literature and marshals overwhelming evidence of Ibn Ezra's ambivalent but unmistakably positive debt to astrology. A comparison of Langermann's exposition of Ibn Ezra's enigmatic doctrine of cosmic "poles . . . holding the cosmos together" and Ibn Ezra's remarks on the equally mysterious priestly ephod ("Long" commentary on Exodus 28:6) dramatically reveals the ascendancy of astrological considerations in Ibn Ezra's thought. For additional discussion of Ibn

Ezra's cosmology and symbolic understanding of various laws, see Heinemann, *Ta'ame ha-Mitzvot be-Sifrut Yisrael*, 1: 65–72. For additional discussion of Ibn Ezra's preoccupation with astrology, see Grieve, *Studien zum jüdischen Neuplatonismus*, 42–44 inter alia.

97. "Long" commentary on Exodus 25:18 (Vatican Ebr. 38, fol. 55a).

98. In his commentaries, Ibn Ezra explicitly referred to Halevi some twenty times. For a sampling of these references, including the one found in the "Long" commentary on Exodus 20:1, see Melammed, *Bible Commentators*, 2:674.

99. See Halevi's *Kuzari* 4:27 ("stay away from astrology"). For Halevi's negative attitude toward astrology and passionate response to the religious worldview represented by Ibn Ezra, see Langermann, "Some Astrological Themes," 65–74.

100. "Long" commentary on Exodus 20:20 (Vatican Ebr, 38, fol. 48a).

101. This summary combines features from both of Ibn Ezra's commentaries on the Pentateuch. See the "Long" commentary on Exodus 32:1 (in the facsimile edition of Vatican Manuscript Ebr. 38 published by Etan Levine, fol. 60b). Ibn Ezra made the same points, but more elliptically, in his "Short" commentary on the same verse; see *Ibn Ezra 'al ha-Torah*, 2:335–336.

102. "Short" commentary on Exodus 32:1, p. 336. For Ibn Ezra's considerable debt to Saadia, see Melammed, *Bible Commentators*, 2: 654–664. For Saadya's noncommittal use of astrological lore to illumine the enigmatic doctrines of the *Book of Creation*, see Saadia ben Joseph Fayyumi, *Sefer Yetzirah*, 86–88. Arabic original, Hebrew translation.

103. "Short" commentary on Exodus 32:1, p. 336.

104. "Long"' commentary on Exodus 32:1 (Vatican Ebr. 38, fol. 61a).

105. Studying the same texts, Moshe Idel came to the reasonable conclusion that "according to Abraham ibn Ezra, the form of the calf was intended to imitate an astral form, although he does not reveal what this form was." By eliminating Taurus and pointing us in the direction of Aquarius, Ibn Ezra made it that much simpler to find what the astral form might have been, if it was there at all. See Moshe Idel, "Hermeticism and Judaism," 63.

106. Twersky, "Aspects of the Social and Cultural History," 185. To supplement the helpful overview and bibliographic references given by Twersky, see Mark Cohen, *Under Crescent and Cross*, xxi, 102–103, 124–125, and 142–143.

107. *Itinerary*, 32–36 (English), 2–6 (Hebrew).

108. For a textbook overview, see Krauss and Horbury, *Jewish-Christian Controversy*, 236–238.

109. See Lasker and Stroumsa, *The Polemic of Nestor the Priest*, 1: 19–31.

110. Ibid., sections 127–134. In vol. 1, they are found on pages 77–78 (from the Arabic), 123–124 (from the Hebrew). In vol. 2, *Pulmus Nestor ha-Komer*, 69–72 (Arabic), 107 (Hebrew).

111. In Lasker and Stroumsa's numbering, this is section 173. In volume 1, it is found at page 86. In volume 2, *Pulmus Nestor ha-Komer*, it is found at page 84. I adopted their English translation but altered it slightly.

112. For an overview and bibliographic references, see Schreckenberg, *Die christlichen Adversus-Judaeos-Texte (11.–13.Jh.)*, 238–242; Krauss and Horbury, *Jewish-Christian Controversy* 1: 216; and Trautner-Kromann, *Shield and Sword*,

49–61. For the original Hebrew text, see Rosenthal, ed., *Milhamot ha-Shem*. Subsequent citations are all taken from Rosenthal's edition.

113. *Milhamot ha-Shem*, 56. For the apostolic and patristic sources of this argument, see Rosenthal's helpful references. For the biblical precedent, see John 3:14 ("As Moses lifted up the serpent in the wilderness, so must the Son of Man be lifted up.")

114. *Milhamot ha-Shem*, 57. Jacob ben Reuben's second rebuttal rejects allegory. It forcefully reminds the Christian that the serpent's function was strictly limited to the specific sin of rebellion against Moses committed by the people. The serpent was an antidote, but not for death in general. The third rebuttal focuses on the significance of placing the serpent high up on a pole. With downcast eyes, ashamed of their sin, the people bowed their heads. Compelled to raise their heads in order to see the serpent, they would be reminded of God in heaven who would forgive them if they sought divine mercy. The fourth rebuttal traps the Christian in the snares of his own theology. Conceding that all humans are born tainted with Adam's sin and subject to death, the Christian must agree that Jesus was equally tainted with sin and subject to death because he too emerged from "the womb of a woman." Jacob ben Reuben concluded: "Woe to those who believe in such a deity in whom is found sin and guilt." See *Milhamot ha-Shem*, 57–59.

115. *Milhamot ha-Shem*, 100.

116. Indicating where to look for the classical Christian responses, Rosenthal refers to Williams, *Adversus Judaeos*, 162, 167, 174, 177, 185, 272, 374, and 379.

Chapter Seven

1. For example, the fifteenth-century Joseph Albo recounted the thirteenth-century pilgrimage experience in Israel of Moses ben Nahman (Nahmanides): "Nahmanides also testifies that when he was in Palestine he found in 'Akko an ancient silver coin with the jar of manna and the rod of Aaron engraved upon it, and with characters all around that he could not read." See Joseph Albo, *Sefer ha-'Ikkarim* 3:16; 3:144–45 in Husik's edition. For additional textual evidence of late medieval pilgrimage, see Adler, *Jewish Travellers*, 100–328.

2. For the ambivalent and reluctant medieval Christian discovery of beautiful "art" in the remains of pre-Christian Europe, see Camille, *Gothic Image*, 77–87.

3. See Grayzel, *The Church and the Jews in the XIIIth Century*, 315 ("they shall moreover not presume to enter churches in the future. And lest they have occasion to enter, we strictly forbid them to deposit and keep their property in churches.," Council of Oxford, 17 April 1222) and 323 ("furthermore, Christians shall not receive the money of Jews in order to hide it in Churches for greater safety," Bishop of Worcester, 1229).

4. See, for example, Grayzel, *The Church and the Jews in the XIIIth Century*, 317.

5. From the "Regulations of Lord William of Bley, Bishop of Worcester" promulgated in 1229, cited in Grayzel, *The Church and the Jews in the XIIIth Century*, 321. For additional evidence of Chrisitian fury over "extortionate usury" leading to the appropriation and alleged desecration of ecclesiastical goods by Jewish moneylenders, see the sources collected by Grayzel: Innocent III (p. 107); Synodical

Rules of Odo (p. 301); Council of Treves (p. 319); and regulations of Alexander of Staveny, bishop of Coventry (p. 329). For twelfth-century precedents, see Chazan, *Medieval Jewry in Northern France*, 44, 48, 67, 96. Chazan cites Rigord, the twelfth-century chronicler, who wrote: "Certain ecclesiastical vessels consecrated to God—the chalices and crosses of silver and gold bearing the image of Lord Jesus Christ crucified—had been pledged to the Jews by way of security when the need of the churches was pressing. These they used so vilely, in their impurty and scorn of the Christian religion."

6. See, for example, Grayzel, *The Church and the Jews in the XIIIth Century*, 315, 319, 321.

7. I borrow the phrase from Henry Kraus, *Living Theatre of Medieval Art*. In the chapter titled "Anti-Semitism in Medieval Art," Kraus summarizes contemporary scholarship proving that hostility toward the Jews was integral to the theater and its diverse audiences: "As the tide of anti-Semtism swept through Western Europe during the twelfth and thirteenth centuries, it was reflected in all media of religious art and liturgy" (p. 149).

8. Berger, *Jewish-Christian Debate*, 68–69.

9. Ibid., 213–214, 331–332. Perhaps the starkest expression of the demythologizing, symbolic approach to Christian images is to be found in the late thirteenth-century dispute of Mallorca. To the Jewish charge that "churches are filled with idols and images . . . that [Christians] adore," Ingetus, the Christian interlocutor responds passionately, verging on heresy: "We do not adore [*adoramus*] idols and images. . . . but seeing them with bodily eyes, the eyes of the heart see, causing them to recall the passion of Christ. . . . Were I to possess a crucifix or some wooden image, and were I to lack something to heat the water for a fellow Christian or Jewish friend who becomes ill, I would put that very same crucifix or wooden image into a fire and burn [it]." For the Latin text and discussion of the historical significance, see Limor, *Die Disputationen zu Ceuta (1179) und Mallorca (1286)*, 290–291.

10. Kimhi, *Book of the Covenant*, 72. For the complete original Hebrew text, see Kimhi, *Book of the Covenant and Other Writings*, 60. For a critical discussion of the author and provenance of the passage, see Krauss and Horbury, *Jewish-Christian Controversy*, 222. For the Hebrew original of the passage cited, an English translation, and detailed commentary, see Trautner-Kromann, *Sword and Shield*, 87–88.

11. Rabbi Joseph ben Rabbi Nathan Official, *Sepher Joseph Hamekane*, 47–48. For discussion and reference to the parallel sources in English translation, see Berger, *Jewish-Christian Debate*, 73–74, 261. For further discussion of Rabbi Joseph and his polemic, see Trautner-Fromann, *Shield and Sword*, 90–101; Schreckenberg, *Die christlichen Adversus-Judaeos-Texte*, 265–269.

12. For a slightly different view of the prominence of Jewish–Christian arguments over images, see Funkenstein, *Perceptions of Jewish History*, 171 n. 3.

13. For the Hebrew original, see Judah Rosenthal, "Disputation between Elijah Hayyim of Genazzano and a Franciscan Friar," 442–443. For further discussion, see Krauss and Horbury, *Jewish-Christian Debate*, 214–215.

14. Berger, *Jewish-Christian Debate*, 67–68, 256.

15. For a complete English translation of the passage, see *Ramban (Nachmanides): Commentary on the Torah: Exodus*, 549–573. For the Hebrew original with annotations, see Rabbenu Moshe ben Nahman, *Perushe ha-Torah*, 1: 505–516. For critical discussion of the Kabbalistic salient in Nahmanides's thought, see Scholem, *Origins of Kabbalah*, 365–393, 404–414, 449–450; and the essays collected in *Rabbi Moses Nahmanides (Ramban)*; and Idel, *Kabbalah*, passim.

16. For a discussion of the theosophical-theurgic trend in Kabbalah, see Idel, *Kabbalah*, 112–249. For an illuminating and detailed exposition of the typical combination of formalist analysis and symbolic referentiality, see Green, *Keter*.

17. For an overview of his homiletical work, see Bettan, *Studies in Jewish Preaching*, 89–129. For the Kabbalist salient in his worldview, see Gottlieb, *Kabbalah in the Writings of R. Bahya Ben Asher Ibn Halawa*. In Hebrew.

18. Bahya ben Asher, *Rabbenu Bahya*, 2:328–332.

19. For the passage in Gersonides's commentary on Exodus 32, see Levi ben Gershom, *Perush 'al ha-Torah*, 112b. For background and bibliographic references to Gersonides, the philosopher, see Sirat, *A History of Jewish Philosophy*, 282–308 and passim; Julius Guttmann, *Philosophies of Judaism*, 236–254; Touati, *La pensée philosophique*; and Eisen, *Gersonides on Providence, Covenant, and the Chosen People*. For an English translation of his philosophic classic, see Levi ben Gershom, *Wars of the Lord*.

20. For the intense intellectual demands on late medieval teachers and preachers created by the growing stock of divergent opinions, see Bonfil, *Rabbis and Jewish Communities in Renaissance Italy*, 143–154, 270–323; and Hacker, "The Sephardi Sermon in the Sixteenth Century," 108–127. In Hebrew.

21. For an overview of his homiletics, see the still useful chapter, "Issac Arama: The Preacher's Preacher," in Bettan, *Studies in Jewish Preaching*, 130–191, and the pages devoted to him in Saperstein, *Jewish Preaching*. For monographic treatment of his religious philosophy, see Wilensky, *The Philosophy of Isaac Arama* (in Hebrew). For a summary of the contents of his essay on the golden calf, see Fox, "R. Isaac Arama's Philosophic Exegesis," 87–102.

22. Isaac Arama, *Sefer 'Aqedat Yizhaq*, 2:192b. The essay comprises chapter 35 and extends from 184b to 196. Because this section of the essay explicitly cites the collection of rabbinic midrashim found in *Exodus Rabbah* 43, it is likely that Arama's parable was inspired by the passage he found there: "A King (other versions: a naval officer) entered his house and found his wife enbracing a three-legged table on which statues are placed (*delphiqe*). He became angry. His companion said to him, 'Were the thing capable of impregnating (*molid*), it would be proper for you to be angry.' The King replied: 'The thing has no such potency, but I wanted to teach her not to behave in this way.' Thus God spoke [to Moses regarding the calf]: "I know that it amounts to nothing, but I did not want them to be involved with idolatry.' [Moses] then said to [God]: 'If it amounts to nothing, then why are You angry with Your children?' Hence, [Scripture reports], 'O Lord, why are You angry with Your people?' "

23. For a biographical overview and discussion of his political philosophy, see Netanyahu, *Don Isaac Abravanel*. For current references to the scholarly literature and insight into Abravanel's intellectual horizons, see Lawee, "On the Threshold of the Renaissance," 283–319.

24. Abravanel's oblivion might be explained by his unfamiliarity with Kabbalistic lore. Discussing the Kabbalists, Abravanel admitted that "[he] was not among them, nor did [he] study Kabbalistic teachings." See Isaac Abravanel, *Sefer Yeshu'ot Meshiho*, 51b. When the allusions were less subtle, dealing with major cosmological topics like the sephirot, he was able to correlate Kabbalistic doctrines with philosophical concepts regarding emanation and the celestial movers. See *Sefer 'Ateret Zeqanim*, 82–83; and *She'elot Leha-Hakham Sha'ul HaCohen*, 12b. For a discussion of Abravanel in the context of philosophic interpretations of Kabbalistic lore, see Idel, "Magical and Neoplatonic Interpretations of the Kabbalah," 226–227. For an overview of current scholarship regarding Abravanel's relationship to the Kabbalah, refuting Benzion Netanyahu's tendentious misreadings, see the persuasive comments of Eric Lawee, " 'Inheritance of the Fathers," 480–481, 493, 532–554. Abravanel's oblivion to Nahmanides's subtle allusion corroborates Lawee's conclusion that Abravanel was "uninitiated."

25. Yizhaq Abravanel, *Perush ha-Torah*, 526–535. For comments of the formal structure of Abravanel's biblical commentaries, see Saperstein, *Jewish Preaching*, 74.

26. I have summarized a portion of Abravanel's commentary on I Kings 12. The predecessors whose views he evaluated include David Kimhi, Levi ben Gershom, and Judah Halevi. For the Hebrew original, see Don Isaac Abravanel, *Perush 'al Nevi'im Rishonim*, 556–558. For the Mosaic blessing upon Joseph, see Deuteronomy 33:16–17.

27. See his comments on 1 Kings 6–7 in *Perush 'al Nevi'im Rishonim*, 496–513. Especially interesting are his observations regarding the various woods used, their dimensions, the slope of the wall, the techniques used to anchor wooden beams in the stone walls, the diverse procedures for overlaying wood panels with gold, the appearance of overhanging porticos and walkways along the walls of the Temple, and the array of sculptural techniques employed by the Israelite craftsmen as they compare with techniques used by craftsmen in Abravanel's own time and places. For data regarding his reliance on Christian commentators, see Gaon, *Influence of the Catholic Theologian Alfonso Tostado*.

28. *Zohar*, ed. Reuven Margaliot, 2:29b–30a. For Midrashic sources attesting to the image of Sarai, see Ginzberg, *Legends of the Jews*, 2:146, 5:369–370.

29. For parallel evidence of paintings and sculptures as reagents in sexuality and therefore subject to censorship, see the examples assembled and analyzed by Freedberg, *Power of Images*, 317–377.

30. Alter, *Genesis*, 1644–165.

31. Levi ben Gershom, *Perush 'al Ha-Torah*, 38a.

32. Ovadiah Sforno, *Be'ur 'al ha-Torah*, 78. In rabbinic Bibles that include Sforno's commentary, the passage is connected to Genesis 30:39. For a useful overview of premodern psychology, see Harvey, *Inward Wits*.

33. For a brief account of his life and thought, see Sirat, *A History of Jewish Philosophy*, 372–374.

34. Shi'mon ben Zemah Duran, *Sefer Magen Avot*, 43a–43b. For the Talmudic traditions regarding Rabbi Yohanan's renowned beauty and presence near bathhouses, see *Berakhot* 20a and *Bava Mezia' 84a.

35. Rabbi Solomon ibn Adret, *Sefer She'elot ve-Teshuvot*, Responsa 168 (pp. 61–62); 413 (pp. 144–150), and 825 (p. 280). For detailed references to the Talmudic literature, see Sperber, *Magic and Folklore*. For an overview of the medieval period, see the still unsurpassed Trachtenberg, *Jewish Magic and Superstition*, esp. 132–152 ("Amulets"), 193–207 ("Medicine").

36. For a bibliographic overview of the texts, see the relevant sections in Steinschneider, *Die Hebraischen Übersetzungen*. For a sample of the texts themselves, see the various Arabic, Hebrew, and English editions of Ibn Rushd's commentary on *Parva Naturalia* edited by Henry Blumberg and published under the auspices of the Medieval Academy of America. For thematic discussion, see Kaufmann, *Die Sinne*.

37. Berger, *Jewish-Christian Debate*, 224, 340.

38. Judah Halevi, *Kuzari* 3:5.

39. For a provocative phenomenological discussion of Loyola's Exercises, see Barthes, *Sade/Fourier/Loyola*, 38–75.

40. Medieval Jewish intellectuals tended to specialize. If they favored philology and grammar over the other branches of learning, they became Biblicists. If they advocated the superiority and autonomy of traditional rabbinic law and lore, they became Talmudists. If they were inclined to humanistic and universal rationalism, they became Philosophers. If they were attracted to myth and mysteries, they became Kabbalists. Many intellectuals, however, were eclectic. They synthesized various combinations of philology, rabbinic tradition, secular philosophy, and mysticism. For elegant and subtle expositions of this taxonomy, stressing the core of talmudic nomocentricity, see the following publications, all of them authored by Isadore Twersky: "Talmudists, Philosophers, Kabbalists," 431–459; "Some Non-Halakhic Aspects of the *Mishneh Torah*," 95–118; and "Religion and Law," 69–82. See also Dan, *Jewish Mysticism and Jewish Ethics*.

41. For an overview of the leading authorities, major texts, and halakhic processes with bibliographic references, see Hecht et al., eds., *Introduction to the History and Sources of Jewish Law*.

42. For a useful collection of medieval sources and contemporary analysis written from a strictly traditional point of view, see Schwartz, *Madrikh Torani le-'Omanut*.

43. For a description of the premodern consensus, see chapter 3 above.

44. Boaz Cohen, "Art in Jewish Law," 172, 175–176.

45. In addition to reviewing the handful of examples assembled by Boaz Cohen in the article cited in the previous note, see Kotlar, *Art and Religion*, 152–195 (in Hebrew). Kotlar collected more than thirty medieval texts. The pattern they reveal is identical to the one suggested by Boaz Cohen's smaller sample of evidence: occasional rabbinic stringency opposed to prevailing rabbinic leniency regarding images in places where public worship is conducted. This exclusive focus on synagogue decor lends support to Lionel Kochan's slightly exaggerated, ahistorical contention that "the context of the prohibition [against images] is always and everywhere that of worship. Remove this context as a qualifying factor and the prohibition falls away." No proposition about rabbinic discourse seems "always and everywhere" the same. See Kochan, *Beyond the Graven Image*, 93. For his review of the evidence regarding synagogue decoration, see pp. 99–103. For his

review of the evidence regarding the permissibility of incomplete statuary of the human figure, see pp. 126–128.

46. Karo, *Shulhan 'Arukh: Yoreh De'ah*, 139–141. For a more complete translation, see my "Defending, Enjoying, and Regulating the Visual." Also included are a complete translation of Rabbi Meir of Rothenburg's responsum on illuminated prayerbooks and the relevant passages from Maimonides's code, the *Mishneh Torah*.

Bibliography

Premodern Sources

Abraham ibn Ezra. *Abraham ibn Ezra's Commentary to the Pentateuch: Vatican Manuscript Vat. Ebr. 38.* Ed. Etan Levine. Jerusalem: Makor, 1974.

———. *The Beginning of Wisdom: An Astrological Treatise by Abraham ibn Ezra.* Ed. Raphael Levy and Francisco Cantera. Baltimore: Johns Hopkins University Press, 1939.

———. *Ibn Ezra 'al ha-Torah.* Ed. A. Weizer. 2 vols. Jerusalem: Mossad Harav Kook, 1976.

———. *Long Commentary on the Pentateuch.* (i.e., the Rabbinic Bible: *Miqra'ot Gedolot Rav Peninim.* 5 vols. Jerusalem: Lewin-Epstein, 1964.)

Adler, Israel. *Hebrew Writings concerning Music.* Munich: G. Henle Verlag, 1975.

Albo, Joseph. *Sefer ha-'Ikkarim (Book of Principles).* Trans. Isaac Husik. 5 vols. Philadelphia: Jewish Publication Society, 1946.

Averroes [Ibn Rushd]. *Averroes' Commentary on Plato's Republic.* Ed. and trans. E. I. J. Rosenthal. Cambridge: Cambridge University Press, 1956.

———. *Averroes' Tahafut al-Tahafut.* Trans. Simon Van Den Bergh. 2 vols. London: Luzac, 1954.

———. *Epitome of the Parva Naturalia.* Trans. Harry Blumberg. Cambridge, Mass.: Medieval Academy of America, 1961.

Avicenna [Ibn Sina]. *An-Najat fi-al-Mantiq wa-l-Ilahiyat.* Ed. Abd ar-Rahman Amira. Beirut, 1992.

———. *Traites Mystiques d'Abou Ali al-Hosain b. Abdallah b. Sina: L'Allégorie mystique Hay ben Yaqzan.* Ed. F. A. Mehren. Leiden: E. J. Brill, 1889.

Bahya ben Asher. *Rabbenu Bahya: Be'ur 'al Hatorah.* Ed. Charles Chavel. 3 vols. Jerusalem: Mossad Harav Kook, 1977.

Bahya ibn Paqudah. *The Book of Direction to the Duties of the Heart.* Trans. Menahem Mansoor. London: Routledge & Kegan Paul, 1973.

———. *Al-Hidaya 'ila Fara'id al-Qulub des Bachja ibn Josef ibn Paquda.* Ed. A. S. Yahuda. Leiden: E. J. Brill, 1912.

———. *Sefer Torah Hovot ha-Levavot.* Trans. Moses Hyamson. 2 vols. Jerusalem: Feldheim, 1970. Translation based on the Hebrew translation of Judah ibn Tibbon.

Barnabas. *The Apostolic Fathers: A New Translation and Commentary.* Vol. 3, *Barnabas and the Didache.* Trans. Robert Kraft. Toronto: Thomas Nelson, 1965.

Benjamin of Tudela. *The Itinerary of Rabbi Benjamin of Tudela.* Ed. and trans. A. Asher. 2 vols. New York: Hakesheth, n.d.

Berakhiah ha-Naqdan. *The Ethical Treatises of Berachya Son of Rabbi Natronai ha-Nakdan Being The Compendium and The Masref.* Ed. and trans. Hermann Gollancz. London: David Nutt, 1902.

Berger, David, trans. *The Jewish-Christian Debate in the High Middle Ages: A Critical Edition of Nizzahon Vetus.* Northvale: Jason Aronson, 1996.

Calvin, John. *Institutes of the Christian Religion.* Trans. Henry Beveridge. Grand Rapids, Mich.: Eerdmans, 1989.

Carmi, J., ed. *The Penguin Book of Hebrew Verse.* New York: Penguin, 1981.

Cicero. *Tusculan Disputations.* Trans. J. E. King. Cambridge: Harvard University Press, 1943.

Crescas, Hasdai. *Sefer Or Hashem.* 1545. Reprint, Jerusalem: Makor 1970. With an introduction by E. Schweid.

Crispin, Gilbert. *The Works of Gilbert Crispin, Abbot of Westminster.* Ed. Anna Sapir Abulafia and G. R. Evans. London: Oxford University Press, 1986.

Gruenwald, I. "A Preliminary Critical Edition of *Sefer Yezirah.*" *Israel Oriental Studies* 1 (1971): 156–157.

Duran, Profiat. *Maase Efod: Einleitung in das Studium und Grammatik der Hebräischen Sprache von Profiat Duran.* Ed. J. Friedländer and J. Kohn. 1865. Reprint, 1970. In Hebrew.

Elijah Hayyim of Genazzano. "The Disputation between Elijah Hayyim of Genazzano and a Franciscan Friar." In *Mehquarim u-Meqorot,* ed. J. Rosenthal, 1: 156–177. 2 vols. Jerusalem: Ruben Mass, 1967.

Fackenheim, Emil. "A Treatise on Love by ibn Sina." *Mediaeval Studies* 7 (1945): 208–228.

al-Farabi. *Fusul al-Madani* (Aphorisms of the statesman). Ed. and trans. D. M. Dunlop. Cambridge: Cambridge University Press, 1961.

————. *Siyasa al-Madiniya* (The political regime). In *Sefer he-Asif,* ed. Z. Philipowski. Leipzig: K. F. Kohler, 1849.

al-Ghazali. *The Incoherence of the Philosophers.* Trans. and ed. Michael E. Marmura. Provo: Brigham Young University Press, 1997.

Harvey, Steven. *Falaquera's "Epistle of the Debate": An Introduction to Jewish Philosophy.* Cambridge: Harvard University Press, 1987.

Isaac Abravanel. *Perush ha-Torah.* Ed. Avishai Shottland. 5 vols. Jerusalem: Horev, 1997.

————. *Perush 'al Nevi'im Rishonim.* Reprint. Jerusalem: Sefarim Torah ve-Da'at, 1976.

————. *She'elot Leha-Hakham Sha'ul HaCohen.* 1574. Reprint, Jerusalem: Makor, 1967.

————. *Sefer 'Ateret Zeqanim.* 1894. Reprint, Jerusalem: Makor, 1968.

————. *Sefer Yeshu'ot Meshiho.* 1871. Reprint, Jerusalem: Makor, 1967.

Isaac Arama. *'Aqedat Yizhaq.* 5 vols. 1849. Reprint, Jerusalem: Makor, 1988.

Jacob ben Asher. *Arba'ah Turim.* 4 vols. 1900. Reprint, Jerusalem: Jacob ben Asher, 1975. With traditional commentaries.

Jacob ben Reuben. *Milhamot ha-Shem.* Ed. Judah Rosenthal. Jerusalem: Mossad Harav Kook, 1963.

John of Damascus. *On the Divine Images: Three Apologies against Those Who Attack the Divine Images.* Trans. David Anderson. Crestwood, N.Y.: St. Vladimir's Seminary Press, 1980.

Joseph Bekhor Shor. *Commentary to the Pentateuch by R. Joseph Bechor Shor.* 2 vols. Reprint, Jerusalem: Makor, 1978.

———. *Perushe Rabbenu Yoseph Bekhor Shor 'al Hatorah.* Ed. Y Nebo. Jerusalem: Mossad Harav Kook, 1994.

Joseph ben Nathan Official. *Sepher Joseph Hamekane.* Ed. Judah Rosenthal. Jerusalem: Mekize Nirdamim, 1970.

Joseph ben Yehudah ibn Aqnin. *Divulgatio Mysteriorum Luminumque Apparentia.* Ed. and trans. Abraham Halkin. Jerusalem: Mekize Nirdamim, 1964.

Josephus. *The Life and Works of Flavius Josephus.* Trans. William Whiston. New York: Holt, Rinehart, and Winston, n.d.

Judah Halevi. *The Book of Refutation and Proof of the Despised Faith (The Book of the Khazars) Known as the Kuzar.* Ed. David H. Banet. Jerusalem: Magnes, 1977. In Arabic.

———. *Juda Hallevi: Le Kuzari, Apologie de la Religion Mepreisse.* Trans. Charles Touati. Louvain/Paris: Peeters, 1994.

———. *Kitab al Khazari: Book of Kuzari by Rabbi Judah Halevi.* Trans. Hartwig Hirschfeld. Brooklyn: P. Shalom, 1969. In Arabic, Hebrew, and English.

———. *Sefer ha-Kuzari.* 1880. Reprint, Warsaw: R. I. Goldman, 1959. With commentaries by Judah Moscato and Israel Halevi.

Judah Messer Leon. *The Book of the Honeycomb's Flow, Sepher Nopheth Suphim by Judah Messer Leon.* Ed. and trans. Isaac Rabinowitz. Ithaca: Cornell University Press, 1983.

Karo, Joseph. *Shulhan 'Arukh.* 4 vols. Reprint, Jerusalem, 1975. Includes traditional commentaries.

Ibn Khaldun. *Muqaddimat Ibn Khaldun.* Beirut, 1982.

———. *The Muqaddimah: An Introduction to History.* Ed. N. J. Dawood. Trans. Franz Rosenthal. Princeton: Princeton University Press, 1969.

Kimhi, Joseph. *The Book of the Covenant.* Trans. Frank Talmage. Toronto: Pontifical Institute of Mediaeval Studies, 1972.

———. *The Book of the Covenant and Other Writings.* Ed. Frank Talmage. Jerusalem: Bialik Institute, 1974. In Hebrew.

Leone Ebreo (Judah Abravanel). *Dialoghi d'amore.* Ed. S. Caramella. Bari: Gius Laterza & Figli, 1929.

Levi ben Gershom (Gersonides). *Commentary on Song of Songs.* Trans. Menachem Kellner. New Haven: Yale University Press, 1998.

———. *Milhamot Hashem.* 1560. Reprint, Riva di Trento. Possibly a pirated reprint.

———. *Perush 'al ha-Torah.* 2 vols. Venice: Daniel Bomberg, 1547. Possibly a pirated reprint.

———. *Perushe ha-Torah le-Rabbenu Levi ben Gershom (Ralbag).* Ed. Y. L. Levi. 5 vols. Jerusalem: Mossad Harav Kook, 1994.

———. *The Wars of the Lord.* Trans. Seymour Feldman. 2 vols. Philadelphia: Jewish Publication Society, 1984–1987.

Luther, Martin. *Ausgewählte Werke.* Ed. S. S. Borcherdt and George Merz. Munich: Chr. Kaiser Verlag, 1957.

Luther, Martin. *Luther's Works.* Trans. Conrad Bergendoff. Philadelphia: Muhlenberg, 1958.

Meir ibn Gabbai. *Sod ha-Shabbat (The Mystery of the Sabbath) from the Tola'at Ya'qov of R. Meir ibn Gabbai.* Trans. Elliot K. Ginsburg. Albany: State University of New York Press, 1989.

Mishnah: Shishah Sidre Mishnah. Ed. H. Albeck. 6 vols. Jerusalem: Mossad Bialik, 1958.

Moses ibn Ezra. *Kitab al-Muhadara wal-Mudhakara.* Ed. and trans. A. S. Halkin. Jerusalem: Mekize Mirdamim, 1975.

Moses Maimonides. *Acht Kapitel.* Ed. Maurice Wolff. Leiden: E. J. Brill, 1903.

————. *Dalalat al-Ha'irin.* Ed. S. Munk. Jerusalem: Azriel, 1929.

————. *The Eight Chapters of Maimonides on Ethics.* Trans. Joshua Gorfinkle. New York: Columbia University Press, 1912.

————. *Le Guide des égares.* Trans. S. Munk. Reprint, Paris: G.-P. Maisonneuve & Larose, 1963.

————. *Guide of the Perplexed.* Trans. S. Pines. Chicago: University of Chicago Press, 1969.

————. "Maimonides' Treatise on Logic (Makalah fi sina 'at al-mantik)." Ed. Israel Efros. *Proceedings of the American Academic for Jewish Research* 8 (1938).

————. *The Medical Aphorisms of Moses Maimonides.* Trans. F. Rosner. Haifa: Maimonides Research Center, 1989.

————. *Medical Works.* Ed. Suessmann Munter. 4 vols. Jerusalem: Mossad Harav Kook, 1961. In Hebrew.

————. *Mishneh Torah.* 5 vols. Reprint, New York, 1954. With traditional commentaries.

————. "Moses Maimonides' Two Treatises on the Regimen of Health." Ed. and trans. A. Bar-Sela, H. E. Hoff, and E. Faris. *Transactions of the American Philosophical Society* 54 (1964): 3–50.

————. *Sefer ha-Mitzvoth of Maimonides (The Negative Commandments).* Trans. Charles B. Chavel. 2 vols. London: Soncino, 1967.

————. *Sefer Moreh Nevukhim.* Trans. Samuel ibn Tibbon. Reprint, Vilna, 1904. With commentaries by Ephodi, Shem Tov, Ibn Crescas, and Isaac Abravanel.

Moses ben Nahman (Nahmanides). *Perush ha-Torah le-Rabbenu Moshe ben Nahman.* Ed. Charles D. Chavell. 2 vols. Jerusalem: Mossad Rav Kook, 1960.

————. *Ramban (Nachmanides): Commentary on the Torah.* Trans. Charles D. Chavell. 5 vols. New York: Shilo, 1971–1976.

Migne, J. P., ed. *Patrologiae Cursus Completus, Series Latina.* 221 vols. Paris, 1844–1865.

Narboni, Moses. "Moses Narboni's Epistle on Sh'ur Qomah." Trans. Alexander Altmann. In *Jewish Medieval and Renaissance Studies,* ed. Alexander Altmann. Cambridge: Harvard University Press, 1967.

Nestor the Priest. *The Polemic of Nestor the Priest: Introduction, Translations, and Commentary.* Ed. and trans. Daniel J. Lasker and Sarah Stroumsa. 2 vols. Jerusalem: Ben-Zvi Institute for the Study of Jewish Communities in the East, 1996.

Ovadiah Sforno. *Be'ur 'al ha-Torah le-Rabbi 'Ovadiah Sforno.* Ed. Z. Gottleib. Jerusalem: Mossad Harav Kook, 1984.

Petahiah of Regensburg. *Sibbuv ha-Rav Petahiah mi-Regensburg.* Ed. Eliezer Gruenhut. Frankfurt am Main: J. Kauffman, 1905.

Philo. *On the Giants.* Trans. F. H. Colson and G. H. Whitaker. Cambridge: Harvard University Press, 1968.

Plato. *Republic.* Trans. G. M. A. Grube. Rev. C. D. C. Reeve. Indianapolis: Hackett, 1992.

Pseudo-Dionysius. Trans. Colm Luibheid and Paul Rorem. New York: Paulist, 1987.

Ravitzky, A. *Crescas' Sermon on the Passover and Studies in His Philosophy.* Jerusalem: Israel Academy of Sciences and Humanities, 1988. In Hebrew.

Rupert of Deutz. *Commentaria in Canticum Canticorum.* Ed. H. Haacke. Turnhout: Brepols, 1974.

Rosenthal, Judah. "Rashi's Commentary on the Song of Songs." In *Samuel K. Mirsky Jubilee Volume,* ed. Simon Bernstein and Gershon A. Churgin, 130–188. New York: Jubilee Committee, 1958. In Hebrew.

Saadia Gaon. *The Book of Beliefs and Opinions.* Trans. Samuel Rosenblatt. New Haven: Yale University Press, 1948.

———. *Sefer ha-Nivhar be-'Emunot ve-De'ot.* Ed. and trans. Joseph Kapah. New York: Sura, 1970.

———. *Sefer Yetzirah.* Ed. and trans. Joseph Kapah. New York: American Academy for Jewish Research, 1972.

Samuel ben Meir (Rashbam). *Rashbam's Commentary on Exodus: An Annotated Translation.* Ed. and trans. Martin Lockshin. Atlanta: Scholars, 1997.

Schirmann, H. *Ha-Shirah ha-Ivrit be-Sepharad uve-Provans.* Tel Aviv: Dvir, 1959.

Sefer ha-Bahir. Ed. R. Margaliot. Jerusalem: Mossad Harav Kook, 1994.

Shem Tov Falaqera. *Moreh ha-Moreh.* Ed. M. Bisliches. Pressburg: Antonn Edlen V Schmidt, 1837.

Shi'mon ben Zemah Duran. *Sefer Magen Avot.* 1785. Reprint, Jerusalem: Makor.

Solomon ben Isaac (Rashi). *The Pentateuch and Rashi's Commentary.* Trans. Abraham ben Isaiah and Benjamin Sharfman. 5 vols. Brooklyn: S. S. & R. Publishing, 1949.

Solomon ben Zemach Duran. *Sefer HaRashbash.* Livorno: Stamperio d'Abraham Meldola, 1742.

Solomon ibn Adret. *Sefer She'elot ve-Teshuvot.* Reprint, Bene Beraq, 1959.

Solomon ibn Gabirol. *Selected Religious Poems of Solomon ibn Gabirol.* Ed. I. Davidson. Trans. I. Zangwill. Philadelphia: Jewish Publication Society, 1944.

Stern, Menahem, ed. *Greek and Latin Authors on Jews and Judaism.* 3 vols. Jerusalem: Israel Academy of Sciences and Humanities, 1974.

Talmud Bavli. 20 vols. 1880–1886. Reprint, New York: Pardes, 1954.

Torah Shelemah. Ed. Menahem Kasher. 39 vols. New York: American Biblical Encyclopedia Society/Jerusalem: Torah Shelemah Society, 1949–1985.

Ibn Tufayl. *Hayy ben Yaqdhan.* Trans. Leon Gauthier. Beyruoth: Imprimerie Catholique, 1936.

Vasari, Giorgio. *Le Vite de Piú Eccellenti Pittori Scultori e Architettori.* Vol. 1. Milan: Edizioni per il Club del Libro, 1962.

———. *Lives of the Most Eminent Painters, Sculptors, and Architects.* Trans. Gaston du C. de Vere. 10 vols. London: Macmillan/Medici Society, 1912–1914.

Walzer, Richard. *Al-Farabi on the Perfect State*. Oxford: Oxford University Press, 1985.

Wolfson, H. A. *Crescas' Critique of Aristotle*. Cambridge: Harvard University Press, 1929.

Zohar. Ed. R. Margaliot. 3 vols. Jerusalem: Mossad Harav Kook, 1964.

Modern Sources

Abrams, M. H. *Doing Things with Texts: Essays in Criticism and Critical Theory*. New York: W. W. Norton, 1991.

Abulafia, Anna Sapir. "Invectives against Christianity in the Hebrew Chronicles of the First Crusade." In *Crusade and Settlement*, ed. Peter W. Edbury. Bristol: University College Cardiff Press, 1985.

Abrahams, Israel. *Jewish Life in the Middle Ages*. New York: Atheneum, 1969.

Adler, Elkan Nathan. *Jewish Travellers in the Middle Ages*. 1930. Reprint, New York: Dover, 1987.

Alsop, Joseph. *The Rare Art Traditions: The History of Art Collecting and Its Linked Phenomena Wherever These Have Appeared*. New York: Harper & Row, 1982.

Alter, Robert. *Genesis: Translation and Commentary*. New York: W. W. Norton, 1996.

Altmann, Alexander. *Von der mittelalterlichen zur modernen Aufklärung*. Tübingen: J. C. B. Mohr, 1987.

Amishai-Maisels, Ziva. "Chagall and the Jewish Revival: Center or Periphery." In *Tradition and Revolution: The Jewish Renaissance in Russian Avant-Garde Art, 1912–1928*. Ed. Ruth Apter-Gabriel. Jerusalem: Israel Museum, 1987.

———. "The Jewish Awakening: A Search for National Identity." In *Russian Jewish Artists in a Century of Change 1890–1990*, ed. Susan Tumarkin Goodman, 54–70. Munich: Prestel, 1995.

Ansky, S. *Semyon An-Sky: The Jewish Artistic Heritage, An Album*. Trans. Alan Myers. Moscow: "RA," 1994.

Arendt, Hannah. *The Life of Mind: One-Volume Edition*. New York: Harcourt Brace Jovanovich, 1978.

Arnold, Matthew. *Culture and Anarchy*. Ed. Samuel Lipman. New Haven: Yale University Press, 1994.

———. *Culture and Anarchy*. Ed. R. H. Super. Ann Arbor: University of Michigan Press, 1965.

Arnold, T. W. *Painting in Islam: A Study of the Place of Pictorial Art in Muslim Culture*. Oxford: Oxford University Press, 1928.

Asad, Talal. *Genealogies of Religion: Discipline and Reasons of Power in Christianity and Islam*. Baltimore: Johns Hopkins University Press, 1993.

Ashtor, E. *The Jews of Moslem Spain*. Trans. Aaron Klein and Jenny M. Klein. 3 vols. Philadelphia: Jewish Publication Society, 1973–1984.

Astell, Ann W. *The Song of Songs in the Middle Ages*. Ithaca: Cornell University Press, 1990.

Auerbach, Erich. *Mimesis: The Representation of Reality in Western Literature*. Trans. Willard T. Trask. Princeton: Princeton University Press, 1968.

Avi-Yonah, Michael. "Jewish Art." In *Encyclopedia of World Art*. New York: McGraw-Hill, 1963.

Baer, I. *History of the Jews in Christian Spain*. Trans. Louis Schoffman. 2 vols. Philadelphia: Jewish Publication Society, 1966.

Baron, Salo W. *The Jewish Community*. 3 vols. Philadelphia: Jewish Publication Society, 1942.

―――. *A Social and Religious History of the Jews*. 2d ed. 18 vols. New York: Columbia University Press, 1952–1983.

Barrett, William. *Irrational Man: A Study in Existential Philosophy*. Garden City, N.Y.: Doubleday, 1958.

Barrett, William, and Henry D. Aiken, eds. *Philosophy in the Twentieth Century: An Anthology*. 4 vols. New York: Random House, 1962.

Baudrillard, Jean. *Simulacra and Simulation*. Trans. Sheila Faria Glaser. Ann Arbor: University of Michigan Press, 1994.

Baxandall, Michael. *Painting and Experience in Fifteenth-Century Italy*. Oxford: Oxford University Press, 1988.

Belting, Hans. *Likeness and Presence: A History of the Image before the Era of Art*. Trans. Edmund Jephcott. Chicago: University of Chicago Press, 1994.

Ben-Sasson, H. H., ed. *A History of the Jewish People*. Cambridge: Harvard University Press, 1976.

Benjamin, Walter. "The Work of Art in the Age of Mechanical Reproduction." In *Illuminations*, ed. Hannah Arendt and trans. Harry Zohn, 217–252. New York: Schocken, 1968.

Bennet, Tony. The *Birth of the Museum: History, Theory, Politics*. New York: Routledge, 1995.

Berenson, Bernard. *Aesthetics and History in the Visual Arts*. New York: Pantheon, 1948.

Berger, John. *Ways of Seeing*. New York: Penguin Viking, 1977.

Berger, Peter L. *The Sacred Canopy: Elements of a Sociological Theory of Religion*. Garden City, N.Y.: Anchor, 1969.

Berkowitz, Michael. "Art in Zionist Popular Culture and Jewish National Self-Consciousness, 1897–1914." *Studies in Contemporary Jewry: An Annual* 6 (1990): 3–42.

Berman, Lawrence V. "Greek into Hebrew: Samuel ben Judah of Marseilles, Fourteenth-Century Philosopher and Translator." In *Jewish Medieval and Renaissance Studies*, ed. Alexander Altmann, 289–320. Cambridge: Harvard University Press, 1967.

Bettan, Israel. *Studies in Jewish Preaching*. Cincinnati: Hebrew Union College Press, 1939.

Birnbaum, Solomon. *The Hebrew Scripts*. 2 vols. Leiden: E. J. Brill, 1971.

Black, Deborah L. *Logic and Aristotle's "Rhetoric" and "Poetics" in Medieval Arabic Philosophy*. Leiden: E. J. Brill, 1990.

Bland, Kalman P. "Antisemitism and Aniconism: The Germanophone Requiem for Jewish Visual Art." In *Jewish Identity in Modern Jewish History*, ed. Catherine M. Soussloff, 41–66. Berkeley: University of California Press, 1999.

―――. "Beauty, Cultural Relativism, and Maimonides in Medieval Jewish Thought." *Journal of Medieval and Early Modern Studies* 26 (1996): 85–112.

Bland, Kalman P. "Defending, Enjoying, and Regulating the Visual." In *Judaism in Practice*. Ed. Larry Fine. Princeton: Princeton University Press, forthcoming.

———. "Medieval Jewish Aesthetics: Maimonides, Body, and Scripture in Profiat Duran." *Journal of the History of Ideas* 26 (1993): 533–559.

———. "Moses and the Law According to Maimonides." In *Mystics, Philosophers, and Politicians: Essays . . . in Honor of Alexander Altmann*. Ed. J. Reinharz and D. Swetschinski, 49–66. Durham, N.C.: Duke University Press, 1982.

Bloch, Marc. *The Historian's Craft*. Trans. Peter Putnam. New York: Vintage Books, 1953.

Blumenkranz, Bernhard. *Les Auteurs Chrétiens Latins du moyen age sur les Juifs et la Judaïsme*. Paris: Mouton, 1963.

———. *Le Juif médiéval au miroir de l'art chretien*. Paris: études Augustiniennes, 1966.

Bolt, John E. "Jewish Artists and the Russian Silver Age." In *Russian Jewish Artists in a Century of Change, 1890–1990*, ed. Susan Tumarkin Goodman, 40–53. Munich: Prestel, 1995.

Boman, Thorlief. *Das hebräische Denken im Vergleich mit dem griechischen*. Göttingen: Vandenhook & Ruprecht, 1954.

———. *Hebrew Thought Compared to Greek*. London: SCM Press, 1960.

Bonfil, Robert. *Jewish Life in Renaissance Italy*. Trans. Anthony Oldcorn. Berkeley: University of California Press, 1994.

———. *Rabbis and Jewish Communities in Renaissance Italy*. Trans. Jonathan Chipman. New York: Littman Library Oxford University Press, 1990.

Borges, Jorge Luis. *Labyrinths*. Ed. Donald A. Yates and James E. Yirby. New York: New Directions Book, 1964.

Bori, Pier Cesare. *The Golden Calf and the Origins of the Anti-Jewish Controversy*. Trans. David Ward. Atlanta: Scholars, 1990.

Bothe, Rolf. *Synagogen in Berlin: Zur Geschichte einer zerstörten Architektur*. Berlin: Verlag Willmuth Arenhövel, 1983.

Bourdieu, Pierre. *The Field of Cultural Production: Essays on Art and Literature*. Ed. Randal Johnson. New York: Columbia University Press, 1993.

Bouwsma, William J. *John Calvin: A Sixteenth-Century Portrait*. Oxford: Oxford University Press, 1988.

Brann, Ross. *The Compunctious Poet: Cultural Ambiguity and Hebrew Poetry in Muslim Spain*. Baltimore: Johns Hopkins University Press, 1991.

Brennan, Teresa, and Martin Jay, eds. *Vision in Context: Historical and Contemporary Perspectives on Sight*. New York: Routledge, 1996.

Braunstein, Susan L. "Sigmund Freud's Jewish Heritage." In *Sigmund Freud and Art: His Personal Collection of Antiquities*. Ed. Lyn Gamwell and Richard Wells. Albany: State University Press of New York Press/London: Freud Museum, 1989. With an introduction by Peter Gay.

Brenner, Michael. *The Renaissance of Jewish Culture in Weimar Germany*. New Haven: Yale University Press, 1996.

Breslin, James E. B. *Mark Rothko: A Biography*. Chicago: University of Chicago Press, 1993.

Bynum, Caroline Walker. *The Resurrection of the Body in Western Christianity, 200–1336*. New York: Columbia University Press, 1995.

Bryer, Anthony, and Judith Herrin, eds. *Iconoclasm*. Birmingham, U.K.: University of Birmingham Centre for Byzantine Studies, 1975.

Bryson, Norman. *Vision and Painting: The Logic of the Gaze*. New Haven: Yale University Press, 1983.

Bryson, Norman, Michael Ann Holly, and Keith Moxey, eds. *Visual Theory: Painting and Interpretation*. New York: Harper Collins, 1991.

Buber, Martin. *Eclipse of God* New York: Harper & Row, 1957.

———. *Juedischer Kuenstler*. Berlin: Juedischer Verlag, 1903.

———. *Moses: The Revelation and the Covenant*. Atlantic Highlands, N.J..: Humanities Press International, 1989. With an introduction by Michael Fishbane.

———. *On Judaism*. Ed. Nahum N. Glatzer. New York: Schocken, 1972.

Burke, Peter. *The Italian Renaissance: Culture and Society in Italy*. Princeton: Princeton University Press, 1986.

———. *Varieties of Cultural History*. Ithaca: Cornell University Press, 1997.

Butler, Judith. *Bodies That Matter*. New York: Routledge, 1993.

Camille, Michael. *The Gothic Idol: Ideology and Image Making in Medieval Art*. Cambridge: Cambridge University Press, 1989.

Carmilly-Weinberger, Moshe. *Fear of Art: Censorship and Freedom of Expression in Art*. New York: R. R. Bowker, 1986.

Carruthers, Mary. *The Book of Memory: A Study of Memory in Medieval Culture*. Cambridge: Cambridge University Press, 1990.

Cassirer, Ernst. *The Philosophy of the Enlightenment*. Boston: Beacon, 1955.

Cassuto, David, ed. *Judaism and Art*. Ramath Gan: Bar-Ilan University, 1988. In Hebrew.

Chagall, Marc. *Marc Chagall and the Jewish Theater*. New York: Solomon J. Guggenheim Museum. 1992.

Chazan, Robert. *Church, State, and the Jew in the Middle Ages*. New York: Behrman House, 1980.

———. *Daggers of Faith: Thirteenth-Century Christian Missionizing and Jewish Response*. Berkeley: University of California Press, 1989.

———. *European Jewry and the First Crusade*. Berkeley: University of California Press, 1987.

———. *Medieval Jewry in Northern France: A Political and Social History*. Baltimore: Johns Hopkins University Press, 1973.

———. *Medieval Stereotypes and Modern Antisemitism*. Berkeley: University of California Press, 1997.

Chenu, M. D. *Nature, Man, and Society in the Twelfth Century*. Chicago: University of Chicago Press, 1968.

Christensen, Carl H. *Art and the Reformation in Germany*. Athens: Ohio University Press, 1979.

Clifford, James. *The Predicament of Culture: Twentieth-Century Ethnography, Literature, and Art*. Cambridge: Harvard University Press, 1988.

Cohen, Arthur A. "From Eastern Europe to Paris and Beyond." In *The Circle of Montparnasse: Jewish Artists in Paris, 1905–1945*, ed. Kenneth E. Silver and Romy Golan. New York: Universe Books, 1985.

Cohen, Boaz. *Law and Tradition in Judaism*. New York: Jewish Theological Seminary, 1959.

Cohen, Elisheva. *Moritz Oppenheim: The First Jewish Painter.* Jerusalem: Israel Museum, 1983.

Cohen, Evelyn M. "The Decoration of Medieval Hebrew Manuscripts." In *A Sign and a Witness: 2,000 Years of Hebrew Books and Illuminated Manuscripts,* ed. Leonard S. Gold, 47–60. New York: New York Public Library/Oxford University Press, 1988.

Cohen, Gerson D. *The Blessing of Assimilation in Jewish History.* Boston: Hebrew Teachers College, 1966.

———. "Esau as Symbol in Early Medieval Thought." In *Jewish Medieval and Renaissance Studies,* ed. Alexander Altmann, 19–48. Cambridge: Harvard University Press, 1967.

Cohen, Hermann. "Heinrich Heine und das Judentum." In *Hermann Cohens Jüdische Schriften,* ed. Bruno Strauss, 2: 2–44. Berlin: C. A. Schwetschke, 1924. Reprint, 1980.

———. *Religion der Vernunft aus den Quellen des Judenthums.* Köln: Joseph Melzr Verlag, 1928.

———. *Religion of Reason out of the Sources of Judaism.* Trans. Simon Kaplan. New York: Frederick Ungar, 1972. Introductory essay by Leo Strauss.

Cohen, Jeremy. "Towards a Functional Classification of Jewish Anti-Christian Polemics in the High Middle Ages." In *Religionsgespräche im Mittelalter,* ed. Bernard Lewis and Friedrich Niewöhner. Wiesbaden: Otto Harrassowitz, 1992.

Cohen, Judith. "Jubal in the Middle Ages." *Yuval* 3 (1974): 83–99.

Cohen, Mark R. *Under Crescent and Cross: The Jews in the Middle Ages.* Princeton: Princeton University Press, 1994.

Cohen, Naomi W. *Not Free to Desist: The American Jewish Committee, 1906–1966.* Philadelphia: Jewish Publication Society, 1972.

Cohen, Richard I. "An Introductory Essay—Viewing the Past." *Studies in Contemporary Jewry: An Annual* 6 (1990): 3–42.

———. *Jewish Icons: Art and Society in Modern Europe.* Berkeley: University of California Press, 1998.

———. "Self-Image through Objects: Towards a Social History of Jewish Art Collecting and Jewish Museums." In *The Uses of Tradition: Jewish Continuity in the Modern Era,* ed. Jack Wertheimer, 203–242. New York: Jewish Theological Seminary of America, 1992.

Cook, John W. "Picturing Theology: Martin Luther and Lucas Cranach." In *Art and Religion: Faith, Form, and Reform,* ed. Osmund Overby, 22–39. Columbia: University of Missouri, 1984.

Corbin, Henry. *Avicenna and the Visionary Recital.* Trans. W. R. Trask. New York: Pantheon, 1960.

Coulton, G. C. *Art and the Reformation.* Cambridge: Cambridge University Press, 1953.

Crary, Jonathan. *Techniques of the Observer: On Vision and Modernity in the Nineteenth Century.* Cambridge: MIT Press, 1990.

Crouch, Joseph. *Puritanism and Art: An Inquiry into a Popular Fallacy.* London: Cassell, 1910.

Curtius, E. R. *European Literature and the Latin Middle Ages.* Trans. Willard R. Trask. Princeton: Princeton University Press, 1953.

Dan, Joseph. *Jewish Mysticism and Jewish Ethics.* Seattle: University of Washington Press, 1986.

Danto, Arthur C. *Embodied Meanings: Critical Essays and Aesthetic Meditations.* New York: Noonday, 1994.

———. *The Transfiguration of the Commonplace: A Philosophy of Art.* Cambridge: Harvard University Press, 1981.

Danton, Robert. *The Kiss of Lamourette: Reflections in Cultural History.* New York: W. W. Norton, 1990.

Davidson, Herbert "Maimonides' *Shemonah Peraqim* and Alfarabi's *Fusul Al-Madani.*" *Proceedings of the American Academy for Jewish Research* 31(1963): 33–50.

———. "Medieval Jewish Philosophy in the Sixteenth Century." In *Jewish Thought in the Sixteenth Century,* ed. Bernard D. Cooperman, 106–145. Cambridge: Harvard University Press, 1983.

Davis-Weyer, Caecilia. *Early Medieval Art, 300–1150.* Englewood Cliffs, N.J.: Prentice-Hall, 1971.

Dawidowicz, Lucy S. *The Golden Tradition: Jewish Life and Thought in Eastern Europe.* Boston: Beacon, 1967.

Derrida, Jacques. "Interpretation at War: Kant, the Jew, the German." *New Literary History* 22 (1990–1991): 39–95.

Dethier, Hubert. "Love and Intellect in Leone Ebreo." In *Neoplatonism and Jewish Thought,* ed. Lenn F. Goodman, 353–386. Albany: State University of New York Press, 1992.

Dewey, John. *Art as Experience.* New York: Perigee, 1934.

Dimont, Max. *The Indestructible Jews.* New York: NAL/World Publishing, 1971.

———. *Jews, God, and History.* New York: Simon & Schuster, 1962.

Dodds, Jerrilyn D. "Mudejar Tradition and the Synagogues of Medieval Spain: Cultural Identity and Cultural Hegemony." In *Convivencia: Jews, Muslims, and Christians in Medieval Spain,* ed. Vivan Mann, Thomas Click, and Jerrilyn Dodds, 113–132. New York: George Braziller, 1992.

Driver, Samuel R., and Adolph Neubauer. *The 'Suffering Servant' of Isaiah according to the Jewish Interpreters.* London: James Parker, 1877.

Duffy, Eamon. *The Stripping of the Altars: Traditional Religion in England, 1400–1580.* New Haven: Yale University Press, 1992.

Eagleton, Terry. *The Ideology of the Aesthetic.* Cambridge: Basil Blackwell, 1990.

———. *Ideology: An Introduction.* Verso: London, 1991.

Eco, Umberto. *The Aesthetics of Thomas Aquinas.* Trans. Hugh Bredin. Cambridge: Harvard University Press, 1988.

Eidelberg, Shlomo. *The Jews and the Crusades: The Hebrew Chronicles of the First and Second Crusades.* Madison: University of Wisconsin Press, 1977.

Eire, Carlos M. N. *War against the Idols: The Reformation of Worship from Erasmus to Calvin.* Cambridge: Cambridge University Press, 1986.

Eisen, Robert. *Gersonides on Providence, Covenant, and the Chosen People: A Study in Medieval Jewish Philosophy and Biblical Commentary.* Albany: State University of New York Press, 1995.

Eliade, Mircea. *The Myth of the Eternal Return or, Cosmos and History.* Trans. Willard R. Trask. Princeton: Princeton University Press, 1974.

Eliade, Mircea. *The Sacred and the Profane*. New York: Harvest, 1959.

Elkins, James. *The Object Stares Back: On the Nature of Seeing*. New York: Simon & Schuster, 1996.

Emery, R. "New Light on Profayt Duran the 'Efodi.' " *Jewish Quarterly Review* 58 (1967–1968): 328–337.

Epstein, Marc M. *Dreams of Subversion in Medieval Jewish Art and Literature*. University Park: Pennsylvania State University Press, 1997.

Ettinghaus, Richard, and Oleg Grabar. *The Art and Architecture of Islam: 650–1250*. New York: Viking Penguin, 1987.

Ezrahi, Sidra DeKoven. "Our Homeland, The Text . . . Our Text the Homeland: Exile and Homecoming in the Modern Jewish Imagination." *Michigan Quarterly Review* 31 (1992): 463–497.

Ezrahi, Yaron. *The Descent of Icarus: Science and the Transformation of Contemporary Democracy*. Cambridge: Harvard University Press, 1990.

Fackenheim, Emil L. *Encounters between Judaism and Modern Philosophy*. New York: Basic, 1973.

Faur, José. *Golden Doves with Silver Dots: Semiotics and Textuality in Rabbinic Tradition*. Bloomington: Indiana University Press, 1986.

Febvre, Lucien. *The Problem of Unbelief in the Sixteenth Century: The Religion of Rabelais*. Trans. Beatrice Gottlieb. Cambridge: Harvard University Press, 1982.

Feher, Michel, ed. *Fragments for a History of the Human Body: Part Three*. Cambridge: Zone MIT Press, 1989.

Finkel, Avraham Y. *The Responsa Anthology*. Northvale, N.J.: J. Aronson, 1990.

Fishbane, Michael. "Israel and the Mothers." In *The Other Side of God*, ed. Peter L. Berger, 28–47. Garden City, N.Y.: Anchor, 1981.

Fishbane, Michael, ed. *The Midrashic Imagination: Jewish Exegesis, Thought, and History*. Albany: State University of New York Press, 1993.

Feuerbach, Ludwig. The *Essence of Christianity*. Trans. George Eliot. New York: Harper, 1957.

———. The *Das Wesen des Christenthums*. Ed. Wilhelm Bolin and Friedrich Jodl. Stuttgart-Bad Cannstatt: Frommann Verlag, 1960.

Formstecher, Solomon. *Die Religion des Geistes*. Frankfurt am Main: J. C. Hermann, 1841.

Foster, Hal, ed. *Vision and Visuality*. Seattle: Bay Press, 1988.

Foucault, M. *The Archaeology of Knowledge*. Trans. A. M. Sheridan-Smith. New York: Vintage, 1973.

Fox, Marvin. "R. Isaac Arama's Philosophic Exegesis of the Golden Calf Episode." In *Minhah le-Nahum: Biblical and Other Studies Presented to Nahum M. Sarna in Honour of His 70th Birthday*, ed. Marc Brettler and Michael Fishbane, 87–102. Sheffield: Journal for the Study of Old Testament Press, 1993.

Frankfort, H., et al. *Before Philosophy*. Baltimore: Penguin, 1946.

Freedberg, David. *The Power of Images: Studies in the History and Theory of Response*. Chicago: University of Chicago Press, 1989.

Freud, Sigmund. *Der Mann Moses und die monotheistische Religion, Drei Abhandlungen*. Amsterdam: Verlag Allert De Lange, 1939.

———. *Moses and Monotheism*. Trans. Katherine Jones. New York: Vintage, 1939.

Frey, J. B. "La Question des images chez les Juifs a la lumière des récentes découvertes." *Biblia* 15 (1934): 265–300.

Friedlander, M. *Ibn Ezra Literature: Essays on the Writings of Abraham Ibn Ezra.* London: Trübner, 1877.

Funkenstein, Amos. *Perceptions of Jewish History.* Berkeley: University of California Press, 1993.

Gallwitz, Klaus, ed. *Makart.* Baden-Baden: Staatliche Kunsthalle, 1972.

Gaon, Solomon. *The Influence of the Catholic Theologian Alfonso Tostado on the Pentateuch Commentary of Isaac Abravanel.* New York: Sephardic House, 1993.

Gardner's Art through the Ages. Ed., Horst De La Croix, Richard G. Tansey, and Diane Kirkpatrick. 9th ed. New York: Harcourt Brace Jovanovich, 1991.

Garside, Charles, Jr. *Zwingli and the Arts.* New Haven: Yale University Press, 1966.

Gager, John. *Moses in Greco-Roman Paganism.* Nashville: Abingdon, 1972.

Gay, Peter. "The Social History of Ideas: Ernst Cassirer and After." In *The Critical Spirit: Essays in Honor of Herbert Marcuse.* ed. Kurt H. Wolff and Barrington Moore Jr., 106–120. Boston: Beacon, 1967.

———. "Encounter with Modernism: German Jews in Wilhelminian Culture." In *Freud, Jews, and Other Germans: Masters and Victims in Modernist Culture.* New York: Oxford University Press, 1978.

Gellrich, Jesse M. *The Idea of the Book in the Middle Ages: Language Theory, Mythology, and Fiction.* Ithaca: Cornell University Press, 1985.

Geller, Jay. "(G)nos(e)ology: The Cultural Construction of the Other." In *People of the Body: Jews and Judaism from an Embodied Perspective*, ed. Howard Eilberg-Schwartz, 243–282. Albany: State University of New York Press, 1992.

Gelles, Benjamin J. *Peshat and Derash in the Exegesis of Rashi.* Leiden: E. J. Brill, 1981.

Gilman, Sander. "The Jewish Body: A Foot-note." In *People of the Body: Jews and Judaism from an Embodied Perspective*, ed. Howard Eilberg-Schwartz, 223–241. Albany: State University of New York Press, 1992.

———. *The Jew's Body.* New York: Routledge, 1991.

Ginzberg, Louis. *The Legends of the Jews.* Trans. Henrietta Szold. 7 vols. Philadelphia: Jewish Publication Society, 1937.

Goetschel, Roland. *Meir ibn Gabbay: Le Discours de la Kabbale Espagnole.* Leuven: Peeters, 1981.

Goitein, S. D. *A Mediterranean Society: The Jewish Communities of the Arab World as Portrayed in the Documents of the Cairo Geniza.* 6 vols. Berkeley: University of California Press, 1967.

Goldberg, David Theo. *Anatomy of Racism.* Minneapolis: University of Minnesota Press, 1990.

Goldstein, Bluma. *Reinscribing Moses: Heine, Kafka, Freud, and Schoenberg in a European Wilderness.* Cambridge: Harvard University Press, 1992.

Goodenough, Erwin J. *Jewish Symbols in the Greco-Roman Period.* 12 vols. New York: Pantheon, 1953–1968.

Goodman, Lenn E. *Rambam.* New York: Viking, 1976.

Goodman, Nelson. *Ways of Worldmaking.* Indianapolis: Hackett, 1978.

Goodman, Susan Tumarkin. "Alienation and Adaptation of Jewish Artists in Russia." In *Russian Jewish Artists in a Century of Change, 1890–1990*, ed. Susan Tumarkin Goodman, 28–39. Munich: Prestel, 1995.

Goody, Jack. *The Domestication of the Savage Mind*. Cambridge: Cambridge University Press, 1977.

Gottlieb, Efraim. *The Kabbalah in the Writings of R. Bahya Ben Asher Ibn Halawa*. Jerusalem: Kiryath Sefer, 1970. In Hebrew.

Grabar, Oleg. *The Formation of Islamic Art*. New Haven: Yale University Press, 1987.

Graetz, Heinrich. *The Structure of Jewish History and Other Essays*. Trans. and ed. Ismar Schorsch. New York, 1975. With an introduction by Ismar Schorsch.

Grayzel, Solomon. *The Church and the Jews in the XIIIth Century*. New York: Hermon, 1966.

Green, Arthur. *Keter: The Crown of God in Early Jewish Mysticism*. Princeton: Princeton University Press, 1997.

———. *New Directions in Jewish Theology in America*. Ann Arbor: Jean and Samuel Frankel Center for Judaic Studies, 1994.

Greenberg, Clement. *Art and Culture: Critical Essays*. Boston: Beacon, 1965.

———. *The Collected Essays and Criticism*. Ed. John O'Brian. 4 vols. Chicago: University of Chicago Press, 1993.

Gregory, Richard L. *Eye and Brain: The Psychology of Seeing*. Princeton: Princeton University Press, 1990.

Grieve, Hermann. *Studien zum jüdischen Neuplatonismus: Die Religionsphilosophie des Abraham Ibn Ezra*. Berlin: Walter De Gruyter, 1973.

Grossman, Avraham. *The Early Sages of Ashkenaz: Their Lives, Leadership and Works*. Jerusalem: Magnes, 1988. In Hebrew.

———. *The Early Stages of France: Their Lives, Leadership and Works*. Jerusalem: Magnes, 1996. In Hebrew.

———. "The Jewish-Christian Polemic and Jewish Biblical Exegesis in Twelfth-Century France." *Zion* 51 (1986): 29–60. In Hebrew.

———. " 'Redemption by Conversion' in the Teachings of Early Ashkenazi Sages." *Zion* 59 (1994): 325–342. In Hebrew.

Groys, Boris. "From Internationalism to Cosmopolitanism: Artists of Jewish Descent in the Stalin Era." In *Russian Jewish Artists in a Century of Change, 1890–1990*, ed. Susan Tumarkin Goodman, 81–88. Munich: Prestel, 1995.

Güdemann, M. *Geschichte des Erziehungswesens und der Kultur der Juden in Frankreich und Deutschland*. 1880. Reprint, Amsterdam: Philo, 1966.

Guérer, Annick Le. *Scent*. Trans. Richard Miller. New York: Turtle Bay, 1992.

Guilbaut, Serge. *How New York Stole the Idea of Modern Art: Abstract Expressionism, Freedom, and the Cold War*. Trans. Arthur Goldhammer. Chicago: University of Chicago Press, 1983.

Gutmann, Joseph. *Hebrew Manuscript Painting*. New York: George Braziller, 1978.

———. "Is There Jewish Art?" In *The Visual Dimension: Aspects of Jewish Art*, ed. Clare Moore. 1–19. Boulder: Westview, 1993.

———. "Jewish Art." In *The State of Jewish Studies*. Ed. Shaye J. D. Cohen and Edward L. Greenstein. Detroit: Wayne State University Press, 1990. pp. 193–211.

———. *No Grave Images*. New York: Ktav, 1971.

Gutmann, Joseph, ed. *The Temple of Solomon: Archaeological Fact and Medieval Tradition in Christian, Islamic, and Jewish Art*. Missoula: Scholars, 1976.

Guttmann, Julius. *Philosophies of Judaism: A History of Jewish Philosophy from Biblical Times to Franz Rosenzweig*. Trans. David W. Silverman. New York: Schocken, 1973.

Ha-'Am, Ahad. *'Al Parashat Derakhim*. Ed. J. Frankel. Tel Aviv: Dvir, 1963.

Ha-'Am, Ahad. *Selected Essays of Ahad Ha-'Am*. Trans. Leon Simon. New York: Atheneum, 1970.

Habermas, Jürgen. "Der deutsche Idealismus der jüdischen Philosophen." In *Philosophisch-Politische Profile*, 37–66. Frankfurt am Main: Suhrkamp Verlag, 1971.

———. "The German Idealism of the Jewish Philosophers." In *Philosophical-Political Profiles*, 21–43. Trans. Frederick G. Lawrence. Cambridge: MIT Press, 1983.

Hacker, Joseph R. "The Sephardi Sermon in the Sixteenth Century—Between Literature and Historical Sources," *Pe'amim* 26 (1986): 108–127. In Hebrew.

Hacking, Ian. *The Emergence of Probability*. Cambridge: Cambridge University Press, 1975.

Halbertal, Moshe, and Avishai Margalit. *Idolatry*. Trans. Naomi Goldblum. Cambridge: Harvard University Press, 1992.

Hammer-Schenk, Harold. "Die Architektur der Synagoge von 1780 bis 1933." In *Die Architekturder Synagoge*. ed. Hans-Peter Schwarz. Stuttgart: Klett-Cotta, 1988.

———. *Synagogen in Deutschland: Geschichte einer Baugattung im 19 und 20 Jahrhundert, 1780–1933*. Hamburg: H. Christians, 1981.

Handelman, Susan. *Slayers of Moses: The Emergence of Rabbinic Interpretation in Modern Literary Theory*. Albany: State University of New York Press, 1982.

Harrison, Charles, and Paul Wood. *Art in Theory: 1900–1990*. Cambridge: Blackwell, 1993.

Hartman, Geoffrey H. "Religious Literacy." *Conservative Judaism* 40 (1988): 21–31.

———. *The Unmediated Vision: An Interpretation of Wordsworth, Hopkins, Rilke, and Valéry*. New Haven: Yale University Press, 1954.

Hartman, and Geoffrey H., and Sanford Budick, eds. *Midrash and Literature*. New Haven: Yale University Press, 1988.

Harvey, L. P. *Islamic Spain, 1200–1500*. Chicago: University of Chicago Press, 1990.

Harvey, E. Ruth. *The Inward Wits: Psychological Theory in the Middle Ages and the Renaissance*. London: Warburg Institute—University of London, 1975.

Harvey, Warren Zev. "Crescas versus Maimonides on Knowledge and Pleasure." In *A Straight Path: Studies in Medieval Philosophy and Culture . . . in Honor of Arthur Hyman*, ed. Ruth Link-Salinger, 113–123. Washington, D.C.: University Press of America, 1988.

Harvey, Warren Zev. "Ethics and Meta-Ethics, Aesthetics and Meta-Aesthetics in Maimonides." In *Maimonides and Philosophy*, ed. Shlomo Pines and Yirmiyahu Yovel, 131–138. Dordrecht: M. Nijhoff, 1986.

———. "Kabbalistic Elements in Crescas' Light of the Lord." *Jerusalem Studies in Jewish Thought* 2 (1982–1983): 75–109. In Hebrew.

Haskell, Frances. *History and Its Images: Art and the Interpretation of the Past*. New Haven: Yale University Press, 1993.

Hecht, N. S., et al., eds. *An Introduction to the History and Sources of Jewish Law*. Oxford: Clarendon, 1996.

Hegel, G. W. F. *Aesthetics: Lectures on Fine Art*. Trans. T. M. Knox. 2 vols. Oxford: Clarendon, 1975.

———. *Early Theological Writings*. Trans. T. M. Knox. Chicago: University of Chicago Press, 1948.

Heine, Heinrich. "*Geständnisse*," In *Heinrich Heine*. Ed. Mazzino Montinari. Vol. 12. Berlin: Akademie-Verlag, 1988.

———. *Religion and Philosophy in Germany* (Zur Geschichte der Religion und Philosophie in Deutschland). Trans. John Snodgrass. Albany: State University of New York Press, 1986.

Heinemann, Yitzhaq, et al. *Three Jewish Philosophers*. New York: Meridian, 1960.

———. *Ta'ame ha-Mitzvot be-Sifrut Yisrael*. 2 vols. Jerusalem: Jewish Agency, 1959.

Heinzl, Brigitte. *Hans Makart: Zeichnung-Entwürfe*. Salzburg: Salzburger Museum Carolino Augusteum, 1984.

Herlitz, Georg, and Bruno Kirschner, eds. *Jüdisches Lexicon*. 4 vols. Berlin: Jüdischer Verlag, 1929.

Herselle Krinsky, Carole. *Synagogues of Europe: Architecture, History, Meaning*. Mineola, N.Y.: Dover, 1996.

Hertzberg, Arthur. *The French Enlightenment and the Jews*. New York: Columbia University Press, 1968.

———. *The Zionist Idea: A Historical Analysis and Reader*. New York: Atheneum, 1984.

Heschel, Abraham Joshua. *The Earth Is the Lord's and The Sabbath*. New York: Harper Torchbooks, 1966.

Heyd, Milly, and Ezra Mendelsohn. " 'Jewish' Art? The Case of the Soyer Brothers." *Jewish Art* 19–20 (1993/1994): 194–211.

Himmelfarb, Gertrude. *On Looking into the Abyss: Untimely Thoughts on Culture and Society*. New York: Vintage, 1995.

Hodgson, Marshall. *The Venture of Islam: Conscience and History in a World Civilization*. 3 vols. Chicago: University of Chicago Press, 1974.

hooks, bell. *Black Looks: Race and Representation*. Boston: South End, 1992.

———. *Art on My Mind: Visual Politics*. New York: New Press, 1995.

Horkheimer, Max. *Critical Theory: Selected Essays*. Trans. Matthew J. O'Connell. New York: Continuum, 1995.

Howarth, Herbert. "Jewish Art and the Fear of the Image: The Escape from an Age-Old Inhibition." *Commentary* 9 (1950): 142–150.

Howe, Irving. *World of Our Fathers: The Journey of the East European Jews and the Life They Found and Made*. New York: Simon & Schuster, 1976.

Hume, David. *Enquiries concerning the Human Understanding and concerning the Principles of Morals.* Ed. L. A. Selby-Bigge. Oxford: Clarendon, 1902.

———. *Selected Essays.* Ed. S. Copley and A. Edgar. Oxford: Oxford University Press, 1993.

———. *A Treatise of Human Nature.* Ed. L. A. Selby-Bigge. Oxford: Oxford University Press, 1902.

Humphreys, R. Stephen. *Islamic History: A Framework for Inquiry.* Princeton: Princeton University Press, 1991.

Husik, Isaac. *A History of Mediaeval Jewish Philosophy.* New York: Macmillan, 1916.

Hyman, Arthur, and James J. Walsh, eds. *Philosophy in the Middle Ages.* Indianapolis: Hackett, 1983.

Idel, Moshe. "Hermeticism and Judaism." In *Hermeticism and the Renaissance: Intellectual History and the Occult in Early Modern Europe.* Ed. Ingrid Merkel and Allen G. Debus, pp. 59–76. Washington: Folger Books, 1988.

———. *Kabbalah: New Perspectives.* New Haven: Yale University Press, 1988.

———. "The Magical and Neoplatonic Interpretations of the Kabbalah in the Renaissance." In *Jewish Thought in the Sixteenth Century,* ed. Bernard Cooperman, 186–242. Cambridge: Harvard University Press, 1983.

———. "Music and Prophetic Kabbalah." *Yuval* 1 (1968): 151–169.

Idelsohn, A. Z. *Jewish Music in Its Historical Development.* New York: Schocken, 1929.

Ivry, Alfred L. "Remnants of Jewish Averroism in the Rennaissance." In *Jewish Thought in the Sixteenth Century,* ed. Bernard D. Cooperman, 243–265. Cambridge: Harvard University Press, 1983.

Jacobs, Louis. *Jewish Biblical Exegesis.* New York: Behrman House, 1973.

Jaeger, Werner. *The Theology of the Early Greek Philosophers.* Oxford: Oxford University Press, 1947.

Janson, H. W. *History of Art.* 4th ed. New York: Harry N. Abrams/Englewood Cliffs: Prentice-Hall, 1991. Revised and expanded by Anthony F. Janson,

Japhet, Sara, and Robert B. Salters. *The Commentary of R. Samuel Ben Meir Rashbam on Qoheleth* [Ecclesiastes]. Jerusalem: Magnes. 1985.

Jay, Martin. *The Dialectical Imagination: A History of the Frankfurt School and the Institute of Social Research, 1923–1950.* Berkeley: University of California Press, 1996.

———. *Downcast Eyes: The Denigration of Vision in Twentieth-Century French Thought.* Berkeley: University of California Press, 1993.

———. "Scopic Regimes of Modernity." In *Vision and Reality,* ed. Hal Foster. Seattle: Bay Press, 1988.

Jenks, Chris, ed. *Visual Culture.* New York: Routledge, 1995.

Jonas, Hans. *The Phenomenon of Life: Toward a Philosophical Biology.* New York: Delta, 1968.

Jones, Peter. "Hume's Literary and Aesthetic Theory." In *The Cambridge Companion to Hume,* ed. David F. Norton. Cambridge: Cambridge University Press, 1993.

Jospe, Raphael. *Torah and Sophia: The Life and Thought of Shem Tov ibn Falquera.* Cincinnati: Hebrew Union College Press, 1988.

Kamin, Sarah. *Jews and Christians Interpret the Bible*. Jerusalem: Magnes, 1991. In Hebrew.

——. *Rashi's Exegetical Categorization in Respect to the Distinction between Peshat and Derash*. Jerusalem: Magnes, 1986. In Hebrew.

Kampf, Avram. *Jewish Experience in the Art of the Twentieth Century*. South Hadley, Mass.: Bergin & Garvey, 1984.

Kanof, Abram. *Jewish Ceremonial Art and Religious Observance*. New York: Abrams, 1970.

——. *Jewish Symbolic Art*. Jerusalem: Geffen, 1990.

Kant, Immanuel. *Anthropology from a Pragmatic Point of View*. Trans. Victor L. Dowell. Rev. and ed. Hans H. Rudnick. Carbondale: Southern Illinois University Press, 1978.

——. *Critique of Judgment*. Trans. Werner S. Pluhar. Indianapolis: Hackett, 1987.

——. *Kant's Gesammelte Schriften*. Konglich Preussischen Akademie der Wissenschaften. Berlin: Georg Reimer, 1917.

——. *Religion within the Limits of Reason Alone*. Trans. and intr. Theodore M. Greene and Hoyt H. Hudson. New York: Harper Torchbooks, 1960.

Kaplan, Mordecai. *Judaism as a Civilization*. New York: Thomas Yoseloff, 1934.

Katz, Jacob. *The Darker Side of Genius: Richard Wagner's Anti-Semitism*. Hanover, N.H.: University Press of New England, 1986.

——. *Exclusiveness and Tolerance: Jewish–Gentile Relations in Medieval and Modern Times*. New York: Schocken, 1961.

——. *From Prejudice to Destruction: Anti-Semitism, 1700–1933*. Cambridge: Harvard Univesity Press, 1980.

——. *Halakhah and Kabbalah: Studies in the History of Jewish Religion, Its Various Faces, and Social Relevance*. Jerusalem: Magnes, 1986. In Hebrew.

Kaufmann, David. "Art in the Synagogue." *Jewish Quarterly Review* 9 (1897): 254–269

——. *Die Sinne: Beiträge zur Geschichte der Physiologie und Psychologie im Mittelalter aus Hebräischen und Arabischen Quellen*. Budapest: F. A. Brockhaus, 1884.

Kaufmann, Thomas DaCosta. *Court, Cloister, and City: The Art and Culture of Central Europe, 1450–1800*. Chicago: University of Chicago Press, 1995.

Kaufmann, Walter. *Religion from Tolstoy to Camus*. New York: Harper and Row, 1961.

Kayser, Stephen. "Defining Jewish Art." In *Mordecai M. Kaplan Jubilee Volume*. New York: Jewish Theological Seminary, 1953.

——. *Jewish Ceremonial Art*. Philadelphia: Jewish Publication Society of America, 1955.

Kellner, Menahem, ed. *The Pursuit of the Ideal: Jewish Writings of Steven Schwarzschild*. Albany: State University of New York Press, 1990.

Kern, Stephen. *The Culture of Time and Space, 1880–1918*. Cambridge: Harvard University Press, 1983.

Kieval, Herman. *The High Holy Days*. New York: Burning Bush, 1959.

Kohn, Hans. *The Idea of Nationalism: A Study in Its Origins and Background*. New York: Collier, 1944.

Kook, Abraham Isaac. *Letters*. Jerusalem: Mosad Harav Kook, 1962. In Hebrew.

———. *The Lights of Penitence, the Moral Principles, Lights of Holiness: Essays, Letters, and Poems*. Trans. and intr. Ben Zion Bokser. New York: Paulist, 1978.

———. *Rav A. Y. Kook: Selected Letters*. Trans. Tzvi Feldman. Ma'aleh Adumim, Israel: Yeshivat Birkat Moshe, 1986.

Kotlar, David. *Art and Religion*. Jerusalem: M. Neumann, 1971. In Hebrew.

Krakowski, Edouard. *L'Esthetique de Plotin et son influence*. Paris: E. De Boccard, 1929.

Kraeling, Carl H. *The Synagogue*. New Haven: Yale University Press, 1956.

Kraemer, Joel L. "Alfarabi's *Opinions of the Virtuous City* and Maimonides' Foundations of the Law." In *Studia Orientalia Memoriae D. H. Baneth*. Ed. J. Blau. Jerusalem: Magnes, 1979.

Kraus, Henry. *The Living Theatre of Medieval Art*. Bloomington: Indiana University Press, 1967.

Krauss, Samuel, and William Horby. *The Jewish-Christian Controversy from the Earliest Times to 1789*. Tübingen: J. C. B. Mohr (Paul Siebeck), 1995.

Krautheimer, Richard. *Batte Keneset Bime ha-Benayyim*. Trans. Amos Goren. Jerusalem: Bialik Institute, 1994. With an introduction by Moshe Barasch.

———. "And Gladly Did He Learn and Gladly Teach: To Gerard E. Caspary for January 10, 1989." In *Rome: Tradition, Innovation, and Renewal A Canadian International Art History Conference, 8–13 June 1987 in honour of Richard Krautheimer . . . Leonard Boyle*, O.P. offprint.

———. *Mittelalterliche Synagogen*. Berlin: Frankfurter Verlags-Anstalt, 1927.

Kristeller, Paul O. "The Modern System of the Arts." In *Renaissance Thought 2: Papers on Humanism and the Arts*. New York: Harper Torchbooks, 1965.

———. *The Philosophy of Marsilio Ficino*. Trans. Virginia Conant. Gloucester: Peter Smith, 1964.

Kugel, James. *In Potiphar's House*. Cambridge: Harvard University Press, 1994.

Kuhn, Thomas S. *The Structure of Scientific Revolutions*. Chicago: University of Chicago Press, 1970.

Lachterman, David R. "Maimonidean Studies, 1950–1986." *Maimonidean Studies*. 1 (1990): 197–216.

Ladner, Gerhart B. "Origin and Significance of the Byzantine Iconoclastic Controversy." In *Images and Ideas in the Middle Ages: Selected Studies in History and Art*, I, 37–47. Rome: Edizioni di Storia e Letteratura, 1983.

Lambropoulos, Vassilis. *The Rise of Eurocentrism: Anatomy of Interpretation*. Princeton: Princeton University Press, 1993.

Langermann, Y. Tzvi. "Some Astrological Themes in the Thought of Abraham ibn Ezra." In *Rabbi Abraham Ibn Ezra: Studies in the Writings of a Twelfth-Century Jewish Polymath*, ed. Isadore Twersky and Jay M. Harris, 28–85. Cambridge: Harvard University Press, 1993.

Lasker, Daniel J. *Jewish Philosophical Polemics against Christianity in the Middle Ages*. New York: Ktav, 1977.

Lawee, Eric. " 'Inheritance of the Fathers': Aspects of Isaac Abarbanel's Stance toward Tradition." Ph.D. diss., Harvard University, 1993.

———. "On the Threshold of the Renaissance: New Methods and Sensibilities in the Biblical Commentaries of Isaac Abarbanel." *Viator* 26 (1995): 283–319.

Lenz, Fritz, Edwin Baur, and Eugen Fischer, eds. *Human Heredity*. Trans. Eden and Cedar Paul. New York: Macmillan, 1931.

Levanon, Yosef. *The Jewish Travellers in the Twelfth Century*. Lanham, Md.: University Press of America, 1980.

Leveen, Jacob. *The Hebrew Bible in Art*. London: Oxford University Press, 1944.

Levi-Strauss, Claude. *The Savage Mind*. Chicago: University of Chicago Press, 1966.

Levin, David M., ed. *Modernity and the Hegemony of Vision*. Berkeley: University of California Press, 1993.

Levin, David, M., ed. *Sites of Vision: The Discursive Construction of Sight in the History of Philosophy*. Cambridge: MIT Press, 1997.

Levinas, Emmanuel. *The Levinas Reader*. Ed. Seán Hand. Oxford: Blackwell, 1989.

Levy, Ze'ev. "The Status of Aesthetics in Jewish Thought." In *Judaism and Art*, ed. David Cassuto, 83–102. Ramat-Gan: Bar-Ilan University, 1988.

Lewitt, Irène, ed. *The Israel Museum*. New York: Vendome, 1995.

Liebes, Y. "Rabbi Solomon Ibn Gabirol's Use of the *Sefer Yesira* and a Commentary on the Poem 'I Love Thee.' " *Jerusalem Studies in Jewish Thought* 6 (1987): 73–123. In Hebrew.

Liebeschütz, Hans. "Hermann Cohen and His Historical Background." *Leo Baeck Institute Year Book* 13 (1968): 3–33.

Limor, Ora. *Die Disputationen zu Ceuta (1179) und Mallorca (1286)*. Munich: Monumenta Germaniae Historica, 1994.

Lloyd, G. E. R. *Demystifying Mentalities*. Cambridge: Cambridge University Press, 1990.

———. *The Revolutions of Wisdom: Studies in the Claims and Practice of Ancient Greek Science*. Berkeley: University of California Press, 1987.

Malter, Henry. "Shem Tob ben Joseph Palquera, II, His 'Treatise of the Dream.' " *Jewish Quarterly Review* 1 (1910): 480–481.

Mango, Cyril. *The Art of the Byzantine Empire, 312–1453* Englewood Cliffs, N.J.: Prentice-Hall, 1972.

Mann, Barbara Ellen. "Icons and Iconoclasts: Visual Poetics in Hebrew and Yiddish Modernism." Ph. D. diss., University of California, 1997.

Mann, Vivian B., ed. *Gardens and Ghettos: The Art of Jewish Life in Italy*. Berkeley: University of California Press, 1989.

Mann, Vivian B., Thomas Click, and Jerrilyn Dodds, eds. *Convivencia: Jews, Muslims, and Christians in Medieval Spain*. New York: George Braziller, 1992.

Mann, Vivian B., with Emily Bilsky. *The Jewish Museum New York*. London: Scala Books/Jewish Museum, 1993.

Manne, Mordecai Zvi. "The Jewish Painter, Oppenheim." In *Kol Kitve Manne*, ed. A. L. Sheynhoyz, 39–60. Warsaw: Tushia, 1897. In Hebrew.

Marcus, Ivan G. *Rituals of Childhood: Jewish Acculturation in Medieval Europe*. New Haven: Yale University Press, 1996.

———. "The Song of Songs in German Hasidism and the School of Rashi: A Preliminary Comparison." In *Rashi, 1040–1990*, ed. Gabrielle Sed-Rajna, 265–272. Paris: Les Éditions du Cerf, 1993.

Margoliouth, George. "Hebrew Illuminated Mss." *Jewish Quarterly Review* 20 (1907–1908): 118–144.

Marx, Karl. *The Economic and Philosophic Manuscripts of 1844.* Ed. Dirk J. Strunk. New York: International Publishers, 1964.

———. *Karl Marx Friedrich Engels Gesamtausgabe (MEGA).* 29 vols. Berlin: Dietz Verlag, 1975-.

Mata, Ángela Franco. "Antigüedades Medievales Judías En El Arqueológico Nacional." *Boletín del Museo Arqueológico Nacional* 13 (1995): 103–114.

Matter, E. Ann. *The Voice of My Beloved: The Song of Songs in Western Medieval Christianity.* Philadelphia: University of Pennsylvania Press, 1990.

Mayer, L. A. *Bibliography of Jewish Art.* Ed. Otto Kurz. Jerusalem: Magnes, 1967.

Melammed, Ezra Z. *Bible Commentators.* 2 vols. Jerusalem: Magnes Press, 1978. In Hebrew.

Mendelsohn, Ezra. *The Jews of East Central Europe between the World Wars.* Bloomington: Indiana University Press, 1987.

———. *On Modern Jewish Politics.* Oxford: Oxford University Press, 1993.

Mendes-Flohr, Paul, and Jehuda Reinharz, "Buber and the Metaphysicians of Contempt." In *Living with Antisemitism*, ed. Jehuda Reinharz, 133–164. Hanover, N.H.: University Press of New England, 1987.

———. "*Fin-de-Siècle* Orientalism, the *Ostjuden*, and the Aesthetics of Jewish Self-Affirmation." *Studies in Contemporary Jewry* 1 (1984): 96–139.

———, eds. *The Jew in the Modern World.* New York: Oxford University Press, 1980.

Metzger, Thérèse, and Mendel Metzger. *Jewish Life in the Middle Ages: Illuminated Hebrew Manuscripts of the Thirteenth to the Sixteenth Centuries.* New York: Alpine Fine Arts Collection, 1982.

Meyer, Michael A. *The Origins of the Modern Jew: Jewish Identity and European Culture in Germany, 1749–1824.* Detroit: Wayne State University Press, 1979.

———. *Response to Modernity: A History of the Reform Movement in Judaism.* New York: Oxford University Press, 1988.

Misiano, Viktor. "Choosing to Be Jewish." In *Russian Jewish Artists in a Century of Change, 1890–1990*, ed. Susan Tumarkin Goodman, 89–95. Munich: Prestel, 1995.

Mitchell, George, ed. *Architecture of the Islamic World: Its Social History and Meaning.* New York: William Morrow, 1978.

Mitchell, W. J. T. *Iconology: Image, Text, Ideology.* Chicago: University of Chicago Press, 1986.

Moore, George F. *Judaism in the First Centuries of the Christian Era.* 3 vols. Cambridge: Harvard University Press, 1927.

Moore, R. I. *The Formation of Persecuting Society: Power and Deviance in Western Europe, 950–1250.* Oxford: Blackwell, 1987.

Namyeni, Ernest. *The Essence of Jewish Art.* Trans. Edouard Roditi. New York: Thomas Yoselloff, 1957.

Narkiss, B. *Hebrew Illuminated Manuscripts.* Jerusalem: Encyclopedia Judaica, 1969.

Netanyahu, Benzion. *Don Isaac Abravanel: Statesman and Philosopher.* Philadelphia: Jewish Publication Society, 1968.

Newman, Barnett. *Selected Writings and Interviews.* Ed. John P. O'Neill. Berkeley: University of California Press, 1992.

Nirenberg, David. *Communities of Violence: Persecution of Minorities in the Middle Ages.* Princeton: Princeton University Press, 1996.

Nochlin, Linda. "Starting with the Self: Jewish Identity and Its Representation." In *The Jew in the Text: Modernity and the Construction of Identity,* ed. Linda Nochlin and Tamar Garb, 7–19. London: Thames and Hudson, 1995.

———. "Why Have There Been No Great Women Artists?" In *Art and Sexual Politics: Women's Liberation, Women's Artists, and Art History,* ed. Thomas B. Hess and Elizabeth C. Baker, 1–39. New York: Collier, 1973.

Norton, David F. *David Hume: Common-Sense Moralist, Sceptical Metaphysician.* Princeton: Princeton University Press, 1982.

Novak, David. *Jewish-Christian Dialogue.* New York: Oxford University Press, 1989.

Novick, Peter. *That Noble Dream: The "Objectivity Question" and the American Historical Profession.* Cambridge: Cambridge University Press, 1988.

Olender, Maurice. *The Languages of Paradise: Race, Religion, and Philology in the Nineteenth Century.* Trans. Arthur Goldhammer. Cambridge: Harvard University Press, 1992.

Olin, Margaret. "C[lement] Hardesh [Greenberg] and Company." In *Too Jewish? Challenging Traditional Identities,* ed. Norman L. Kleebatt. New York: Jewish Museum, 1996.

Ong, Walter J. *The Presence of the Word: Some Prolegomena for Cultural and Religious History.* Minneapolis: University of Minnesota Press, 1981.

Ozick, Cynthia. "Previsions of the Demise of the Dancing Dog" In *Art and Ardor.* New York: Alfred A. Knopf, 1983.

Panofsky, Erwin. *Abbot Suger on the Abbey Church of St. Denis and Its Art Treasury.* Princeton: Princeton University Press, 1979

Patai, Raphael. *The Jewish Mind.* New York: Scribner's, 1977.

———. *Man and Temple in Ancient Jewish Myth and Ritual.* New York: Ktav, 1967.

Petropoulos, Jonathan. *Art as Politics in the Third Reich.* Chapel Hill: University of North Carolina Press, 1996.

Pines, Shlomo. "The Limitations of Human Knowledge according to al-Farabi, Ibn Baija, and Maimonides." In *Studies in Medieval Jewish History and Literature,* ed. Isadore Twersky, 82–109. Cambridge: Harvard University Press, 1979.

———. "Medieval Doctrines in Renaissance Garb? Some Jewish and Arabic Sources of Leone Ebreo's Doctrines." In *Jewish Thought in the Sixteenth Century,* ed. Bernard D. Cooperman, 365–398. Cambridge: Harvard University Press, 1983.

Powell, Richard J. *Black Art and Culture in the 20th Century.* London: Thames & Hudson, 1997.

Prawer, S. S. *Heine's Jewish Comedy: A Study of his Portraits of Jews and Judaism.* Oxford: Clarendon, 1983.

Pringent, Pierre. *Le Judaïsme et l'image.* Tübingen: J. C. B. Mohr [Paul Siebeck], 1990.

Rand, Harry. "Torah's Incipient Esthetics." *Religious Education* 86 (1991): 20–28.

Rather, L. J. *Reading Wagner: A Study in the History of Ideas*. Baton Rouge: Louisiana State University Press, 1990.

Reines, Alvin J. *Maimonides and Abrabanel on Prophecy*. Cincinnati: Hebrew Union College Press, 1970.

Reinhardt, Ad. *Art-as-Art: The Selected Writings of Ad Reinhardt*. Ed. Barbara Rose. New York: Viking, 1975.

Reinharz, Jehuda, ed. *Living with Antisemitism: Modern Jewish Responses*. Hanover, N.H.: University Press of New England, 1987.

Robbins, Jill. *Prodigal Son/Elder Brother: Interpretation and Alterity in Augustine, Petrarch, Kafka, Levinas*. Chicago: University of Chicago Press, 1991.

Rose, Paul L. *German Question/Jewish Question: Revolutionary Antisemitism from Kant to Wagner*. Princeton: Princeton University Press, 1990.

Rosenthal, Franz. *The Classical Tradition in Islam*. Trans. Emile Marmorstein and Jenny Marmorstein. London: Routledge, 1992.

Rosenau, Helen. *A Short History of Jewish Art*. London: J. Clarke, 1948.

Rosenberg, Harold. *Art and Other Serious Matters*. Chicago: University of Chicago Press, 1985.

———. "Is There a Jewish Art?" *Commentary* 42 (1966): 57–60.

Rotenstreich, Nathan. *Jewish Philosophy in Modern Times: From Mendelsohn to Rosenzweig*. New York: Holt, Rinehart, and Winston, 1968.

———. *Jews and German Philosophy: The Polemics of Emancipation*. New York: Schocken, 1984.

Rosenzweig, Franz. *The Star of Redemption*. Trans. William Hallo. Boston: Beacon, 1972.

Rudolph, Conrad. *The "Things of Greater Importance": Bernard of Clairvaux's Apologia and the Medieval Attitude toward Art*. Philadelphia: University of Pennsylvania Press, 1990.

Roth, Cecil, ed. *Jewish Art: An Illustrated History*. New York: McGraw-Hill, 1961.

Roth, Norman. *Maimonides: Essays and Texts*. Madison: University of Wisconsin Press, 1985.

Rubin, Miri. *Corpus Christi*. Cambridge: Cambridge University Press, 1991.

Ruderman, David B. *The World of a Renaissance Jew: The Life and Thought of Abraham ben Mordecai Farissol*. Cincinnati: Hebrew Union College Press, 1981.

Sammons, Jeffrey L. *Heinrich Heine: A Modern Biography*. Princeton: Princeton University Press, 1979.

Samuels, Ernest. *Bernard Berenson: The Making of a Legend*. Cambridge: Harvard University Press, Belknap Press, 1987.

Saperstein, Mark. *Jewish Preaching, 1200–1800: An Anthology*. New Haven: Yale University Press, 1989.

Sarachek, Joseph. *Faith and Reason: The Conflict over the Rationalism of Maimonides*. 1935. Reprint, New York: Hermon Press, 1970.

Sarna, Nahum. *The JPS Torah Commentary: Exodus*. Philadelphia: Jewish Publication Society, 1991.

Scarry, Elaine. *The Body in Pain: The Making and Unmaking of the World*. New York: Oxford University Press, 1985.

Schade,Werner. *Cranach: A Family of Master Painters.* Trans. Helen Sebba. New York: G. P. Putnam's, 1980.

Schäfer, Peter, ed. *Konkordanz zur Hekhalot-Literatur.* Tübingen: J. C. B. Mohr (Paul Siebeck), 1986.

Scheindlin, Raymond P. "Hebrew Poetry in Medieval Iberia." In *Convivencia: Jews, Muslims, and Christians in Medieval Spain,* ed. Vivan Mann, Thomas Click, and Jerrilyn Dodds, 39–60. New York: George Braziller, 1992.

——. *Wine, Women, and Death.* Philadelphia: Jewish Publication Society, 1986.

Schelling, F. W. J. *The Philosophy of Art.* Ed. and trans. Douglas W. Scott. Minneapolis: University of Minnesota Press, 1989.

Scholem, Gershom. *On the Kabbalah and Its Symbolism.* Trans. R. Manheim. New York: Schocken, 1969.

——. *The Messianic Idea in Judaism.* New York: Schocken, 1971.

——. *Origins of the Kabbalah.* Ed. R. J. Werblowsky. Trans. Allan Arkush. Philadelphia: Jewish Publication Society, 1987.

Schorske, Carl E. *Fin-De-Siècle Vienna: Politics and Culture.* New York: Vintage, 1981.

Schreckenberg, Heinz. *Die christlichen Adversus-Judaeos Texte (11.–13 Jh.).* Frankfurt am Main: Peter Lang, 1988.

——. *Die christlichen Adversus-Judaeos-Texte und ihr literarisches und historisches Umfeld (13.–20. Jh.).* Franfurt am Main: Peter Lang, 1994.

Schwartz, Joel. *Madrikh Torani le-'Omanut.* Jerusalem: Devar Yerushalayyim, 1992.

Schwarz, Karl. *Die Juden in der Kunst.* Vienna: R. Löwit Verlag, 1936.

Schwarzschild, Steven S. "Aesthetics." In *Contemporary Jewish Religious Thought: Original Essays on Criticial Concepts, Movements, and Beliefs,* ed. Arthur A. Cohen and Paul Mendes-Flohr, 1–6. New York: Scribner's, 1987.

Schweid, Eliezer. *A History of Jewish Thought in Modern Times: The Nineteenth Century.* Jerusalem: Kether\Hakkibutz Hameuchud, 1977. In Hebrew.

Sed-Rajna, Gabrielle. *The Hebrew Bible in Medieval Illuminated Manuscripts.* Trans. Josephine Bacon. New York: Rizzoli, 1987.

——. *Jewish Art.* Trans. Sara Friedman and Mira Reich. New York: H. N. Abrams, 1997.

Shatskikh, Alexandra. "Jewish Artists in the Russian Avant-Garde." In *Russian Jewish Artists in a Century of Change, 1890–1990,* ed. Susan Tumarkin Goodman, 71–80. Munich: Prestel, 1995.

Shatzmiller, Joseph. *Jews, Medicine, and Medieval Society.* Berkeley: University of Califorrnia Press, 1994.

Shavit, Yaacov. *Athens in Jerusalem: Classical Antiquity and Hellenism in the Making of the Modern Secular Jew.* Trans. Chaya Naor and Niki Werner. London: Littmann Library of Jewish Civilization, 1997.

Shear-Yashuv, Aharon. *The Theology of Salomon Ludwig Steinheim.* Leiden: E. J. Brill. 1986.

Shear-Yashuv, Aharon, ed. *The Theology of Salomon Ludwig Steinheim.* Leiden: E. J. Brill. 1986.

Sheets-Johnstone, Maxine, ed. *Giving the Body Its Due.* Albany: State University of New York Press, 1992.

Silman, Yochanan. *Thinker and Seer: The Development of the Thought of Rabbi Yehuda Halevi in the Kuzari*. Ramat-Gan: Bar-Ilan University Press, 1985. In Hebrew.

————. *Philosopher and Prophet: Judah Halevi, the Kuzari, and the Evolution of His Thought*. Trans. Lenn J. Schramm. Albany: State University of New York Press, 1995.

Silver, David J. *Maimonidean Criticism and the Maimonidean Controversy*. Leyden: E. J. Brill, 1965.

Simon, Uriel. "Abraham ibn-Ezra—Between the Exegete and His Readers." In *Proceedings of the Ninth World Congress of Jewish Studies: Panel Sessions—Bible Studies and Ancient Near East*, ed. Moshe Goshen-Gottstein, 23–42. Jerusalem: Magnes, 1985. In Hebrew.

Sirat, Colette. *A History of Jewish Philosophy in the Middle Ages*. Cambridge: Cambridge University Press, 1985.

Smalley, Beryl. *The Study of the Bible in the Middle Ages*. Notre Dame: University of Notre Dame Press, 1964.

Smith, Anthony D. *National Identity*. Reno: University of Nevada Press, 1991.

Smolar, Levi, and Moses Aberbach. "The Golden Calf in Postbiblical Literature." *Hebrew Union College Annual* 39 (1968): 91–116.

Solomon, Solomon J. "Art and Judaism." *Jewish Quarterly Review* 13 (1901): 553–556.

Sombart, Werner. *The Jews and Modern Capitalism*. Trans. M. Epstein. Glencoe, Ill.: Free Press, 1951.

————. *Die Juden und das Wirtschaftsleben*. Leipzig: Verlag von Duncker und Humblot, 1911.

Sorkin, David J. *The Transformation of German Jewry, 1780–1840*. New York: Oxford University Press, 1987.

Soussloff, Catherine M., ed. *Jewish Identity in Modern Art History*. Berkeley: University of California Press, 1999.

Southern, R. W. *The Making of the Middle Ages*. New Haven: Yale University Press, 1953.

Sperber, Daniel. *Magic and Folklore in Rabbinic Literature*. Ramat-Gan: Bar-Ilan University Press, 1994.

Spero, Shubert. "Towards a Torah Esthetic." *Tradition: A Journal of Orthodox Thought* 6 (1964): 53–66.

Stahmer, Harold. *"Speak That I May See Thee": The Religious Significance of Language*. New York: Macmillan, 1968.

Stanislawski, Michael. "The Jews and Russian Culture and Politics." In *Russian Jewish Artists in a Century of Change, 1890–1990*, ed. Susan Tumarkin Goodman, 16–27. Munich: Prestel, 1995.

Staniszewski, Mary Ann. *Believing Is Seeing: Creating the Culture of Art*. New York: Penguin, 1995.

Stassoff, Vladmir, and David Gunzburg. *L'ornement hébreu*. Berlin: S. Calvary, 1905.

Steinberg, Leo. *The Sexuality of Christ in Renaissance Art and Modern Oblivion*. Chicago: University of Chicago Press, 1996.

Steinheim, Salomon Ludwig. *Die Offenbarung nach dem Lehrbegriffe der Synagoge.* 2 vols. Leipzig: Leopold Schnauss, 1856.

Steinschneider, Moritz. *Die Hebraeischen Übersetzungen des Mittelalters.* 1893. Reprint. Graz: Academische Druck-u. Verlaganstalt, 1956.

Stern, Sacha, "Figurative Art and *Halakha* in the Mishnaic-Talmudic Period." *Zion* 41 (1996): 397–419.

Stock, Brian. *The Implications of Literacy: Written Language and Models of Interpretation in the Eleventh and Twelfth Centuries.* Princeton: Princeton University Press, 1983.

Stow, Kenneth. *Alienated Minority: The Jews of Medieval Latin Europe.* Cambridge: Harvard University Press, 1992.

Strauss, Heinrich. "Jewish Art as a Minority Problem." *Jewish Journal of Sociology* 2 (1960): 147–171.

Summers, David. *The Judgement of Sense: Renaissance Naturalism and the Rise of Aesthetics.* Cambridge: Cambridge University Press, 1987.

Swartz, Michael D. *Mystical Prayer in Ancient Judaism: An Analysis of Ma'aseh Merkavah.* Tübingen: J. C. B. Mohr (Paul Siebeck), 1992.

Ta-Shma, Israel M. *Early Franco-German Ritual and Custom.* Jerusalem: Magnes, 1992. In Hebrew.

Terry, Allan. *Five Essays on Islamic Art.* Sebastopol, Calif.: Solipsist, 1988.

Tirosh-Rothschild, Hava. *Between Worlds: The Life and Thought of Rabbi David ben Judah Messer Leon.* Albany: State University of New York Press, 1991.

Tishby, Isaiah. *The Wisdom of the Zohar.* Trans. D. Goldstein. 3 vols. Oxford: Oxford University Press, 1989.

Touati, Charles. *La Pensée philosophique et théologique de Gersonide.* Paris: Minuit, 1973.

Touitou, Elazar. "*Peshat* and Apologetics in the Rashbam's Commentary on the Biblical Stories of Moses." *Tarbiz* 51 (1982): 248–273. In Hebrew.

Trachtenberg, Joshua. *Jewish Magic and Superstition: A Study in Folk Religion.* New York: Behrman's Jewish Book House, 1939.

———. *The Devil and the Jews: The Medieval Conception of the Jews and Its Relation to Modern Antisemitism.* New Haven: Yale University Press, 1943.

Trautner-Kromann, Hanne. *Sword and Shield: Jewish Polemics against Christianity and the Christians in France and Spain from 1100–1500.* Tübingen: J. C. B. Mohr (Paul Siebeck), 1993.

Traverso, Enzo. *The Marxists and the Jewish Question: The History of a Debate, 1843–1943.* Trans. Bernard Gibbons. Atlantic Highlands, N.J.: Humanities, 1994.

Twersky, Isadore. "Aspects of the Social and Cultural History of Provençal Jewry." In *Jewish Society Through the Ages*, ed. H. H. Ben-Sasson and S. Ettinger, 185–207. New York: Schocken, 1971.

———. "Did R. Abraham ibn Ezra Influence Maimonides?" In *Rabbi Abraham Ibn Ezra: Studies in the Writings of a Twelfth-Century Jewish Polymath*, ed. Isadore Twersky and Jay M. Harris, 21–48. Cambridge: Harvard University Press, 1993. In Hebrew.

———. *An Introduction to the Code of Maimonides (Mishneh Torah).* New Haven: Yale University Press, 1980.

———. *A Maimonides Reader.* New York: Behrman House, 1972.

———. "Religion and Law." In *Religion in a Religious Age*, ed. S. D. Goitein, 69–82. Cambridge: Association for Jewish Studies, 1974.

———. "Some Non-Halakic Aspects of the *Mishneh Torah.*" In *Jewish Medieval and Renaissance Studies*, ed. A. Altmann, 95–118. Cambridge: Harvard University Press, 1967.

———. "Talmudists, Philosophers, Kabbalists: The Quest for Spirituality in the Sixteenth Century." In *Jewish Thought in the Sixteenth Century*, ed. Bernard D. Cooperman, 431–459. Cambridge: Harvard University Press, 1983.

———, ed. *Rabbi Moses Nahmanides (Ramban): Exploratioins in His Religious and Literary Virtuosity.* Cambridge: Harvard University Press, 1983.

Urbach, Ephraim E. *The Sages: Their Concepts and Beliefs.* Trans. Israel Abrahams. Cambridge: Harvard University Press, 1975.

Urbach, Ephraim E. *The Tosaphists: Their History, Writings, and Methods.* Jerusalem: Bialik Institute, 1955. In Hebrew.

Vajda, Georges. *L'amour de Dieu dans la théologie juive du Moyen Age.* Paris: J. Vrin, 1957.

———. "The Rabbinical Laws of Idolatry in the Second and Third Centuries in the Light of Archaeological and Historical Facts." *Israel Exploration Journal* 9 (1959): 149–265. A more complete Hebrew Version of this article appears in *Eretz-Israel* 5 (1958): 94–96, 189–205.

Virilio, Paul. *The Vision Machine.* Trans. Julie Rose. Bloomington: Indiana University Press, 1994.

Voltaire. *The Complete Works of Voltaire.* Oxford: Voltaire Foundation, 1994.

———. *A Treatise on Toleration and Other Essays.* Trans. Joseph McCabe. Amherst: Prometheus, 1994.

———. *Voltaire on Religion: Selected Writings.* Trans. Kenneth W. Applegate. New York: Frederick Ungar, 1974.

Wagner, Richard. *Richard Wagner Gesammelte Schriften und Dichtungen.* Hildesheim: Georg Olms Verlag, 1976.

———. *Richard Wagner's Prose Works.* Trans. William A. Ellis. London: Kegan Paul, Trench, Trübner, 1895.

Wallace, Michele. "Afterword: 'Why Are There No Great Black Artists?' The Problem of Visuality in African-American Culture." In *Black Popular Culture*, ed. Gina Dent, 333–346. Seattle: Bay Press, 1992.

Weinfeld, Moshe. *Deuteronomy and the Deuteronomic School.* Oxford: Clarendon, 1972.

Weiss, Raymond, with Charles E. Butterworth. *Ethical Writings of Maimonides.* New York: New York University Press, 1975.

Werner, Eric, and Isaiah Sonne. "The Philosophy and Theory of Music in Judaeo-Arabic Literature." *Hebrew Union College Annual* 16 (1941); 17 (1942–1943).

Wharton, Annabel J. *Refiguring the Post Classical City: Dura Europos, Jerash, Jerusalem, and Ravenna.* New York: Cambridge University Press, 1995.

Wieder, Naftali. "Sanctuary as a Metaphor for Scripture." *Journal of Jewish Studies* 8 (1956–1957): 166–67.

Wilensky, Sarah Heller. *The Philosophy of Isaac Arama in the Framework of Philonic Philosophy.* Jerusalem: Mossad Bialik, 1956. In Hebrew.

Williams, A. Lukyn. *Adversus Judaeos: A Bird's-Eye View of the Christian Apologiae until the Renaissance.* Cambridge: University Press, 1935.

Williams, Raymond. *Culture and Society: 1780–1950.* New York: Columbia University Press, 1983.

Winckelmann, Johann Joachim. *Geschichte der Kunst des Altherthums.* Ed. Julius Lessing. Leipzig: Verlag der Dürr'schen Buchhandlung, 1882.

———. *The History of Ancient Art.* Trans. G. Henry Lodge. Boston: James R. Osgood, 1880.

Wischnitzer, Mark. *A History of Jewish Crafts and Guilds.* New York: Jonathan David, 1965.

Winkler, Wolf, ed. *A Spectacle of Spectacles: Exhibition Catalogue.* Trans. Dorothy Jaeschke. Leipzig, 1988.

Wischnitzer, Rachel. "Judaism and Art." In *The Jews: Their History Culture, and Religion,* ed. Louis Finkelstein, 1322–1368. New York: Harper & Brothers, 1960.

Wölfflin, Heinrich. *Principles of Art History: The Problem of the Development of Style in Later Art.* Trans. M. D. Hottinger. New York: Dover, 1950.

Wolfson, Harry A. *Philo: Foundations of Religious Philosophy in Judaism, Christianity, and Islam.* 2 vols. Cambridge: Harvard University Press, 1948.

———. *The Repercussions of the Kalam in Jewish Philosophy.* Cambridge: Harvard University Press, 1979.

Wolfson, Elliot R. *Through a Speculum That Shines: Vision and Imagination in Medieval Jewish Mysticism.* Princeton: Princeton University Press, 1994.

Yates, Frances A. *The Art of Memory.* London: Routledge, 1966.

———. *Giordano Bruno and the Hermetic Tradition.* 1964. Reprint. Chicago: University of Chicago Press, 1979.

Yovel, Yirmiyahu. *Dark Riddle: Hegel, Nietzsche, and the Jews.* University Park: Pennsylvania State University Press, 1998.

———. *Spinoza and Other Heretics: The Adventures of Immanence.* Princeton: Princeton University Press, 1989.

Yerushalmi, Yosef Hayim. *Freud's Moses: Judaism Terminable and Interminable.* New Haven: Yale University Press, 1991.

———. *Zakhor: Jewish History and Jewish Memory.* Seattle: University of Washington Press, 1989.

Young-Bruehl, Elisabeth. *Hannah Arendt: For Love of the World.* New Haven: Yale University Press, 1984.

Yuval, Israel J. "Vengeance and Damnation: From Jewish Martyrdom to Blood Accusations" *Zion* 58 (1993): 25–89. In Hebrew.

Zimmels, H. J. *Ashkenazim and Sephardim.* Oxford: Oxford University Press, 1958.

Zirlin, Yael. "Celui qui se cache derrière l'image: Colophons des enlumineurs dans le manuscrit hébraïqe." *Revue des études Juives* 155 (1996): 33–53.

Index

CPSIA information can be obtained at www.ICGtesting.com
Printed in the USA
LVOW071712301112

309544LV00004B/152/P

9 780691 089850